Writers and their Background

GEOFFREY CHAUCER

Howgh she þ quuent was mayden marie
And saw his loue floure and fructifie

¶ Al þogh his lyfe be queynt þe resemblaunce
Of him hath in me so fressh lyflynesse
Þat to putte othir men in remembraunce
Of his psone I haue heere his lyknesse
Do make to þis ende in soithfastnesse
Þat þei þt haue of him left þought & mynde
By þis peynture may ageyn him fynde

¶ The ymages þt in þe churche been
Maken folk þenke on god & on his seyntes
Whan þe ymages þei be holden & seen
Were oft unsyte of hem causith restreyntes
Of youghtes gode Whan a þing depeynt is
Or entailed if men take of it heede
Thoght of þe lyknesse it wil in hym brede

¶ Yit some holden oppynyou and sey
Þat none ymages schuld ymaked be
Þei erren foule & goon out of þe wey
Of trouth haue þei scant sensibilitee
Passe ou þt now blessid trinitee
Uppon my maistres soule mcy haue
ffor him lady eke þ mcy I craue

¶ More othir þing Wolde I fayne speke & touche
Heere in þis booke but such is my dulnesse
ffor þt al voyde and empty is my pouche
Þat al my lust is queynt wt heuynesse
And heuy spirit comaundith stilnesse

Writers and their Background

GEOFFREY CHAUCER

EDITED BY DEREK BREWER

OHIO UNIVERSITY PRESS · 1975

© G. BELL & SONS LTD. 1974

PRINTED BY OFFSET AND BOUND IN THE

UNITED STATES OF AMERICA

FOR OHIO UNIVERSITY PRESS, ATHENS, OHIO

BY EDWARDS BROTHERS, INC., ANN ARBOR, MICHIGAN

LC 74-84295

ISBN 8214-0184-X

REPRINTED 1976

REPRINTED 1982

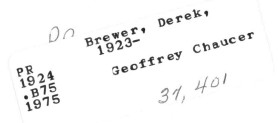

Contents

The Contributors

PROFESSOR L. D. BENSON
Professor of English, Harvard University

DEREK BREWER
Fellow of Emmanuel College, Cambridge, and Lecturer in English in the University of Cambridge

PROFESSOR NORMAN DAVIS
Merton Professor of English in the University of Oxford

PROFESSOR E. T. DONALDSON
Professor of English, Yale University

PETER DRONKE
Fellow of Clare Hall, Cambridge, and Lecturer in Medieval Latin in the University of Cambridge

PROFESSOR F. R. H. DU BOULAY
Professor of Medieval History, Bedford College, University of London

BRUCE HARBERT
Lecturer in English, Merton College, Oxford

PROFESSOR V. A. KOLVE
Professor of English, University of Virginia

JILL MANN
Fellow of Girton College, Cambridge

PROFESSOR M. MANZALAOUI
Professor of English, University of British Columbia, Vancouver

PROFESSOR HOWARD SCHLESS
Professor of English and Comparative Literature, Columbia University, New York

PROFESSOR GEOFFREY SHEPHERD
Professor of English, University of Birmingham

PROFESSOR JAMES I. WIMSATT
Professor of English, University of North Carolina

Abbreviations

BD:	*The Book of the Duchess*
CT:	*The Canterbury Tales*
HF:	*The House of Fame*
KT:	*The Knight's Tale*
LGW:	*The Legend of Good Women*
PF:	*The Parliament of Fowls*
TC:	*Troilus and Criseyde*

General Editor's Preface

THE STUDY OF LITERATURE is not a 'pure' discipline since works of literature are affected by the climate of opinion in which they are produced. Writers, like other men, are concerned with the politics, the philosophy, the religion, the arts, and the general thought of their own times. Some literary figures, indeed, have made their own distinguished contributions to these areas of human interest, while the achievement of others can be fully appreciated only by a knowledge of them.

The volumes in this series have been planned with the purpose of presenting major authors in their intellectual, social, and artistic contexts, and with the conviction that this will make their work more easily understood and enjoyed. Each volume contains a chapter which provides a reader's guide to the writings of the author concerned, a Bibliography, and Chronological Tables setting out the main dates of the author's life and publications alongside the chief events of contemporary importance.

In this volume Dr Brewer has brought together a distinguished team of Chaucer scholars who have produced by an exercise of their own individual and expert knowledge a study that does justice to the genius of the poet himself and the complexity of the civilisation of which he was a part. The present volume is a brilliant illustration of the need to relate (to use T. S. Eliot's phraseology) tradition and the individual talent and it will be greeted as an important achievement by the scholar and the general reader alike.

R. L. BRETT

Editor's Preface

EACH OF THE ESSAYS in the present volume is an authoritative and original account of its subject matter by an experienced scholar. The names of the contributors are sufficient advertisement of their quality. Surprisingly enough, the life of Chaucer seems never to have been considered extensively and in relation to original material as an historical fact, in its own right, by an historian of the period who is not primarily a literary historian and critic, before Professor Du Boulay's essay in this volume.

While there has been a huge increase in the second half of the twentieth century in the attention paid to Chaucer, to which Professor Benson's chapter offers a guide, knowledge about *Chaucer's* knowledge, understanding of the concepts and information available to him, or of the conditions of life and culture which to some extent conditioned him, though not exactly neglected, and indeed in some specialist aspects the subject of notable books, has nevertheless not on the whole attracted quite so much effort as has an often unduly self-contained, unhistorical, literary criticism. Not all readers of Chaucer can hope to have his voracious intellectual appetite for religion, philosophy, science, and the literatures of three languages other than his own, and even if we have, we have not his genius. But we ought to remember that no great literature lives in a vacuum, or can be read with an empty mind; that literature needs subject-matter, since it does not itself provide one; that any literary appreciation requires historical depth of perspective, and comparative experience, preferably in another language. The subjects in which Chaucer was interested, even when they were other works of literature, are remarkably various and often difficult, certainly more remote to the native English-speaking reader than Chaucer's own work. Yet acquaintance with Chaucer's own work inevitably leads to these other subjects, so important to him in various ways; leads, that is, to a desire to know and grasp the nature and history of English as it came to him already a richly multiple inheritance, to know and grasp the major Latin,

French and Italian writings, the interrelated religion, philosophy, science and art of his day, the significance of his general historical ambience. If ever there was an exercise in the European cultural tradition, it is the reading of Chaucer. The English, even the British, are no longer the majority among the readers of Chaucer, and the French and Italians have never really taken to him; a very large amount of the important work on Chaucer has been done by Americans and Germans; but there is at this point of time a peculiar interest for the English in the phenomenon of Chaucer, at once so English and so European in quality, when the British themselves have at last turned back to join other West European countries in a union that has many medieval echoes.

When Chaucer's works are sensitively and sympathetically read they can, of course, guide us themselves to their own understanding, but they also point us to wider vistas which, when reached, reveal, among other things, more of Chaucer's own works themselves. Also, when read without comparative and historical knowledge, the works themselves are often sensitively *mis*-read. It is the aim of the present book, through the work of specialists writing in the fullness of their knowledge for those less specialized, to enable readers to follow Chaucer, further than has so far been possible, in his own interests, achievements and background, to convey some of the more important ideas and information that will be helpful in understanding Chaucer's intellectual and linguistic inheritance and how he used what was available. The basis of the knowledge of Chaucer's life, language, manuscripts, of his literary, scientific and other sources of information, concepts and attitudes, is here brought up to date and presented in relation to the significant literary achievement which is the ultimate source of our interest. The editor confidently claims that the essays of his colleagues now presented here constitute an important book in the progress of Chaucer studies which will serve many different interests for years to come.

It is important to note that all the essays were separately written and contributed at the request of the editor; none was written with respect to any other contribution. No cross-references have been attempted.

The editor wishes to record his thanks to the distinguished contributors, at least one of whom completed his work under personal difficulties, for agreeing to undertake the essays, and for patiently enduring the long delays that occurred after some of the essays were submitted, of a kind that seem to be inevitable in such a volume of collaborative authorship. He also wishes to thank Mr B. A. Windeatt for editorial assistance.

Quotations are taken, unless otherwise noted, from *The Works of Geoffrey Chaucer*, edited by F. N. Robinson, 2nd edition, Boston: Houghton Mifflin; London: Oxford University Press, 1957.

DEREK BREWER

	The main events of Chaucer's life	The main events of literary and intellectual importance	The main events of historical importance
c.1300		Machaut born	
1304		Petrarch born	
1307			Accession of Edward II
c.1313		Boccaccio born	
c.1320		Wycliffe born	
1321		Dante died	
1326		Trevisa born	
1327			Accession of Edward III
c.1330		Gower born	
1337			Declaration of war against France (Hundred Years' War)
c.1340–5	Chaucer born		
c.1340		Auchinleck MS written	
c.1346		Deschamps born	Crécy
1348–9			Black Death
1348–58		Boccaccio's *Decameron*	
c.1352		*Winner and Waster*	
1356			Poitiers
1357	Page to Countess of Ulster		
1359–60	Military service, captured and ransomed		Treaty of Bretigni
c.1362		First (A text) version of *Piers Plowman*	
1366	Spanish journey		
c.1366	Married		
1367	Yeoman in King's Household		
c.1368		Hoccleve born	
1369	Campaign in France *The Book of the Duchess* Esquire of King's Household		War with France renewed. Deaths of Queen Philippa and Duchess Blanche
c.1370		Lydgate born	
1372–3	Journey to Italy		
1374	Comptroller of Customs	Death of Petrarch	
1374–80	*The House of Fame*		
1375		Death of Boccaccio	
1376–7	Journeys abroad on King's secret affairs		

1377		Death of Machaut	Accession of Richard II
c.1377		Second (B text) version of *Piers Plowman*	
1378	Second Italian journey, to Lombardy		
c.1380		*Sir Gawain and the Green Knight*	
1381			The Peasants' Revolt
c.1380–2	*The Parliament of Fowls*		Richard marries Anne
1382–5	Translation of Boethius' *Consolation; Troilus and Criseyde; Palamon and Arcite* (*The Knight's Tale*)		
1384		Death of Wycliffe	
1385	Appoints permanent deputy. J.P. in Kent		
1385–6	*The Legend of Good Women*		
1386	Knight of the Shire for Kent, then loses controllerships		Council of Regency: impeachment of Suffolk
1386–90		Gower's *Confessio Amantis*	
c.1387– 1400	*The Canterbury Tales*		
1388		Thomas Usk executed	The Merciless Parliament
1389	Clerk to the King's Works		Restoration of Richard's power
c.1390		Third (C text) version of *Piers Plowman*	
1391	Relinquishes Clerkship: appointed Subforester		
1392			Death of Anne
1394	Extra grant for good service		
1399	Grants confirmed by Henry IV		Deposition and murder of Richard and accession of Henry IV
1400	Dies 25 October		

1: *Gothic Chaucer*

DEREK BREWER

Lo here the forme of olde clerkis speche
In poetrie, if ye hire bokes seche.

WHAT IS THE general nature of Chaucer's works and its relation to his times? The Canterbury pilgrims know what *they* want: entertaining stories giving *sentence* (or *doctrine*) and *solaas* (or *mirth*). For them, story telling is an agreeable *game*, or it conveys serious information—not both at the same time. The Knight and Harry Bailly the innkeeper, good representative men, express these commonsense ideas (CT, I, 788–801). Like many such ideas, on examination they appear less clear. The first testing comes in 'The Miller's Prologue'. All pilgrims, but especially, says Chaucer, the 'gentils', think 'The Knight's Tale' 'noble'. Then the Miller also proposes to tell what he too describes as a 'noble' tale. It will be, he says, 'a legende and a lyf', that is, a Saint's life—probably the most generally popular fourteenth-century genre—but his 'legend' will be of a carpenter and his wife. Everyone assumes that the Miller's tale will be a *lewed dronken harlotrye*, so we can expect parody, at least, and the literal-minded Reeve expects slander. Despite the protests, we may assume that as a tale it is *solaas*. Yet most of the audience oppose it and we can assume no such organic relationship between *sentence* and *solaas* as that suggested by the Horation *dulce et utile*, or by the Neoclassical 'instruction by delighting', which has been familiar since the Renaissance and is often urged, if in perverse ways, even in the twentieth century. Chaucer himself emphasizes that the tale the Miller will tell has nothing to do with *gentilesse, moralitee* or *hoolynesse*: a *cherles tale*, told by a *cherl*, of *harlotrie*, as the Reeve's tale also will be. A blunt warning. We shall need a subtle argument for the improving effect of the study of literature if we accept the poet's own clear description and interpretation of it. The subject-matter is immoral; and it is not hypocritically offered as a cautionary tale. We may well disapprove. The poet, however, turns the tables on us if we disapprove. He writes (and we may notice the inconsistent abandonment of the illusion of oral delivery):

> *Turne over the leef and chese another tale*   (I, 3177)

—which receives an echo in modern controversies over the presentation of obscene television shows—you can always switch off. Such an argument can of course also be used in defence of public hanging, drawing and quartering, (no one *has* to look). This fourteenth-century poet, like a modern artist, adopts a morally neutral stance in judgment of his subject-matter: again, like the modern artist, his only obligation, he says, is to the way things are; as he puts it, he feels he must not 'falsen' his 'mateere'.

There are some differences from modern times. Chaucer is joking, and is satirizing his audience. His matter is a story, not 'reality'. You know, he implies, that you want to hear this dirty story, and don't in the least care about *sentence* in this case, even if you did think 'The Knight's Tale' 'noble'. He will satisfy us, but take no responsibility. Nevertheless, at this point he remains within the fictional plane. That is, we do not for a moment believe that he is really reporting the actual courtly words in rhyme of a real peasant Miller on a specific pilgrimage; it would obviously be impossible, indeed ridiculous, and is therefore amusing. We may similarly expect, for the same literary reason, not actually to be told of real immorality in the tale. On the other hand, Chaucer truly is disclaiming responsibility for telling immoral tales. He is denying the instructions of the dominant, or 'official' culture, essentially ecclesiastical in literary matters, which (quoting St. Paul, Rom. XV. 4) required that all that is written should be written for our doctrine; should be morally improving. He also amused himself over that same requirement at the end of 'The Nun's Priest's Tale', though the free play of mind in that poem has not always been observed by critics intent on making too earnest of his game.

Chaucer ultimately repented his revolt against the official culture, as we know from the 'Retracciouns' at the end of *The Canterbury Tales* (not present in all the manuscripts), in which he repudiated not only the obviously immoral tales like 'The Miller's Tale', but *all* his secular writing. Moreover, the 'Retracciouns' deny the possibility of purely self-enclosed fiction. They assert that literature has an effect on us. In them the poet breaks out of the self-enclosed fictional frame of *The Canterbury Tales* to address us directly, a real man speaking to men, no narrative pose or irony, no jokes, but in real sincere earnest. This major inconsistency in *The Canterbury Tales* has been somewhat neglected, but it is only one of many inconsistencies, of different kinds, in Chaucer's works.

The range of inconsistencies and internal incompatibilities within *The Canterbury Tales* is formidable and deserves recognition for what it is. Much criticism has been devoted to arguing round or through such difficulties in a local way, or in condemning them as artistic flaws, but we might do better to follow our intuitions: that is, to accept the dislocations first as natural enough, then to see that they imply important differences from what we usually expect in art and culture which it is worth our while to recognize. The recognition of difference will increase our enjoyment and understanding. We shall see what it is to be a Gothic poet, rather than a Neoclassical or Romantic or a modern poet. We shall become more conscious of Chaucer's immense, though not unlimited, variety, and of the problem of unity, or at least, of whatever is the opposite of disintegration, in his work. We shall learn to meet in Chaucer's work a frequent ambivalence at all levels, and to find an art that ebbs and flows into life like the tide on an indented coast, with no clear demarcations.

In the subject matter of *The Canterbury Tales* *sentence* and *solaas* may be distinct and incompatible. 'The Miller's Tale' has plenty of *solaas*, but no *sentence* even in mockery. The very notion of *sentence* may be mocked, as it is explicitly in 'The Nun's Priest's Tale'. 'The Parson's Tale' has only *sentence* and the Parson quotes St. Paul to deny the value of all fiction (CT, X, 33–4). He himself aims at truth, though what he calls his 'meditation' (it is not the sermon it is often called), turns out after all to be typical old-fashioned layman's moralizing. The Parson disdains *solaas* and *mirth*. Such *sentence* opposes *solaas*, as Chaucer's 'Retracciouns', already referred to, condemn all his secular works. Apparently incompatible subject-matter is contained within the *Tales*.

There are also many inconsistencies of form in Chaucer's works. The 'Retracciouns' apart from its subject-matter is a glaring example of the author breaking the fictional frame and speaking to us directly and sincerely. It is not surprising that many scribes omitted it. More scrupulous modern editors and readers cannot so easily disregard it, because Chaucer clearly makes it run straight on from 'The Parson's Tale', and because it is fully consonant with the Parson's remarks in his Prologue. We find similar breaking of the fictional frame in one way or another elsewhere: for example in 'The Prologue to The Man of Law's Tale', where there are references to the real-life Chaucer himself; the ending of 'The Clerk's Tale' in the so-called 'Lenvoy de Chaucer' whose fictional status, and compatibility with the tale it follows, are very dubious; and in 'The Merchant's Tale', where a character inside the tale refers to the Wife of Bath who exists outside the tale on a different fictional level altogether (IV, 1685). When to these examples are added addresses to both the real and fictional audiences; comments by the poet himself and meant literally about his own narrative art; and such self-description by the ostensible narrator as being himself a dull man in the middle of 'The Squire's Tale', supposedly told by a very sprightly young man (V, 278–90); then we have a formidable list of inconsistencies and discontinuities of various kinds. Yet there are more; for example there are major inconsistencies in the presentations of character, as in the learned references made by the unlearned Harry Bailly and the Wife of Bath, or in the extraordinary changes in the Pardoner's attitudes at the end of his tale. There are also varying inconsistencies between the pilgrims and the tales they tell. There are further inconsistencies of narrative level and point of view within the tale; and local inconsistencies of tone. The varieties of tone themselves may constitute an inconsistency best described as indecorum; yet they are quite deliberate, like the jumble of religious references with gross improprieties.

To sum up, it is as if we have to do with a picture that does not obey our laws of perspective, though our natural enjoyment leads us to reject the notion of the poet's mere clumsiness, and suggests that other, unfamiliar, shaping principles may be at work. The analogy between Chaucer's works in this respect and the quality of the Gothic visual arts contemporary with him, with their disregard for perspective and their discontinuities of naturalistic representation, is close and fruitful. It has been argued by several critics. We are justified in adopting the term 'Gothic' to denote by analogy the literature contemporary with Gothic art.[1] Chaucer is therefore part of 'English Gothic Literature'.

[1] The Gothic analogy is now something of a commonplace. It was introduced into Chaucer criticism by C. A. Muscatine, *Chaucer and the French Tradition*, California 1957, following German art and literary historians. R. M. Jordan, *Chaucer and the Shape of Creation*, Harvard 1967, and D. W.

Chaucer was aware of the problem of inconsistency. In *Troilus and Criseyde* he quotes Geoffrey of Vinsauf's recommendation of the need for overall planning of a work (I, 1065–71), though with reference to conducting love intrigues, not poems. Again, Pandarus advises Troilus not to mingle in a letter:

Ne jompre ek no discordant thyng yfeere (II, 1037)

There was a well-known medieval doctrine of decorum of style to subject-matter. But this limited stylistic decorum does not govern subject-matter, nor changes of style and subject-matter within a work. Inconsistencies and discontinuities are unquestionably present in Chaucer's work.[1] In any case Chaucer would not be the only poet who practised something different from what he preached, even if Pandarus's instructions to Troilus on writing love-letters were to represent Chaucer's general views on art.

Our problems with form are matched by our puzzles over Chaucer's status as a poet. He is both irresponsible and responsible as an artist, and in neither way quite fits a modern reader's prepossessions. His disclaimer of responsibility for retailing improper fictions has already been quoted. On many other occasions, even where no question of impropriety is involved, he is apparently anxious to shift responsibility to his 'auctor', his 'authority' e.g.:

Wherfore I nyl have neither thank ne blame.
Of al this werk . . .
For as myn auctour seyde, so sey I.

(TC, II, 15–18)

But Chaucer is artistically even more irresponsible, because he has apparently no concept of the inviolability of artistic form, of the impossibility or indeed the heresy of paraphrase, of the enormous importance of the *mot juste*. He does not, as Sidney, Neoclassical, and Romantic critics do,

Robertson, *Preface to Chaucer*, Princeton 1963, valuably though at times controversially extends it. A salutary warning against misuse is given by E. Salter, 'Medieval Poetry and the Visual Arts', *Essays and Studies of the English Association 1969*, 1969, pp. 16–32.

[1] Also noted by N. E. Eliason, 'The Language of Chaucer's Poetry', *Anglistica*, XVII, Copenhagen 1972.

proclaim the sheer *importance* of literature, its supremacy over all other forms of human discourse and activity, and consequently the supreme calling of the poet as artist. At a high point in *Troilus and Criseyde* when the lovers are at last brought to the point of consummation, not only does he indulge in a touch of indecorous levity, but he actually invites the reader or hearer to increase or diminish his language according to preference and personal experience (TC, III, 1335–36).

This is a licence that we modern critics, in so far as it concerns his *meaning*, have not hesitated to take up, but on the part of the poet it implies a wonderfully fluid, easy-going attitude to artistic integrity. At the end of the same poem Chaucer invites Gower and Strode to correct it where need is. Like his Manciple and Parson he seems not to claim to be 'textueel' (IX, 235; X, 57; cf. VII, 959–61). Words are slippery things. On the other hand, even because of their slipperiness, in actual practice he is most anxious—no problem of sincerity here!—that scribes should get his words exactly right (Adam Scriveyn; TC, V, 1795; CT, I, 2062–63; more amusingly:

> *What was comaunded unto Lamuel*
> *Nat Samuel but Lamuel, seye I.*

> (CT, VI, 584–5)

Even with this, one scribe muddled the second Lamuel). But that anxiety is the great craftsman's concern, not a literary concept of the perfect unparaphrasibility of poetry and the high status of poets. He is entirely casual about his own reputation or posthumous fame (HF, 1876–7). He constantly adopts a deferential attitude towards his audience. He is an entertainer; almost, we may think, the last of those minstrels who did not turn to musical instruments. He mocks his own achievement through his Man of Law, who knows no stories but those

> *That Chaucer, thogh he kan but lewedly*
> *On metres and on ryming craftily*
> *Hath seyd hem in swich Englissh as he kan.*

> (II, 47–9)

It is as if he regards them as not well done, but is surprised to find them done at all. He worked hard when he was young, he writes, but as an old man he reflects, with a sincerity hard to doubt, that:

> *al shal passe that men prose or ryme.*
>
> (*Scogan*, 41)

Chaucer has in the end no more care for literature than had Shakespeare.

Quite different ideas were available to him. Contrast with Chaucer's Gothic disengagement towards literature the views of Petrarch expressed in Italy about the time of Chaucer's birth. Petrarch had an exalted, almost Neoclassical, view of the poet's superiority, of which a concise statement is available in the oration he delivered when crowned Laureate at Rome 8 April 1341. Petrarch writes, in part:

> poets under the veil of fictions have set forth truths, physical, moral and historical—thus bearing out a statement I often make, that the difference between a poet on the one hand and a historian or a moral or physical philosopher on the other is the same as the difference between a clouded sky and a clear sky, since in each case the same light exists in the object of vision, but is perceived in different degrees according to the capacity of the observers. Poetry, furthermore, is all the sweeter since a truth that must be sought out with some care gives all the more delight when it is discovered. Let this suffice as a statement not so much about myself as about the poetic profession. For while poets are wont to find pleasure in a certain playfulness, I should not wish to appear to be a poet and nothing more . . .
>
> The poet's reward is beyond question multiple, for it consists, firstly, in the charm of personal glory, of which enough has been said already, and secondly, in the immortality of one's name . . .
>
> (Translated by E. H. Wilkins, *PMLA* 68, 1953, 1241–50)

The similarity of these views with those of Sidney, who, in his *An Apology for Poetry*, 1595 (ed G. T. Shepherd 1965), creamed off the works of European scholars of literature in the sixteenth century, is obvious. But they also represent a medieval tradition, expressed for example by Alanus de Insulis (*De Planctu Naturae, Migne*, Pl, CCX, col. 451 BC), in the twelfth century and by many commentators on Virgil. It is natural for men with powerful minds who devote themselves to literature, whether creatively or (especially) critically, to exalt its importance. It certainly happens today. And they are not entirely wrong. But how different from Chaucer.

The kind of responsibility Chaucer feels towards literature complements his irresponsibility. When taking a responsible view he cites the

Pauline view already referred to in his 'Retracciouns', 'Al that is writen is writen for oure doctrine', and appears to understand it to mean that 'anything that is written ought to be written in order to improve us'. He comes down to the narrowest interpretation of *doctrine*; in his own work, as he mentions, to the translation of Boethius, legends of saints, homilies, morality, devotion. All other writings are 'enditynges of worldy vanitees' and to be recalled. They are worthless; it was irresponsible to produce them: serious literary responsibility condemns fictions, even if they are products of high literary art.

We are therefore in a curious position with regard to Chaucer's works. Our own responses, and six centuries of mature readers, including all our greatest poets but Tennyson, encourage us to believe that here is great poetry, and that great poetry is of high human value. Yet the poet himself did not share this view and the poems seem by our usual standards of form to be as fragmented as a shattered mirror, which the poet cannot be bothered to pick up. This must be wrong. We had better shatter and reconstitute our own ideas.

In fact this has already been done for us in modern literature and art. The drama nowadays has broken away from its self-contained Neoclassical unity that lasted from the seventeenth century till as late as the 1920s and has spilt over the proscenium arch to involve the real audience in its fictions. Illusion and reality are no longer clearly divided. A variety of dramatic forms abandon the fixity of a rigid printed text. Again, poetry has become oral to enthusiastic audiences and also frequently abandons fixed forms of metre, syntax, logic, meaning itself. Chaucer's inconsistencies and discontinuities are not remarkable by comparison with those of many modern poets. The novel now frequently abandons its original eighteenth-century concern with realistic representation of the natural social world.

Music offers us another useful analogy. The harmonic scales that underlie both 'Classical' and 'Romantic' music, with their strong emotional and imaginative associations, were developed first about the sixteenth century in Europe and came to dominate high musical culture. Medieval music was modal, whether the Gregorian chant, courtly song or folk-song. Under the triumph of the harmonic scale (and who would wish it away?) from among traditional forms only folk-song survived, largely unrecognized by high art until towards the end of the nineteenth century. The twentieth century has seen a revolution in music from

Stravinsky onwards which has quite altered our understanding of earlier music. Folksong has been recovered especially by the ballad-scholars, and our ears are open again to the still strange, but now marvellously attractive cadences of medieval musicians once entirely forgotten or derided. The principles of unity and fixity of note, of tonal compatibilities, of dominance and subordination, of associations of feeling, in this music are quite different from what Europeans and North Americans learnt from the seventeenth century onwards. Having been emancipated by modern music we can now hear and enjoy medieval music in its own right, fortunately without having to abandon the subsequent great classics.

It need hardly be added that the visual arts in our time have seen a similar destruction of once accepted absolute standards. Since the fifteenth century in painting Europeans became accustomed to the framed picture constituting its own self-enclosed world, dominated by a single visual point of view, giving a regular perspective of receding depth and consonant proportion, aiming with homogeneous materials to present an idealized naturalistic image. At the end of the nineteenth century began a process explosively developed in the twentieth century that destroyed the frame, scattered the single point of view and perspective, portrayed what could never be naturally seen by one pair of eyes at one moment, used miscellaneous materials, denied representationalism its supreme value, and exalted the casual and accidental, the crude, rough, the non-ideal. Once again it was possible to turn back to medieval art, in this case especially to manuscript illumination, and see it afresh in something like its own terms. The art of the thirteenth to the fifteenth centuries, the Gothic period, has attracted interest in its mixture of realistic and non-realistic forms, of partially disregarded frames and varied levels of representation, of multiple points of view, its indecorous mixture of serious and comic, religious and grotesque. Such a work as the famous Beatus Page of the St. Omer Psalter in the British Museum (Add. MS. 39810, f. 7) with its almost incredibly rich mixture of various elements offers a real analogy to such a work as *The Canterbury Tales*, and can, by being compared with later types of picture following different conventions, really clarify the nature of Chaucer's work, and of our response. It is by such analogies that we are justified in referring to English Gothic literature, and to Gothic Chaucer.

The history of criticism reinforces our sense of radical changes in forms of artistic culture which first changed away from the medieval and then, in the twentieth century, turned if not towards the medieval, nevertheless moved as it were in a parallel direction.[1] The great changes in English literature are in the seventeenth and twentieth century, but the first period of change was heralded by a New Criticism, the Neoclassical, whose first theoretical spokesman in England was Sir Philip Sidney in his *Apologie for Poetry*. Here is the insistence on decorum, on an idealized nature, on simplicity of *genre* (e.g. not to mix comedy and tragedy), on a single dominant point of view, with exaltation of the status of the poet, already foreshadowed by Alanus, and emphasized by Petrarch. Poetry becomes fully the instrument, in some ways the highest expression, of the official culture, conveying the official moral system, the official philosophy. What was once only the possession of Latin has now become the attribute of the fully-fledged vernacular. The formal Neoclassical ideal was stretched, not broken, by Romanticism and it remained dominant until the middle of the twentieth century. Nor is it, we may hope, utterly defeated: yet its weakening allows us to see medieval literature more in its own terms, as they now appear more nearly parallel with ours.

We live today in a time of the breaking of forms, and social institutions experience a turmoil which also offers some parallels, if remote ones, with the situation in the fourteenth century in England. It seems likely that universities, for example, those characteristically medieval inventions, are today becoming more like their medieval counterparts. They had taken on a new shape, at least in England, in the sixteenth century, and were designed as educational institutions for an *élite*, quite as much as institutions for research and the advancement of learning. Few readers of this book will need to be reminded that nowadays the forms and functions of universities are rapidly changing away from such hierarchical patterns and that in the late 1960s and 1970s they rather more resemble the disorderly congeries of the fourteenth century. In each case central authority is weak, though in different ways. In the fourteenth century it was the means of control in a technologically primitive society with a high level of illiteracy which caused weakness, though authority made absolute claims. Nowadays authority is weak for other reasons. The parallel of the medieval situation with *The Canterbury Tales*, in terms of authoritative *doctrine* and rebellious or unconforming *solaas* is clear. One aspect of this is the development of individualism. By the end of the fourteenth century the historical development of the sense of the indivi-

[1] *Chaucer: The Critical Heritage*, ed D. S. Brewer, 2 vol forthcoming.

dual as someone potentially apart from and even hostile to the social frame had proceeded a very long way.[1]

Different choices between varieties of life in the world and in religion were becoming open to many men. Even within each way of life either conformity and social cohesion or independence and alienation were possible. When at the same time traditional social constrictions and the claims of older authority were immense, the resulting tensions issued in open rebellion, like the Peasants' Revolt of 1381, or in deeply dissident religious movements like Lollardy (associated by many at the time with the Peasants' Revolt). I am not arguing for a strong similarity between the changing social structures of today and the fourteenth century, only for a distant analogy which allows us some degree of sympathetic insight into those earlier social and artistic forms. It is now a commonplace that late twentieth-century advanced Western national societies, and certainly that of England, are pluralist in culture; fourteenth-century English society may be described as unintentionally or reluctantly pluralist. There is enough similarity, for all the obvious differences between the modern and the ancient period, to enable us, in our day, to respond with particular sympathy to the extraordinary variety, and to the tensions, which seem to be reflected in the art of the fourteenth century, and specifically in Chaucer's work.[2]

Chaucer's genius is more versatile than that of any other major English writer. Although much of this versatility must be due to personal causes, it could not have flourished as it did except in a culture which favoured pluralism. The fourteenth century was peculiarly favourable to variety and miscellaneity, to sustaining simultaneously incompatible or conflicting cultural elements. Of course all human culture does this: no culture, no person, is a completely harmonious self-consistent whole. But some periods seem notably more tense than others, just as the Gothic style, more than most styles, accepts conflicting elements. To be able to speak of a certain style, even of a culture, implies some containment of fissipa-

[1] Cf. Colin Morris, *The Discovery of the Individual 1050–1200*, 1972, who shows how modern individualism develops from and in the culture of the twelfth century.

[2] The problems of analyzing the nature of Chaucer's work more closely than as analogy or reflection as a product of social pressures are very difficult. Cf. Professor Du Boulay's essay, below, and D. S. Brewer, 'Class Distinction in Chaucer', *Speculum* 43, 1968, 290–305.

rous elements, a kind of unity such as certainly existed in the fourteenth century in England, and in the Gothic style. But within the containment may be differing degrees of inconsistency, and consequent variety or multiplicity, and a versatile genius has consequently much scope. The fourteenth century offered Chaucer this scope, particularly in his specially favoured environment around Westminster and London. Even Gower makes use of it. Westminster was becoming the permanent centre of the King's court, and was also important in religion. London was only two miles away and was the centre of the nation's commercial life, and of legal, perhaps liberal, learning at the Inns of Court. Within this small area between City and Court were gathered remarkably varied possibilities, and the experience of severe strains.

If, in the light of modern experience and a contemplation of fourteenth-century culture, we therefore abandon the attempt to discover a relatively simply unified, non-Gothic, dominant pattern in the literary culture represented by Chaucer's works and their social circumstances, we can allow ourselves to distinguish several competing centres of power. I have already referred to one of these, the dominant ecclesiastical official culture, represented most effectively for our interests by 'The Parson's Tale' and the 'Retraccioun', but found elsewhere in many places in Chaucer's work. Another centre of power was the courtly vernacular. The courtly element was itself also partly an official culture, but was secular not ecclesiastical, orientated towards this-worldly personal human relationships, activities and enjoyments. These two official cultures were in close but uneasy relationship. They were allied in many respects. For example they shared a hierarchical view of society, and the court and the kingdom were largely administered by clerics. But they were hostile in other respects, for example in some (not all) of the notions about love and sexuality, or on the value placed on personal armed combat. Moreover, Lollardy, in origin as much courtly as anything else, and certainly lay rather than ecclesiastical, as the Lollard knights witness, shows how the lay courtly culture could attack the ecclesiastical on its own moral grounds as well, probably, as on grounds of financial greed.[1]

[1] For an introductory discussion of the Lollard knights in relation to Chaucer see D. S. Brewer, *Chaucer in his Time*, 1963: for the latest detailed historical account, K. B. McFarlane, *Lancastrian Kings and Lollard Knights*, Oxford 1972.

Both ecclesiastical and courtly official cultures were complex in themselves as well as being both allies and rivals. The official ecclesiastical culture comprised, but did not exactly control, the purely intellectual culture represented by philosophy and science, and it developed with intellectual discovery. Moreover the central Christian teaching has always been based on paradox and irony, of divinity that is human, of power that is not ordinary power, of losing one's life to gain it, of life that is death and death life. The Synoptic Gospels are perhaps the most variously paradoxical and ironic documents in the world's writings. Christianity itself began with that status of an unofficial culture to which in the latter part of the twentieth century, it seems rapidly to be returning, and even when the medieval Church's version of Christianity was dominant it necessarily contained within itself the ironic seeds of self-criticism and change, even of destruction and renewal. For the moment however our consideration must be limited to the more dominating aspects of the official ecclesiastical culture as represented in Chaucer.

All rationalizations, literal interpretations and institutional embodiments of the Gospels tend to rigidify their fluidity, to choose a dominant version that ossifies in the process of time, to simplify. A prime example of such simplification occurs at the end of *The Parson's Tale* with the evocation of the eternal delights of heaven, and the need to live a miserable life in this world in order to achieve the delights and avoid the horrors, of the next.

Heaven is the official ecclesiastical culture's view of the good life. Since all official cultures become so by repudiating certain areas of experience and kinds of behaviour, which may then be called unofficial counter-cultures, Hell is the official ecclesiastical culture's view of unofficial counter-cultures. When the official culture is narrowly ecclesiastical, Hell tends to be equated with the secular, and that is no doubt partly what the Parson is doing, in a way very typical of the Gothic period. Since the courtly was also secular we easily arrive at the famous joke in the thirteenth-century French poem *Aucassin et Nicolette* where the hero wishes to go to Hell when he dies, for there are all the courtly lovers and the beautiful people.[1]

[1] In Paradise, says Aucassin, are only old priests and cripples crawling in front of altars, etc., dying of hunger and thirst and cold and disease; while in hell are the fine clerks, and the knights killed in tournaments and 'rich wars', and other worthy men, and beautiful courteous ladies who have had

The Parson's concept of Heaven is rather static. There is more movement in Hell. Hell is presented in his meditation as a horrible pit down
into which a soul damned at judgment shall be drawn by a multitude of
devils. It is a place of mental and bodily pain, burning and darkness,
crowding and confusion of people, without respect for rank or sex, with
poverty and mutual hatred; a general anarchy of misery. Similarly, the
Deadly Sins are all represented as of demonic energy, unloving, greedy,
grasping, selfish, divisive, competitive and individualistic, taking always
short-term gratifications instead of long-term benefits. The Parson has a
regrettable, entirely human, interest in Hell, and hardly describes
Heaven. If Heaven is the opposite of Hell it is calm, bright, joyous, com-
fortable. There is an accepted hierarchy and distinction where each has
his justified place, but co-operation and mutual love allow the individual
to sink his sense of himself in the whole. Virtue, similarly, is co-
operation, self-sacrifice, postponement of personal gratifications in a
long perspective.

The pattern of Heaven and Hell, official culture and unofficial culture,
is repeated in Chaucer's poetry. What is approved of tends to be static,
aiming at serenity, unmoved, or detached from the world, like
Chaucer's heroines, or the quietist longings expressed in the short moral
Boethian personal poems, or the views expressed by Theseus in 'The
Knight's Tale'. The competitive, quarrelsome, active elements are contrasted with heavenly serenity, and tend to be secular (like the young
men in 'The Knight's Tale') as opposed to ecclesiastical or philosophical;
or, within the secular world, they are the ribald, unruly lower-class elements, contrasted with the upper-class. In passing, it may be remarked
that there is a striking dearth of references in Chaucer's work to Purgatory: of a mere total of five, two refer to wives being their husband's
purgatory on earth: another is Arcite's denial that he is in purgatory
when in prison—he is in hell. Of the remaining two references, both by
the Parson, one is merely casual and assimilates Purgatory effectively to
Hell (X, 715–20); the other is the briefest passing reference (X, 805–10).
Chaucer's imagination prefers the Either/Or, the *pro* or *con*. Genial he
may be, but not compromising.

In so far as the official ecclesiastical culture recognized Hell, it was in-

two or three lovers, with those barons; and there are gold and silver and
fine furs, harpers, minstrels and the king of this world. *Aucassin et Nicolette*
ed M. Roques, VI, 24–39, CFMA, Paris 1932.

clusive; in so far as it repudiated Hell, it was exclusive. In a sense it was both, as was Chaucer's poetry; illogical but natural. An acceptance paradoxically encloses a rejection. The official culture is inevitably in contact, because in conflict, with the unofficial. Each needs the other to maintain its sense of its own identity. The recalcitrant, relaxed, evasive, amorphous or rebellious nature of unofficial counter-cultures means that they take on meaning largely in opposition to the dynamics of effort, will and control of the official culture (though unofficial cultures also have some important positive qualities of their own). And also, of course, the official culture necessarily works on the unofficial cultures and is itself affected by their responses. The two kinds of culture are defined in related opposition to each other. Each is denied complete victory or defeat, and sometimes they change places, as seems to be happening in the late twentieth century. Mutual definition in conflict appears in the fourteenth century when official and unofficial cultures are seen in the form either as ecclesiastical versus secular, or as courtly-secular versus low-class secular. Chaucer's poetry represents these conflicts of embrace: ecclesiastical versus secular conflict appears most vividly in the 'Retracciouns' with almost total victory going to the ecclesiastical. The courtly versus the low-class conflict appears in the derisive term *cherles tale*, imputing to the lower classes the vulgarity of what is after all a courtly *fabliau* such as 'The Miller's Tale'. Courtly versus lower-class contempt appears in the presentation of the vulgar behaviour of the lower classes in the same *fabliaux*, in the competitive quarrelsome behaviour of the lower classes on the Canterbury pilgrimage, and in a number of casual references—e.g.:

> O stormy peple! unsad and evere untrewe!   (CT, IV, 995)

Yet Chaucer's poetry is also notable for the hospitality it offers to the unofficial cultures; to secular and lower-class elements, to folk-tale, folk-humour even of a coarse kind (as in some of the *fabliaux*), and in the laughter he raises often enough against the official culture, by satirizing clerics, for example. The benefit comes from the failure in Chaucer's poetry of the official culture to crush its opposite, and therefore from the fact of co-existence, the almost-balance of *pro* and *con*.[1]

---

[1] It has long seemed to me probable that the relative dullness of English literature of the fifteenth century (for all the important developments and expansions that took place at that time, and with the interesting special

The relative weakness of the official ecclesiastical culture in many places is nowhere more apparent than in its treatment of sexual love and of women, where the courtly secular is both unofficial and at its best. The sentiment of love is plainly rooted in biological sexual desire which is not a cultural phenomenon but a given condition of life. Nevertheless, our feelings are also culturally conditioned. The Middle Ages, as is well known, developed the sentiment of sexual love with an elaboration far beyond anything previously or even subsequently known and has influenced culture subsequently throughout the world. Now when all qualifications are made about the interreactions of secular with religious influences in the medieval elaboration of the sentiment of love, it can hardly be disputed that the incapacity of the Church to recognize much medieval treatment of sexual love as a genuine attempt to control, stabilize, humanize and even sanctify sexual desire, was a great failure and a great disaster, equivalent to the split caused by the Reformation, with which it was closely connected (Luther's marriage may be recalled). In the case both of love and of the Reformation we see the triumph of the logic of the official culture in excluding what it disapproved of (or alternatively we find incompatibilities within the total pluralistic culture so developed as to produce absolute divisions between elements that had previously co-existed). It is as if there were an attempt by Heaven not only to repudiate Hell but to banish it by logic from the cosmos: in other words, since this is not possible, to deny co-existence and plurality, to pretend that Hell does not exist. Such concealment is always dangerous to Heaven itself. In practice this situation did not arise in the fourteenth century because of the weakness of ecclesiastical prohibitions against the semi-official strength of the courtly culture which was devoted to the love of ladies, and because after all, the Church recognized love in a

exception of Malory's *Morte Darthur*) is a dullness caused by the successful imposition of the criteria of the dominant ecclesiastical culture, with its absolutist claims. This dates from the successful quelling of Lollardy in the University of Oxford by Archbishop Courtenay in 1387, but extends more widely as the fifteenth century progresses. (Cf. D. S. Brewer, *Chaucer in his Time*, 1973, pp. 228–35).

Malory was probably saved by his sturdy lack of intellectual interests, by his practicality, and by his firm grounding in the old-fashioned courtly secular culture of the Arthurian romances, operating in subtle relation with a simple but profound moral concern which is indeed part of his fifteenth-century ambience.

more general sense as the root of all being. The relative weakness of the Church as an authoritarian body which had only come to insist on priestly celibacy in the eleventh century allowed many priests to have unofficial wives, and many respectable clerics to write, in holiday moments, less respectable love-songs, even in Latin.

Nevertheless, another strange aspect of the dichotomy between official and unofficial cultures was that it was also a sexual dichotomy; since the official culture was exclusively masculine most of the feminine element in life must be unofficial—an extraordinary state of affairs, however much mitigated by qualifications in theory and practice. The dichotomy was reinforced, in an age when physical strength was very important in every sphere of life, by the greater physical weakness of women worn out by unlimited child-bearing. It was further reinforced by their deprivation of education. Even so, it was not completely inevitable. The Anglo-Saxons had given much greater equality to women than did later medieval men, who seem to have had a great desire for much greater specialization of human roles. (And English women have always had notoriously greater freedom than their Continental sisters.) The fact remains that in the Middle Ages women were largely identified with the unofficial culture, with temptation to sin, distraction of the ongoing masculine intellect, disorderliness. Abelard's love for Heloise is the tragic emblem.

One must not exaggerate, simply because no culture could obliterate the most vital element in the human condition. Since men need women, the official Gothic ecclesiastical culture adopted with passionate intensity one supreme feminine element, that represented by Mary the Mother of Christ, Mother and Virgin. Heaven was full of women. A curious sidelight on the developing 'feminism' in fourteenth-century England is that apparently the 'sex' of angels in general came to be represented as feminine about the middle of the century.[1] So the feminine image split, and as far as Chaucer's poetry goes we may say that he has broadly two positive images of the feminine to each of which he gives full, if apparently contradictory, assent: that of the official culture, represented by the Virgin-Mother, by St. Cecilia, perhaps Emily in 'The Knight's Tale' as courtly-official, and so on; and that of the unofficial culture, or cultures, an image represented by Venus on the courtly mythological level, by

[1] According to F. Bond, *Wood Carvings in English Churches*, I. 'Misericords', 1910, p. 150.

Criseyde, and on a lower social and moral level, by Alisoun and The Wife of Bath (Venus's daughter).

Chaucer is the most notably feminist author in English until Richardson, and has had few rivals since. Both the official and unofficial feminine images are important in his works, and it is characteristic that both should be so. We may well feel however that less interest attaches to his *positive* presentation of the official image, for though it is not weak, it is less artistically worked, and far less extensive. More interest attaches to his presentation of the official but *negative* image of women, that is, of the long tradition of fiercely jocular clerical Latin anti-feminist satire. This is the unofficial image of woman seen from the official side—Hell from Heaven. (And it must be remembered that images of Hell were also often comic, at the same time as horrific, in medieval culture.) Admittedly a man need not be a celibate cleric in order to mock women, wives and marriage, as extremely secular modern vaudeville comics and newspaper strip-cartoonists know. Antifeminism is quite natural in societies which to any extent specialize the roles of the sexes: but the satire that Chaucer enjoyed was mainly formulated in official Latin clerical writings from St. Jerome onwards, and although it appears elsewhere in Chaucer's work is brought to a climax in 'The Wife of Bath's Prologue'. This Prologue is a confession designed to make her appear as a comic, man-eating monster, embodying in part that ancient masculine fear of sex and of women that is less often recognized today than it should be. But as we should expect in Chaucer, he is equivocal. In his dramatically expressive portrait of the Wife in her Prologue, though he uses Latin material, he transposes it into the language of broad vulgar English free-wheeling feminine humanity. The Wife of Bath is triumphantly human and sympathetic, gloriously selfish and materialistic, always sacrificing long-term benefits in Heaven for short-term gratification on earth.[1] There are

---

[1] It may be that the most satisfactory, though still crude, method of distinguishing between higher and lower cultures, or official and unofficial cultures, is the degree to which they encourage long-term views and deferred benefits. Short-term gratifications, on the other hand, such as involve spontaneity, gathering rose-buds while we may, seizing the passing joy as it flies, taking no thought for the morrow, all seem to be characteristics of what are at least historically unofficial, or popular, cultures, and are not all unchristian. Some of these are negative, mere reluctance to be organized, but others are positive, which is why popular culture always

some inconsistencies in her presentation, including the uncertain impression we have that her fifth husband is alive at the beginning of her 'confession' and dead at the end—but that, though inconsistent, is very fitting, as reflecting the sense of flux, the absence of a fixed point of view. No sensible reader worries. The incompatibilities can live together. As a result, the satire against women of the official culture is joined by the laughter by and about women and also against the would-be dominant male, of an unofficial culture with a powerfully aggressive feminine element. Yet the official culture's hierarchical scale of values is even accepted. The Wife gladly agrees that virginity is superior to marriage, that she is barley-bread in comparison to wheat. She is no revolutionary. But she has had her world as in her time which is more than monks have had. The advantage of short-term gratifications is that you have at least made sure of them. A bird in the hand is worth a bird of paradise after death. Fundamentally the Wife of Bath is satisfied, though far from sated.

We also have a useful pointer here to the nature of laughter in Chaucer. It arises, as is generally the case, from the juxtaposition of incongruous elements; in particular in Chaucer from juxtapositions of official and unofficial aspects of culture. Such juxtapositions are so extraordinarily frequent in Chaucer, by contrast with his contemporaries, as to be a principle defining quality of his work.

First we may note how he presents himself. Laughter was traditionally associated with satire, and the classical justification of satire is that it is corrective. Certainly there is less kindliness in laughter than the rather sentimental English view usually assumes. It is painful to be laughed at and probably most people go out of their way to avoid it. Therefore clowns, and all those who for professional or other reasons attract laughter against themselves, almost always promote a double vision of themselves, whereby they dissociate their 'true' personality from that part that deliberately invites laughter. Comic actors can frequently be seen creating such a double image of the self. Chaucer does the same thing when

---

has some real value in itself.

Medieval official ecclesiastical culture took an extremely long view in postponing all benefits till after death, and in positively avoiding, at least in theory, short-term gratifications. (A full treatment of this topic would have to consider how strong a short-term gratification is the act of postponement; as well as many other problems. All that can be made here is a general suggestion.)

he projects a comic image of himself in his poems. Such apparently self-mocking self-description inevitably implies a superior part of himself which is associated with the audience, like them being later in time than the events being described, and it is this superior part of himself which tells us about his earlier, foolish, lesser, less essential, self. Who could *really* take Chaucer to be the 'dul man' he so often represents himself to be? This division between superior and inferior selves, in those poems in which he presents his own self as actually one of the *dramatis personae* (e.g. the love-visions, 'The Prologue' to *The Canterbury Tales*, but *not Troilus and Criseyde*) in itself corresponds to a division between higher and lower cultures, in this case, between the official aspects of the courtly secular culture, and the ignorant, consequently rejected, therefore unofficial, aspects.

On the other hand, though to be laughed at is painful, it is less painful than exclusion or assault. Laughter on the part of those who laugh is a substitute for more hostile action. If we laugh we do not fear, even if we usually do not love either. While we laugh we do not attempt to remove the object or cause of laughter. We tolerate it if it is superior to us, or patronize it if inferior, and we may even feel in part kindly towards the object, attribute to it some value, because we get enjoyment from laughing at it. Partly for this reason we like the Wife of Bath. Laughter therefore has a unitive function between those who laugh and those who are laughed at, though a unity arising from difference. In Chaucer most laughter is superior; either of the official culture against the unofficial, as with the official antifeminism of 'The Wife of Bath's Prologue' against her crudeness, or of the courtly against the inferior uncourtly, most obviously in *The Miller's Tale*, and *Sir Thopas*, or the learned against the ignorant, as in 'The Reeve's Tale'. But the laughter is by definition not simple condemnation; it implies acceptance, even pleasure. Furthermore, a certain amount of laughter in Chaucer's poetry is of the unofficial against the official. The Wife of Bath really does have a joke against the official culture: she has much more fun. Chaucer's genius is such that both kinds of laughter can coexist in the same passage. The portrait of Alisoun in 'The Miller's Tale' is funny because Alisoun is a ridiculous low-class imitation of a great lady of romance: but the parody also mocks the rhetorical abstractions of formal descriptions. Such two-way action is of the essence of mock-rhetorical writing, not limited to Chaucer, but found extensively in *The Nun's Priest's Tale*, where there is also ambivalent humour over the subjects of serious speculation, Fate, Free Will, Fore-knowledge Absolute. Both 'The Friar's Tale' and 'The Summoner's Tale' are mockery by unofficial secular cultures against important aspects of the dominant ecclesiastical official culture. To be laughed at is the forfeit which the official culture may have to pay for dominating the unofficial; or which the unofficial may pay for being unpunished. The greatness of the poetic humour of Chaucer consists in the variety and complex blends of contrasts of several different kinds which he combines in one poetic narration, but the key lies in the fundamental contrasts between various kinds of official and unofficial cultures. Most laughter arises, however, when the balance between the official and the unofficial is fairly even.

To return to the general interplay between the two in Chaucer's works, the balance between official and unofficial culture may well be very unequal. The 'Retracciouns' reveal a very heavy preponderance of the official, and there is, in consequence, no humour, irony or ambivalence. Much of the writing about women, on the other hand, is somewhat weighted towards the unofficial. In the use of language, since the vernacular was Chaucer's sole choice, and was essentially the language of women, the mother-tongue in every sense, the linguistic balance is almost entirely against the official, and there is nothing intrinsically comic in his using the vernacular. Yet a major comic paradox of 'The Wife of Bath's Prologue' is that while almost the whole of its content is derived from official clerical Latin writing against women, the work itself is in English and in several ways asserts the rights of women. Very few women in fourteenth-century England, if any at all, knew Latin —not even nuns who entuned the Latin offices full seemly through their noses every day. The Church had always had occasional recourse to the vernacular for preaching to the laity and for a few didactic works aimed at the laity and at religious women. But the serious central developing thought and work of the official ecclesiastical culture was only in Latin, restricted to men. The intimate clash in Chaucer between the two language cultures and their intrinsic attitudes is beautifully and comically illustrated in 'The Nun's Priest's Tale':

> *For al so siker as* In principio,
> Mulier est hominis confusio—
> *Madame, the sentence of this Latyn is,*

'*Womman is mannes joye and al his blis.*'

(CT, VII, 3163–66)

There could be no neater illustration of the contrast (which is also found in one or two macaronic lyrics outside Chaucer). Which version is correct, or preferred by Chaucer? For if the English is a mistranslation of the Latin, the Latin is also in a sense a mistranslation of the English, and each language has its own characteristic validity. History and natural feeling are all nowadays on the side of the vernacular, secular, unofficial version. The story and the poem give no answer one way or the other. In a sense Chantecleer—like Chaucer, perhaps—believes both, without insincerity. So sharp a juxtaposition of opposites creates not so much a sense of the relativity or fluidity of truth as of the limitations of any specific formulation of it, and the consequent call for a complementary formulation. Interpretations of 'The Nun's Priest's Tale' as being an intentional allegory of the Fall, that is, as a conscious instrument of the official culture, are surely wrong, but an echo of Eve's delinquency may legitimately be heard in the passage just quoted. If so, then Adam's fault must be remembered too, and Chantecleer's silliness is evidently masculine enough. Moreover, women do indeed bring men *joye and solas* (though this is rather an egotistical way of praising them), as well as trouble. Both the Latin and the English 'sentences' are extremes, and one extreme calls for the other as modification: *pro* needs *con*. Once again, there is no compromise, no grey middle term between black and white, but the sentences when set side by side, for all their logical incompatibility express in a way a complex truth. Unity is found in the complexity, as achieved by juxtaposition, by the metonymy of close association itself, by the complementarity of the pattern, and by the fact that it is contained by one speaker. If the speaker, Chantecleer or Chaucer, is prepared to entertain both terms at once, even with apparent self-contradiction, that may be unity enough. The English language also asserts some capacity for containment, for in this very poem it demonstrates an ability to handle the topics of the official culture. The vernacular is now adequate to convey complex thought and feeling, and has absorbed terms taken directly or through French from Latin into the English stock, so that it can handle much—not all—of the intellectual material normally treated in Latin. Chaucer necessarily withdraws from a full takeover of the Latin intellectual culture by the vernacular:

I wol nat han to do of swich mateere. (CT, VII, 3251)

The time was not yet ripe and the official intellectual culture remained mostly Latinate though on an ever narrower basis until the eighteenth century. Chaucer had all the same made an important advance of the vernacular.

He was also associated with another development of the vernacular which was apparently more hostile to official Latin culture. This was Lollardy. The early celebrated group of Lollard Knights were close courtly associates with each other; one of them, Sir John Clanvowe, was a poetic disciple of Chaucer's, and presumably a friend, as others may well have been. The complications of and the changes in Lollardy need not be discussed here. It is enough to recall that it was variously hostile to many beliefs and institutions of varied importance, like the doctrine of transubstantiation, the wealth and political power of the Church, marriage, Sunday observance, pilgrimage, as well as to a lot of general jollity. The demand to have the Bible, the central official sacred Latin book, in the 'unofficial' vernacular, proved to be Lollardy's most explosive characteristic, and developed into its principal requirement and defining quality. For all the scholastic Wyclif's importance, the movement was essentially secular in origin. At first the gentry adhered, but persecution shook most of them off, and in the fifteenth century Lollardy was almost entirely a lower-class movement. It was thus doubly unofficial. Early in the fifteenth century the very use of English, let alone the possession of a Bible in English, was regarded by the Church as presumptive evidence of dangerous heresy.[1] The opposition of Lollardy to the official culture is also paradoxical, as can be expected from the paradoxical nature of Christianity, because much of Lollardy arose from simply taking literally certain parts of the Church's own message. The presence of Wyclif and other priests in the early days of the movement helps to mark its equivocal nature. Yet it was a real development in spiritual culture, aiming, like many such movements, even in our own day, at a new sincerity, spontaneity and inwardness of spiritual life in the world, a new but not unspiritual secularity that has obvious parallels with that over-

[1] For Clanvowe see K. B. MacFarlane, ref. page 12; V. J. Scattergood, 'The Authorship of "The Boke of Cupide"', *Anglia* 82, 1964, 137–49; B. Cottle, *The Triumph of English 1350–1400*, 1969. For the heresy, see M. Deanesly *The Lollard Bible*, Cambridge, 1920, pp. 319, 352, 366. I am obliged to Mr. T. J. Heffernan for drawing my attention to these last references.

whelming interest in personal human relationships, in the uninhibited
movements of the human heart, especially sexual love, that characterizes
so much of Chaucer's work, and the unofficial secular culture.

Chaucer's unofficial vernacular culture also carried, what was very
different from Lollardy, some elements of folk-culture, that is, of oral
tales, and their inherent concepts.[1] There is a strong folk-element seen
especially clearly in the plots of several of the *Tales*, notably the comic
and improper *fabliaux*. To speak of folk-tale in the fourteenth century
does not exclude courtly or clerical participation and the situation
cannot be read along class-lines. The folk-tale plots of 'The Miller's' and
'Reeve's Tales' are widespread through Europe in several languages and
well established in writing. The earliest account of the folk-tale pear-tree
episode of 'The Merchant's Tale' is the twelfth-century Latin *comoedia
Lydia* written in a highly elaborate literary style. Like other such episodes
it is also found in the East and may have originated in India. Nevertheless, the official culture as represented so conveniently for us in Chaucer's
understanding by 'The Parson's Tale' did not approve such frolicking
even when its indecency was concealed within the learned language, and
though it may occur in Latin it must be regarded as 'unofficial', in opposition to the dominant notions of what was right and proper. Yet
Chaucer in *The Canterbury Tales* invokes these ribald elements more
liberally, in terms of the number of tales (not of the actual bulk of material), than any others. They have a coarse and hearty humour that mocks
pretensions to dignity, justice and superiority (whether of age, or learning) or to marital possession, or to official ecclesiastical position. They
share with other folk-tale plots in the Tales ('The Clerk's Tale' of Griselda, 'The Wife of Bath's Tale') a certain qualified optimism, a belief in
'joy after woe', more characteristic of the basic irrepressible humanity of
the uneducated folk the world over, than of sophisticated clerks, who
inclined to pessimism then as now. But these folk-tale plots may also be
told in a way, characteristic of courtly 'folk', that satirizes class inferiors,

[1] A largely unexplored subject, but see F. L. Utley, 'Folklore, Myth and
Ritual' in *Critical Approaches to Medieval Literature: Selected Papers from the
English Institute 1958–9*, New York 1960, pp. 83–109. There is useful
material in *Sources and Analogues of the Canterbury Tales*, ed W. F. Bryan and
G. Dempster, Chicago 1941; *Originals and Analogues of Some of Chaucer's
Tales*, Chaucer Society Publications, Part I, 1872, Part II, 1875, Part III,
1876, Part IV, 1886, Part V, 1887. See also *The Literary Context of Chaucer's
Fabliaux*, ed L. D. Benson and T. M. Andersson, New York 1971.

as 'The Miller's Tale' and 'Sir Thopas' do. They are ambivalent.

The complex cultural pluralism here briefly and schematically sketched as it appears focused in Chaucer's works contains other pluralisms. Fortunately we may disregard the political, legal, administrative and practical elements of Church and State, Latin and Anglo-French, since they hardly appear in the literature. The inner complexities of the official Latin culture have also necessarily been largely neglected, though the internal conflicts between multiple pagan sources of knowledge and the equally multiple elements of the specifically Judaeo-Christian sources and inspiration had once been severe, even if by the fourteenth century they were mostly reconciled. Some other characteristics of the official culture need to be mentioned. First it was historically based, and had an intense consciousness of time past and future. It saw a purpose in history, and was concentrated upon an end. Beginnings and ends were important, but especially the end. Doomsday was absolute judgment. The last moments of a completely ill-spent life might redeem it. 'The ende is every tales strengthe.' (TC, II, 260). 'The RetraccIouns' thus count in moral terms for more than all the rest of Chaucer's works. But this absolutism allows much flux, much divagation, before the end. Associated with the historical teleological pattern is an intense idealism. The end represented the achievement of the highest ideal. 'Be ye perfect' (Matt. V. 48). There was a purposeful seeking and a consequent tension in official culture. Since official culture was idealistic, the unofficial culture usually represents relaxation, recreation, sport, frivolity. If the official culture was a seeking, a straining after long-term spiritual benefit, the unofficial culture could only be a finding of short-term physical gratification. But it is worth emphasizing that the official culture was intellectually optimistic, as on the whole the unofficial cultures, perhaps through mere unthinkingness, were also optimistic—folk-tales tend to have happy endings, and after the Crucifixion comes the Resurrection. Historians, with the exception of Professor Du Boulay[1] have tended to emphasize the pessimism of the later Middle Ages, but this may well be to exaggerate certain tendencies in the image of modern literary despairs. If there was optimism, it did not imply a foolish blindness to misery and wickedness. There was often a rationally low estimate of the world, traditionally expressed by Chaucer:

[1] Cf. F. R. Du Boulay, *An Age of Ambition*, 1970.

> The world hath mad a permutacioun
> Fro right to wrong, fro trouthe to fikelnesse.
>
> ('Lak of Stedfastnesse', 19–20)

But there is nothing in the Middle Ages to match both the sense of a purposeless, valueless, arbitrary, 'accidental' universe, and the literally suicidal despair, that marks so much of the literary (though not the scientific) culture of the West in the latter part of the twentieth century. For the official culture of the Middle Ages certainly the world of appearances, of naturalistic experience, just like the world of literature and our very thoughts, was not only corrupt but transient and ultimately unimportant, and

> al shal passe that men prose or ryme.
> Take every man hys turn, as for his tyme.
>
> ('Scogan', 41–2)

There was no easy evasion of suffering: rather it was *through* suffering, through meeting the worst, that the best, which lay behind appearances, might be achieved, and which was all the time wanting us to achieve it, helping us.

> And Trouthe thee shal delivere, it is no drede.
> ('Truth, Balade de Bon Conseyl' 7, repeated at 14, 21, 28)

Truth is not only 'what is true', but God himself. The individual soul was offered in the long term a prospect of eternal delight, at what was in comparison a slight cost in short-term gratification. Boethius in *The Consolation of Philosophy* had expressed that duality most attractively to Chaucer, as he did to thinking laymen for a thousand years or more through the Middle Ages and later. Chaucer constantly draws on Boethius for material and attitude in what are nevertheless his most personally sincere lyrics, 'The Former Age', 'Fortune', 'Truth', 'Gentilesse', 'Lak of Stedfastnesse'; whose uniqueness and success in the general body of English literature deserve more notice. It is also worth noting that Chaucer finds the secular Christian wisdom of Boethius more personally sympathetic, eight centuries after Boethius's death, than contemporary fourteenth-century ecclesiastical formulations of ordinary religious devotion, or than those expressions of transcendental mystical experience which in his very lifetime reached their greatest height in English with the work of Hilton, Dame Juliana, and the author of *The Cloud of Unknowing*. Boethius, like Chaucer a Christian man of the world, admirably expresses the world's charm yet transience, the need for the individual's mind to rise above the most adverse immediate circumstances, even death by torture, and in so doing to express an ultimate optimism about the goodness and purpose of Creation. Granted many variations, this was the general temper of medieval official culture, that needs always to be born in mind.

Finally, it must be remembered that the official culture was essentially intellectual, cognitive. I do not mean that it excluded feeling and imagination for it obviously did not, but that it primarily sought knowledge and truth. The nature of salvation was thought to depend on getting the truth about the universe, and about oneself. This was the reason for the passionate conviction of the importance and significance of life in general and of how the individual thought and conducted himself. This was why heresy was so important and so frightening, and why it was persecuted. It was no exaggeration to say at least in theory that the persecutor was being cruel to be kind. The modern abandonment of the sense of absolute truth in Christianity by so many modern Christians as well as by atheists should not make us forget that once all Christians felt as strongly about truth as scientists do now. It is well recognized that modern science arises from the medieval Christian view of the universe, even though it has broken that view.[1] Knowledge of the physical universe was not as important as theological knowledge, but it was part of that order. The unofficial cultures were of course unintellectual or anti-intellectual, and suffer for it, like the miller in 'The Reeve's Tale,' who despises clerks.

It is clear that the literary form which could most fully realize the complicated cultural situation must be an encyclopaedic one, and we are not surprised to find various encyclopaedic forms dominating the literary culture of the time. The Bible has some claim to be regarded as encyclopaedic and it was basic and universal; the many *Summa* of the schoolmen offer an example of another kind; but more specific to the literature of the Gothic period in Europe are such encyclopaedic poems (to select only two examples that deeply influenced Chaucer) as *Le Roman de la Rose* and *La Divina Commedia*. The poems of his exact contemporaries

[1] For one of the latest accounts see R. Hookyas, *Religion and the Rise of Modern Science*, Edinburgh 1972.

Gower's *Confessio Amantis* and Langland's *Piers Plowman* are also encyclopaedic in scope. Chaucer's own personal taste clearly ran to learning,
and he achieves an intellectual range greater than that of any other poet,
let alone major poet, in English. The man matched the age. Such univer-
sality of interest and resource in a poet could not have occurred at any
other period of our history. Even Milton is surpassed.

The encyclopaedic tradition in literature has been identified by Professor Northrop Frye in *Anatomy of Criticism* as 'Menippean Satire' or
alternatively, 'Anatomy'. *The Canterbury Tales* contains even the mixture of prose and verse which Professor Frye shows is typical of purer
elements of the *genre*. It is not surprising that, though he overlooks
Chaucer's work when establishing his concept of the form, Professor
Frye describes Chaucer's favourite serious reading, Boethius's *Consolation of Philosophy*, as 'pure anatomy'.[1] Frye notes that Chaucer was one of
the favourite authors of the writer of 'the greatest Menippean satire in
English before Swift', Robert Burton (*op. cit.* p. 311). Nigel Longchamp,
whose work was known to, and which provides interesting comparisons
with, Chaucer, wrote in the *Speculum Stultorum* a pure Menippean satire.

The terms 'anatomy' and 'Menippean satire', not quite synonymous,
come together because a taste for widespread learning, combined with
an interest in the world, seem to lead to satire. Satire is the natural product of an idealistic intellectual culture, simply because practically every
thing in this world is less than ideal.

The intellectual and idealistic bias of 'encyclopaedism' does not encourage mere 'imitation' in words of the social or natural world of experience, however great may be the interest in the world. Some of what
Professor Frye writes of the *genre* admirably illuminates this aspect of
Chaucer's work:

> The Menippean satire deals less with people as such than with
> mental attitudes (e.g. *Troilus*). Pedants, bigots, cranks, parvenus,
> virtuosi, enthusiasts, rapacious and incompetent professional men of
> all kinds (e.g. *many of the Canterbury pilgrims, the Eagle of 'The House
> of Fame', the birds of 'The Parliament'*) are handled in terms of their
> occupational approach to life as distinct from their social behaviour.
> The Menippean satire thus resembles the confession . . . (*as of The
> Wife of Bath and the Pardoner*).
>
> (*op. cit.* p. 309, *with insertions in italics by the present writer*)

[1] Northrop Frye, *Anatomy of Criticism*, Princeton, N. J. 1957, p. 312.

Though it would be fruitful to continue to analyze Chaucer's works, severally or generally, as Menippean Satire, or Anatomy, it is important to note the other literary form which is so influential in Chaucer: that of romance. Though the origins of romance are earlier than the Middle Ages, romance is the dominant form of Gothic secular literature, though its religious form was even more widespread, as Saint's Life. Secular romance is a courtly form which lives almost entirely in the vernacular, and to that extent has strong unofficial elements, seeking satisfaction in the world here and now, especially in sexual love. The mainspring of Chaucer's early poetry, as I have shown elsewhere, is to be sought in the English vernacular romances current in his boyhood.[1] Romance may be defined by reference to its interest in individual satisfactions and personal relationships (of physical love or physical contest) and also by its happy ending, its optimism, in which it reflects not only popular but official culture. Furthermore, in its typical form, the Quest, romance clearly images the idealistic, purposeful, even yearning, strain of the official culture. Romance also has two aspects, inner and outer. The outer aspect, of arms and adventure, hardly interests Chaucer at all. The inner aspect, of the hero's quest for a love which shall be a spiritual, imaginative and emotional adventure, not merely sexual, absorbs Chaucer deeply, and develops into something more in himself and in his culture; a quest for knowledge, of tidings, stories, people, intellectual matters, an inclusiveness of human experience, leading eventually to a concern for the highest spiritual achievement, for salvation, as imaged rather indirectly in the apotheosis of Troilus and more directly, but alas, all too negatively, in the Parson's 'meditation' about the way to the 'Jerusalem celestial'. Thus do romance and anatomy in the end unite, with the inclusiveness of anatomy and the happy ending of romance.

The combining of anatomy and romance produces further ironic developments in later romance, and especially in Chaucer. The analytical mind fostered by anatomy, which juxtaposes so many miscellaneous elements, causes them to interact. If anatomy is sustained by the long-term optimism of romance, romance is also subjected by anatomy to corrosive comparisons and hence qualifications. Spontaneity is shown not to last: transience begins to look like lack of value. Anatomy and romance may come to seem mutually incompatible and hostile. The classic confronta-

[1] 'The Relationship of Chaucer to the English and European Traditions', in *Chaucer and Chaucerians*, ed D. S. Brewer, 1966, pp. 1–38.

tion of romance with anatomy, in Chaucer's work before *The Canterbury Tales*, though often foreshadowed in shorter poems, is *Troilus and Criseyde*, that ironic romance, where confrontation as well as salvation is at last focused in the ending. Troilus finds his happy ending, intrinsic to romance, and, it seems, in accord with the official culture: but it has been postponed till after death, and by comparison his earthly love-affair shrinks a little; its gratifications were immediate, but transient, as of the lower culture.

The Canterbury Tales offers other confrontations, and the final disastrous victory in the 'Retracciouns' for the severest aspect of the official ecclesiastical culture. By a paradox, anatomy in this conclusion is denied its inclusiveness, romance its happy ending in this life. Satire itself turns into outright condemnation.

Yet this last word is again paradoxically not final to later time. The process of time which brings such transmogrifications also, in literature at least, preserves them. The works of intervening time are not destroyed, but coexist with the end that denies them, as was characteristic of the sustained tensions of the culture of the time and to be expected from the human condition. Neither flux nor stasis has absolute rule, but must coexist in a state of ironical tension. Given the nature of Gothic literary culture, its supreme expression must be an irony.

The peculiar precarious balances, inconsistencies and tensions of the Gothic period are not unique. They arise out of the human condition, are endemic within it, and are found in all periods. This is one reason for the continuous relevance of the major and indeed minor works of the Gothic period. It seems however that Gothic art in general, and the verbal art of the late fourteenth century, and of Chaucer, in particular, were at a point of balance between a multiplicity of forces, new and old, that was able to contain unusual diversity. Langland, the *Gawain*-poet, and to a less extent Gower, all witness to this multiplicity, but none so fully as Chaucer. (The others all have rather less detachment, rather more urgency to find and communicate a view, a certainty, a commitment, than Chaucer has except at the very end of his writing career, but they are all sufficiently ambivalent.) Irony is the very literary figure to express, even to create, this ambivalent culture. Irony being the statement of two different, often opposing meanings, in one set of words, it conveys both the oppositions, or incompatibilities, or inconsistencies, and their yoking together, that we find everywhere in Chaucer. Unity may sometimes seem no more than mere contiguity, but the acceptance of contiguity expresses an attitude that is itself a unifying; it is that toleration, that love, which so many critics have rightly found in Chaucer. There were other attempts to unify, important over large areas, made by the age itself. The construction of hierarchies of value that allowed for that 'principle of plenitude' explored by Professor Bennett[1] is one of the most important. And it must be emphasized that by no means all that Chaucer writes is to be taken as ironical at the literal level. There is a very great deal that we are meant to accept simply and as it were naïvely in its literal obvious sense. If in the end we fail to find a completely watertight general scheme to express our understanding, we need not be surprised. Neither Chaucer, nor English Gothic literature, nor human life, is to be so contained. A pregnant phrase has been attributed to Professor Noam Chomsky: 'All grammars leak.' All systems of thought are inadequate to contain the richness of human life.

For a poet to reflect (or create) so fully such a cultural situation brings some losses, or rather, involves the absence of some literary pleasures. The inconsistencies and discontinuities noted in Chaucer at the beginning of this essay, while they can reflect and create a valid sense of life even more penetratingly by the absence of organic or logical connection and of overall naturalistic representation, nevertheless cannot give us the sort of realistic representations bound by chains of cause and effect which the novel provides, and for which, especially when we are young, we naturally hunger. Chaucer's own advances in naturalistic realism are huge, and deserve recognition, but they are still set against a conceptual abstract view of 'reality', and are therefore still a part of his *pro* and *con*, and he writes no satisfactorily complete novel. There is another absence, perhaps more serious, though again more important when we are young. That 'sober certainty of waking bliss' (or, as usually preferred nowadays, certainty of brutal disaster), that guidance and sense of exalted commitment, given by some Neoclassical, but especially by Romantic and post-Romantic writers, up to D. H. Lawrence and beyond, who assume the heavy responsibilities of the imaginative verbal artist to be more than philosopher, historian or priest, is not much to be found in Chaucer's contemporaries, as Mr. Burrow has pointed out, and least of

[1] J. A. W. Bennett, *The Parlement of Foules*, Oxford 1957.

all in Chaucer himself.[1] Such commitment is a Neoclassical and later, not a Gothic function, of the poet. We return to Chaucer's 'irresponsibility' as a poet, only qualified when he himself condemns all his best imaginative work. He only takes absolute responsibility, only offers guidance and absolute commitment and exaltation, in a rejection that we ourselves can only—supreme paradox!—reject. Within his imaginative work, he takes no responsibility. He throws it on to the reader. We are treated as equals. This is why we can reject his rejection and remain true to the experience of reading him. Chaucer requires, and we must supply, not disciples, not partisans, but responsible readers.

[1] J. A. Burrow, *Ricardian Poetry*, 1971. See also D. S. Brewer, *Chaucer*, 3rd (Supplemented) edition, 1973, pp. 165 ff.

2: The Historical Chaucer

F. R. H. DU BOULAY

THE WORLD IN WHICH Chaucer lived was small in terms of people but large in terms of geography. A magical journey backwards in time would place us in an England where the most terrifying noise would not be made by bomb or jet but the yelling of a murderous crowd, and where for every twenty people on today's streets there would be only one. The south-east was already more heavily populated than the rest of the country, but the London throngs would have seemed comparatively thin. Perhaps the age-structure of the population would also have appeared different. Many children died, and to be fifty was to be quite old. When Chaucer began his literary career the bubonic plague had recently taken a specially heavy toll of the very young, so that by modern standards English life was carried on by a large majority of people who were between twenty and forty years old. The children, as was customary, fitted into the work of the adult world without the doting attention of today. Above all, the effective leadership of society was in the hands of relatively few men. The historian who reads the records of government, law and commerce between 1340 and 1400 is constantly surprised by meeting the same people and noticing how often they knew each other and were connected with the same affairs. In his brilliant *Some New Light on Chaucer*, Professor J. M. Manly tried to identify some of the characters in *The Canterbury Tales* with real people, and even if he does not always carry conviction it is a remarkable sign of society's smallness that such attempts at identification could be made. Another illustration of this close community is furnished by the account-book of Gilbert Maghfeld, a London merchant and money-lender. His customers between 1390 and 1395 included nobles, knights, clerks and merchants from England and abroad, and of these no less than thirty to forty are known to have been associated in some way with Chaucer.[1]

Though lightly peopled, the world of Chaucer was mobile. War, diplomacy, trade, administration and the impulses of religion shifted men and women of even humble station about the country and far beyond its shores. The framework of a pilgrimage from Southwark to Canterbury which Chaucer chose for his best-known collection of tales is not out of keeping with historical truth, but the theme of the journey appears even more clearly after a closer look at the pilgrims. There were thirty-two of them, and out of these at least thirteen not counting Chaucer himself were regular travellers by profession or taste. The knight as a chivalric crusader had seen Granada, North Africa, Armenia, Russia, Lithuania and Prussia.[2] The squire like his literary creator had fought in Flanders, Artois and Picardy. The monk coursed over the countryside with a string of hunters. Unlike the monk the friar belonged to a religious order in which travel was part of the vocation itself, necessary for study, preaching and organized begging. The merchant's business trips to the Low Countries were a commonplace activity upon which depended the export-import trade and credit transactions of Merchant Venturers and other groups from English towns. The Serjeant-at-Law made his assize-circuits just as his modern counter-part does and incidentally helped by so doing to bring to remoter shires the English of the king 'that is lord of this langage'.[3] As a well-to-do landowner the franklin had been commissioned as sheriff and justice of the peace and elected as a parliamentary 'knight' for his shire, so that he was familiar with constant journeying, at least within the realm. The shipman like the friar was so much a medieval byword for rootlessness that he was regarded as a good spy in war and a bad surety in the courts.[4] Chaucer's example was evidently experienced on both the Bordeaux and Baltic routes. The reeve was an agricultural overseer from Norfolk and accus-

[1] J. M. Manley, *Some New Light on Chaucer*, New York 1926; for remarks on Maghfeld's account-book and excerpts from it see *Chaucer's World*, compiled by Edith Rickert, ed Clair C. Olson and Martin M. Crow, New York 1948, pp. 185–93.

[2] For maps of the crusading journeys to Prussia and Lithuania undertaken in the 1390s by Henry of Derby and his knightly companions, see *Richard II*, ed F. R. H. Du Boulay and Caroline M. Barron, 1971, pp. 163, 166.

[3] *The Works of Geoffrey Chaucer*, ed F. N. Robinson, 2nd edn, 1957, p. 546.

[4] *The Paston Letters, 1422–1509*, ed James Gairdner, 1900–08, I, Nos. 146, 195.

tomed to presenting biannual accounts to his lord's auditors. The summoner was a specialized postman whose round covered an entire diocese
and made him an embarrassingly familiar figure. The pardoner was one
of a whole crowd of 'Rome-runners', and the maniple, if he were like
many other estate-officials, was probably the servant of more than one
lord and liable to serve in several parts of England in any one year.

The rustic members of this company have been called the manorial
aristocracy, and it is true that we do not meet the poorest villagers among
them, nor did Chaucer write about the mass of small-holders as did
Langland about the cottage-dwellers he felt to be his neighbours. But
even Langland envisaged pilgrimage, and the estate-documents of the
time leave no doubt that the manorial poor travelled too, bound on
errands or carrying-services for their masters, service in wars, or in
search of wage labour.

Of course this pilgrimage to Canterbury was a literary construct, yet
behind it lay a constant historical reality which can to some extent be
measured. Offerings at the shrine of Becket in Canterbury Cathedral
amounted during the fourteenth century to some £300 or £400 a year,
more during the second half of the century, and they only declined permanently after 1420.[1] If aristocratic pilgrims were more noticed in the
monks' records they sometimes cost the cathedral more than they gave:
most of the donors were the anonymous, humble people who were
doubtless often able to make the journey because their fortunes were
improving through the forces of economic change.

For Chaucer's lifetime spanned a period of economic transition so
important that neither his career nor his writing can be properly understood without some brief reference to it. It is basically a question of
demography. The first and most lethal epidemic of plague occurred in
1348–9, when Chaucer was a small boy. During his middle years there
were further epidemics, so that within a generation the population of
Britain like that of Europe as a whole had been severely reduced. Historians often argue that the horrors of pestilence made late medieval men
and women preoccupied with death and filled their art and literature
with fantasies of mortality, but the most striking historical consequence
seems to have been a sharper appetite for a better life. As people died the
pressure of population on land was relieved. The survivors inherited

[1] C. Eveleigh Woodruff, 'The financial aspect of the cult of St. Thomas of
Canterbury', *Archaeologia Cantiana* XLIV, 1932, esp. pp. 18–25.

property more quickly. Poorer fields could go out of cultivation, leaving men in possession of the most productive arable. In general the price of basic foodstuffs remained low while the wages of labourers rose. The unskilled man who got 1d a day in 1300 got 4d or 5d by 1400. In short, labouring men benefited from the very fewness of their numbers and could expect to have more to spend after rents had been paid and food bought or grown. It is not surprising that lords and knights thought their inferiors were becoming uppish and attempted, though without success, to control wages and prevent the flaunting of fine clothes and personal possessions by folk whose fathers had known better how to keep to their station.

Chaucer's age was consequently one of unusual tension, born of betterment rather than oppression. The Great Revolt of 1381 was only the biggest explosion in a fire of change. Up the ladder of society inferior answered back to superior with sharp criticism and occasional blows, whether it was bondmen against lords and lawyers, commons against the tax-men, middling townsmen against the big financiers, laymen against rich, endowed clergy, or warlike nobles against a young king who wanted peace with France and respectful acquiescence for his tactless spending on personal friends. These conflicts sometimes merged into each other and are in any case too complex for full discussion here, but a word must be given to the problem of social class which clearly coloured Chaucer's own assumptions.

The fundamental distinction in English society was between those who were *gentils* and those who were not, in very much the same way as this was true at least up until the early twentieth century. A squire in a noble household was usually *gentilhomme* no less than the king himself. By about 1425 this simple class distinction was being frequently expressed in the English language by the word 'gentleman' which was taking the place of the older Latin *generosus* and French *gentil*. This is not to say that more numerous gradations in rank were of no account. It was an aristocratic society in which king, nobles, prelates and knights all received particular expressions of deference. It was also a world of social mobility which in fact sharpened the sense of status. Merchants who had just climbed into *gentilesse* could be despised by those who had forgotten any remoter taint of trade. Even the de la Poles, dukes of Suffolk and most splendid of medieval *arrivistes*, could now and then be reminded without much delicacy how they were 'worshipful men grown to fortune of the world'.[1] But the bisection of society into gentle and simple was understood clearly enough and is the basic historical reality of late medieval class structure. It makes no difference that Chaucer wrote moralizing lines to the effect that a real gentleman is a man who behaves decently. 'Handsome is as handsome does' is an acceptable motto to the most snobbish societies, just as in our own somewhat more relaxed days 'nature's gentleman' remains a wholly intelligible alternative for a rough diamond. To this extent the social historian must differ from the literary scholar who sees equal reality in literary statements of four-teenth-century class distinction.[2] The idea of 'degree', according to which men were ranked by their function in society was certainly at-tractive to the theological cast of mind that understood society's God-given architecture in terms of men's vocations and mutual dependence. But it was of no more social significance than are ranks and regiments in the armed services of today. As to the theoretical division of men into those who fight, those who pray and those who work (such as the knight, the clerk and the ploughman), this was only a more primitive version of 'degree': if it is 'the only class system known to medieval theory', then it must be answered that the class distinctions which possess the greatest everyday importance are those least subject to theory.

Hence, when we enquire about Chaucer's place in Society (which must have been of more account to him than society), we may accept that he was a gentleman because he had a courtly upbringing and worked, behaved and wrote like one. True, his origins were mercantile, his position modest, his ambitions even a trifle eccentric in their artistic solitariness. But he was not a hired craftsman who came in at the back door and downed his ale with the life-long servants. He 'communed with gentle wights'.

The sort of people who gathered for their entertainment round a public reader would have been aware of changes that were taking place in language. Three of these changes were leaving their mark upon the fourteenth century. English was moving towards a standardized form, French was being forgotten, and the ability to read and write in English was becoming more widespread amongst lay people. In a well-known passage of *Troilus* Chaucer alludes to the variations which still existed in

[1] For all this, see the present writer's *An Age of Ambition*, 1970, chap. 4.

[2] A skilful literary analysis is by D. S. Brewer, 'Class distinctions in Chaucer', *Speculum* XLIII, 1968, pp. 290–308.

English and hopes that what he is writing will be understood.

> *And for ther is so gret diversite*
> *In Englissh and in writyng of oure tonge,*
> *So prey I God that non mysywrite the,*
> *Ne the mysmetre for defaute of tonge . . .*

Yet the very apostrophe suggests the marvellous possibility of a wider comprehension:

> *And red wherso thow be, or elles songe,*
> *That thou be understonde, God I biseche!*
>
> (V, 1793–98).

And no one who has glanced at the provincial literature of the same age can doubt that the future lay on the sophisticated London tongues of Chaucer and his friends, not with the up-country authors of *Pearl*, *Gawayne* or *Sir Orfeo*. There is a historical point here too. In the mid-fourteenth century the richer classes of London society were being reinforced by immigrants from the east midlands who brought their speech with them and fused it with existing London language as the vehicle of communication between Englishmen of position. These people were merchants who dealt in major commodities like wool and wine, so that the economic drift to the south-east accomplished changes in society and speech as well as in production and government. Once more, the de la Poles of Hull provide a leading instance, but so too does the Chaucer family of Ipswich whose migration to the capital helped the victory of the very language used by its most famous member. The fact that French was concurrently becoming a foreign tongue is probably a parallel development rather than a consequence of this slowly forming linguistic identity. Enmity with France never stopped the interchange of ideas and people across the Channel, but the standardization of speech into its modern shapes was occurring none the less, and indeed in France and Germany as well as England. It was encouraged the more vigorously in England because London stood as a capital city in a relatively small country, whereas France was larger and even more regionalized, and Germany had no capital at all. So to London wealth and substantial people were drawn, and thence flowed the torrent of administration and law, expressed in the dialect of Europe's most centralized government. All the standard history books tell how English began to be used in

London courts and parliaments in the 1360s. French was becoming an accomplishment rather than a habit, and a sidelight on this comes from the will of James de Peckham, a Kentish gentleman who died in the same year as Chaucer. His codicil of 30 September 1400 ordering the bequest of 10 oxen and 200 sheep added that 'my executors shall distribute all my books in French to those who know how to use them'.[1]

With language went literacy in the sense of an ability to read and even write in the mother tongue. The great collections of private correspondence like the Paston Letters begin to survive from about this time. If Chaucer himself had been an exception as a literate layman it would hardly have made sense for him to describe so naturally the exchange of love-letters between Troilus and Criseyde:

> *The lettres ek that she of olde tyme*
> *Hadde hym ysent he wolde allone rede,*
> *An hondred sithe atwixen noon and prime . . .*
>
> (V, 470–2).

So too does his midnight remedy invite a flash of sympathy from fellow insomniacs: 'to rede, and drive the night away'. (*The Booke of the Duchess* 49).

Evidence does not exist to make possible any geography of literacy, though we may guess that more people who could read and write lived in the south-east and east of England than elsewhere. But certainly the most advanced institutions of government had their home in and about London. The king himself was often on the move, accompanied by friends and counsellors. But the established departments of state were organized in permanent buildings spread out over the metropolis, like the Exchequer and Chancery at Westminster, and the Wardrobe's permanent offshoots, the Great and Privy Wardrobe which housed bulk supplies and armaments in Baynard's Castle and the Tower within the City walls. Household departments both stationary and itinerant possessed seals as the essential instruments to authenticate orders, commissions and grants of property and privilege. To remove the seals from the effective control of the king was an organized baronage's chief answer to his supposed misrule, yet at the same time the action most

[1] Lambeth Palace Library, Register of Archbishop Arundel, I, fos. 176b–177a: '. . . *volo ut executores mei distribuant omnes libros meos gallicos scientibus illos occupare* . . .'

likely to arouse the king's vengeful anger. During the reigns of Edward III (1327–77) and Richard II (1377–99), the internal politics of England turned principally round the problem of controlling such commissions and grants, in peace and in war, and of how the groups of politically influential men combined with and against each other in ever-changing factions: nobles, parliamentary knights, bishops and merchants; king's friends and king's critics, allies or enemies of each other according to a thousand personal interests, but never parties in a modern sense. There is no place here for a detailed chronicle, but it may be helpful to explain two basic characteristics of political life. Medieval government at every level was organized through households; and the disposition of property was the stuff of politics.

Public affairs in modern times are carried on in offices and committees which operate for the most part in office hours and rely heavily upon administrative standing orders and the services of secretaries. In the fourteenth century the household of an important man was also to a great extent the place where political decisions were taken. Private and public life were not yet clearly distinguished. This is true of insignificant country lords with small estate councils and a handful of armed retainers, of merchants who slept near their bales and accounts, and of the king himself whose advisers might talk gravely with their master in a private room whilst his immense entourage prepared the meals, mended the waggons, or rollicked in halls and yards. Our imaginative picture of minstrels and large-scale catering is sound enough if we remember also that the household was a moving centre of government where messengers to and from the outside world sped like bees. Charters, letters and writs drawn up with professional care in Chancery or Exchequer often awaited their ultimate authority from this pell-mell dwelling.

The subject-matter of public business was in a curious way equally private. At tense moments educated men might speak of the crown in distinction from the king, or of 'the law and course of parliament', but the underlying realities were cornfields, flocks of sheep, rents, pensions from the Exchequer, rake-offs from customs houses or judicial courts, and, perhaps above all, the capital gains that accrued from rich marriages. The king's task was to walk on the knife-edge between all-round generosity and the insolvency which left him desperate.

One of the medieval historian's greatest difficulties is to discover in detail the jealousies and ambitions which set men at daggers drawn or brought them for a time into sworn friendship, but the generalized picture is quite a simple one. The royal household and noble households were the same in kind but different in degree. Their outward form was a family structure of men and women living according to rank yet with a good deal of informality, and in a milieu where kindness to a young knight or an unexpected flirtation might have the most serious political undertones. Everybody wanted security and income, and these things were in the gift of the dynasts: offices, pensions, manors or the hand of a girl with an inheritance whence might spring another young family to struggle and jockey in its turn for livelihood and power. All this is quite different from modern family life of which the function at its best is fulfilled by twenty years of intimate parental care. The medieval *familia* embraced other people's children as well who from early adolescence shared in the work of the adult world, whether they were apprentices, religious postulants or pages.

To call Chaucer's age violent is not very illuminating as this is true of almost all epochs, but the particular forms violence took are of interest. In the first place there was endemic warfare. When Chaucer was born the young Edward III had just reopened the war with France which was fundamentally about the king of England's lands and status across the Channel. The 'Hundred Years War' (1337–1453) sounds like a distinct episode but was in fact a fresh series of phases in a conflict so old that it was part of the folk-memory. In the middle years of the fourteenth century war took the form of sea fights, raids across the Scottish border and, more centrally, long-range expeditions or *chévauchées* into France under a king with unusual gifts of affability and comradeship with his own nobility. Thousands of people were involved besides the knights, men-at-arms and archers, from the clothiers who made uniforms for the retinues to the craftsmen who supplied bowstrings and the shipmen who ferried grain for the armies overseas.[1] But war is never a unifying activity for long, and cracks soon widened in the fabric of English society. These were of two kinds: the little fissures of outrage committed by men habituated to the violent seizure of what they wanted; and the crevasses which opened when the dramatic victories of Crécy and Poitiers were over and the slog had to be paid for by taxation, when financiers were caught profiteering, and (worst of all) when a new young king, wilful, cliquish and extravagant, actually wanted to make peace with his ancient

[1] H. J. Hewitt, *The Organization of War under Edward III*, 1966.

adversary and use his soldiers nearer home. Two examples of political shock may be chosen for their bearing on Chaucer's life.

In 1376 a group of highly-placed courtiers and London financiers was impeached in parliament for peculation, at the instigation of Peter de la Mare, knight of the shire for Herefordshire and the earliest known Speaker of the Commons. The incident is complex because it was part of an aristocratic wrangle, and is also especially famous for the earliest eye-witness account of a debate amongst the parliamentary Commons. But to the point here is the person of Richard Lyons, the chief merchant culprit, for he was a man of similar background to Chaucer's and a London neighbour, though he had made himself of much greater political importance. Little is known of Lyons's origins apart from the fact that he was illegitimate. But by 1359 he was buying houses and shops in London and in the 1360s was a prominent vintner with a group of taverns which sold sweet wine. He had a country property in Essex as well and was to represent Essex in the parliament of 1380. In the 1370s he was lessee of much of the petty custom and subsidy in English ports and able to lend the government money and buy the government's debts at a heavy discount. Professor Myers calls him 'not so much a thief as a rich individual who could help to rescue a virtually bankrupt government'.[1] After his impeachment his wealth was confiscated, but he soon got it back. The present interest lies in seeing how an obscure vintner could become so rich and how his heart lay where his treasure was. His confiscated possessions were worth nearly £2500 and he owned a fairly large ship. In 1380 he bought exemption for life from being made sheriff, escheator, coroner, J.P. or collector of taxes against his will. Probably these tasks would have interfered too much with business, and the exemption is suggestive of the fact that these important offices were not always either desired or voluntary. Lyons's end was neither happy nor dignified, for he was murdered in Cheapside by the rebels of 1381, his house at Over-hall in Essex was wrecked and a woman called Isabella spent fruitless years of litigation in claiming to be his widow, though the executors argued that the marriage had been annulled in 1363. Stow saw his tomb in St. James Garlickhithe, with his effigy showing 'hair rounded by his ears and curled, and a little beard forked', like the king he served. Com-

[1] A. R. Myers, 'The Wealth of Richard Lyons' in *Essays in Medieval History presented to Bertie Wilkinson*, ed T. H. Sandquist and M. R. Powicke, Toronto 1969.

pared with Lyons, we may reflect that Chaucer had the better part in remaining a politically modest figure.

Ten years after the Good Parliament the court was again attacked, this time by the impeachment of Michael de la Pole, earl of Suffolk and Chancellor. The opposition of the autumn and winter of 1386 was led by Thomas of Woodstock (duke of Gloucester since 1385) and the earl of Arundel. The most recent research has shown that it was indeed the king himself, not yet twenty, who was the real target of attack,[1] for his extravagance and political partisanship; and the crisis of the next two years during which many of the king's friends were executed or exiled was a most violent confrontation in which the king's possession of the throne and perhaps of his life itself hung in balance. It has proved all too tempting for scholars to argue that Chaucer's surrender of his post in the customs was a minor consequence of this massive political purge, but as we shall see this seems on balance unlikely. The events of 1386–8 are more useful as a prominent instance of political upheaval which help to explain the prudence of Chaucer's life but did not involve any punishment for his associations.[2]

The Church which might have stood as a city of peace in so unquiet a world shared in fact in all that world's frictions and political malice. This is not to deal out the almost total disapproval bestowed upon late medieval Catholicism by disdainful critics like G. M. Trevelyan. In parishes, monasteries and even in the lives of certain bishops there are examples of fidelity, study and the works of charity. But the deep connections between secular and ecclesiastical government involved the Church in precisely the same imperfections as the world itself of which it was part, and attracted criticisms which reasonably condemned many blemishes. It may at the same time be remembered that the criticisms themselves are a sign of grace, and that not every revolted conscience belonged to a heretic or cynic.

In 1305 the papacy had moved to Avignon, and fourteenth-century Englishmen had grown accustomed to thinking of a *curia* where the cardinals were mostly French as an institution hostile to English interests.

[1] J. J. N. Palmer, 'The Impeachment of Michael de la Pole in 1386', *Bulletin of the Institute of Historical Research* XLII, 1969, pp. 96–101.
[2] This is the place to applaud the general sound historical sense displayed in a now quite old work: J. R. Hulbert, *Chaucer's Official Life* (Ph.D. dissertation), Chicago 1912.

Papal taxation had been loudly resented even in the early thirteenth century; the resentment did not abate even after kings in the fourteenth century had moderated its impact upon their subjects. The claims of popes to provide their direct nominees to church benefices and the unremitting hostility of English parliaments to such papal provisions are prominent in the records of the fourteenth century. If this was material enough for an English political anti-papalism, the Great Schism which began in 1378 was an enormous aggravation. It is arguable that before 1378 the popes had the will of peace-makers between England and France, but afterwards the divided papacy was yet another *casus belli*.

Perhaps a gaze too firmly fixed on Rome or Avignon causes optical illusions in students of Chaucer. Understanding of Englishmen's attitudes must in the best analysis be sought in England itself. Here was a society both religious and anti-clerical, and to miss the fact that both these attitudes co-existed is to misread the age. Indeed, it is doubtful whether anticlericalism can occur in an irreligious society.

In the fourteenth century there were at least three different kinds of hostility to clergy. Occasionally there was anger against senior prelates who were also high government officials, like the bishops of Chichester and Lichfield, Chancellor and Treasurer respectively, who were dismissed for inefficiency by Edward III in 1340 and replaced by laymen on the grounds that their clerical order gave them undue protection against punishment. Similarly, William of Wykeham, bishop of Winchester, was thrown out of the Chancellorship in 1371, and Simon of Sudbury, archbishop of Canterbury and Treasurer of England, had his head cut off by the rebels in 1381. Secondly, bitter feelings were often shown towards the friars. The *Summoner's Tale* is a well-known joke in this vein, but the belief that the friars had betrayed their ministry to the poor is expressed with more solemn indignation in *The Vision of Piers the Plowman*. Yet hatred of the mendicants was more keenly felt by other kinds of clergyman than by laymen. The friars were competitors with the secular clergy for the alms and esteem of parishioners and for academic privileges in the universities. No amount of literary vilification can hide the fact that lay men and women continued to leave bequests of money to the orders of friars right up until the Reformation, so that friar-baiting was in a sense a clerical variety of anticlericalism. Third, and most important, was a disgust with the wealthy, established, sacerdotal Church which was felt with varying intensity by a wide range of people, from outright Lollard

heretics to those who were entirely orthodox in fundamental belief and
practice, yet devoted in their hearts to the simplicities of the New Testament and the application of moral principles to everyday life. It is difficult to avoid the conclusion that Chaucer himself moved in these circles,
and equally difficult to show that in Richard II's reign there was any
clear dividing line between Lollards and what, for lack of a better term,
may be called orthodox evangelicals.

The careers of the so-called Lollard knights reflect these ambiguities.
In the chronicles at least ten distinguished laymen are named and portrayed as supporters of heresy and heretics themselves. The interpretation
of their activities is still controversial but any account of Chaucerian society must at least face the same problem.[1] Seven of these men formed a
closely-knit group of friends, namely, the knights Richard Stury, Lewis
Clifford, Thomas Latimer, William Nevill, John Clanvowe, John Mon-
tagu (earl of Salisbury from 1397) and John Cheyne. All were courtiers
and members of the king's household. Stury, Clifford, Nevill and Clanvowe were knights of the king's Chamber and thus members of an intimate circle of which Chaucer, as an esquire of the Chamber, was also
part. In 1372 when Chaucer was certainly occupying this position he was
about 30 years old; Stury would then have been about 45, Clifford about
40, Nevill and Clanvowe roughly Chaucer's age. They were therefore
more or less contemporaries, and they lived the same kind of life. By
1378 they were mostly veteran campaigners who knew other lands and
had also, except for Latimer, travelled on diplomatic missions. In September 1385 the same Wardrobe account records the issue of black cloth
for mourning the king's mother to Clanvowe, Clifford, Clifford's son-
in-law, La Vache, and Chaucer. Several of this circle had literary tastes.
Clifford had brought Chaucer a copy of a poem written in his honour by
Eustache Deschamps, praising him for his wisdom and his ability as
translator of the *Roman de la Rose*, which is, incidentally, more a satire in
its English form against false love and corrupt morals than a work of

[1] W. T. Waugh, 'The Lollard Knights' in *Scottish Historical Review* XI,
1914, pp. 55–92 held that most of them were never serious Lollards and all
made orthodox ends. Conversely, the genuine and lasting Lollardy of these
knights was argued by the late K. B. McFarlane in a paper read to the *Canterbury and York Society* on 13 December 1962 and now published in fuller
form in *Lancastrian Kings and Lollard Knights*, Oxford 1972.

courtly love.[1] Stury also owned a copy. Montague was a versifier praised by Christine de Pisan. Clanvowe was himself a sincerely moralizing author who will be referred to again. The group were also knights, and individually much more well-to-do than Chaucer. Although Clifford began as an almost landless man in a Devonshire village, by 1389 he had nearly £400 a year in annuities and was exchanging them quickly for land, an intelligent business move which Chaucer too may have been making when in 1388 he granted his Exchequer annuities to John Scalby. Several of the knights married heiresses and some invested in the English lands of Norman abbeys confiscated by the king, and thus had an interest in the disendowment of the Church at a time when Lollards were demanding the same thing. But financial success formed no barrier between these men and Chaucer. Nevill and Clanvowe acted as witnesses to a deed in Chaucer's interest.[2] Clifford was his close friend and the father-in-law of Sir Philip La Vache whom Chaucer in his popular poem *Truth* advised to shun the servitude of this world. Whether the knights were Lollards in any exact sense must remain an open question. They were called such in the chronicles, but chroniclers were emotionally hostile even to implicit criticisms of the Church. True, Latimer was accused of heresy before the king's council, and when Wycliff's disciple, master Nicholas Hereford, was arrested Nevill asked to have his custody 'because of the honesty of his person'. Clifford, Latimer and Cheyne drew up wills which used phrases dear to Lollards, like referring to their bodies as 'stinking carrion', and requesting burial in cheap cloth and without funeral pomp, and to supervise the execution of these wills they chose Lollard overseers. Yet it remains possible that as a group they showed in exaggerated form the sentiments felt by many orthodox contemporaries. What betrays this attitude to the historian is less the ambiguous record of action than the common feeling behind Chaucer's own poem *Truth* (before 1390?) and the English tract by Clanvowe later entitled *The Two Ways* (1391?)[3] The message of Chaucer is that the world is a wilderness, not a home, through which the wise man goes as a pilgrim in dread of avarice and self-advancement:

[1] D. W. Robertson, *Chaucer's London*, New York 1968, p. 209.

[2] *Chaucer Life-Records*, ed M. M. Crow and C. C. Olson, Oxford 1966, p. 343.

[3] V. J. Scattergood, 'The two ways: an unpublished religious treatise by Sir John Clanvowe', in *English Philological Studies* X, 1967, pp. 33–56.

> *Hold the heye wey, and lat thy gost thee lede:*
> *And trouthe thee shal delivere, it is no drede.*

In Clanvowe's pamphlet the meaning is the same and even the imagery similar. No more than Chaucer does he attack or defend the Church's institutions, but begs Christians to avoid the 'broad way' that leads to hell and enter the 'narrow way' to heaven. Insistent that salvation lies through a life in which scriptural teaching is observed he speaks with the same voice as Chaucer in his moments of direct simplicity or, for the matter of that, of Langland when he uses the metaphor of pilgrimage and prefers Do-Wel to triennials. It is an authentic English voice of late fourteenth-century spirituality.

> For that that is cleped richesse it is greet trauail to geten it and it is greet drede to keepen it and to departe therfro it is greet heuynesse, so that fro the first getynge to the laste forgoying it is alle sorewe . . .

Nothing in the rhythmic phrases of Clanvowe is wholly out of accord with what little of his private mind Chaucer himself permits us to hear. So we come from the world of Chaucer to the man himself.

There can be no intention here to rehearse in detail the well-known fragments of Chaucer's biography, but rather to offer the view of a single historian about what in that life is important to understanding the poet. His life indeed begins and ends in historical obscurity, and even the extraordinary labours which have culminated in the *Life Records* leave us in a twilight unimaginable to students of post-Plantagenet England. The first frustration is of a natural wish to know about the domestic life of a poet who wrote so much of marriage and children. The most that can be said is that Chaucer was probably married to Philippa de Roet from about 1366 to 1387, by which time she was dead, and that he had a son called Thomas who rose higher in the world than his father, probably also a son called Lewis, and just possibly a surviving daughter called Elizabeth. To attempt deductions from the poetry about Chaucer's happiness or otherwise in the married state seems a waste of time like so much other effort which, unsupported by real evidence, has been put into the Chaucer industry. Yet enough is known of the fourteenth-century milieu to allow a reflection that Chaucer was lucky in having legitimate parents, a settled home, a father who did not die till his son was about 22, and a marriage which lasted some 21 years. Despite the Christian teaching about monogamy and fidelity it was an age when family life was often brief and fragile. Parents frequently died young, leaving the survivor to re-marry quickly. Bastardy was exceedingly common. Children were likely to be shunted off to fend for themselves at quite an early age. Chaucer's own maternal grandmother Mary was married three times. His father John was abducted by an aunt who tried to marry him off at the age of about 11. In fact, many of Chaucer's contemporaries had a rough youth, such as Langland who was illegitimate and resented it, or Boccaccio legitimized after his birth and estranged from a father 'old, coarse and mean'.[1] Richard Lyons was also illegitimate; Dante and Petrarch exiles; Boccaccio, Dante and Petrarch had step-mothers; Boccaccio and Petrarch had many illegitimate children. Even Chaucer's sister-in-law was a mistress for many years before she became John of Gaunt's third wife, and her very marriage attracted sneers rather than rejoicing.

Like the great Italians, Chaucer started from a mercantile background and was educated in letters—we do not know where—at an early age. Literary originality was rare among the old landed families. But he did not have the advantages or disadvantages of being a tonsured cleric and in this he was unlike Langland, Froissart, Boccaccio, Petrarch, Hoccleve and Lydgate. Although the literate layman was becoming quite a common figure as a reader it was still exceptional for a layman to be a professional poet, let alone a great one. In this he is perhaps to be compared only with Dante.

Undoubtedly the career of Chaucer was made possible by his acceptance into courtly households. It is not necessary to suppose either that he was a faintly bourgeois usher or the partisan of any longlasting political faction. He had a foot in several worlds: the courtly, the mercantile and the literary, but as already explained he lived naturally as a gentleman, like many other Englishmen of the governing class, with jobs to do and the usual rewards in return. Further, it was easy to pass from one household to another. Chaucer began as an adolescent in the household of Elizabeth, countess of Ulster, wife of Lionel, duke of Clarence, who was the second son of Edward III and one of Richard II's uncles. By 1367 he was in Edward III's household and from then on until his death he was connected with the royal court in one way or another even though he

[1] John Larner, *Culture and Society in Italy, 1290–1420*, 1971, p. 216.

did not always travel about with the king as one of his personal entourage. Another point is worth making. There were times when political and personal hostility (much the same thing) existed between some of the magnates and the king, and even between Richard II and his uncle John of Gaunt, and as everyone knows Gaunt's son Henry ultimately deposed his cousin. But factions however savage were transient, and although royal or noble servants connected with unpopular policies might on occasion be dismissed or even destroyed, there were whole substrata of courtiers, officials and servants who did not suffer if they did not seem to pose any political threat or to have committed any political crime. Guilt by association was not taken very far. It is hard to believe that Chaucer was not liked and valued, and not because he was a wary trimmer but for his genial skill in bringing 'mirth and solas' to his neighbours and a personal inability to get seriously diverted from practising his gift. This seems the explanation of his professional and financial survival. Doubtless he was welcome in the great Lancastrian family. In 1386 his wife was admitted to the fraternity of Lincoln Cathedral in the presence of Gaunt and along with Henry of Derby and a galaxy of Lancastrian luminaries. It was both a distinguished occasion and a family affair. This sort of thing did not prevent Chaucer continuing in the service of Richard II, and even riding through England on his urgent business within a year of Derby's landing. On the day of Henry IV's coronation Chaucer, still king's esquire, received a handsome rise in his pension.[1] There is no contradiction in all this, for it is a sequence of rewards for uncomplicated service and friendship, the bright lining of political storm-clouds.

Much of Chaucer's employment was too fleeting, too ordinary or of too little significance in his life to merit discussion in a short essay, but his work at the London Customs House is worth a moment's attention. He was appointed Controller of the wool custom, the wool subsidy and the petty custom in London in 1374, increasingly allowed deputies to do the work at the wool quay, and replaced in these posts in December 1386. It is sometimes said that these were important posts from which he was dismissed when the Wonderful Parliament placed the king's government in commission under the power of Gloucester, Arundel and Warwick. Neither of these suppositions is likely. It is true that the wool custom was one of the chief props of the crown's finances despite the decline in

[1] *Life Records*, pp. 91, 62, 525.

exports of raw wool, by reason of the high tariff and the relative ef-
ficiency of its collection by the best civil service in Christendom. But the
really important officials were the Collectors and not the Controllers.
The Collector was usually a London merchant-financier who lent the
crown money and spent his time in the customs service in repaying himself out of the £18,000 or so annual revenue which flowed through his
hands. His work was in the technicalities of the credit system while the
actual collecting was done by deputies. The Controller (*contrarotulator*)
was intended to act as a check on the Collector, returning to the Exchequer his own counter-roll which detailed the exports and imports. In
fact, of course, he was so inferior in wealth and status that he was no effective check. The idea was that the Collector had one half of the customs seal (the cocket) and the Controller the other half, and that the
application of this seal to documents of consignment would show that
the customs had been paid. But the Controller's half had to be surren-
dered to the king's creditors, and when this happened the Controller was
virtually deprived of office and the creditor was made Controller in all
but name. In 1379, for instance, the City of London held half the cocket
seal, which meant that the great financier John Philipot held one half of
the seal as Collector and the other as Mayor.[1] No doubt the job of Controller needed expertise, especially in accounting at the Exchequer, and
it yielded a salary equivalent to the income of a simple country knight.
But it was 'a modest office for a modest man'. Nor, despite parliamentary petitions that life-holders of Controllerships should have their
appointments annulled, is there evidence that any of them was dis-
charged after investigations or purges. Chaucer's service for $12\frac{1}{2}$ years
had in 1386 already run beyond the usual term. Once more the attempt
to dramatize the events of his external life must fail.

The years 1385–6 saw the beginning of serious political disturbance in
England, and at the same time a number of changes occurred in
Chaucer's life, so that scholars have naturally assumed some connection
between the two. The changes are interesting, but the assumption does
not carry strong conviction. In 1385 Chaucer got a permanent deputy at
the wool quay and also became one of the J.P.'s for Kent. In the late
summer of 1386 he was elected knight of the shire for Kent in the parlia-

[1] An expert study is Olive Coleman's 'The Collectors of Customs in
London under Richard II' in *Studies in London History presented to P. E. Jones*,
1969, pp. 181–96.

ment that was to meet at Westminster on 1 October, he gave up his house at Aldgate, and by December had ended his employment at the Customs House altogether. No direct evidence survives to tell us what property he acquired in Kent, but what most likely happened is that now, past his fortieth year and perhaps with a sick wife, he went to live in north Kent and hoped to give more time to his writing in agreeable surroundings. Of course the idealization of May and the cult of the daisy were stock literary forms. But it is hard to reject as mere devices the expressed delight at the tranquillity of gardens in the Prologue to the *Legend of Good Women*, whether that poem was written before or after Chaucer's exit from the city. At this point it will be timely to say something of Chaucer's connection with Kent. The county was as much the scene of his life as London. On occasion he uses Kentish dialect forms, the road to Canterbury he knew in actuality as well as imagination, and close investigation shows that many of the people he knew lived near Greenwich, the Cray valley or within sight of the North Downs, then a prosperous residential area and even now offering a certain freshness to the London worker.

As early as 1375 Chaucer had a considerable financial profit out of Kent through the custody of a Canterbury heir called Edward Staplegate,[1] but by the time he was appointed J.P. for the county in 1385 he probably possessed property in the part of Kent nearest to London.[2] When in 1387 he was placed on a commission to enquire into the abduction of a young heiress, the session was held at Dartford and the other three commissioners possessed land and interests in the same area. The centre of the enquiry was indeed Bexley, North Cray, Sidcup and Chislehurst, whence came plaintiff, defendant and jurors as well as commissioners, and the wills of some of their descendants are extant and derive from the same region.[3] Again in 1388 the transfer of a small action

[1] *Life Records*, Ch. 12.
[2] The only other esquires in this list of Kentish J.P.'s were Hugh Fastolf who was Deputy Constable of Dover Castle and William Topcliffe who was a lifelong servant of the archbishop and probably lived in Maidstone, F. R. H. Du Boulay, *The Lordship of Canterbury*, 1966, pp. 394, 396, 398.
[3] William Hall (1512) and Thomas Hall (1526), yeomen of Bexley (Public Record Office, filed will and Prerogative Court of Canterbury (PCC) Will Register 20 Porch); William Swetesyre (1527), yeoman of North Cray (ibid., 23 Porch). For these, see my pamphlet *Medieval Bexley*, Bexley

for debt against Chaucer suggests that the Exchequer considered Kent to be his home. Frequently during the 1390s official records hint at Chaucer's association with the Woolwich and Greenwich areas, and a manuscript of 'Lenvoy a Scogan' dating from *c.* 1393 has a marginal note which says that Chaucer was then living in Greenwich. This is made virtually certain by the series of deeds dated 1395–6 transferring Spittlecombe in East Greenwich from Archbishop Arundel to Gregory Ballard. The technical details do not matter here, but the witness-list fairly clearly numbers Chaucer among the Greenwich residents. Chaucer was also one of the attorneys appointed by Ballard to take possession in his behalf which would have been most conveniently done by a local inhabitant. There is an additional point. Gregory Ballard was a busy official who during his life served both the king and Archbishop Arundel, the king's enemy. He was butler to Richard II in the 1390s (a post later held by Thomas Chaucer) and both Treasurer (1398–1401) and Steward of the estates (1400–12) to the archbishop. His will made in October 1415 shows him a well-to-do inhabitant of Greenwich, accustomed to travel, and leaving a widow, one son and at least four menservants.[1] When Arundel suffered forfeiture in 1397 Ballard received this property from the king, yet again became the archbishop's counsellor when Arundel was restored to favour. His career illustrates the kind of friend Chaucer had in prosperous north Kent: a modest landholder with professional skills, accustomed to riding over southern England and giving official orders, and surviving the cross-winds of political fortune.

The years 1385–6 formed a dividing-point in Chaucer's life. Hitherto his work had been carried on in contact with communities, whether in great households or in the bustle of city life. Thereafter his appointments required him to travel about but to live less closely surrounded by his fellow men. From 1389 to 1391 he was Clerk of the King's Works with

Corporation Public Libraries 1961. The case clearly concerned the Bexley Halls, so *Life Records* p. 379 note 3 is wrong, but p. 381 is on the right lines. Rickhill, the chief commissioner and a man connected with the death of the duke of Gloucester in 1397, was from Rochester, where his second wife, Rose, died in 1418 or 1419 (*Register of Henry Chichele, archbishop of Canterbury, 1414–43*, ed E. F. Jacob, II, Oxford 1938, pp. 161–2). Thomas Carshill (Cressell), one of the defendants, had a descendant, Richard Cressell, gent., still living in Chislehurst in 1508 (PCC Will Register 12 Bennett).

[1] *The Lordship of Canterbury*, pp. 394, 398; *Register Chichele* II, pp. 114–15. These works add to the information in *Life Records*, p. 509 note 2.

responsibilities for buildings and repairs at various royal residences; from at latest 1391 till the end of his life he was one of the deputy foresters of North Petherton, Somerset. There is no evidence that as Clerk of the Works he was unsatisfactory, and his duties in Somerset, if any, are quite obscure. The impression is that as he grew older he continued to be favoured on all sides, received posts which made decreasing demands on him, and was granted emoluments to maintain him at a decent standard of living. The debts which have attracted such attention were nothing unusual, but rather indicate a certain affluence, for his income tended to rise and was paid with remarkable regularity for the times, and the ability to borrow money was then as now a sign of creditworthiness. His service as Justice of the Peace for Kent in 1385–9 has left no trace of any personal activities, nor does the commission mark him out from scores of country gentry who were thus associated with magnates in the shires, but his election to parliament in 1386 merits comment. It was the last time that Chaucer found himself at the centre of public affairs. Any personal part played by him is quite unknown (again, the same is true of many others) but the occasion can be made to illustrate with some satisfying detail the society in which he found himself.

During the thirteenth and fourteenth centuries the king's government was always trying to persuade men of suitable substance to take up knighthood and thus formally qualify themselves for various kinds of public duty in their localities. This is true of Londoners as well as of rural landholders, but resistance to so expensive a distinction was stubborn. Consequently, many of the parliamentary 'knights of the shire' were not true knights at all, ceremonially girt with the sword and styled *chivaler*, but squires and gentlemen more interested in their estates than in the warrior pursuits so admired by monastic chroniclers and other deskromantics who liked to deplore the softness of the times. Likewise, election to parliament was not always the prized honour it later became. Absence from one's domestic concerns might be awkward; travel had its risks, and so too did business among the powerful and demanding men who surrounded the king; and four shillings a day would not seem much when faced with the need to furbish accommodation, as were the four citizens of London who travelled to the Cambridge parliament of 1389 and had to spend £112 7s 0d restoring and equipping a ruined house for their stay.[1]

[1] *English Historical Documents, 1327–1485*, ed A. R. Myers, 1969, pp. 451–2.

In any parliament there were men who had never been there before and some who would serve once only. For all that, the parliamentary knights were becoming an influential body in petitioning the king, arguing about taxation and at critical moments supporting the king's aristocratic opponents. Politics were still 'lords' matters', and the political leaders were the higher nobility. Between the ordinary run of barons and knights there was no very sharp social division. It was a strongly held opinion that the knights in parliament ought to have some property in the shires they represented. The rule of primogeniture in aristocratic inheritance meant that a knight could well be a lord's close kinsman and even if he were not many knights were followers and retainers of the lords. Likewise, a knight could have ties of business or relationship with a burgess, although the townsmen enjoyed less prestige than the knights when they met in parliamentary sitting. In brief, the Commons in parliament were by Chaucer's day becoming a homogeneous group, yet one in which wide differences of career and importance could be found.[1]

In the parliament which met on 1 October 1386 only 38 out of the 71 shire representatives present were real knights.[2] No pattern can be discerned. Both representatives for Sussex and Buckinghamshire happened to be knights, but neither for Kent or Bedfordshire. If anything, the north, the east midlands and the west country produced on this occasion more knights than the south-east. But there was a tendency for men of greater wealth to be knights, whether they had inherited it, married it or been granted it for good service. A constant feature in the lives of shire knights is that they also at some time acted as sheriff, Justice of the Peace and commissioner for the various tasks of local government. A few instances must suffice to show how diverse were the men whose characteristics might seem at first glance so similar. Ralph Carminew of Cornwall was elected but never sat in the parliament at all because he was pulled over a cliff on 9 October by a pair of greyhounds he was leading. He had been to parliament twice before, but his fellow Cornishman, John Bevyle, sat only the once even though he was unusually young at this time; as sheriff of Cornwall he complained of his 'great losses and costs in office', but he married an heiress and became richer than his

---

[1] The following biographical details have been made available before their official publication by courtesy of the *History of Parliament Trust*, London, and special thanks are due to its Secretary, Mr. E. L. C. Mullins.

[2] *Calendar of Close Rolls, 1385–89*, H.M.S.O., pp. 298–9.

father. Walter atte Lee of Hertfordshire sat for parliament eleven times and was a king's knight and vigorous soldier, but Thomas atte Lee, esquire, his colleague and probable kinsman, never came to parliament again although he was a favoured retainer of the king. Sir Thomas Broke of Somerset, who sat twelve times, owed his position largely to marriage with the rich widow of a Bristol merchant who had sixteen manors in the west country. They lived in a stone mansion at Holditch (now in Dorset) where they had a deer-park. The family became connected with the Cobhams, notorious for Lollardy, and Broke himself requested in his will (1415) a simple grave that might be trampled by people going to church, and left no bequests to religious institutions. The knights for Northumberland were quite different again: Sir Bertram de Mont-boucher and Sir Robert de Claveryng were both campaigners much oc-cupied with the unremitting border struggle against the Scots. Chaucer's Kentish colleagues were less distinguished. Hardly anything is known of the Rochester burgesses, Piers Pope and John Fleming, not even their connection with Rochester. One of the Canterbury burgesses, called L. H. Holt, was in 1387 a trustee for the property of Edmund Staplegate, former ward of Chaucer.[1] The other shire representative was William Bettenham of Hawkhurst who owed large sums of money, including £66 13s 4d to Sir Richard Stury. He must have been related to Stephen Bettenham, esquire of Cranbrook, and it is interesting that whereas Wil-liam obtained a papal licence to have a private altar, Stephen showed signs of the evangelical views that were common in Kent, for he asked in his will that money should be given to the poor rather than spent on a funeral feast 'which is rather called the solace of the living and dissipation of goods than refreshment and salvation of souls'. He cannot have been a wholehearted Lollard as he did not forbid obsequies but merely wished to avoid a multiplicity of masses for his soul.[2] Chaucer could almost have made a variegated pilgrimage out of his fellow-parliamentarians.

Nothing is more natural than the wish to give genius a human face. Yet five hundred documents excavated with monumental labour and printed in the *Life Records* still leave the figure veiled. There can be little surprise at the exasperation of scholars with Chaucer's habit of slipping

[1] See p. 39 above. Edmund Staplegate was also a landlord of James de Peck-ham who arranged masses to be said for him. See the will referred to on p. 39, n. 1.

[2] *Register Chichele*, II, pp. 33–6.

into the background of historical events. Some have preferred the most fearful precision of conjecture rather than a blurring of the biographical edges and have argued for almost anything but the commonplace: domestic misery, political cowardice, insolvency, incompetence, rape, or even a *diseur's* subjection to the patronizing tolerance of courtiers. Criticism is disfigured by such rash dramatizations; nor does Chaucer's fame need the aid of worldly distinction. There is indeed a biographical singularity about him if we will see it. It is, I dare to say, in a personal modesty which was real and not simply a device of rhetoric designed to charm an audience. Geoffrey Chaucer did not struggle for the kind of advancement which his son Thomas achieved. There is no question of an actual poverty or public neglect (though the absence of his last will is one of the worst gaps in the evidence), for his financial means never failed and his son cannot have begun a well-heeled life on nothing. But the poet's own life-work was truly in poetry which he generated in quiet reading and expressed as professional entertainment. To a society not surfeited with mental recreation he brought mirth and solace. Implicit in the solace was an assumption that even a story has a 'signification', a morality that assured his hearers of values beyond mere storytelling. In the fourteenth century it was impossible that it should be otherwise, and Chaucer did not speak a language wholly different from that of Langland or the preachers, mystics, or religious lyricists. In a sense his outlook was a spiritual one, while entirely compatible with the conventions of courtly love, mild pessimism, irony, a sense of destiny and pleasurable indecency. For the historian the literature's integrity is matched by that of the man when he is compared with the great Italians he admired and used. Despite similarities in mercantile origins, life at courts, public position and dedication to letters, we miss in Chaucer the spiritual violence of Dante, the bitterness of Boccaccio, the vanity of Petrarch. It is a dubious excuse to argue that he did not suffer as they did; that he was able to stand outside the pain of his own utterances, unlike Boccaccio for whom *Il Filostrato* was a shield 'for his secret and amorous grief'. If Troy was London, the *Troilus* is incredible as a mere entertainment, indited without sentiment as the author claimed.[1] The fifth book of *Troilus and Criseyde* is the Everest of Chaucer's Himalayas and cannot have been climbed without cost. When at nightfall the warden of the gates began to call in the townsmen and

---

[1] *Troilus*, II, 13, and, for the closing of the gate, V, 1177–80.

their beasts, and Troilus at last gave up his gazing for the woman who did not come, the poet was communicating an experience satisfying to the historian, who is fiction's enemy, and the historian must be silent and content.

3: Chaucer and Fourteenth-Century English

N. DAVIS

I T IS A MAJOR commonplace of English linguistic history, which
for all its familiarity needs to be stated again in a study of this kind,
that the fourteenth century saw English at last set firmly on a course
which would rapidly lead to the consolidation of a literary language
accepted throughout the country and potentially flexible and expressive
enough to make possible the great achievements of the sixteenth century.
When William Caxton—who was far from satisfied with the condition
of the language in his own day—printed his second edition of *The Canterbury Tales* in 1484, he began with a Proem in which he praised 'that
noble and grete philosopher Gefferey Chaucer' especially because 'to
fore that he by hys labour enbelysshyd, ornated, and made faire our Eng-
lisshe, in thys royame was had rude speche and incongrue, as yet it appie-
reth by olde bookes.' Which old books he had in mind he did not say,
and, presumably guided by this opinion, he printed nothing in English
earlier than Chaucer. That there were indeed books composed in what
might be called 'rude' language is true enough, but Caxton must have
been unlucky if he came across nothing else. The exact force of his
'incongrue' is uncertain—the word had not been much used before his
time. It might refer to inept applications of words, inharmonious sentences, or unfamiliar grammatical forms. It might very justly refer to the
diversity of dialects, but this is not likely because Caxton was still complaining about that in 1490.

Whatever the limitations of Caxton's reading, we now know that
—leaving out of account pre-Conquest work, which nobody in the fifteenth century could be expected to appreciate even if they were aware
of it—long before Chaucer the English language had been proved capable of being used in both prose and verse very effectively, and at its best

with grace and subtlety. Many modern readers have some acquaintance with the witty fluency of *The Owl and the Nightingale*, which though probably written over a century before Chaucer was born approaches the quality of some of his own work; admittedly it stands alone in the verse of its time. But the text as it is presented by the surviving manuscripts requires for its full enjoyment a certain amount of work even today, when readers have the advantage of a grounding in Middle English; and it is easy to see that such things as dialectal verb forms and obsolete pronouns would seem 'incongrue' enough to a man like Caxton who had worked his way out of the 'brode and rude Englissh', as he called it, of the Kent of his youth. He might have done better with some of the romances of the Auchinleck Manuscript (written about 1330), which there is reason to think that Chaucer himself had read, such as the delicately handled *Sir Orfeo* or the vigorous and entertaining *Kyng Alisaunder*, distinguished by its lively dialogue and especially its lyrical seasonal 'headpieces'—

> *In tyme of hervest mery it is ynough—*
> *Peres and apples hongeth on bough,*
> *The hayward bloweth mery his horne,*
> *In everyche felde ripe is corne,*
> *The grapes hongen on the vyne.*
> *Swete is trewe love and fyne!*[1]

This manuscript is believed to have been produced in a London bookshop, but its language is not homogeneous and is not the simple direct ancestor of the kind of English that Chaucer wrote. The principal long verse texts of the late thirteenth or early fourteenth centuries are very diverse in their original dialects and made more so in the various manuscripts in which they were copied: *Cursor Mundi* and the *Northern Homily Cycle* come from undetermined areas in the north, the *South English Legendary* and the *Chronicle* formerly attributed to 'Robert of Gloucester' from the south-west, Robert Manning's works from the east midlands. These are all written in rhymed verse. Somewhat later, the main texts of the 'alliterative revival' can be placed in the north-west, and some at least of the romances in 'tail-rhyme' (a form which achieved a distinctive popularity in English) in the east. None of these varieties would have

---

[1] Ed G. V. Smithers, *EETS*, 227, 1952, lines 5745–50. In this and other quotations obsolete characters are replaced by their modern equivalents.

seemed in its day like the beginning of a generally current literary language, though looking back now we can see that many of the ingredients which later became general were present in Robert Manning:

> *A man yn Southfolke ones deyde*
> *Besyde Sudbyry, men seyde.*
> *For that man swych grace was dyght*
> *That hym was graunted to come anyght*
> *For to speke wyth hys wyfe*
> *To amende the defaute of hys lyfe:*
> *"Yyf a messe were for me doun*
> *With gode mannes devocioun,*
> *Y hope," he seyd, "to blis go,*
> *And be delyverd of alle my wo."*[1]

This short four-stress couplet was much the most important metre in the verse of this date. Short poems of the type vaguely called 'lyric' were usually in stanzas, some complex in structure and of changing pace:

> *Lutel wot hit any mon*
>   *Hou derne love may stonde*
> *Bote hit were a fre wymmon*
>   *That muche of love had fonde.*
> *The love of hire ne lesteth nowyht longe;*
> *Heo haveth me plyht ant wyteth me wyth wronge.*
>   *Ever ant oo for my leof icham in grete thohte;*
>   *Y thenche on hire that y ne seo nout ofte.*[2]

Some lyric writers had developed a highly mannered vocabulary of simile and symbol:

> *Heo is lilie of largesse,*
> *Heo is parvenke of prouesse,*
> *Heo is solsecle of suetnesse,*
>   *Ant ledy of lealté.*[3]

In addition to this background of verse a considerable tradition of

[1] Ed F. J. Furnivall, *EETS*, 119, 1901, lines 10397–406.
[2] *The Harley Lyrics*, ed G. L. Brook, Manchester 1948, no. 32, lines 1–8.
[3] *Ibid.*, no. 14, lines 51–4. For an excellent appraisal of the qualities of pre-Chaucerian verse see Miss P. M. Kean's summary in the first chapter of her *Chaucer and the Making of English Poetry*, 2 vol 1972.

English prose writing went back to the early thirteenth century. Much of it was obviously skilled and cultivated, though the word *prose* is not recorded in English before Manning. The earliest work had become antiquated in language before Chaucer's day, and was written in a pronounced western dialect which evidently seemed alien to many later readers: a partly modernized version of the *Ancrene Riwle* was transcribed into the Vernon Manuscript in his lifetime. Good prose in the generation before Chaucer was written by Richard Rolle, whose northern dialect is not marked enough in most manuscripts to make understanding and appreciation difficult for readers from other areas. But there was much less variety in the prose tradition than there was in the verse. Before the third quarter of the fourteenth century it was limited to religious use in devotional treatises and in sermons, and indeed continued to be predominantly so until the end of the century. It is an important element in the history of English that up to this time, as far as records show, the language was not much written for ordinary business or private purposes. This lack of use for familiar communication must have done much to delay the attainment of a widely accepted form of written language.

A major change of tone and content appeared, in Chaucer's middle years, with the rise of the Wycliffite movement, which produced many prose texts of a controversial rather than a devotional cast, in addition to important series of sermons and the translation of the Bible in an earlier and a later version. The number and quality of surviving manuscripts of the sermons show that they were carefully produced and widely known,[1] but the authors cannot usually be identified: the attribution of many pieces to Wyclif himself rests on inadequate evidence. About the same time prose of secular content began to be written in English, notably by John of Trevisa in his translations of the *Polychronicon* of Ranulph Higden and the *De Proprietatibus Rerum* of Bartholomeus Anglicus, and a little later by the anonymous translator of *Mandeville's Travels*; and the beginnings of specialized scientific writing can be seen in translations of astronomical treatises.[2] Chaucer's own translation of Boethius, though not of purely secular interest as these works are, may be seen as part of the same trend to bring books of international scholarly concern within

[1] See Anne Hudson, 'A Lollard Sermon-Cycle and its Implications,' *Medium Ævum*, XL, 1971, 142–56.

[2] Examples are given in *The Equatorie of the Planetis*, ed D. J. Price, Cambridge 1955, Appendix III.

reach of readers of English. In this he was working with few examples before him of lucid and idiomatic English prose, and he cannot be said to have made a success of it. Despite the claims that have been made for the artistry with which Chaucer composed his prose,[1] nearly all of it is laboured and artificial except for the special case of the *Astrolabe*. There is much of interest in the vocabulary, especially of the *Boece* and 'The Parson's Tale', but in other characteristics the progress of English prose owes disappointingly little to Chaucer.

The works of translation and controversy of the late fourteenth century were part of a general movement towards the use of English in many fields in which French or Latin had earlier been customary. It was at this time that English began to appear in documents of many kinds, such as wills, indentures, the statutes of guilds, and records of local government, though it was not until the 1420s that it was generally adopted for these purposes. Again, the last years of the fourteenth century saw the earliest extant private letters written in English.[2] As critics have often remarked, Chaucer's choice of English for all his work, at the courtly level at which he wrote, was advanced in comparison with the decision of his friend Gower to write in French and Latin as well. But in view of the spread of English in every sphere of life it was certain to become the predominant vernacular language very shortly; and in fact Gower was the last of the writers of Anglo-Norman.

Despite the re-establishment of English throughout the country everyone was aware that it was not in all things the same language in all places: pronunciation and grammar and vocabulary differed locally much more than they came to do in later ages, and there was not yet any broad agreement among educated men about the usages to be preferred in literary work—the great movement towards homogeneity in the written language set in during the fifteenth century. Clerks who copied texts would often alter some of the forms of their exemplar to others more familiar to themselves or to the readers they had in mind, and this would often dis-

---

[1] The best statement, with references, is by Margaret Schlauch, 'The Art of Chaucer's Prose', in *Chaucer and Chaucerians*, ed D. S. Brewer, 1966, 140–63.

[2] There must in fact have been many earlier ones which do not survive, for conventions were established by the time Chaucer wrote *Troilus and Criseyde*. See N. Davis, 'The *Litera Troili* and English Letters', *RES*, XVI, 1965, 233–44.

turb the rhyme or the rhythm of verse. There was evidently a large degree of tolerance among readers for forms which were readily comprehensible even if different from local custom, for many literary manuscripts embody more than one form of numerous words. These variants depend ultimately on differing local pronunciations and inflections, but were apparently expected to be acceptable enough to the people for whom the scribes worked. Much of this inconsistency must be merely a matter of spelling, for someone reading a text aloud would presumably for the most part use his own customary pronunciation of each word and maintain it however the individual occurrence of it was written. But variation went further than this, for some poets, including Chaucer, used more than one form of some words in rhyme, which of course demands the acceptance of more than one pronunciation. This tolerance had its limits. Though the London language itself was changing rapidly under the influence of immigrants from the Midlands and East Anglia, so that variant forms and accents must have been familiar to everyone, Chaucer's treatment of the dialect of the students in 'The Reeve's Tale' as a laughing matter shows that that particular dialect fell outside the range of acceptable literary usage in London.

Many features of his language a writer has no choice but to accept as he finds them. He cannot introduce new sounds that are no part of the system of speech of his hearers, or inflections with no established place in the grammar (though he may exploit archaic and regional variants), and syntax he can modify only in particular circumstances and in very limited ways which will only exceptionally spread to users of the language at large. His effective freedom of choice and to some extent of innovation lies in the use of words and their combinations, and this choice itself may be restricted by the form in which he has decided to write.

Chaucer's own words prove that he was greatly interested in form and its demands: he complains of the scarcity of rhymes in English, and apologizes for irregularities in syllables.[1] Until the introduction of printing made multiple copies widely available most people's experience of poetry necessarily lay in hearing it read aloud, so that the sound of verse was even more important to its appreciation than it is in later periods, and there was no opportunity for 'eye-rhyme' based on likeness of shape rather than sound. Chaucer's works in verse are all obviously intended to

[1] *Complaint of Venus*, 80; *House of Fame*, 1098.

rhyme, and it is worth while to inquire at the outset what kind of restriction this set upon his writing.[1]

It may be taken as settled that in the London language of the late fourteenth century the long vowels and diphthongs had not yet moved to the positions which later set them apart from most of the corresponding sounds in other European languages. In words involving these Chaucer had some opportunities for rhyme that the language later lost, and on the other hand he lacked some that it later acquired. For example, the rhyme

> *Of yeddynges he baar outrely the pris.*
> *His nekke whit was as the flour-de-lys*   A(I), 237–8)[2]

was a good one because *pris* was pronounced with the vowel which *fleur de lis*, because of its strong French connection, still retains. Not everything is as clear-cut as this. The letters *e* or *ee*, *o* or *oo*, could each represent two vowels, one of a 'close', the other of an 'open' quality, depending on the history of the words in which they appeared. The close and the open vowels were significantly distinct sounds (phonemes), and would not correctly rhyme together. Some pairs that make good rhymes in later English do not normally rhyme in Chaucer's language: for instance *mete* 'food', which had an open vowel (as the later spelling *meat* implies), does not rhyme with *mete* 'meet'; *hepe* 'heap' does not rhyme with *wepe* 'weep'. Some words rhyme with both types: *dede* 'deed' is paired with *rede* 'red', historically with an open vowel (A(I), 2636), and also with *blede* 'bleed', with a close one (B, 3696=VII, 2506); *slep* 'sleep', which usually rhymes on the close sound, very often in *kep* 'attention' (e.g. BD 5, 137, 223), is paired with *hep* in BD 296. This is easily accounted for because these and words of similar descent had had different vowels in different Old English dialects, and both types survived as alternatives in Middle English, no doubt essentially as regional variations but known to and accepted by London writers. Thus, though the absence of spelling distinction obscures this, they are of the same standing as the alternatives Chaucer uses in a number of words containing a vowel descended from an Old English *y* (like modern French *u*). This vowel is normally *i* in

[1] For an informative study of some of its effects see M. Masui, *The Structure of Chaucer's Rime Words*, Tokyo 1964.

[2] References to *The Canterbury Tales* are by fragment-letter, as in Skeat's edition and the Tatlock-Kennedy *Concordance*, and line number, with Robinson's fragment-numbers added.

Chaucer, but sometimes *e* as it was in the south-east of England—a variant familiar in London—and it rhymes accordingly: *liste* 'please' rhymes with *upriste* 'rising' (A(I), 1052), the alternative *leste* with *beste* (TC III, 452); *fir* 'fire' normally rhymes with words like *desir* (A(I), 1502, 2320), but, as *feere*, with *deere* and *heere* at TC III, 978. But not all Chaucer's rhymes between *e*-sounds of different descent are covered by known variants in Old English—most conspicuously, the noun *see* 'sea', which would be expected to have an open[1] vowel and certainly had it in early modern English, very often rhymes with the verb *see* and other words which historically had a close one (e.g. A(I), 59, 3031); and the adjective *clene*, which should have an open vowel, sometimes rhymes on the close sound in the participle *(y)sene* 'seen' (A(I), 133, F(V), 995). Special explanations have been offered for these apparent exceptions, based on the environment of the vowels; but difficulties remain, notably in the rhyme *lief* 'lief' with *leef* 'leaf' at A(I), 1837. Similar rhymes occur in other Middle English texts, mainly of the east and north, and the explanation appears to be that in some areas the open sound had already become identical with the close as it did generally much later. Chaucer was again making use of the alternative.[2] A similar but not identical problem appears in some rhymes involving the sounds written *o (o)*. Here the same spelling served for open and close sounds which can usually be readily identified because they have remained distinct in modern English though still sometimes spelt in the same way, as in *go* and *do*. Chaucer usually keeps these apart in rhyme, but not always: he normally rhymes *goon* 'go' with such words as *oon* 'one' and *stoon* 'stone' (A(I), 2510, 3022), but occasionally with *doon* 'do' (A(I), 2963, T C II. 410); *bothe*, which usually rhymes with *wrothe* (A(I), 1180, 1839), is paired with *sothe* at G(VIII), 168; *hom*, which ought to rhyme with such words as 'foam' and 'roam' (both of which Chaucer uses, though not in rhyme), he rhymes only on

---

[1] The phonetic terms 'close' and 'open' refer to the shape of the mouth cavity in articulation. The 'close' vowels are produced with the tongue higher and tenser, and the jaw opening narrower, than the 'open' vowels. In modern French the close and open *e* sounds are heard respectively in *été* and *tête*, the *o* sounds in *tôt* and *tort*. English now provides no exact parallel, but the difference may be crudely suggested by the contrast of the vowels in *hay* and *hair*, *go* and *gore*.

[2] See E. J. Dobson, *English Pronunciation 1500–1700*, Oxford 2nd edn 1968, § 121.

the past tense *com* and the noun *dom* (BD 77, B, 3128=VII, 1938), both
with the close sound. As with the abnormal *e*-rhymes, Chaucer is not
alone in this: there are many similar rhymes in other fourteenth-century
texts of the east and south-east.[1] Again it seems that there was a type of
pronunciation with the close vowel which was current for a time as an
acceptable rhyming device, though it never developed into a feature of
the literary language as the close pronunciation of the 'open *e*' words did.

These apparently irregular features of rhyming technique Chaucer
thus shared with some of his contemporaries, though not with all. Some
other matters of pronunciation affected his range of rhyme-words. For
example, in words like *right* and *sight* the fricative consonant represented
by the spelling *gh* was still pronounced, so that rhymes as useful, and later
popular, as that of *sight* with *white* or *delight* (in which the *gh* conceals the
descent from French *delit*) were not available. An important general
limitation is that some common word-endings, such as *-able*, *-age*,
-a(u)nce, *-ence*, occur only in words of French origin, so that the choice of
one such word in rhyme requires another, with significant effect on the
texture of the diction. A special case of a similar kind arose from the
limited currency at the ends of words of some sounds which have since
become commoner; most conspicuously perhaps that spelt *oi* or *oy*,
whether final or followed by *-e*, which does not occur in words descended from Old English—modern words ending in *-oy* are mostly
from French or Dutch. A number now familiar, such as *buoy*, *toy*, *decoy*,
employ, Chaucer never used, and among others he made some clear distinctions: *boy* and *coy* on the one hand rhyme only with *Seinte Loy* (A(I),
120, D(III), 1564), who appears nowhere else in his work and makes the
impression of owing his place to the rhyme; *joye* and *anoye* on the other
rhyme only with *Troye*. In *Troilus and Criseyde* the word *Troye* occurs in
rhyme in no less than 31 places, in every one of which it rhymes with *joye*
except at V, 393 where the rhyme-word is the verb *rejoie*. (At IV, 1307 it
rhymes also with *anoye*, at V, 779 with *acoye*.) In Chaucer's other works it
rhymes a further nine times, without exception on *joye*. It appears that
because of the 'scarcity' of rhymes the mention of Troy at the end of a
line brings with it the mention of joy. Since *Troilus and Criseyde* is set in
Troy the name is naturally frequent; and it is the pressure of the rhyme
scheme that is likely to lead to the prominence of *joye* rather than

[1] See G. V. Smithers, 'A Note on *Havelok the Dane* 2008–2009,' *English and
Germanic Studies*, II, 1948–9, 1–9.

Chaucer's wish to devise 'a sort of refrain expressive of joy or sorrow as the occasion may arise', as Professor Masui has suggested.[1] This is a good illustration of the admittedly commonplace fact that the choice of a complex stanza form in a language with limited rhyming resources may in part determine what a poet says.

Just as an understanding of Chaucer's rhymes requires some knowledge of the history of the sounds of stressed syllables, and their possible variations, discussion of the rhythm of his lines requires attention to the history of the sounds constituting the unstressed syllables of inflectional endings. In the two centuries or so before Chaucer was born English in all areas had moved far towards simplifying inflections—further in some areas than others; and changes were still going on in Chaucer's time in his own dialect. In nouns, for example, most plurals had adopted the ending *-es*, which remained an additional syllable in words monosyllabic in the singular (not only those ending in certain sounds like modern *houses* and *bridges*), but could be reduced to the consonant alone in longer words such as *frankeleyns* (A(I), 216) or *maydens* (A(I), 2275); many French words especially retained the simple *-s* plural, as *nacions, servantz* (A(I), 53, 101). In verbs the present tense singular retained the *-(e)st* and *-(e)th* long characteristic of the second and third persons, but Chaucer in his early work adopted, evidently for the sake of rhyme again, the northerly *-es* in three places in the third person (BD 73, 257, HF 426) and once in the second (HF 1908). He made some use also of the alternative syncopated forms of the third person of verbs with stems ending in a dental consonant, as

> "*Lo, yond he* rit!" "*Ye,*" *quod she,* "*so he doth.*"
>
> (TC II, 1284)

but

> *Fro thennesforth he* rideth *up and down*
>
> (TC V, 561)

This is manifestly on account of the metre. Other optional forms were available in past participles, which could be used with or without the prefix *y-*, and those of strong verbs with or without the ending *-n*; rarely also the stem itself could vary, so that for 'slain' Chaucer could, and did, use *slayn* (A(I), 992), *yslayn* (A(I), 2708, *slawe(n)* (E(IV), 544, B,

---

[1] Structure, § 142. See also E. G. Stanley, 'Stanza and Ictus. Chaucer's Emphasis in "Troilus and Criseyde"', in *Chaucer und seine Zeit. Symposion für Walter F. Schirmer* (Tübingen, 1968), pp. 123–48, esp. p. 134.

2016=VII, 826), *yslawe* (A(I), 943). This variation is ultimately one of dialect, *y*- being typical of the south, -*n* of the north; but the types over-lapped and were variously accepted by different authors. It is especially remarkable that Gower used the *y*- prefix very rarely, in contrast to its frequency in Chaucer; but he differed also in using -*ende* as a suffix of the present participle, instead of Chaucer's -*ynge*. The most versatile verbal ending was -*n*, which served not only in the past participle of strong verbs but also in the infinitive and the plural of the present and past tense indicative and subjunctive of verbs of all classes. But it could be, and very often was, dropped in all these, and this option was important in adjusting syllables to a verse line.

The commonest inflectional ending was -*e* (presumably pronounced as a 'central' vowel like that of German or southern dialects of French). In nouns it could act as a case-ending after a preposition, mainly in set phrases like *to bedde*; in adjectives it was normal after a determining word, and to mark the plural; in verbs it marked the first person singular of the present, the singular of the subjunctive and some imperatives, and the past singular of weak verbs, and it could also occur in all those parts which in their full form ended in -*n* but could optionally drop it. In ad-dition, final -*e* was an integral part, not an inflection, of many words which had ended in a vowel in Old English or Old French. This was the position in early Middle English. Mainly in the course of the fourteenth century the vowel gradually ceased to be pronounced, first in the north and later more extensively, until by the middle of the fifteenth century it had become silent everywhere. Scribes nevertheless often continued to write -*e* in traditional places, and sometimes wrote it where it had never been pronounced.

The place of this vowel in Chaucer's verse, especially at the end of the line, has been much debated and there is no room here to review the arguments; but the general question is so important to a judgement of Chaucer's technique that one must attempt to reach an opinion about it. It is not a simple question, because it depends so much on what we expect the movement of a line of verse to be, and there is danger of circular argument. From the late eighteenth century onwards the prevailing opinion has been that Chaucer's metre was based on the alternation of unstressed and stressed syllables in the same way as later verse commonly though inappropriately called iambic, whether in four-stress couplets as in *The Book of the Duchess* and *The House of Fame* or in five-stress lines in couplets or in stanzas. The longer line might contain nine, ten, or eleven syllables, and occasional reversal of stress and variation in the number of unstressed syllables must of course be admitted. A great number of Chaucer's lines as presented in good early manuscripts read entirely naturally when taken in this way, and indeed will not read in any other way without distortion. In some the rhythm depends on the sounding as separate syllables of the endings *-es* and *-ed*, as in 'His bootës claspëd faire and fetisly' (A(I), 273). This is readily understood because these endings are still current in many words and remembered as archaisms in others. (Chaucer's choice of optional variants, as in the third person singular of verbs as noticed above (p. 67), confirms his concern for patterns of this kind.) In many others it depends on the pronunciation of inflectional or etymological final *-e*, which offers more difficulty partly because it is irregularly written in the manuscripts, partly because the sound is now unknown in English, but mainly because it cannot invariably be pronounced to accord with the metre in positions where it would be historically in place. A brief example must suffice. The word *love*, Old English *lufu* and its inflections, would properly have two syllables in early Middle English. In the line 'Han felt that Love dorste yow displese' (TC, I, 27) a regular five-stress reading requires that both *Love* and the verb *dorste* should have two syllables; but in 'Love that of erthe and se hath governaunce' (TC, III, 1744) the opening of the line would be spoilt by a disyllabic *Love* because of the two light syllables following, and it must be read as a monosyllable. From lines of this kind it appears that though in most places where it is justified by historical grammar the *-e* is sounded, in a good many it is better not. Such irregularity does not invalidate the general rightness of accepting the sound as essential to the pattern of alternating stresses. The use of alternative forms of various kinds can be seen to be a common feature of Chaucer's language, and the irregularities in the pronunciation of *-e* should be regarded in this light.

When it occurs in rhyme, as it very often does, the unstressed *-e* seems if regularly sounded to hamper the easy flow of informal language, especially in dialogue, in which Chaucer excels, and one would often willingly dispense with it. But there is no denying the strength of the evidence that Chaucer generally did not rhyme together words with and without it, and that he did several times exploit the eccentric-looking but evidently traditional type of rhyme seen in *Rome: to me* (A(I), 671–2). The most remarkable of these is in *Troilus and Criseyde* I, 2–5, in which *Troye* rhymes with *fro ye*. This is the only place in all Chaucer's work where *ye* takes the place of the normal objective form *yow*. It must be a weakened form appropriate to informal spoken use. This may seem out of place in so apparently solemn an introduction—'Thesiphone, thow help me for t'endite . . .'—but Chaucer presumably meant the tone at this point to be light-hearted, as it clearly was a few lines later, 'Have he my thonk, and myn be this travaille!' Certainly these combinations of preposition and pronoun, with the stress on the former, mainly occur in more or less humorous contexts, such as Pandarus's *by me* rhyming with *tyme* and *pryme* at II, 991; but they need not always have this colour—usually they do not in Gower, who uses them often, and Hoccleve can have meant nothing of the kind when he concluded stanza 281 of *The Regement of Princes*, addressing 'mi maister Chaucer, flour of eloquence',

> *Allas, that thou thyn excellent prudence*
> *In thi bed mortel mightist noght byquethe!*
> *What eiled Deth? Allas, why wold he sle the?*

Comparatively recently the view that in most of his work Chaucer intended to write essentially the same kind of five-stress lines as many later English poets has been challenged,[1] but the rhythms produced by the competing theory of 'four-beat' lines are so often unsatisfactory that they cannot be accepted. It has never been seriously doubted that when Chaucer used the short, four-stress couplet for *The Book of the Duchess* and *The House of Fame* he was following the practice of many earlier English poets, such as the authors of *The Owl and the Nightingale*, *Cursor Mundi*, *Havelok*, and many other romances, in adapting to English the octosyllabic couplet so widely used in French. The movement of the line could not be exactly the same, for French writers counted syllables and English were more concerned with stresses, perhaps affected by the shape of the native alliterative line; but the resemblance is close and the dependence not in doubt. Some of the hesitation about Chaucer's longer line arises because he was the first to use an apparently decasyllabic line in English on any appreciable scale—before him there were a few isolated

[1] Most radically by J. G. Southworth, *The Prosody of Chaucer*, Oxford 1962. I. Robinson in *Chaucer's Prosody*, Cambridge 1971, though more sympathetic to Southworth than I am, reaches a position which in practice is not very different from that set out here; but his advocacy of wider acceptance of 'trochaic' movement does not in general persuade.

lines such as lines 5–6 of the stanza quoted on p. 60 above—and the structure was evidently not identical with that of the strictly syllabic French
decasyllable which had been used for a long time in France and was
popular in Chaucer's day. C. S. Lewis thought that English readers
would find such an innovation hard to understand.[1] But syllabic metres
had been adapted to English from the *Ormulum* onwards; and though
Chaucer was indeed highly original in introducing, as he effectively did,
the five-stress line into English poetry, it is not apparent why it should
have been too much for the comprehension of his audience any more
than the much earlier adaptation of octosyllabics to English stress had
been for their ancestors.

The grammar of Chaucer's language and the pronunciation of inflectional syllables can of course give some of his lines a texture different
from that of later English. For example, 'And pynnës for to yevën fairë
wyvës' (A(I), 234), even admitting the archaic *for to*, requires eleven syllables where the modern equivalent has seven—a distinctly lower
'semantic density'.

To the formal resources of English verse in the fourteenth century
Chaucer brought the five-stress line and the seven-line stanza, which he
found so congenial that he used it for *Troilus and Criseyde* in spite of the
eight-line stanza of his source. To its verbal resources he made an evidently great but scarcely determinable contribution: scarcely determinable because while he was writing many others were writing too, and
the exact dates of most of their works, and of Chaucer's, are not known
so that priority cannot be demonstrated. In writing of Chaucer's diction,
critics ever since Hoccleve have dwelt on his 'eloquence', and Caxton's
'enbellyshyd, ornated, and made faire' is usually taken to be another way
of praising his 'augmenting' of the English vocabulary, as the sixteenth
century would have put it, with new learned or fashionable words from
French or Latin. No doubt in part it is; but there are other ways of
improving a language than by introducing into it words from another,
and Chaucer's 'eloquence' consisted no less in the 'decorum' with which
he applied the existing resources of the language.[2] Study of Chaucer's
vocabulary has been directed very largely to his use of words of
Romance origin and especially the number of them that he may have

[1] 'The Fifteenth-Century Heroic Line', *Essays and Studies*, XXIV, 1938,
28–41, especially p. 32.

For a good discussion of this question see P. M. Kean, *Chaucer*, II, chap. VI.

brought into English.[1] Praise of his handling of the language was un-
alloyed until the beginning of the seventeenth century, when dissenting
voices arose from those who disliked what they thought was excessive
use of French and Latin—'a great mingler of English with French', said
R. Verstegan in 1605. It is significant that this type of criticism came long
after his own day, and after the 'ink-horn' disputes of the sixteenth century which concentrated attention on vocabulary and its origins. Widely
divergent views on Chaucer's contribution to the Romance element in
English continue to be expressed. A typical recent statement is this:
'Chaucer revolutionized "poetic diction" by "augmenting" his English
with a vast number of new words of Latin, French, and Italian origin.'[2]
The tone of this is strikingly different from that of F. N. Robinson in
what is probably the most widely-used edition of Chaucer's *Works*:[3] 'He
not only did not invent or alter the grammatical inflections, but he also
appears to have added few words to the English vocabulary. At least Mr.
Henry Bradley, in the light of his experience in editing the *New English
Dictionary*, was very cautious about attributing such contributions to the
poet.' In fact Bradley was less cautious than Robinson. What he wrote
was: 'It would be easy to give lists of words and expressions which are
used by Chaucer, and, *so far as we know*, not by any earlier writer. We
cannot doubt that a large proportion of these were really brought into
literary use by him; . . . Yet in individual instances we can seldom feel
sure that in the use of this or that word he had not some English example
before him.'[4] Less cautious in a different sense was Sir Walter Raleigh:
'Least of all great English poets did Chaucer mould and modify the
speech he found. . . . His English is plain, terse, homely, colloquial English, taken alive out of daily speech.'[5] It often is, where this is appropriate,
but most readers know that very often it is not; especially in the set pieces
such as 'Infortunat ascendent tortuous' (B(II), 302) but also in the lighter
vein of 'dysordynaunce of naturel acustumaunce' (HF, 27–8) and many
similar things. If Chaucer's English had been consistently so homely,

---

[1] The history of this study is surveyed by J. Mersand in his *Chaucer's
Romance Vocabulary*, New York 2nd edn 1939.

[2] D. S. Brewer, 'The Relation of Chaucer to the English and European
Traditions' in *Chaucer and Chaucerians*, 1–38; quotation p. 26.

[3] First published in 1933, but left unaltered in the second edition of 1957.

[4] *The Making of English*, 1904, p. 226.

[5] *On Writing and Writers*, 1926, p. 115.

Hoccleve, Lydgate, Caxton, Dunbar, and others far nearer to colloquial Middle English than we are would not have repeated so approvingly that he had embellished and adorned the language.

The details given in Joseph Mersand's book[1] about the priority of particular words are often unacceptable, partly because views of the dating of numerous works have changed since it was written, partly because new information, especially that collected for the *Middle English Dictionary*, supersedes what he could learn from the *Oxford English Dictionary*. Substantially fewer Romance words than he lists as innovations by Chaucer can in fact be attributed to him; yet it remains true that in spite of the necessary particular revisions there are still a great many words in Chaucer that are not recorded in works demonstrably earlier. But there is a more important general objection to be made to the approach to vocabulary defined in the book: 'The only way to determine the nature of Chaucer's vocabulary is to count every word he used, to investigate the etymology of every word, and, finally, to arrange, add, and compute carefully' (p. 37). These last activities should not come 'finally' at all. The significance of Romance words varies infinitely. We need to know not only the bare fact of etymology but the associations and status of every word, and whether specific applications of it would seem to contemporary hearers in any way out of the ordinary. In the early stages of Middle English every Romance word is significant because it necessarily implies a recent shift in patterns of association: when the Peterborough Chronicler writes of *pais* or *iustise* he departs from the ambience of old words like *grith* and *right*, with far-reaching consequences. But by Chaucer's time a great deal of this sort of innovation was ancient. Many Old English words had fallen out of use or become restricted in application, and Romance words had become the normal, or the only, means of expressing some concepts. For something as common as *air*, which Chaucer used 37 times (usually *eir* or *eyr* in the manuscripts) he had no choice. The descendant of the equivalent Old English word *lyft* was *lift*, which survived mainly in the north though also in Gower, but with the meaning 'sky' from the thirteenth century on. The position is wholly different with such a word as *effect*, which is not recorded before Chaucer but was used by him no less than 76 times, according to the *Concordance*, in a wide range of senses. To cite a few examples, several are not far from the Latin senses, as in 'falleth al the effect contraire' (TC, I, 212),

[1] See p. 72, n. 1 above.

where the meaning is 'consequence'. or 'to this effect and to this ende'
(B, 3073=VII, 1883), where it is 'intended consequence, purpose', or 'th'
effect, as fer as I kan understonde' (TC, II, 1220), where it is 'substance';
several technical senses follow the Latin of Boethius, as '[the whiche
names ben ful ofte reproved] by the effect of the same thynges' (*Boece* II,
pr. 6, 114), rendering *ipsarum rerum effectu*, where the meaning is 'quality'
or 'nature'; some phrases also are already established, especially *in effect*,
'in fact, effectively', very much as in later use, some fifteen times. This
word was also used by contemporaries or near-contemporaries such as
Gower, Trevisa, and Usk, and looks like a term current in educated
circles which only by accident came to be recorded first in Chaucer's
work. Different again are individual words that Chaucer highlights and
plays with: so in the 'words between the Summoner and the Friar' at the
end of 'The Wife of Bath's Prologue', 'This is a long preamble of a tale!'
says the Friar, to which the Summoner retorts,

> *What spekestow of preambulacioun?*
> *What! amble, or trotte, or pees, or go sit doun!*
>
> (D(III), 831, 837–8)

Neither *preamble* nor *preambulacioun* is known earlier than this; Chaucer
used them nowhere else, and none of his contemporaries used them
either. He thus brought them into use for a special effect, but he can
hardly be said to have established them in the literary language. These
few examples are enough to show how little light is cast on the composition of Chaucer's vocabulary by treating words so various in currency as
if they were in some way of equivalent quality by the mere fact of
Romance derivation.

   Not enough work has yet been done on distinctive qualities of
Chaucer's native vocabulary;[1] and the particular ways in which he com-
bined native and Romance words are often worth attention. One of the
simpler blends appears in the opening line of 'The Nun's Priest's Tale',
'A poure wydwe, somdeel stape in age' (B, 4011=VII, 2821). Here the
French words *poure* and *age* were in normal use in Chaucer's time, but

---

[1] Valuable steps in the right direction are taken by J. A. Burrow on *list* in *N
& Q*, CCXIII, 1968, 326–7, and *worly* in *Chaucer Review*, III, 1969, 170–3.
Important earlier studies of special sectors are J. R. R. Tolkien, 'Chaucer as
a Philologist: *The Reeve's Tale*', *TPS*, 1934, 1–70, and E. T. Donaldson,
'Idiom of Popular Poetry in the Miller's Tale', *English Institute Essays 1950*,
reprinted in *Speaking of Chaucer*, 1970, pp. 13–29.

were not quite on an equal footing; for *poure*, in English from about 1200, had long since supplanted the native *arm* in this meaning, but *age* overlapped in the particular sense of 'old age' with the still current native *elde*—which indeed appears once in Chaucer in the general sense as well: 'Yong was this quene, of twenty yer of elde' (*Anelida* 78). Thus 'Whan tendre youthe hath wedded stoupyng age' (E(IV), 1738) may be compared with 'For youthe and elde is often at debaat' (A(I), 3230). The word that stands out in this line is not a French one but *stape*, which is used again in the same phrase *stapen in age* in 'The Merchant's Tale' (E(IV), 1514). The participle is old, but has not been found earlier in this sense. The other noticeable word, *somdeel*, was widely current and evidently unremarkable at that time.

In these lines *age* was the natural word to use, irrespective of its form. In other places choice between a pair of words closely similar in meaning, one Romance and one native, is clearly determined by sound rather than sense. The best example is probably the pair *voice* and *steven*, as in the couplet

> *The voys of peple touchede the hevene,*
> *So loude cride they with murie stevene* (A(I), 2561–2)

and in a different sense ('favourable report'),

> *That swich a vois was of hym and a stevene*
>
> .   .   .   .
>
> *That it up rong unto the yate of hevene* (TC, III, 1723–5)

Vois was Chaucer's normal word, and had been familiar in English from the late thirteenth century onwards. The Old English equivalent had been *stefn*, which was evidently still quite well known—it survives in northern dialect into modern times. Chaucer used *stevene* nine times, against seventy of *vois*—all nine at the end of the line, eight of them rhyming with *hevene*, the other with the verb *nevene* 'name'. *Vois* rhymes only three times, all with *croys* 'cross'. From this it is plain that *stevene* for Chaucer was a convenient word for rhyme. Gower used it in the same way, and writing of the Sirens associated it similarly with *vois*:

> *with so swete a stevene*
> *Lik to the melodie of hevene*
> *In wommanysshe vois thei singe* (*Confessio* I, 493–5)

It is worth while to compare these London uses with the practice of the

Gawain poet. He did not use *vois* at all, only *steven*, a total of ten times.[1]
Here is a real difference of usage, the *Gawain* poet retaining the Old English
word alone but the London writers exploiting it only occasionally
for the rhyme and normally replacing it by the French.

In a different relation from the pairs so far considered are *joy* and *bliss*.
Here again an English word survives after a French synonym is adopted,
but in this case there is little specialization and the words are often used
almost indifferently, or linked in a set phrase, *joye and blis*, which
Chaucer used a dozen times.[2] The phrase varies in tone from the serious
account in 'The Knight's Tale' of Theseus 'with alle joye and blis' (A(I),
1684) to the familiar asseveration 'So have I joye or blis' used by the Friar
to the Wife of Bath (D(III), 830) and by Chauntecleer to Pertelote
(B, 4256=VII, 3066). It was an established phrase long before Chaucer
—used perhaps a century earlier in *Cursor Mundi* (which also has *bliss and
joy*), then in *The Land of Cokaygne*, 'Robert of Gloucester', and elsewhere; also contemporaneously in *Pearl*, and continuing in later poetry:
'All my redeemd may dwell in joy and bliss' (*Paradise Lost*, XI, 43). Professor Potter observes that 'joy is of earth, . . . bliss . . . is of heaven'.
This is by no means regularly so, as the phrase *joy and bliss* itself sufficiently shows, as well as other pages such as

> O sodeyn wo, that evere art successour
> To worldly blisse, spreynd with bitternesse!
> The ende of the joye of oure worldly labour! (B(II), 421–3)

and probably 'Womman is mannes joye and al his blis' (B, 4356 = VII,
3166) where the two are indistinguishable. There is nevertheless a strong
trend in that direction, helped by the fortuitous likeness of *bliss* and *bless*.
Beyond the semantic field, too, the words were not of precisely equal
value to Chaucer: his choice sometimes turned on a rhyme, pointed or
witty:

> And seyde, "I am, al be it yow no joye,
> As gentil man as any wight in Troie"
> > (Diomede, in TC, V, 930–1)

[1] This word is of course to be distinguished from the other of the same
form, meaning 'appointed time', which Chaucer used three times (in
rhyme) and the *Gawain* poet nine times.
[2] Cf. S. Potter, 'Chaucer's Untransposable Binomials', *Neuphilologische
Mitteilungen*, LXXIII, *Studies Presented to Tauno F. Mustanoja*, 1972, 309–14.

> *"For every wo ye shal recovere a blisse."*
> *And hym in armes took, and gan hym kisse*
>
> (Criseyde, in TC, III, 181–2)

Joye often occurs in association with other near-synonyms than *blis* —notably *solas*, an old-established word which Chaucer, except for two occurrences in 'The Parson's Tale', always placed in rhyme; *felicitee*, which was a new word in his time and may well have been introduced by him, though Langland and Gower also used it; *gladnesse*, which in contrast to these French words was an ancient compound apparently in unbroken use since Old English. With *gladnesse* we encounter some significant peculiarities of Chaucer's diction in his prose, for eight examples of it are in *Boece* (out of a total 41), where it renders *laetitia* or *iucunditas*. *Felicitee* he used there too, but strangely not to render *felicitas*, which is frequent in Boethius but becomes mostly *welefulnesse*, once *blisfulnesse*. *Felicitee* once renders *beatitudo*, but this is otherwise almost regularly *blisfulnesse*—never simple *blis* despite its familiarity in other places. It is remarkable that *blisfulnesse* appears 85 times, *welefulnesse* 31 times, in *Boece* and neither of them anywhere else in Chaucer's work. The near-regularity with which these are kept apart, for *beatitudo* and *felicitas* respectively, and also distinguished from *gladnesse* for *laetitia/iucunditas*, proves how carefully he could attend to distinctions between words of closely connected meaning. They and other compounds of similar shape strikingly show that he did not as a matter of course simply take over a Romance word from the text he was translating, even when, as with *felicitee*, he had used the word already, but he thought out a new compound which he believed to represent the sense: 'Socrates in his opinyoun of felicite, that I clepe welefulnesse', as he puts it in a gloss in *Boece* I pr. 3. Yet when largely re-working the passage about *caduca ista felicitas* in Book IV pr. 4 in Criseyde's speech in *Troilus and Criseyde* III, 813ff. he used instead *selynesse* (known earlier in *Cursor Mundi*) beside *felicitee*:

> *"O God!" quod she, "so worldly selynesse,*
> *Which clerkes callen fals felicitee . . .".*

He used *selynesse* in two other places in the same passage—(825, 831)—but nowhere else at all.

Fluctuations of this kind show that the choice of a Romance word rather than a native one was seldom a simple matter of 'augmenting' the vocabulary of English. Still in the Boethian field, Chaucer showed considerable ingenuity in setting beside some of his more technical Romance terms, as a kind of etymological gloss, their English equivalents; but in a way far removed from the crude doublets of so much prose translation of the time, including his own. A good example is in the passage about Providence in *Troilus and Criseyde* IV, extending from line 958 to line 1078, of which the following extracts are typical:

> "For certeynly, this wot I wel," he seyde,
> "That forsight of divine purveyaunce
> Hath seyn alwey me to forgon Criseyde,
> Syn God seeth every thyng, out of doutaunce,
> And hem disponyth, thorugh his ordinaunce . . ."   (960–4)

> "They seyn right thus, that thyng is nat to come
> For that the prescience hath seyn byfore
> That it shal come; but they seyn that therfore
> That it shal come, therfore the purveyaunce
> Woot it byforn, without ignoraunce."   (997–1001)

In the first passage *forsight* and its seeing explain *purveyaunce*; in the second *prescience* sees, and is treated interchangeably with *purveyaunce*, which knows. Here Chaucer freely uses *forsight*, in line 989 *forseynge*, and in 1071 *forwoot*, beside these learned nouns and the verbal forms *purvey* and *purveyinge* (e.g. 1066, 1015). This makes the impression of a conscious effort to exploit the different modes of expressing the Boethian ideas; yet it was not a new device, for the author of *Cursor Mundi* had thought of it long before: 'He purvaid al in his forsight' (284). When Chaucer put a briefer version of the same discussion into the mouth of the Nun's Priest he did not use the Romance words at all, only the English *forwityng* and *forwoot* (B, 4424, 4433;=VII, 3234, 3243).

This last case leads to a consideration of special uses by Chaucer of native words. Something may be seen of this in one of his most elaborately worked passages, the Proem to Book III of *Troilus and Criseyde*, which depends so closely on Boccaccio and yet is adapted with extreme subtlety. There is room for only one example:

> O verray cause of heele and of gladnesse,
> Iheryed be thy myght and thi goodnesse!   (6–7)

Except for the French-derived *verray cause*—both words long established and widely used in English—the diction is not directly suggested by the Italian, 'Certa cagion del valor che mi muove . . ., Sempre lodata sia la tua virtute'. All the other words are native, and most of them are unremarkable; but *iheryed* stands out, together with its noun which appears at the end of the Proem, 'to Venus *heryinge*' (48). The verb is ancient, used in Old English both of praising God (as in the oldest of all English religious poems) and of commending people. Words available for these uses shifted a good deal in Middle English, owing partly to the introduction of the French *preise(n)*, partly to the rise of *worshipe(n)* as a verb applied to both divine and human. Chaucer used *preise(n)* freely, but only in the human application. In the sense 'worship, praise' (God or gods) his commonest choice was *herye(n)*—22 cases in all taking noun and verb together (two in prose), against only ten of *worshipe(n)*. In favouring this word he differed noticeably from contemporaries. As far as our present knowledge of *Piers Plowman* texts goes, Langland used *herye(n)* very seldom; all A-text manuscripts read some form of it at XI, 247, but there are few other well-attested occurrences. Gower did not use it at all. In the Wycliffite Bible translations the early version in some places has *herien* where the later has *worschipen* or *onouren*. The *Gawain* group has the word only twice, in *Purity* (one miswritten in the manuscript); *Erkenwald* has it once. The general impression made by the recorded occurrences in the fifteenth century is that *hery* was old-fashioned if not obsolescent soon after 1400, and the limited records in the late fourteenth century suggest that it was already going out of use. It evidently held a special significance or tone for Chaucer, and presumably for his hearers.

Still more striking juxtapositions of old and new appear in the famous stanza in *Troilus and Criseyde* III:

> *But O Fortune, executrice of wyrdes,*
> *O influences of thise hevenes hye!*
> *Soth is that under God ye ben oure hierdes,*
> *Though to us bestes ben the causes wrie.*   (617–20)

Executrice and *influence* are both first recorded here, and *executrice* elsewhere only in the testamentary sense; but *wyrdes* (only here in *Troilus*), *hierdes*, and to some extent *wrye* ('hidden') are old, deep-seated words of very different atmosphere. The strange later history of *weird* is well known, but with that we are not concerned; there was nothing eerie about the word at this time. But already it had come to be comparatively little used in the south, being largely supplanted by *destiny*, as Chaucer himself put it in *The Legend of Good Women*, 'The Wirdes, that we clepen Destiné' (2580). He used it in only two other places, both in *Boece* rendering *fatum, fata*—a word that he ventured to adopt as *fate*, but tentatively: he tried it only three times, all in *Troilus* V. In Middle English *wyrd* is mainly northerly (*Cursor Mundi*, Rolle, *Gawain*), but Langland and Gower did use it. It must already have carried some archaic or dialectal tone, for after this time it was largely restricted to Scottish authors, from whom of course the future development derives. *Wrye* is not a rare word in Chaucer, occurring fourteen times in various forms, mainly in the literal sense 'cover'; but it seems not to have been used by Langland, Gower, or the *Gawain* poet, and it ceased to be used after about the middle of the fifteenth century. It must surely have been obsolescent in the ordinary language of Chaucer's time. The diction of this highly rhetorical stanza is a very original blend of new Romance and mannered English words which must have given it a powerfully telling effect in its own day.

Such heightening need not involve any new Romance words at all. In another great apostrophe, in *Troilus and Criseyde* IV,

> O soule, lurkynge in this wo, unneste,
> Fle forth out of myn herte, and lat it breste   (305–6)

the words are English, or at any rate Germanic, and the strength lies in the bold compound *unneste*, part of the image of the flight of the soul —apparently Chaucer's invention, 150 years before it is next registered. It is one of a number of 'reversive' verbs in *Troilus and Criseyde* formed with the prefix *un-*: *unbodye* V, 1550, *unloven* V, 1698, *unswelle* IV, 1146, V, 214, none of them found before Chaucer. This is an original and effective use of the native resources of English.

A group in some ways comparable comprises verbs formed with the prefix *to-*, which most commonly signifies destruction by disintegration, but is sometimes merely intensive: 'The helmes they tohewen and toshrede' (A(I), 2609); 'What discordable cause hath torent and unjoyned the byndynge or the alliaunce of thingis?' (*Boece* V m. 3, rendering (ineptly—how can such prose be taken seriously?) 'Quaenam discors foedera rerum causa resoluit?') Chaucer used about seventeen of these compounds, some of them only once. (Their number is not precise because the construction of one or two sentences is doubtful.) They are a feature of the language of the time, most of those in Chaucer being found in earlier and contemporary authors as well and many going back to Old English. Strangely, this prefix ceased to be productive soon after this date, and words containing it are rare after 1500. Comparable also are verbs with the prefix *for-*, which also goes back to Old English, where it generally implies spoiling or wasting. Many compounds of this type survive, though the prefix is no longer productive—e.g. *forbear, forbid, forgo*. More were current in Middle English, such as *fordo* 'destroy', *forlese* 'abandon', and others less common were also used by Chaucer, such as '*forslewthen* wilfully thy tyde' ('idle away your time', B, 4286 = VII, 3096), and 'Accidie . . . *forsleweth* and *forsluggeth* and destroyeth alle goodes temporels' (I(X), 685). Related to this use of the prefix are participles like the frequent *forwaked*, as in 'Wery forwaked in hire orisouns' (B(II), 596), of which Chaucer employed a considerable range including a few for the first or only time: *forstraught* 'distracted' (B, 1295 = VII, 105), the striking 'With broken vois, al hoors *forshright*' ('exhausted by shrieking', TC, IV, 1147), and if the first part of *The Romaunt of the Rose* is indeed his, *forsongen* 'exhausted by singing' in line 664. It is sometimes hard to distinguish from these forms others in which *for* evidently functions as a preposition indicating cause, best known in 'col-blak for old . . . shoon for blak' in 'The Knight's Tale' (A(I), 2142, 2144). But the latter is shown to be the correct analysis when a qualifying word follows *for*, as 'for pure ashamed' (TC, II, 656) and Gower's 'for pure abaissht' (*Confessio*, IV, 1330). It appears that the intensifying function of the prefix was taken to be causal instead, and the new construction developed—a fourteenth-century idiom which had no significant descendants.

Two other features of Chaucer's native vocabulary are worth notice. First, he is the earliest recorded user of a number of compounds of the type *lette-game* 'spoil-sport' (TC, III, 527), formed from a phrase in which the second element is a noun, object of the preceding verb. The pattern was French, as in *traille-baston*, anglicized and imitated in the fourteenth century. Chaucer provides the earliest quotation of *letgame*, though Usk has it at more or less the same date. A generation later it is in the *Promptorium Parvulorum*, which suggests that it was a colloquialism adopted rather than devised by Chaucer. A notable example apparently not yet found elsewhere is *trede-fowel*, in the Host's words to both the

Monk and the Nun's Priest: 'Thou woldest (han) been a tredefowel aright' (B, 3135, 4641=VII, 1945, 3451).[1] In some cases one or other of the elements is of Romance origin, as *pykepurs* (A(I), 1998) and *combreworld* (TC, IV, 279—elsewhere only in Hoccleve). These words are in general only scantily recorded, but some of them, and similar formations, appear in contemporary writers, especially Langland, who has *cuttepurs* in the A-text, *pyke-herneys* and *Spille-love* (as a name) in the B, *pykepurs* and *spille-tyme* in the C.[2]

Second, Chaucer provides the first record of a miscellaneous group of words, most of them of obscure origin but at any rate not French or Latin, which have a distinctly colloquial air. Space permits only a small selection. The past participle *bi-daffed* 'fooled, taken in' in Chaucer's address to wives at the end of 'The Clerk's Tale' (E(IV), 1191)—which includes *archewyves*, obviously his own facetious coinage, imitated by Lydgate—is apparently based on the noun *daffe* 'fool', familiar from earlier in the century and frequent in Langland. *Gnof* in the opening lines of 'The Miller's Tale', "A riche gnof that gestes heeld to bord" (A(I), 3188), must surely be a popular term of Germanic origin, probably allied, as the dictionaries suggest, to Frisian *gnuffig* 'thick, coarse'. It has not been found elsewhere until 1566. *Gruf* is more widely known in slightly varying forms and constructions: 'They fillen gruf and criden pitously' in 'The Knight's Tale' (A(I), 949) is matched by similar uses in 'The Prioress's Tale' (B, 1865 = VII, 675) and *Troilus* (IV, 912). As a simple adverb the word is first known in Chaucer; other late Middle English texts have *on (the) grufe*, modelled on Old Norse *á grúfu* 'prone'. A group of words meaning 'look' (especially intently) offers problems of origin and relation, as well as text. In 'The Miller's Tale' (A(I), 3841) 'Into the roof they *kiken* and they *cape*'. (So Robinson; some manuscripts read *gape*.) Middle Dutch had a verb *kiken*, *kieken*, which was used in the phrase *kiken ende capen*. Old English also had a verb *capian* with the right sense, which survived into Middle English; and it seems likely that the Dutch phrase was associated with this and adapted to English use. Of similar import is *pike* in 'Pandarus . . . gan in at the curtyn pike' (TC, III,

---

[1] *OED* takes a different view of this formation, putting it under *tread* sb. IV, 12; but this is much less likely.

[2] *Cacchepole* in B XVIII, 73, and frequent in documents, is not in the same category because it derives from an Anglo-Norman compound of much older descent.

60). This is of quite unknown origin, but probably to be associated in some way with *kiken*. The phonetic relation of both words to later *keek* (now northern) and *peek* is abnormal; but the fact that the other verbs of similar meaning, *peep* and *peer*, have the same vowel may suggest that the high front vowel seemed appropriate to the sense, and so resisted the normal diphthongization. Other words of an apparently colloquial kind, not found earlier, are *knakke* 'trick' (three times), *knarry* 'gnarled', *labbe* 'talker' and the participle *labbyng* (the verb *labbe* is in Langland), *motre* 'mutter', *mullok* 'refuse', *toty* 'dizzy' in 'Myn heed is toty of my swynk to-nyght' (A(I), 4253). These are words of varying status and future fortunes, but they have in common a short and simple shape and an accommodation of sound to sense that suggests origin and currency in the spoken language. A few other words that appear for the first time in Chaucer can be more fully explained than these: for example the adjective *new(e)fangel* (which occurs twice, not yet with *-ed*) and the noun *newfangelnesse* (four times) are compounded of elements recognizably English; *wantrust* 'lack of confidence' (twice in Chaucer and of short life) is comparable to the earlier and frequent *wanhope* 'despair', and both of them have parallels in Middle Dutch. A surprising 'first occurrence' is *haselwode*, which Chaucer used three times, all in *Troilus* and all in the mouth of Pandarus, in expressions of incredulity—

> *"From haselwode, there joly Robyn pleyde,*
> *Shal come al that that thow abidest heere."* (V, 1174–5)

The appearance of so many colloquial or informal words first in Chaucer is no doubt largely to be explained by the comparatively few works before his time in which his kind of realistic dialogue found a place. It nevertheless makes clear how precarious it is to credit Chaucer (or any other) with the 'introduction into English' of particular words simply on the evidence collected by the lexicographers. All the words mentioned in the last paragraph are 'first found in Chaucer', but none of them, except perhaps *wantrust*, can have been new to English, though they may well have been new to works of literary pretension.

Finally, as a contrast to novelty, some familiar phrases that Chaucer used have a long history and wide currency, and may be noticed briefly as yet another element in his linguistic resources. So *cares colde*, which he used ten times (six in *Troilus*), always in rhyme, beside *colde care* once, is something of a cliché about this date—it is in *William of Palerne, Pearl,*

Patience, Gower. As it stands it does not seem to be traceable before the thirteenth century, but the association is as old as *cealdum cearsiðum* in *Beowulf* 2396. It depends on venerable alliterative tradition; and the figurative use of *cold* is of course an ancient Germanic one, surviving vividly in 'Wommennes conseils been ful ofte colde' in 'The Nun's Priest's Tale' (B, 4446=VII, 3256). Similarly alliterative is 'He swor hire yis, *by stokkes and by stones*' (TC, III, 589). The use of stocks and stones as objects to swear by descends from earlier application of these words to heathen idols, and the collocation is at least as old as Ælfric. It is very common in Middle English—three times in *Purity,* for example. Also in origin alliterative is *word and ende* 'beginning and end, completely,' used of a narrative as in 'al this thyng he tolde hym, word and ende' (TC, II, 1495) and three other places. This is a common four-teenth-century corruption of earlier *ord and ende,* known from Alfred to the fifteenth century.[1] Of a different pattern and more recent origin, though depending on the old alliterative habit, are comparisons such as 'stille as ston', 'as stille as any ston', which Chaucer used ten times. This particular simile was excessively common: B. J. Whiting in *Proverbs, Sentences, and Proverbial Phrases* gives about 175 references from the early thirteenth century to Douglas. But Chaucer did not treat it with the humorous condescension that he shows to 'romantic' phrases like *bright in bour* or *over stile and stoon* in 'Sir Thopas': the tone is usually serious enough, even solemn in 'In crepeth age alwey, as stille as stoon' (E(IV), 121).

These remarks on Chaucer's vocabulary have done no more than touch upon some of its qualities that seem to deserve more attention than they have received. Many kinds of comparative study are needed, though some can be only provisional until the *Middle English Dictionary* completes its stately course—perhaps about the end of the century. Meanwhile it should be apparent that Chaucer not only added new Romance elements to the accepted written English of his day, but retained or revived words and phrases of ancient tradition, and accommodated popular terms new to literature. In the words used by T. S. Eliot of the 'auditory imagination', his language 'fuses the old and the obliterated and the trite, the current, and the new and surprising.'[2]

---

[1] C. T. Onions, *MLR* XXIV, 1929, 389 ff.
[2] *The Use of Poetry and the Use of Criticism,* 2nd edn 1964, p. 119.

4: The Manuscripts of Chaucer's Works and Their Use

E. T. DONALDSON

A READER OF A MODERN edition of Chaucer's works will be conscious of the great length of time that has passed since Chaucer wrote them, but he may well be unaware of the enormously complicated history that the works have had between their composition and their appearance on the printed page. As a result, he may not be as sceptical as perhaps he ought to be that what appears on the page is in all respects what Chaucer wrote. The invention of printing and subsequent developments in the publication of books have greatly simplified the process by which an author's final draft becomes a book; yet even modern writers sometimes complain that the printed version of their work contains infidelities to what they actually wrote—and this can occur despite all the aids to accuracy that now exist: a typewriter capable of producing a highly legible manuscript that can be cleanly corrected before going to the printer; generally two—and if necessary more—opportunities for the author to correct the printer's work before the final printing; and a desire for accuracy that is (ideally) shared by author, publisher, and printer. If so carefully controlled a short-term process can succeed in producing in print at least an occasional reading that is not what the author wrote, then it follows that a process largely uncontrolled and extending over almost six centuries will produce a very large number of such readings. If Chaucer himself were to read his works in even the best of modern editions he would probably charge the editor with innumerable infidelities, and address him a stanza even more scathing than the one he addressed to Adam his scribe, whose 'negligence and rape' in copying cost Chaucer painful hours of correction.

The majority of the readings that Chaucer might deplore would be due to errors that came into being through the dissemination of his works in manuscripts—errors made by scribes during successive copyings; unhappily, no manuscript of any of his works that was genuinely close to Chaucer—perhaps none that was written during his lifetime—has survived.[1] But even if we had a manuscript overseen by Chaucer himself, the very act of adapting it to the conventions of modern English and modern printing would to some extent falsify the text. Yet such adaptation seems necessary in order not to throw up obstacles in the way of the reader's comprehension. In most medieval English handwritings—and probably in Chaucer's—the letters *v* and *u* were written as *v* initially and *u* elsewhere, but it seems merely confusing now to print *vse, loue,* or *vnauysed* ('unadvised') for *use, love* and *unavysed.*[2] Similarly, Chaucer may have used (we do not know) the old letters þ (thorn) and ȝ (yogh), but when these occur in the manuscript serving as the basis for an edited text, most editors of Chaucer have preferred to alter them to their modern equivalents *th* and *gh/y.* Again, while capitalization in general followed the same practice in Middle English writing as we use today, it followed it at best sporadically and with some recurrent differences. Editors will naturally capitalize the name of the Christian deity, though this appears in the manuscripts also always as *god;* on the other hand a proper name such as Satan's will appear now as *Sathanas,* and as *sathanas,*[3] and the editor will probably alter his text to achieve consistency, as he will

[1] The earliest major manuscripts of Chaucer's works are the Ellesmere and Hengwrt copies of *The Canterbury Tales* and the Corpus Christi College, Cambridge and Campsall copies of *Troilus,* all of the first decade of the fifteenth century. Campsall bears the arms of a Prince of Wales, presumably Henry V who was Prince of Wales from 1399 to 1413. The dating of manuscripts is a very delicate and complex task requiring great expertise, and even the greatest palaeographers do not always agree. It should be noted that the date of a manuscript is no index to its textual character: a very early manuscript may be highly faulty and a late one relatively free of corruption.

[2] Since the letters *i* and *y* had the same value in Middle English, a scribe might write *vnauysed* or *vnauised.* The preference for *y* in such a word as this is discussed below, p. 90.

[3] The *th* in this word, as so often in proper names, represents the sound *t.* The reason for this is probably that in French, through which many classical names came into English, *th* was sounded as *t* and hence could be substituted for it, the extra later presumably adding some kind of distinction.

when, in the manuscript before him, most lines of verse begin with a capital, but many do not. In some scripts certain combinations of letters, as with the word *with Inne* ('within'), produce a capital which if reproduced may seem to the modern reader merely quaintly distracting.[1] The same seems true of *ff*, which is the common form of F capital that has now disappeared except in a few personal names. Even the editor who is trying to reproduce a text exactly is occasionally forced into falsification; with some letters, like *a* in many handwritings, the difference between the small form and the capital is only a matter of size, a fact that is apt to produce a small *a*, a large *a*, and a middle-sized *a*, too large to be small and too small to be a capital. Finally, editors of any text designed to be read for pleasure will expand the many abbreviations that occur in medieval manuscripts—those for *per-, pro-, con-, ser-, -er, -es*, etc.—and will not always be sure that they have expanded correctly.[2]

A far more serious risk of falsification is presented by the lack of punctuation in medieval poetic manuscripts, and presumably in Chaucer's autographs. There are, to be sure, occasional full stops, but these are apt to be placed haphazardly: sometimes they occur sensibly at the end of substantial blocks of text, marking what we should consider verse paragraphs, but at other times they will be used merely to mark the end of a line of verse, even where the line is not grammatically discrete from what follows it. In consecutive verse scribes often indicate paragraphs (and in stanzaic verse a new stanza) by placing a paragraph sign (¶) to the left of the first letter, or else by writing a very large capital (sometimes rubricated) for the first letter. Unfortunately in consecutive verse these are sometimes misplaced,[3] so that editors must be wary in reproducing them.

Note the spelling, common in the Chaucer manuscripts, *Ptholome*, 'Ptolemy'.

[1] The capital *I* is a substitute for *y* which would normally be written in the neighbourhood of minim letters: see below, page 90. Note that words with two elements (*with Inne*) often appear as two words, which most editors will silently join in accordance with modern convention.

[2] The loop that represents final *es, is* is in some handwritings indistinguishable from the flourish that scribes liked to put on terminal consonants such as *k, g, t, d,* etc. As a result, in uncontrolled situations it is often impossible to tell whether a word like *thing* is singular or plural.

[3] An instance is line 1648 of 'The Knight's Tale', which, because of a mis-

Of punctuation within the line there is virtually none, unless the caesura mark (/) that occurs in some manuscripts is to be considered punctuation (as it doubtless is in prose, where it occurs where we should use a full stop, a comma, or a semicolon). Since in a line of verse it generally occurs at the natural pause (infrequently at the end of the line), it seems to have more to do with the rhythm than with the sense of the language, though some readers profess to find it useful for both. We are uncertain whether Chaucer himself used this mark, and it is in any case of little service in determining the relationship of one line of verse to another. For instance, in the following couplet as it appears in the Hengwrt manuscript,[1]

> *She was a worthy womman / al hir lyue*
> *Housbondes at chirche dore / she hadde fyue,*

the caesura marks do nothing for the sense (and little for the rhythm), and the really urgent question, which is how we are to relate the sense of the first line to that of the second, is unanswered. Modern readers are trained to expect punctuation to clarify sense relationships, and an editor cannot leave the first line unpunctuated at the end. But what mark to choose? A random sampling of seven editions shows three editors preferring a semicolon after *lyue*, two a comma, and two a colon. Significantly enough, none uses a full stop, evidently because no one wishes to discourage the reader from observing a relationship between the Wife of Bath's being a worthy woman and her having had five husbands. The comma allows the relationship without emphasizing it; the semicolon tends to minimize it; and the colon points to it—perhaps too obtrusively. As so often happens, Chaucer's lack of clarification—in this case, punctuation—has forced the reader to make his own interpretation, and seven readers have made three different interpretations. Chaucer might well say all were false, since his two sentences originally stood both unconnected and undivided, neither related nor inhibited from relationship.

Since all punctuation involves editorial interpretation that may falsify

---

placed paragraph indicator, is generally printed as if it completes a paragraph when, in fact, it begins a new one.

[1] As reproduced in *A Six-Text Print of the Canterbury Tales*, ed F. J. Furnivall, The Chaucer Society, 1870: General Prologue, lines 459–60.

Chaucer's meaning, it might be argued—indeed, some modern critics do argue—that his text ought to be presented without punctuation; but given the difficulty of the language, many beginning readers might understandably founder early. It would, for instance, be natural to stumble over the following lines as they appear in the Ellesmere manuscript:[1]

> And whan he rood / men myghte his brydel heere
> Gynglen / in a whistlynge wynd als cleere
> And eek as loude as dooth þe Chapel belle
> Ther as this lord / was kepere of the Celle
> The reule of seint Maure / or of seint Beneit /
> By cause that it was old / and som del streit /
> This ilke Monk / leet olde thynges pace
> And heeld / after the newe world the space

This is a trackless forest for a reader unassisted by punctuation: he must somehow recognize that the first four lines constitute a complete statement, to be followed by a (mental) full stop, and that the fifth and sixth lines begin a sentence that alters its syntax in mid-course, for anacoluthon occurs after *streit*, requiring a (mental) dash, and the sentence continues with its apparent subject 'rule' of the fifth line subsumed into the object, 'old things', of the seventh. But a reader might well be misled by *Ther as* in line four, taking it as meaning 'whereas', 'inasmuch as', and concluding that it introduces a new statement to the effect that the Monk's contempt for monastic rule was somehow associated with his being the warden of a subordinate religious house which absorbed much of his energy. In that case the reader will miss the poetically weighty point that the chapel bell with which the Monk's bridle bells successfully vie is that of the cell of which he is in charge. That the most esteemed editor of Chaucer, one who makes very few mistakes, makes this one [2] illustrates both the fact that punctuation can falsify Chaucer's meaning and also the fact that without punctuation even a very expert reader can get lost. For beginning readers punctuation seems essential; for more advanced ones it may operate as an irritant, but one that provokes them to thought; and the reader is always free to repunctuate according to his own informed reading.

[1] *Ibid.*, lines 169–76.
[2] F. N. Robinson, ed, *The Works of Geoffrey Chaucer*, 2nd ed, Cambridge, Mass. 1957, pp. 18–19.

Even if an editor had before him a manuscript whose text had been corrected by Chaucer himself he would not necessarily be immune from falsification of the sense. In most late medieval English handwritings the letters *i, n, u* (that is, *u* and *v* in post-initial positions), and *m* were formed by upright strokes called minims, and in *n, u,* and *m* these minims were generally not joined at their tops or bases. The result is that combinations of letters such as *im* or *mu* could conceivably read in a number of different ways. In order to avoid confusion scribes frequently wrote *y* for *i* in the neighbourhood of other minim letters (note *whistlynge wynd* in the passage quoted above), though not invariably (note *seint*).[1] They might also substitute the letter *o* for phonetically short *u* in certain words containing minim letters, a substitution that has permanently affected English orthography: modern *love, son, some* all represent short *u*. But even with these safeguards, minim confusion remained a rich source of scribal error and will occasionally plague modern editors, especially because of the similarity of post-initial *u* or *v* to *n*. An interesting example of this orthographical ambiguity occurs at the very beginning of *The Canterbury Tales* in the portrait of the Knight: 'At many a noble armee hadde he be'.[2] This is the reading of all standard editions, but conceivably the *m* of *armee* could stand for original *iu*, giving *arivee*, 'disembarkation', 'landing', which is as good a meaning as 'armed naval expedition', and *noble arivee* is a more usual metrical pattern than *noblē armee*. Indeed, ten of the twenty-eight manuscript authorities for the line either have an unmistakable form of *arivee* such as *aryue* or else a corruption of it (*ryuer*).[3] Perhaps such patent attempts to eliminate the possibility of the reading *armee* should have moved editors to avoid it; but the word *arivee* is not elsewhere attested in Middle English,[4] and editors are hesitant to introduce a rare word into

[1] The classic example of a minim word is Latin *minimum*—fifteen minims. It should be noted that scribes often distinguished *i* by placing a stroke over it ('), the ancestor of the modern dot; but like the modern dot, it was frequently misplaced.

[2] *General Prologue*, line 60.

[3] This information, like all the detailed data for variant readings in *The Canterbury Tales*, is drawn from J. M. Manly and E. Rickert, eds, *The Text of the Canterbury Tales*, 8 vol, Chicago 1940; the present reference is V, 6. For a discussion of a word in which a number of editors may have misread an initial *n* as *u*, see the present writer's note, 'The Miller's Tale, A3483–6', *MLN*, 69 (1954), 310–14, reprinted in *Speaking of Chaucer*, 1970, pp. 131–3.

[4] See *OED*, *arrive*, sb., for sixteenth-century and later uses.

their texts. Since, however, Chaucer's works contain many rare words, some future editor may prefer *arivee*. But it is probable that we shall never be certain which Chaucer intended.

So far we have been dealing with what editors would consider peripheral—if inevitable—circumstances capable of causing falsification of Chaucer's text. The last example, however, brings us toward the chief problem, which is the interpretation of the variant readings of the manuscripts. As mentioned earlier, no manuscript survives of any of Chaucer's works that may be ascribed to him or that may have been overseen by him. From his verse rebuke to Adam, we know that by the time he translated Boethius and composed *Troilus* Chaucer was employing a scribe to whom he gave his own final draft for copying. In mitigation of Adam's alleged inaccuracy, one should remark that Chaucer's own final drafts may not have been altogether easy to read. Poets are notoriously bad copyists of their own work, for the urge to improve what they have written almost insures that no copy made by their own hand is free of crossings-out and insertions. The vellum or paper on which a final auctorial copy might be made was expensive, and this may have tempted the poet to write small and to waste no space; the ink was obdurate and erasure difficult; and even the relatively wealthy Chaucer may have had to work in poor light and with cold fingers. As a result, Adam may have been the recipient of some rather difficult material of which to make a fair copy, and even though this was laboriously corrected by Chaucer, there were probably errors he left uncorrected and perhaps some that he introduced in the very process of correcting others.

It is probable that this corrected copy would serve as the base for any other copies that Chaucer himself may have wished made. We know nothing about his disposition of his works, which was probably not always uniform, but it is reasonable to suppose that he would want to give a copy to his patron—if, indeed, he had a patron—and that he would want one for himself from which he could read aloud if called upon; and he might wish one or more further copies to circulate among friends and benefactors. This handful of copies would constitute for Chaucer what we should consider the whole process of publication, at least of the first edition of any of his works. (Chaucer revised the Prologue to *The Legend of Good Women* after it was in circulation; he seems also to have revised the Physician-Pardoner link in *The Canterbury Tales*; and there is some evidence, though it is not accepted by all scholars, that he revised *Troilus*, perhaps twice.)[1] Further proliferation of copies was a haphazard and uncontrolled process. Manuscripts of a popular work given or loaned by Chaucer might be copied and recopied by their recipients, and the new copies in turn copied, and so on down through generations of scribes even beyond the introduction of printing and into the sixteenth century. And while it is not inevitably true that every copying would increase the amount of error, most would; and it is true that almost no line of descent of any given text escapes at least one hasty or unprofessional transcription which infects all its descendants. It follows that many surviving manuscripts are highly faulty, and that all are faulty to some degree. Together they form the raw material upon which a modern edition is built.

The number of preserved copies of Chaucer's individual works varies tremendously (from one to sixty-two). This variation is due partly to the accidents of time and history—war, Reformation,[2] overuse and abuse, partly to the work's popularity, and perhaps partly to the author's own disposition of it. The alternate (?later) version of the Prologue to *The Legend of Good Women* survives in only one manuscript, presumably because Chaucer failed to circulate it.[3] This is the only considerable piece

[1] Both versions of *The Legend* are generally printed in standard editions, but there is no general agreement on which is the revision. The evidence for revision of the Physician-Pardoner link is persuasive: see Manly-Rickert, II, 325–8. Evidence for other revision in *The Canterbury Tales* is less impressive; in the section devoted to revision in Manly-Rickert, II, 475–518, the presumed early versions seem to represent characteristic scribal mishandling of the presumed revised versions. For the supposed revisions of *Troilus*, see R. K. Root, ed, *Troilus and Criseyde*, Princeton 1926, pp. lxx–lxxxix, and Root's *The Textual Tradition of Chaucer's Troilus*, The Chaucer Society, 1916.

[2] In his *Animadversions* (upon Speght's 1598 edition of Chaucer), ed F. J. Furnivall, The Chaucer Society, 1876, p. 10, Francis Thynne says that he had heard from John Thynne that at a session of Parliament of which John was a member Chaucer's works were spared from proscription only because they were fables; many persons must have shared Parliament's disapproval.

[3] Information on the numbers of manuscripts is drawn from Robinson's textual notes; from Carleton Brown and R. H. Robbins, *The Index of Middle English Verse*, New York 1942, and from Robbins' and J. L. Cutler's

of his poetry to be attested by a single copy, though four of his short poems are similarly slimly attested: the delightful *jeux d'esprit*, 'To Rosamond' and 'Chaucer's Words to Adam', the very Chaucerian, though unascribed, 'Merciles Beute', and the imperfect 'Womanly Noblesse'. Some of these may have been uncirculated because they had been written for specific recipients, as were the two Envoys, 'To Bukton' (preserved in two manuscripts) and 'To Scogan' (preserved in three). *The Book of the Duchess* may also have been at least a semi-private poem, confined to the household of John of Gaunt, for it survives in only three manuscript copies. *The House of Fame* similarly survives in three, but hardly appears to have been a private poem; one might suppose that it had not been given wider circulation because it appears to have been left unfinished, but this reasoning is contradicted by the abortive *Anelida and Arcite*, which is contained in eight manuscripts, and its Complaint in four more. One might guess that *The Book of the Duchess* and *The House of Fame* were written before Chaucer had become an eminent and popular poet, a manuscript of one of whose works would be a prized possession: perhaps when he wrote them he could not afford to pay an Adam to have them recopied.

With the exception of the doubtfully authentic translation of the *Roman de la Rose* (one manuscript), the obviously experimental *Complaint to His Lady* (two manuscripts), and the imperfect Boethian paraphrase, *The Former Age* (two manuscripts), all Chaucer's other works that have survived at all have survived in some quantity. There are between eight and ten copies each of the three Complaints, *To Pity*, *Of Venus*, and *Of Mars*, and of the moral balades *Fortune* and *Gentilesse*. The most frequently represented of the short poems are *Truth*, surviving in more than twenty manuscripts, the pious 'An ABC' (sixteen, some fragmentary), and *Lak of Steadfastness* (fifteen). Of the larger works, *Troilus and Criseyde* survives in sixteen manuscripts, plus bits and pieces in eight more; *The Parliament of Fowls* in fourteen; *The Legend of Good Women*, though unfinished, in twelve; and the translation of Boethius in ten. It may come as a surprise that Chaucer's second most frequently preserved work after *The Canterbury Tales* is his *Treatise on the Astrolabe*, appearing in twenty-five manuscripts; but this could be because scientific translations were

Supplement, Lexington, 1965; and, for some of the shorter poems, from A. I. Doyle and G. B. Pace, 'A New Chaucer Manuscript', *PMLA*, 83, 1968, 22–34.

not so avidly read as creative works and hence did not suffer the wear-and-tear that must have destroyed many manuscripts of Chaucer's literary productions.

Even though a large number of copies of *The Canterbury Tales* must have disintegrated through overuse or have been lost through the accidents of time, an extraordinary number of manuscripts have survived that contain at least portions of his longest poem: eighty-five. Thirty of these are either fragmentary, ranging from a single leaf to a number of leaves with lines from one or more tales, or else are miscellanies or anthologies of moral or religious works which contain only a tale or two from Chaucer's poem. The remaining fifty-five manuscripts, however, are tolerably complete transcriptions of *The Canterbury Tales*. Fifteen of them are 'perfect' in the sense that they contain all the tales, though it should be emphasized that no manuscript is perfect in the sense that it contains every line that Chaucer wrote. Another twenty-four have lost leaves (or, in several cases, their exemplars had) from the beginning or end or both: this is, of course, the characteristic form of disintegration for a much-read manuscript. Seventeen manuscripts lack tales from the middle portions of the poem, and more than half of these are also deficient at the beginning or the end or both. These fifty-five manuscripts, more or less complete, are our principal witnesses to the text of *The Canterbury Tales*.

The sporadic omission of tales from these manuscripts is due either to physical damage or to scribal disturbance of the tradition, and is no indication of unpopularity. While 'The Parson's Tale' is missing from twelve of the fifty-five manuscripts and is defective at the end of seventeen in which it appears this results from the terminal disintegration mentioned above and not from dislike of the Tale; indeed, it appears independently in two miscellanies as well as in two fragmentary manuscripts. For similar reasons the *General Prologue* is entirely missing from eight manuscripts and defective at the beginning of twenty-one, so that only twenty-six have the opening lines of the poem. 'The Cook's Tale', more centrally located, is missing from eleven manuscripts: the reason for this is probably its unfinished state, which prompted some editor early in the copying tradition to supplement it with the un-Chaucerian *Tale of Gamelyn*, a fact that has given rise to the speculation that Chaucer had at one time planned to reshape *Gamelyn* for the Cook. The only other tale that is missing from a relatively large number of manuscripts is

'The Canon's Yeoman's Tale', lacking in nine. This may in part have been due to its position near the end of the series, but there is at least a possibility, suggested by its absence from Hengwrt, one of the earliest surviving manuscripts, that it came into circulation later than the rest of the tales.

The only tales that are not omitted by one or more of the major manuscripts are the Man of Law's and the Clerk's. The former appears also in two fragments, in a religious miscellany, and in a manuscript containing five *Canterbury Tales*, giving 'The Man of Law's Tale' a total representation of fifty-nine manuscripts. This is exceeded only by 'The Clerk's Tale' and 'The Prioress's Tale'. In addition to the fifty-five major manuscripts, 'The Clerk's Tale' appears in four anthologies as well as with 'The Man of Law's Tale' among the five tales mentioned above: these transcriptions, along with a single leaf containing lines from it, make the tale the most frequently represented of all Chaucer's works, with sixty-two appearances in manuscript. Standing second to it is 'The Prioress' Tale' which, while missing from two of the major manuscripts, appears twice in another and in five anthologies as well as in one fragment—a total of sixty appearances. If appearance in anthologies is a measure of popularity, then 'The Tale of Melibee' must also have rated high, for it appears in five; it is, however, omitted from five of the major manuscripts, giving it a total of fifty-five appearances, plus one fragment. This is still above the average of fifty-three for the tales not already mentioned. It might be observed that the tales of Fragments A, B[1], D, (or I, II and III in Robinson) and E (IV) (less 'The Merchant's Tale') are slightly better preserved than the others.

Ideally, the editor of a medieval work must have at his disposal all the surviving transcriptions, preferably in the original or, if that is impossible as it usually is, in photographic reproductions. From among these he will choose for his exemplar—his base or 'copy' text—one which he finds peculiarly satisfactory, not perhaps so much in the correctness of its readings—which he can readily amend—as in its spelling and general air of consistency. Where the dialect of the poet is known, as Chaucer's is, the manuscript should reflect it as closely as possible. The editor will transcribe this manuscript and then will—ideally—collate all the other manuscripts with it and record their variants: it is necessary to emphasize the word 'ideally' here, since the collation of an average of fifty-three manuscripts (plus Caxton's printed text, which has manuscript status, having been based on a lost manuscript)[1] for any given Canterbury Tale is a virtual impossibility in human terms. Indeed, no edition of *The Canterbury Tales* available to a large number of readers has been based on anything but a selection of manuscripts; but the great eight-volume work of Manly and Rickert (though its actual text is not wholly satisfactory) contains the whole corpus of variants from all the manuscripts—an enormous advantage for future editors. Complete collation of the other works of Chaucer is humanly possible, even if, with a poem the length of *Troilus*, enormously laborious; and it has been made easier by the Chaucer Society, which has reproduced in printed form and with good accuracy a large number of the manuscripts of his works: nearly all the authorities for the short poems, all the authorities for *The Book of the Duchess, The House of Fame, The Parliament of Fowls,* and *The Legend of Good Women,* seven of the manuscripts of *Troilus,* and eight of the manuscripts of *The Canterbury Tales.* With such aids at hand, the modern editor may assemble his corpus of variants with what is at least relative ease.

There is one matter in which, paradoxically enough, collation of all the manuscripts and analysis of their variants are of little use to the editor: this is the perennially vexed matter of the part played by final *e* in Chaucer's verse. It is a commonly held hypothesis that Chaucer wrote a fairly regular iambic line, for thousands of his verses, especially those in the longer (presumably pentameter) line fall unequivocally into the pattern:[2]

> *Of which vertú engéndred is the flóur*
> *That slépen ál the nýght with ópen éye*
> *The hoóly blisful mártir fór to séke*

[1] Early prints from manuscripts now lost are normally accorded manuscript status in editing the text. Thus Caxton's prints of *The House of Fame, Boethius, The Parliament of Fowls,* and *Troilus* as well as of *The Canterbury Tales* and six of the shorter poems are treated as manuscripts; so also are Wynkyn de Worde's print of *Troilus;* Notary's print of three short poems; and a number of the poems in William Thynne's 1532 edition of the Works: *Book of the Duchess, House of Fame, Boethius, Troilus, Legend of Good Women,* and ten short poems, as well as the *Romance of the Rose.* The latest edition of a poem granted manuscript status is 'An ABC' in Speght's second (1602) print of the Works.

[2] The lines are quoted from Ellesmere as reproduced in the Chaucer Society Six-Text volume.

But others fall into the pattern only if final *e* is sounded:

> *Whan Zéphirús eek wíth his swétë breéth*
> *The téndre cróppes ánd the yóngë sónne*
> *To férnë hálwes kówthe in sóndry lóndes*
> *Ful óftë týme he hádde the bórd bigónne*

It is evident from the last two lines that while the sounding of some final
e's creates iambic verse, the sounding of others would disrupt it: hence it
is assumed that the *e* on *kowthe, tyme,* and *hadde* is silent. It happens that
these silencings occur in circumstances where the hypothesis allows them
—here elision before a word beginning with a vowel or *h*. A great many
other kinds of patterns where the *e* may be silent are identifiable, but
there remain hundreds of lines in which the letter has to be suppressed for
no other reason than to serve the demands of the hypothesized meter:

> *Thanne lóngen fólk to goón on̦ pílgrimáges*
> *For hé was láte ycóme̦ from his viáge*
> *In hópe̦ to stónden in his lády gráce*
> *Hire̦ nóse̦ tretýs hir éyen gréye̦ as glás*

The abundance of such lines as these permits a rational suspicion about
the rectitude of the whole hypothesis: if the presumed metrical pattern
depends on a seemingly arbitrary sounding or silencing of final *e*, how
may one be really sure that the pattern existed for Chaucer?

There is a fairly good answer to the question, though not one good
enough to allay all suspicion. One may point first of all to the lines that
fit the pattern without involving final *e*. In the second place—though the
argument is not wholly to the point—Chaucer uses a soundable final *e*
only where it is grammatically justified, as in the inflections, inherited
from Anglo-Saxon, of verbs, adjectives, and, occasionally, nouns; or else
where it is historically valid, as in nouns and adjectives that were normally spelled with final *e* in Chaucer's time and dialect. That is,
Chaucer's final *e* has the potentiality of being sounded only where it
served a known linguistic function or had an historical *raison d'être*. Discrimination between words properly with and properly without *e* is
consistent in his rhymes: contrary to the practice of the majority of fourteenth-century English poets, Chaucer and Gower never rhyme an uninflected adjective such as *whit* with an inflected form such as *write*. Other

poets who knew enough of final *e* to use it on occasion correctly within the line seldom heeded it in rhyme; and it is hard to see why, if Chaucer could reduce words like *hope* and *nose* to monosyllables within the line, he could not do it at the end, thus vastly increasing his store of rhymes. The only answer that suggests itself is that he and Gower considered rhyme the true test of a poet's art, refusing to allow themselves liberties in rhyme that they allowed themselves, for ease and naturalness of expression, within the line.

In settling the question of metre the manuscripts are of almost no help. It is true that the earliest manuscripts of *The Canterbury Tales*, Ellesmere and Hengwrt, and the early manuscripts of *Troilus*, Corpus and Campsall, handle final *e* in a way that supports the generally accepted hypothesis,[1] as do certain of the manuscripts of the lesser poems, though the support of none is entire. But at least by 1410, and perhaps earlier, what we identify as Chaucer's scrupulous use of final *e* had become so outmoded that it was wholly alien to most scribes: for them the letter had ceased to be sounded, so that they might drop it or add it at will. In the first line quoted above (from Ellesmere), manuscripts dated as early as 1410–20 read *whiche, vertue,* and *floure*; a relatively early manuscript reads *oft time,* and a somewhat later one *yong sonne*; and even Ellesmere and Hengwrt divide on *Hire/Hir nose*. The editor who wishes to find authority for adding or dropping a final *e* can always find it among the manuscripts, but it is worthless. If he wishes to emend his copy text in this respect he must do it on his own authority. Manly and Rickert print line 8 of the *General Prologue* as follows:[2]

Hath in the Ram his half cours yronne.

This is the reading of the manuscripts that usually support the metrical hypothesis—indeed, it is the reading of all but five of the twenty-six manuscript authorities for the line. The five with *e* read *halfe,* not *halue* (*halve*), which is the reading of most standard editions and is the expected form of the adjective *half* in the weak position. The emendation is caused by the metrical hypothesis, and may be supported only by the rather slender argument that the adjective *half* occurs infrequently in the weak position and that scribes may have tended to think of the word as an

---

[1] Ellesmere and Hengwrt are rather more careful with final *e* than Corpus and Campsall.

[2] III, 3; see also V, 3.

uninflected noun. But such a line as this will shake an editor's confidence in the metrical hypothesis; and if he were editing one of the poems in the shorter line according to a hypothesis that they represent iambic tetrameter, his confidence would be shaken far more often.[1]

Nevertheless, insecure as any metrical hypothesis may be, it is impossible to edit at all without having in mind some fairly strong preconception concerning the metre. This principle may be illustrated by analysis of the variant readings of a single line of *The Canterbury Tales*—an analysis that will also introduce us to more interesting problems that the editor confronts. Line 19 of the *General Prologue* is what one might call a bread-and-butter line of narrative poetry, containing nothing hard or obscure and virtually free of rhetorical flourish—indeed, free of any quality that one might suppose would lead to scribal error. Yet the twenty-seven authorities for the line (twenty-six manuscripts and Caxton's first edition) produce eleven different versions of what Chaucer wrote. Using Hengwrt as his base text, an editor might record the variation in the following way.[2]

> Bifel that in that sesoun on a day

Bifel] It bifel HtLa; So bifel DsEn[1]; So it bifel Ma; And fel Cx. that (1)] than La; it DsEn[1]Ha[3]; *om* Ad[1]CxLd[2]MaPyTc[1]. in] on SeTo; *om* DsEn[1]Ma. on] upon FiLaLd[2]Ph[2]PyTc[1].

This apparatus records in economical shorthand ten variant lines in fifteen manuscripts:

1	Bifel	that	on	that	sesoun	on	a	day	SeTo
2	Bifel	that	in	that	sesoun	upon	a	day	FiPh[2]
3	Bifel	it	in	that	sesoun	on	a	day	Ha[3]
4	Bifel		in	that	sesoun	on	a	day	Ad[1]
5	Bifel		in	that	sesoun	upon	a	day	Ld[2]PyTc[1]
6	And fel		in	that	sesoun	on	a	day	Cx
7	It bifel	that	in	that	sesoun	on	a	day	Ht
8	It bifel	than	in	that	sesoun	upon	a	day	La
9	So bifel	it		that	sesoun	on	a	day	DsEn[1]
10	So	it	bifel		that	sesoun	on	a	day	Ma

[1] Of the poems in the short line, it is easier to read the *Romance of the Rose* as iambic tetrameter than it is to read *The House of Fame*, and easier so to read *The House of Fame* than *The Book of the Duchess*. To what extent the manuscript tradition may be responsible for 'irregularities' is undeterminable.

[2] Variants are from Manly-Rickert, V, 4; spelling has been normalized on the Hengwrt model.

How will the editor determine which of the eleven recorded versions of the line is most probably what Chaucer wrote? In the first place, he will undoubtedly be impressed by the fact that twelve manuscripts are unanimous in reading a perfectly satisfactory line: Hengwrt (Hg) is here supported by Bo^{1}Bo^{2}ChEn^{3}ElHa^{2}Ha^{4}MgPsPwRy^2. But even while he is gratified by such support, he will be aware that wrong readings are not infrequently supported by a vast majority of manuscripts and right readings by very few. Most of the variant readings in this line, however, are in violation of the metrical hypothesis, reading hypermetrical *upon* or *So* or *It bifel* or doing without the conjunction *that*. Since, as we have seen, scribes show no general tendency to improve Chaucer's metre, it is hard to believe that the well-represented metrical line represents a regularizing of an irregular original or, conversely, that Chaucer would have chosen to shape a wholly non-emphatic line in such a way that its metre calls attention to it and in a way that almost any non-poet could remedy. The metrical test will thus eliminate all the alternatives except 1, 3, 6, and 10. The Caxton variant (6) is not impossible metrically, for headless lines with initial stress falling upon a conjunction occur in Chaucer; but the sense seems inferior, for there is no reason why line 19 should be closely tied by *And* to the eighteen-line sentence that precedes it. The variant in 1 hardly affects the sense, but may be rejected on the grounds that 'on that sesoun' is unusual idiom, and *on* may have been written in anticipation of the *on* later in the line—a common type of scribal error. As for 3, while one might feel that *that* is preferable to *it*, the point would be a hard one to argue, for the idiom is unexceptionable; if the authorities were equally divided between *that* and *it* an editor would probably follow his copy-text, which is the proper procedure where there is little to choose between alternate readings.

Taking 10 by itself, one cannot find much objection to it: *So* is not an elegant conjunction, but Chaucer did not scorn it; and to omit the preposition before *sesoun* is perhaps overly colloquial, but Chaucer is often very colloquial. The line as it stands in 10 would not disgrace him. But if one takes 10 together with the obviously unsatisfactory reading of 9 one notices that they both have *So* and *it* and omit the first *that* as well as *on*, and this suggests that the two readings are related. If it could be established that these additions and omissions occurred in a common ancestor of the three manuscripts concerned, then 10 could be rejected as a mere smoothing of the reading inherited by 9: that is, a plausible reading has come into being through alteration of a patently wrong one. Yet proof of such a family relationship can be established only by collecting and analyzing all the variants of every line of *The Canterbury Tales* and finding that the manuscripts DsEn[1]Ma consistently share the same error. And actually Manly and Rickert's analysis of all the variants of *The Canterbury Tales* shows a highly consistent pattern of shared error among the three manuscripts (along with two others not containing this line);[1] as a result, the reading of 10 may be safely disregarded.

Identification of the relationships of manuscripts to each other—that is, classification by family—is the first and all-important step in the so-called genetic method of editing texts that have been preserved in hand-written copies. Since at least a modified or partial use of this method underlies most recent editions of Chaucer, it would be well briefly to discuss the method here. In any given text, analysis of the readings of the manuscripts might produce a stemma, or family tree, as in the following model based upon four surviving manuscripts:

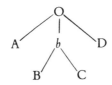

O here represents the author's original, ABCD the surviving manuscripts, and *b* the hypothetical ancestor of BC. This ancestor has been hypothesized because, while A and D each have a number of readings which they share with neither each other nor with BC, BC share many readings against A and D. In this trifid stemma, it seems logical to suppose that when A and D agree against *b* (represented by BC), or A*b* against D, or *b*D against A, the minority reading will be wrong, and the majority right, since in each case the minority will be presumed to have made an error which the majority avoided. If AD consistently agree with each other against *b*, then BC will be considered the more corrupt manuscripts. Finally, if A is in the minority less often than D—that is, there are fewer *b*D readings than A*b*, then A will be presumed to be the

---

[1] See Manly-Rickert, II, 51–7.

most reliable manuscript. Thus certain advantages will have been gained for the editor.

This ideal model has been discussed in terms of shared readings. Yet, strictly speaking, one cannot make a stemma on the basis of shared readings: properly one must deal only with shared error. It is obvious from a glance at the model that A and C might share a right reading where D and B had independently gone astray, but A and C are related only in that they both inherit their readings from O: Chaucer's Adam is as inevitably responsible for all the right readings that are shared by the manuscripts descended from his as his namesake is for shared sin. On the other hand, the grouping of manuscripts by shared error implies that the editor knows the right reading before he begins his classification. In this dilemma, the editor is either forced to use his stemma not as an aid in editing but as a proof—made after the fact—that his editing was systematic, or else to hope, as Manly and Rickert did, that the laws of probability would support relationships worked out on the basis of shared readings without regard to their rightness or wrongness.[1]

Even if the model were assumed to have been made on the basis of shared error a number of uncertainties might arise. Just as the fact that a right reading shared by A and C is no proof of their relationship, so a wrong reading may be shared by them without proving relationship. Scribes, like most human beings, often react to certain situations in similar ways, so that a difficult line of verse may be transcribed a number of times independently in the same incorrect way; and lines of no difficulty are apt to encourage the same errors, as one can see from line 19, cited above, where the six manuscripts reading *upon* are no more significantly related to one another than they are to manuscripts reading *on*. Indeed, errors such as this are so random that editors will frequently ignore them in classifying manuscripts, and will concentrate upon 'significant' error; but this, unfortunately, is the type of error which above all is apt to result from coincidentally similar solutions to the same textual problem. Because of the prevalence of coincidental error, the editor would be fortunate indeed who, in the model above, did not have to ignore in his classification a number of readings where A and B agree against an agreement of C and D—a situation his stemma suggests to be impossible. Similarly, agreement of AD against *b* may at times result from A and D's

---

[1] II, 8. Skeat's Students' Edition uncorrected was the basis for the collation.

having coincidentally made the same error which *b* avoided, and this is a violation of the rule that two are right when they agree against one.

If even so simple a stemma can, conceivably, misrepresent the true situation, then any stemma made for a very long poem with a large number of witnesses will almost inevitably do so. This is especially true because of two factors that the stemma must necessarily exclude: correction and change of exemplar. Many surviving manuscripts of Chaucer's works are heavily corrected, and usually the exemplar from which the corrections are taken is of a different family from the exemplar that served as the basis of the manuscript being corrected. This is easy enough to recognize and allow for in surviving manuscripts; but when a corrected manuscript has been copied and lost, its descendant or descendants will present anomalies—curious grafts on the family tree. Even more disturbing is the fact that scribes frequently changed exemplars while producing a manuscript—sometimes not once, but a number of times. Indeed, in *Troilus*, where R. K. Root hypothesized three early forms of the poem, only ten of the seventeen authorities represent a single pure form: seven represent one form, two another, and one the third; the other seven all represent various mixtures of forms.[1] No stemma can represent such a changing situation; add to this the fact that scribes changing exemplars sometimes used one to correct the other while they were writing, it becomes almost too great an act of faith to suppose that none of the groups we identify most confidently as pure may not themselves go back to a mixed manuscript.

Despite its implicit paradoxes and its frustrations, genetic analysis of the manuscripts of medieval works, including Chaucer's, has proved fruitful by helping to establish which are the more reliable manuscripts of many of the works and which manuscripts are to be treated most cautiously. But as a method of editing a text, it has proved to have grave limitations. In the first place, as a supposedly scientific operation, genetic analysis has preëmpted the editor's attention to the point where the actual text that it was designed to produce has often received rather short shrift. It was in the interest of 'science' that Manly and Rickert settled for trying to reproduce not Chaucer's original but O^1, an intermediate text between the original and all the surviving manuscripts. It was presumably their analysis of manuscripts that forced them to exclude from their

[1] See Root's edition of *Troilus*, pp. lxx–lxxxi.

text many readings which, on the one hand, they admitted to be genuinely Chaucerian but, on the other, they did not believe could have been
honestly inherited by the manuscripts containing them. In settling for
such a text they were behaving with admirable honesty yet with some
overconfidence about the manuscript classifications they had made; and
in particular they seem to have neglected the genuinely scientific principle that a right reading may occur anywhere in a line of transmission
when all the intermediaries between it and the original are hypothetical.
As a result, when Manly and Rickert say of a given right reading
excluded from their text that a number of scribes restored it independently one has a right to wonder whether at least some of the manuscripts
may not have inherited it honestly.[1] Similarly, while it may be all but
certain that some right readings were introduced into a surviving or
hypothesized manuscript by correction, one wonders whether to
exclude these is not to cut off one's nose to save one's face. A correction
made in the fifteenth century may very well have been made from a
better manuscript than now exists, and it seems as sensible to hypothesize
such a manuscript as to hypothesize some of the ancestors of surviving
manuscripts.

The genetic system has resulted not only in too large a distrust for
manuscripts with bad if hypothetical ancestors; it has, conversely,
resulted in too great a respect for reliable manuscripts, whose individual
readings are often preferred to interesting alternatives on the grounds
that in other readings it has been reliable. This reflects a common tendency, to which the genetic analyst is perhaps especially susceptible, to
personify the materials that one has spent so long studying. If one proceeds on the assumption that the whole transmission of a text was
mechanical, one will try to be resolutely impersonal while classifying the
manuscripts; but one will be apt to compensate for this act of dehumani-
zation by ultimately personifying the classified manuscripts, treating
them as if they were reliable or unreliable people who are 'of great authority' or 'of little or no authority' in determining a text. Since the whole
process of the creation and transmission of a work of literary art is
human, it might be better to personify the individual members of the
corpus of variants. Hundreds of these, to be sure, will be describable in
no other terms but 'drab and unimaginative'; others may appear at first

[1] See, for examples from a single Tale, p. 425, note to line 660; 427, to 876;
430, to 1595 and 1900; 437, to 2994; 438, to 3071.

glance as 'attractive', but will, with the passage of time, seem 'attractive but specious': some will seem 'very interesting'—so interesting, indeed, that the editor will have to think long and hard before rejecting or accepting them and, no matter which he does, may never cease to suffer from an uneasy feeling that he has done the wrong thing; and some—a very few—will seem 'precise and witty', a true reflection of the personality of the poet whose work the editor is trying to reproduce in the most accurate form.

The most important requirement for an edition of a medieval text is to have the variants available to the editor, and thanks to the Chaucer Society, to Root, and to Manly and Rickert, the variants of most of the Chaucer manuscripts are available. Future editors ought to consider this vast body of information without too much regard for the classification of manuscripts, rejecting out of hand no interesting variant merely because classification makes its originality seem improbable, though classification may be a contributory reason for ultimately rejecting a variant. But when a reading cries out for recognition, it must be given it regardless of any doubts about how it found its way into the manuscript in which it appears. When an editor is persuaded that a reading is original, he must print it; it may very well be unoriginal, but the only test will be the reaction of hundreds—perhaps generations—of informed and devoted readers of Chaucer.

We conclude this discussion with three examples of interesting readings in *The Canterbury Tales* that long escaped general notice. The first, which has been treated in detail elsewhere,[1] provides a classic example of the good reading that probably came into being as a result of correction. In line 117 of her Prologue, the Wife of Bath refers to the Creator: in O[1], according to Manly and Rickert, she refers to him as a *wight*, 'creature', an epithet that many scribes found so surprising that they altered the line in various ways in order to get rid of it. In this part of her Prologue the Wife is paraphrasing St. Jerome's attack on Jovinian, and at the point where she seems to be calling the Creator a *wight*, St. Jerome refers to him as a *conditor*. The Latin is, of course, the equivalent of English 'carpenter', which in Middle English would be 'wrighte'. It seems likely that an *r* and a final *e* were lost early in the transmission. Still, three manuscripts, all 'of no authority', do read *wrighte*: one of these is a copy of

[1] Donaldson, '*Canterbury Tales*, D117: A Critical Edition', *Speculum*, 40, 1965, 626–33, reprinted in *Speaking of Chaucer*, pp. 119–33.

another, and in the third the word has been visibly introduced by correction.[1] Whether the older manuscript of the related pair could have inherited the reading honestly is not the issue: the quality of the reading demands that it be passed onto readers for ultimate judgement.

The second example (also treated in detail elsewhere)[2] occurs in the last complete line of 'Sir Thopas' where in O[1] the unredoubtable hero is described as 'worthy under wede'. This very trite and common expression in Middle English romance is not one which one would expect to produce scribal variation: once written it seems clear and self-justifying. Yet fifteen of the thirty-seven authorities for the line produce variants for *worthy*: five read *worthily*, five *worthely*, four *worly*, and one *worthly*.[3] The first of these forms represents the adjective, not uncommon in the romances Chaucer is parodying, *worthily*; the second may represent the same, or may represent an alternate spelling for the last form, *worthly*; this is also not uncommon in the romances, having the same meaning as *worthily*; and *worly* is a rather rare variant form of *worthly*. Since Chaucer's parody of the romances is linguistic as well as literary, it seems reasonable to suppose that he wrote not *worthy*, but one of the variant forms. Since *worly* is the most outlandish, while the other forms—as well as *worthy* itself—are more common and respectable, it is probable that he wrote *worly*. This small joke was, indeed, allowed by Manly in his 1928 text of *The Canterbury Tales*,[4] but was eliminated in the Manly and Rickert edition. The elimination was the more surprising, since *worly* and its more recognizable variants are preserved in some of the 'most reliable' of the manuscripts, including Ellesmere and Hengwrt, and appear in four of the seven independent lines of transmission that Manly and Rickert describe for this tale.

The explanation may lie in the inattentiveness to the meaning of variants that is perhaps an inevitable by-product of the tremendous concentration of energy that classification of variants demands. This might also account for the third example. In 'The Shipman's Tale', the lusty and lustful monk is described, in O[4], as 'fre . . . and namely of dispence' when

[1] See Manly-Rickert, VI, 15.

[2] John Burrow, '"Worly under Wede" in *Sir Thopas*', *The Chaucer Review*, III, 1969, 170–3.

[3] See Manly-Rickert, VII, 199. The spellings with medial *e* are from Burrow's article.

[4] *Chaucer's Canterbury Tales*, New York 1928, p. 436.

he visited the merchant, that is, 'generous and especially of expenditure'. But a variant, appearing in fifteen manuscripts representing five out of eight independent lines of transmission, including again some of the most 'reliable' manuscripts, is *manly* for *namely*.[1] The latter is a very common adverb, the former a common enough adjective in contexts where it means 'virile', but perhaps initially puzzling in the present context. In this case—as, indeed, in the last—the principle of *durior lectio* demands that the editor try to account for what seems to be a harder reading varying from a perfectly easy one: if Chaucer had written *namely*, it is difficult to account for a number of scribes substituting *manly* for it. But *manly* has a secondary meaning 'generous';[2] and while in the present context the word might seem redundant in view of the adjective *fre*, it is nevertheless probable that *manly* is what Chaucer wrote. 'The Shipman's Tale' is distinguished for its *double entendres* and its suggestive play on words; the adjective *manly* does double duty for the monk's generosity and his virility which, like everything else in this tale of buying and spending, becomes part of a commercial transaction. Chaucer would have been unlikely to use up space with a rather idle *namely* in a poem at once so economical and so rich.

Perhaps none of these suggestions will find favour with readers at this moment. But as was remarked earlier, it takes a very long time to determine whether a given reading is good or bad. We can only proceed very slowly, and by trial and error, in our attempt to get back to an uncorrupted Adam, and editors should be willing to be found wrong even where they are most persuaded that they are—probably—right. And in the endeavour to reconstruct what Chaucer actually wrote it seems sensible to concern oneself directly with the meaning of the variants rather than with mechanistic systems—with literary criticism rather than with stemmata. This is the human and the humane way. Chaucer's works, the manuscripts that preserve them, and the editions that reproduce them are all part of a great human endeavour that has been carried on for six hundred years now and that may, quite possibly, never end, since nothing human is perfectible. Nevertheless, it is possible that after Chaucer's making we may still 'write more true'.

[1] See Manly-Rickert, VII, 114.
[2] *OED, manly*, a., 4, lists for 'generous' only the clear instance in *Piers Plowman*, B, V, 260, but many of the uses listed in 2 and 1 also imply generosity.

Not included in this discussion of Chaucer's works is the *Equatorie of the Planetis*, ed D. J. Price, Cambridge 1955, a Middle English translation of a Latin translation of an Arabic astronomical treatise, preserved in a single manuscript; this is thought by its editor and by a number of Chaucerians to be Chaucer's work and, indeed, to be partly in Chaucer's hand. But while it seems to contain a reference to Chaucer and was probably written by a contemporary, the evidence for ascribing it to Chaucer himself seems wholly inadequate, depending on Chaucer's known interest in astronomical documents (cf. the *Treatise on the Astrolabe*) and the similarity of the handwriting of the name *Chaucer* in the manuscript to what may be his genuine signature on another document: in view of the close similarity of many late medieval English handwritings this would hardly be conclusive evidence of identity even if it were certain that the signature were Chaucer's own.

5: Chaucer and French Poetry

J. I. WIMSATT

IN ABOUT 1385, apparently responding to Chaucer's request. Eustache Deschamps sent copies of some of his verse to the English poet; to accompany the verse he composed the balade with the refrain 'Grant translateur, noble Geffroy Chaucier.' This balade provides our most important testimony to the contemporary reputation of Chaucer across the Channel. Even allowing for hyperbole, the estimate is a high one:

> O Socrates plains de philosophie,
> Seneque en meurs et Anglux en pratique,
> Ovides grans en ta poeterie,
> Bries en parler, saiges en rethorique,
> Aigles treshaulz, qui par ta theorique
> Enlumines le regne d'Eneas,
> L'Isle aux Geans, ceuls de Bruth, et qui as
> Semé les fleurs et planté le rosier,
> Aux ignorans de la langue pandras,
> Grant translateur, noble Geffroy Chaucier.[1]

[O Socrates full of wisdom, Seneca in morals and Aulus in practice, great Ovid in your poetry, brief in speech, wise in versifying, most

---

[1] *Oeuvres complètes d'Eustache Deschamps*, ed le Marquis de Queux de Saint-Hilaire and Gaston Raynaud, Société des anciens textes français, 11 vol, Paris 1878–1904, II, 138–9. The translation accords with the consensus of previous scholars except as regards 'pandras' (l. 9), which—following a suggestion of my colleague James Atkinson—I render as the future of *pandre*, seen as a cognate or variant of O. F. *espandre* (cf. Mod. F. *répandre*), rather than as a proper noun. The most important of numerous studies of this lyric is T. Atkinson Jenkins, 'Deschamps' Balade to Chaucer,' *MLN*, XXXIII, 1918, 268–78.

lofty eagle who by your philosophy illuminate the kingdom of
Aeneas, the Island of Giants—those whom Brutus destroyed—and
who has sown the flowers of poetry and planted the rose-tree, you
will spread light to those ignorant of French, great translator, noble
Geoffrey Chaucer.]

In the next stanzas Deschamps goes on to identify Chaucer as the worldly
god of love in Albion (l. 12) and to praise specifically his translation of
the *Roman de la Rose*; he claims to depend on him for his own future
inspiration—for a true drink of the spring of Helicon (ll. 22–5).

It is clearly more than Chaucer's version of the *Roman de la Rose* which
lies behind the epithet 'grant translateur'. In the eyes of the French poet,
one would infer, Chaucer's translation involves a 'carrying-across' and
enlarging of accumulated poetic wisdom for the English people, wisdom
which the French poets have recorded, but which has become largely inaccessible to the English with the decline of French among them. With
strong ties both with the English-speaking world of affairs and with
French-speaking polite society, Chaucer is in an ideal position to become
Albion's monarch of love, an arch-Ovid drawing practical and theoretical philosophy into an English poetry of love based in large part on
French models, particularly the *Roman de la Rose* and the works of Guillaume de Machaut.

Chaucer's relationship to the French language, of course, was quite
different from his relationship to other languages he knew. To him Latin
was the great language of learning and Italian a foreign vernacular of
large cultural importance. But French was a second native tongue. Year
after year he listened to French gossip at the court; as a customs official he
transacted much business in French; he wooed a wife in French; and he
read and discussed French literature with French-speaking courtiers such
as Jean Froissart and Oton de Granson. Indeed, not only well-known
poets like these would have discussed literature with Chaucer, but almost
every courtier he encountered would have been an *aficionado* of love
verse and a prospective poet, for poetry was part of the knight's métier.
French remained, of course, an important language of poetry at the
courts of Edward III and Richard II, and at the ducal courts of Edward's
sons.

Chaucer obviously knew and appreciated a substantial body of literature in English, but his various positions and situations in life around
London conduced to his immersion in the French tradition of poetry. It

would have been quite natural for him, like Gower, to have begun his career writing original verse in French. However, he manifested a translator's temperament from the beginning by producing English versions of Deguilleville's 'A.B.C.' and the *Roman de la Rose*. From these he went on to adapt literary materials in English compositions that, while quite original, may be seen as 'translations' in the broad sense implied by Deschamps' balade. Such translation was part of a programme. As Wolfgang Clemen has it, 'From the beginning it was Chaucer's intention to give the idiom of English poetry the entrée to the court, to ennoble it after the French pattern.'[1] The great work of his life was the development of an English poetic tradition; this involved transference into English of the French tradition fed and supplemented by the greater literatures in Latin and Italian.

Chaucer had French sources for almost everything he wrote. Even when he was using Latin and Italian originals he usually found versions in French to assist his composition, as with the *Boece*, the Ovidian stories in *The Legend of Good Women, Troilus and Criseyde*, and 'The Clerk's Tale'. It is not, however, with the *Ovide moralisé*, Beauvau's *Roman de Troyle et de Criseida*, and such that Chaucer's French background manifests its essential role in his work, for these primarily supplement and assist the presentation of materials of other languages. Nor—to look further—is it manifested with the fabliaux which supply the story type and ultimate narrative sources for several of *The Canterbury Tales*; Chaucer's style in his fabliaux is much richer than that which characterizes the French verse tales, and the stories themselves in the late fourteenth century were part of the common literary stock of Europe. Nor again is the vital contribution of estates literature to the plan of the *General Prologue* and the characterization of the pilgrims basically French; estates analysis and complaint are in origin and essence learned and religious, which is to say Latin.

While all such French works—and others, like the sources of 'The Man of Law's Tale' and 'The Tale of Melibee'—certainly participate in Chaucer's carrying-across of the poetic tradition into English, they are not what made it possible for Deschamps to view him as a love poet in the French pattern. In any of these there is little of importance that can be seen as basically French, as contrasted with Latin, or Italian, or Flemish. More identifiably French are the chivalric romances which Chaucer

[1] *Chaucer's Early Poetry*, trans. C. A. M. Sym, 1963, p. 7.

used—the *Roman de Troie*, the *Roman de Thèbes*, and the other romances and lays which possibly lie behind the tales of the Wife of Bath, the Franklin, and the Squire. However, it was not these either which contributed an essential French quality, for their total effect on Chaucer's poetry is of less than major importance. It was instead the romances of love of Guillaume de Lorris, Jean de Meun, and Guillaume de Machaut that were basic. Central elements which Chaucer drew from these made him throughout his career Worldly God of Love in Albion—poet of love par excellence.

It seems appropriate to consider here the specific important ways in which Chaucer's work is indebted to each of these three poets. Many aspects of this debt have been neglected and do not show up in any sweeping impressionistic comparison. Impressionistically, Homer and Joyce no doubt would be found more like Chaucer than the French poets we are considering. However, since our aim is to deal with more immediate relationships, we will concentrate in this essay on the various aspects of Chaucer's use, first of Guillaume de Lorris' poem, then of the work of Guillaume's direct poetic descendant, Guillaume de Machaut, and finally of the poem of Jean de Meun.

As is well known Guillaume de Lorris wrote something over four thousand lines of the *Roman de la Rose* in about 1230. His narrative breaks off with the lover unsuccessful and denied access to the rose. Jean de Meun in about 1270 took up the story and attached a huge seventeen thousand line ending to it. The combined poem was to be one of the most influential writings in history. It integrally affected all of the literatures of Western Europe, and well into the Renaissance it was the best-known work of French literature.

In the fourteenth and fifteenth centuries Guillaume's part was both the chief ultimate source and a main tributary of love poetry in French. The refined tone of the poem suited perfectly the courtly sensibility of contemporary nobility, and its subtle analysis of lovers and the love affair was compatible with the proclivities of the scholastic mind for fine intellectual distinctions. It crystallized the poetic tradition and the courtly code in an archetypal narrative of love. The affair that the story portrays is carried on decorously within the area of experience where aspiration and desire predominate over action and fulfilment. Before the narrative is forced outside this area Guillaume's poem breaks off. The focus of his story thus rests on psychological process, not on physical action.

Despite the poem's influence, the mode of Guillaume's narrative was imitated with but limited success by succeeding poets who constructed allegories around such fixtures of medieval life as the hunt, the law court, and the prison. By Machaut's and Chaucer's time elaborate love allegories were quite out of fashion, and in their stories personifications are rare except on the level of diction. Only in the *Complaint to Pity* does Chaucer employ psychological allegory in which personifications interact significantly.[1] The usual case in his work is that the analysis of the processes of love presented in the *Roman de la Rose* is assumed in stories which feature well-rounded, if often conventional, characters.

Chaucer frequently evokes Guillaume's allegory, nevertheless, through reference to his personifications. The Second Nun, for instance, speaks of 'Ydelnesse / That porter of the gate is of delices' (VIII, 2–3), and the Black Knight comparably refers to the time when 'Yowthe, my maistresse, / Governed me in ydelnesse' (ll. 797–98). In 'The Knight's Tale' the temple of Venus features the 'porter, Ydelnesse,' as well as 'Narcissus the faire' (I, 1940–41) and Jealousy wearing a yellow garland (I, 1928–29). In *Merciles Beaute* the poet complains,

> *So hath your beautee fro your herte chaced*
> *Pitee, that me ne availeth not to pleyne;*
> *For Daunger halt your mercy in his cheyne.*   (ll. 14–16)

This opposition of Pity and Danger, originating in the *Roman*, is found again in the Prologue to *The Legend of Good Women*, where Pity triumphs 'Thurgh innocence and ruled Curtesye' (F, 163). Fortune is the target of Amant's lament in Guillaume's poem and so of several lovers' complaints in Chaucer; and Guillaume's God of Love is a primary inspiration for many references to the God in Chaucer, including his appearance in full glory in the Prologue to *The Legend*.

Such random appearances of personifications of the *Roman* suggest the pervasive presence of the whole of Guillaume's story. Even when references to his personifications are lacking, the inherence of the story in every love narrative of Chaucer is shown by the pattern of events and the actions of the characters. Troilus is shot through his eyes to the bottom of his heart when he sees Criseyde, as Amant is when he sees the Rose; Venus dances with her torch at January's marriage and inflames Damian just as she inflamed Fair Welcome; and the Black Knight endures Fair

[1] See Clemen, pp. 179–85.

White's rebuff—clearly her Danger—until Pity softens her. The dreamer plays the part of Reason to the Black Knight, and Pandarus assumes the role of Friend to Troilus, bringing him Sweet Speech. Jealousy motivates both the carpenter John and old January, whose age properly puts them outside the wall of Mirth's domain.

In his standard study of Chaucer's uses of the *Roman de la Rose* Dean S. Fansler identifies and documents a close parallel between the actions of Troilus and those of the lover as prescribed by the God of Love in his lecture to Amant.[1] I have comparably set forth in another study certain of the obvious correspondences that one finds between the progress of the affairs of the Black Knight, Troilus, and January, and that of Amant.[2] Similar comparisons might be made with characters and stories in all the love narratives of Chaucer and of fourteenth-century French love poets. The countless parallels do not show that these poets consulted the *Roman de la Rose* whenever they wrote love poems, but rather that the complete story attained the status of an archetype, as it were, in their minds and in the minds of their readers.

Not only the pattern of Guillaume de Lorris' narrative, but also its appurtenances became part of the stock of the love poet, most notably the figure of the narrator-lover, the dream aspect, the garden description, the classical exemplum, the discourse on love, and the formal complaint, all of which played important roles in the tradition. Chaucer's works reflect most of these in some degree.

The narrator in Chaucer clearly owes some of his naïveté directly to the Amant-narrator of Guillaume de Lorris; however, as we shall discuss later, he owes much more to the innovations of Guillaume de Machaut. On the other hand, for the details and the ambience of his dreams, Chaucer relies mainly and directly on the *Roman de la Rose*. Machaut's model in this regard was of small importance, and while it is true that the dream frame of *The Book of the Duchess* makes especial use of Froissart's *Paradys d'Amours*, the dream setting and the crucial lines that immediately preface the dream are inspired by the *Roman*.

In the verses before the dream in *The Book of the Duchess* the narrator emphasizes the meaningfulness of his experiences and mentions Macrobius as a notable dream interpreter. The passage is important in itself and also provides a precedent for even more notable passages on the meaning

[1] Chaucer and the *Roman de la Rose*, New York 1914, pp. 149–54.

[2] James I. Wimsatt, *Allegory and Mirror*, New York 1970, pp. 61–87.

of dreams in *The House of Fame* and *The Parliament of Fowls*. All three grow out of the memorable lines with which Guillaume de Lorris begins his poem:

> *Maintes genz dient que en songes*
> *N'a se fables non e mençonges;*
> *Mais l'en puet teus songes songier*
> *Qui ne sont mie mençongier,*
> *Ainz sont après bien aparant;*
> *Si en puis bien traire a garant*
> *Un auctor qui ot non Macrobes,*
> *Qui ne tint pas songes a lobes,*
> *Ançois escrist l'avision*
> *Qui avint au roi Scipion.*[1]

[Many men say that there are nothing but fables and lies in dreams. You can dream such dreams, however, that are not lies at all, but afterwards they prove true. And can bring as a witness for that an author named Macrobius, who did not think dreams deceptive; rather he wrote the vision which King Scipio had.]

For *The Parliament* this passage, in addition to inspiring the discussion of dreams, provides the germ for the whole story of Scipio. Much later in Chaucer's poetic career, too, his rooster-lover again returned to the problem of dreams and Macrobius' testimony.

One may correctly note, of course, that Chaucer drew some of his dream discussion as well as the story of Scipio directly from Macrobius, but, as with a great body of material from the Latin tradition, the relevance of Macrobius' treatise to love poetry was established by the *Roman de la Rose*. The circumstances and manner of Chaucer's dreams leave no doubt that Guillaume is the primary inspiration.

The dreamer in the *Roman* narrates a series of experiences that precede his arrival at the pool of Narcissus: the departure from the bed and the chamber, the trip along the river, the sight of the garden from the outside, and the wandering and caroling within the garden—all of these serve to remove the dreamer from the world of practicality and to fix him within a fictive romantic world. Similar stages in a retreat from reality may be found in *The Book of the Duchess*, where the dreamer goes

---

[1] *Le Roman de la Rose*, ed Ernest Langlois, SATF, 5 vol, Paris 1914–24, ll. 1–10.

from his wonderful chamber, participates in the hunt of Octavian, follows a little dog down a path, proceeds through a marvellous garden, and at last arrives at the tree before which the Black Knight sits. The dreamers in *The House of Fame* and *The Parliament* also make involved journeys before reaching their ultimate destinations, the places where the culminating events of the poems take place. This manner of developing the dream experience is quite effective in creating an other-worldly illusion. Neither Macrobius nor any of the *dits amoreux* aside from the *Roman* suggest a comparable process.

Another feature of Chaucer's dream poems for which Guillaume de Lorris supplies the only model is the placement of a developed exemplum before the main section of the narrative. As Narcissus' fatal love keynotes Amant's painful experiences, so the story of Alcyone looks forward to the elegiac portion of *The Book of the Duchess*, and so too the stories of Dido in *The House of Fame* and Scipio in *The Parliament of Fowls* bear—if somewhat less directly—on the narratives which ensue. In the Seys and Alcyone story especially, Chaucer's treatment reminds one of Guillaume's tale of Narcissus. The humanization of the central figures, particularly in their medieval displays of emotion, is notable.[1] This humanization shows up well in the endings, where Chaucer and Guillaume comparably excise Ovid's metamorphoses, thus eliminating supernatural, potentially diverting episodes. The reasons presented for the deaths of Narcissus and Alcyone, and the phrasing describing it, are remarkably similar:

> *Il [Narcissus] perdi d'ire tot le sen,*
> *E fu morz en poi de termine.*   (ll. 1502–3)

[Narcissus swooned for sorrow, and was dead in a little time.]

> *'Allas!' quod she [Alcyone] for sorwe,*
> *And deyede within the thridde morwe.*   (ll. 2139–2140)

Chaucer imitates effectively—perhaps not consciously—Guillaume's simple pathos.

The effect of Guillaume's style and subject matter on Chaucer is particularly noticeable in the garden description, as has been long recognized. The atmosphere, birds, animals, flowers, and trees of Chaucer's

[1] For Chaucer's humanization of Ovid's Seys and Alcyone, see Clemen, pp. 31–6.

most complete garden, that of *The Book of the Duchess*, all come from Guillaume de Lorris. And even when he uses other poets for his garden description, like Boccaccio in *The Parliament of Fowls* or Machaut in 'The Franklin's Tale' (F, 907–17), the 'paravis terrestre' of the *Roman* clearly is in the background. Like his French contemporaries, Chaucer at times simply depends on a few details to evoke the garden of the *Roman* and to fill out curtailed descriptions. Thus Machaut in the *Remede de Fortune* instead of describing the Parc de Hesdin says simply, 'I could never describe the wonders, the delights, the artifices, the devices, the fountains, the diversions, and the curious things that were enclosed therein.'[1] It was automatic in a context like this for the reader to supply mentally the particular artifices and diversions of the garden of Guillaume de Lorris. In such economical evocations of Guillaume's prototypal garden, the poet could of course be more explicit, as Chaucer is in foreshortening the description of January's garden in 'The Merchant's Tale': 'He that wroot the Romance of the Rose / Ne koude of it the beautee wel devyse' (IV, 2032–33).

As with the garden description, so also the love complaints contained in Guillaume de Lorris' poem were of seminal importance for future love poems. The complaint imagined for Amant by the God of Love (ll. 2449–2504) and Amant's own lament (ll. 3782–96) established the complaint of the stricken beau as a matter of convention. Thus Absalon shows his nice sense of decorum in responding to Alison's demand that he go away and let her sleep:

> *'Allas,' quod Absolon, 'and weylawey,*
> *That trewe love was evere so yvel biset!'*   (I, 3714–15)

Likewise the Merchant, with little sympathy for Damian but a good feeling for protocol, verbalizes for the squire his sufferings and fears:

> *Now wol I speke of woful Damyan,*
> *That langwissheth for love, as ye shul heere;*
> *Therfore I speke to hym in this manere:*
> *I seye, 'O sely Damyan, allas!*
> *Andswere to my demaunde, as in this cas.*
> *How shaltow to thy lady, fresshe May,*

[1] *Les Oeuvres de Guillaume de Machaut*, ed Ernest Hoepffner, SATF, 3 vol, Paris 1908–21, ll. 813–17. Citations of Machaut's poetry, except where noted, are from this edition.

> *Telle thy wo? She wole alwey seye nay.*
> *Eek if thou speke, she wol thy wo biwreye.*
> *God be thyn helpe! I kan no bettre seye.'*   (IV, 1866–74)

For Chaucer's longer complaints, however, both the separate poems and the set pieces in narrative works, Machaut provided a more important precedent than Guillaume de Lorris.

In summary, the direct influence of Guillaume de Lorris on Chaucer's development as England's great poet of love is found most signally in the analysis of the process of love which underlies Chaucer's stories and lyrics, and in such matters as the use of dreams and garden descriptions, and the introduction of dream experiences with exempla. In numerous other respects Guillaume affects Chaucer chiefly through the poetry of his most important French disciple, Guillaume de Machaut.

Born about 1300, Machaut became famous as a musical composer as well as a poet; he has been characterized as the last of the great poet-musicians of medieval France. In both artistic media he successfully innovated and set fashions that were followed for centuries. In lyric poetry he established the so-called 'formes fixes'—most notably the rondeau and balade—and his longer love narratives or *dits* were the first long poems in the tradition of the *Roman de la Rose* which themselves proved imitable. Jean Froissart and Eustache Deschamps, who wrote in the generation after Machaut, and Christine de Pisan, Alain Chartier, and Charles d'Orléans, the major French poets of the early fifteenth century, utilized the forms, modes, and manner of expression of Machaut. Even Villon's ultimate debt is substantial.

From the 1360s when he and Froissart wrote poetry at the English court, Chaucer likewise was strongly influenced by Machaut. One may well conjecture with B. J. Whiting that the slightly older Froissart 'introduced the English boy to Machaut's poetry as well as his own.'[1] Acquainting him with Machaut's work was probably Froissart's greatest service to Chaucer, for the effect that Machaut had on his work is considerably more fundamental and comprehensive than the combined influence of Froissart, Deschamps, Granson, and the other lesser French love poets whom Chaucer utilized.[2]

---

[1] 'Froissart as Poet,' *Mediaeval Studies*, VIII, 1946, 191.
[2] For Chaucer's use of Machaut, see particularly James I. Wimsatt, *Chaucer and the French Love Poets*, Univ. of North Carolina Studies in Comp. Lit.,

Chaucer evidently knew most of Machaut's numerous works. Along with using a representative range of the lyrics, he seems to have employed in some fashion every one of Machaut's ten longer poems, which include eight *dits* of love, the *Confort d'Ami*, and *Prise d'Alexandrie*, a chronicle in verse about Pierre of Cyprus. The works which are most significant for Chaucer's poetry are the four best of the longer *dits*—two debate poems and two *dits* of 'complaint and comfort'—along with the shorter *Dit de la fleur de lis et de la Marguerite*. Our discussion will concentrate on these.

Machaut's two debate poems, the *Jugement du Roi de Behaingne* and the *Jugement du Roi de Navarre*, make a closely-related pair, not only in the fact that both are debate poems which end with judgments made by royal patrons of Machaut, but also in that *Navarre* is a palinode to *Behaingne*, expressly written to redress the alleged injustice of the earlier judgment. *Behaingne*, composed in four-line interconnected stanzas rather than the customary octosyllabic couplets, seems to have been Machaut's most popular poem. The story involves a debate between a knight and a lady, both distracted lovers, who meet by chance in a wood. Her chevalier being dead, the lady thinks her sufferings the worst possible, but the knight argues that his plight is worse, the desertion of his fickle lady depriving him of all hope for consolation. They take their dispute to Jean of Luxembourg, King of Bohemia, who renders a verdict in which he holds the knight the greater sufferer, a judgment that was to be impugned for anti-feminism.

Behaingne is the most important source of *The Book of the Duchess*. It provides numerous close precedents for the behaviour of the Black Knight and for his story, the similarities extending to both language and

No. 43, Chapel Hill 1968, Chaps. IV–VI. For the relationships between Froissart's work and Chaucer's see the same, pp. 118–133, and also James I. Wimsatt, 'The *Dit dou Bleu Chevalier*: Froissart's Imitation of Chaucer,' *Mediaeval Studies*, **XXXIV**, 1972, 388–400. For Chaucer and Granson, see Haldeen Braddy, *Chaucer and the French Poet Granson*, Baton Rouge 1947, and *Chaucer and the French Love Poets*, pp. 143–6. See also Chapters II and III of the latter for various affinities between Chaucer's works and French poems before Machaut. Of general importance for Chaucer's use of French love poetry are Clemen's study of the early poetry, cited above; Charles Muscatine, *Chaucer and the French Tradition*, Berkeley, California 1957; and D. S. Brewer, ed, *The Parlement of Foulys*, 1960, 'Introduction' and appendices.

situation. The first words of the Black Knight and the dreamer, for
instance, are very like those of the knight and the lady in *Behaingne* and
arise from a similar occasion. When the knight comes up, she is distracted by her own thoughts, but when she becomes conscious of him she
apologizes:

> 'Certes, sire, pas ne vous entendi
> Pour mon penser qui le me deffendi;
>   Mais se j'ay fait
> Riens ou il ait villenie ou meffait,
> Vueilliez le moy pardonner, s'il vous plait.'
> Li chevaliers, sans faire plus de plait,
>   Dist doucement:
> 'Dame, il n'affiert ci nul pardonnement,
> Car il n'y a meffait ne mautalent;
> Mais je vous pri que vostre pensement
>   Me vueilliez dire.'   (ll. 70–80)

['Indeed, sir, I didn't hear you because my thinking prevented it;
but if I have done anything low or wrong, please pardon me.' The
knight without further dispute said sweetly: 'Lady, there is no par-
doning necessary here, for there is no wrong nor ill will. But I pray
that you tell me your thought.']

The first conversation between the Black Knight and the dreamer in
Chaucer's poem (ll. 514–28), one readily recognizes, though somewhat
more colloquial and stichomythic, draws largely on this exchange. So
also the Black Knight's complaints, story, and description of White owe
much to the recitations of both debaters in Machaut's poem. There is
even a debate element in the exchanges in *The Book of the Duchess* which
originates in *Behaingne*.

Behaingne, furthermore, seems to have had an effect on the basic mode
of Chaucer's love stories. The love affair of the Black Knight and White
follows a conventional pattern that was established by the *Roman de la
Rose*, but their story is particularly indebted to *Behaingne* not only for
narrative detail but also for the existential status of the participants. In
Behaingne the main figures are idealized but rounded characters; there is
no fragmentation of them into personified aspects. They provide good
models for the non-allegorical but relatively unindividualized figures
that appear in several of Chaucer's works in addition to *The Book of the*

Duchess. Specifically, the lady in Machaut's poem, a swooning complainant against her lot, is the first of Chaucer's models for a long line of ladies—Dido, Anelida, the falcon of the Squire's Tale, the martyrs of *The Legend*—who wear the mask of the suffering lover. And the knight, a loyal and worthy lover whose lady was perfect except that she lacked one virtue—loyalty (l. 699)—is a fine model in character and fortune for the betrayed Troilus. To reinforce this parallel the poem *Troilus and Criseyde* also is like *Behaingne* in that its imputed anti-feminism provoked a poetic retraction. It is surely no simple coincidence, moreover, that Machaut's retraction of *Behaingne*, the *Jugment dou Roy de Navarre*, is the prime source for Chaucer's palinode to *Troilus, The Legend of Good Women.*[1]

The inspiration that *Navarre* provided for *The Legend*, however, as important as it is, is probably not its main contribution to Chaucer's work. Incidental uses of *Navarre* in *The House of Fame* and *The Book of the Duchess* show that Chaucer had the poem in mind in the very time that he was developing his comic narrator. Machaut's own comic persona receives its fullest development in *Navarre* and provides a particularly significant precedent for Chaucer's figure.

Navarre has been known especially for the 458-line prologue in which the poet, having locked himself in his room for fear of the Plague, ruminates on the calamities of the time. In the ensuing narrative he goes out to hunt rabbits in the woods, but he becomes involved in a dispute with a lady he meets named Bonneurté who thinks the decision of the previous judgment poem an insult to women. The poet maintains his contrary opinion adamantly, so they take the matter to the King of Navarre. In the argument before the king Bonneurté's ladies adduce several examples of women who have suffered for love. After hearing the poet's maladroit defence, the king proclaims in favour of Bonneurté and fixes a penance for Guillaume (Machaut is identified by first name in this work as Chaucer is in *The House of Fame*) of a lay, a chanson, and a balade. *Navarre* thus provides a model for *The Legend* in several ways: in the poet's being accused of offending women in previous works, in his

---

[1] For the relationship between *Navarre* and the Prologue, see Robert M. Estrich, 'Chaucer's Prologue to the *Legend of Good Women* and Machaut's *Le Jugement dou Roy de Navarre*,' *SP*, XXXVI, 1939, 20–39. See also *Chaucer and the French Love Poets*, pp. 93–102, for the importance of *Navarre* to Chaucer's works.

being arraigned before a king particularly sympathetic to ladies, in his awkward attempt to defend himself, and in the penance involving poetic composition. Furthermore, of the five exempla cited at length in proof of the virtue and sufferings of women, four (Dido, Ariadne, Medea, and Thisbe) have counterparts in Chaucer's legends and the other (Hero) was envisaged in his plan.

Machaut's narrator in *Navarre*, for whom the stereotyped lover-narrator of Guillaume de Lorris provides but small precedent, is a cowardly and rather obtuse individual. He keeps his windows closed to the Plague until others are dancing in the street. When he is summoned to Bonneurté he fatuously imagines that she is interested in him amorously. And in the debate his arguments border on the outrageous, infuriating his antagonists who are clearly favourites of the king. At one point Guillaume asserts that there is no stability in women; when at this the ladies all murmur against him, he facetiously suggests that they all present their arguments simultaneously. Only in the end, when the judgment goes against him, is he properly humbled.

This figure in *Navarre* is consistent with the narrator in the other love stories of Machaut, particularly the *Dit de la Fonteinne amoureuse* and the *Voir Dit*. Though he differs in certain respects from Chaucer's timid and docile narrator, yet he is a model for comic individualization and is a product of poetic problems comparable to those which faced Chaucer. Machaut like Chaucer was not of the nobility, yet he was patronized by powerful royalty and he depicts such patrons in his poems. By presenting his first-person narrator in the works as obtuse and comical, Machaut took himself out of competition with his royal audience; without seeming presumptuous he could give himself a central part in stories of noble love and could show himself associating with men like Jean of Luxembourg and the Duke of Berry. In this way he was also able to add an individual flavour to narratives in which the conventional aspects if unrelieved could become onerous.

It is notable that Froissart, who followed Machaut in almost everything poetic, did not in his *dits* significantly differentiate his narrator from the conventional Amant of the tradition. In this matter as in most others it is clear that Chaucer was inspired by Machaut directly rather than through Froissart. Machaut's narrator supplies easily the best precedent among Chaucer's sources—of whatever language—for his literary persona, an important aspect indeed of his literary art.

The two other long *dits* of Machaut which are of particular importance to Chaucer's works are also closely related to each other. These are
Remede de Fortune and the *Dit de la Fonteinne amoureuse*, which fathered a
group of poems that I have called narratives of 'complaint and comfort.'
The group includes Chaucer's *The Book of the Duchess*, two of Froissart's
poems, a Granson work, and the anonymous *Songe vert*.[1]

Remede de Fortune has as narrator a mostly conventional Amant who is
one day so tongue-tied with his lady that he goes off to the Parc de
Hesdin to complain against Love and Fortune. His elaborate complaint
at length calls forth Lady Hope, who provides him comfort. In appearance Hope recalls Boethius' Philosophy, and her comfort is drawn in
large part from the *Consolation of Philosophy*, especially the sections on
Fortune.[2] She inspires Amant with the courage to approach his beloved
once more and to confess his devotion. In the end the lady is persuaded to
accept him. Intercalated in the poem are nine lyric set-pieces representing a tableau of current forms, the longest being the complaint.

Among the sources of *The Book of the Duchess*, *Remede de Fortune* is
second only to *Behaingne* in the number of lines directly employed by
Chaucer. In particular the Black Knight's complaint against Fortune, the
moral virtues ascribed to White, and several segments in the Knight's
story are indebted to this *dit*. Even more significant perhaps is the poem's
rather original use of a Boethian situation and of ideas from the *Consolation* which are comparably employed in *Troilus and Criseyde*. For this situation the *Roman de la Rose* supplies a precedent. The description of
Reason in the *Roman* proclaims her a descendant of Lady Philosophy, and
she uses the words of Boethius to dissuade the lover from serving Amour.
Machaut's Hope, however, whose appearance likewise resembles Philosophy's, employs Boethius' wisdom for a rather different purpose: to encourage Amant to persevere in the service of Amour. Pandarus in Book I
of *Troilus* comparably appears in the guise of Philosophy and uses the
words of Machaut's Hope as well as of Philosophy to give heart to
Troilus.[3] This part of Chaucer's poem, inspired basically by *Remede de
Fortune*, is particularly instrumental in characterizing Pandarus and in
preparing for later uses of the *Consolation* in Book IV. Chaucer's great

[1] See *Chaucer and the French Love Poets*, Chaps. VI–VIII.

[2] E. Hoepffner, II, xix–xxx, analyzes the uses of Boethius in *Remede de Fortune*.

[3] See George L. Kittredge, 'Chaucer's *Troilus* and Guillaume de Machaut,'
MLN, XXX, 1915, 69.

flexibility in his employment of Boethian counsellors elsewhere—the dreamer in *The Book of the Duchess*, the eagle in *The House of Fame*, and Theseus in 'The Knight's Tale'—probably also owes something to Machaut's innovation in *Remede de Fortune* as well as to the *Roman de la Rose*.

In the *Dit de la Fonteinne amoureuse* Machaut formalizes the complaint and comfort pattern found in the narrative of *Remede de Fortune*; *Fonteinne* has a lengthy separate complaint at the beginning, and towards the end there is a substantial balancing 'Comfort de l'Amant et de la dame' with the same distinctive stanzaic form. The poem begins with the narrator overhearing the lover's complaint; he laments his impending separation from his beloved, and bemoans the fact that she does not even know of his love. Recalling the story of Seys and Alcyone, he wishes that Morpheus would help him as he helped Alcyone. The narrator records the complaint, then walks out and introduces himself to the lover, who turns out to be a prince. The two go to a park where they sleep beside a wonderful fountain and dream the same dream. In it Venus brings the prince's beloved to him who gives him many kisses and words of comfort; when they awake the prince's suffering has been assuaged.

An acrostic near the beginning of *Fonteinne amoureuse* identifies the lover-prince as the Duke of Berry; the occasion obviously was the enforced separation of the Duke from his new wife in 1361 under the terms of the Treaty of Brétigny. When Chaucer came to write *The Book of the Duchess* he evidently recognized that the central situation in Machaut's work supplied an appropriate model for his own poem designed to comfort a ducal patron on separation from his wife, caused in this case by death. His presentation of John of Gaunt in *The Book of the Duchess* as a complaining lover-knight follows Machaut's poetic presentation of the Duke. Also recalling the French poem is the conception of the narrator as a droll figure who overhears the lover's complaint and comes forward to offer comfort though he has not been previously acquainted with the lover. In addition *Fonteinne amoureuse* suggested the Seys and Alcyone exemplum which Chaucer narrates very much as Machaut does for much the same ostensible reason.[1]

The elaborate complaints which Machaut inserted in both *Remede de Fortune* and *Fonteinne amoureuse* exerted an important influence on

[1] See James I. Wimsatt, 'The Sources of Chaucer's "Seys and Alcyone,"' *Medium Aevum*, XXXVI, 1968, 231–41.

Chaucer's planning of several poems. The Black Knight's complaint, though short, is a separate composition which prompts the comforter to come forward. In addition Chaucer places quite elaborate separate complaints within the stories in *Complaint unto Pity, Complaint of Mars,* and *Anelida and Arcite.* It seems probable to me furthermore that had Anelida's poem been finished her complaint would have resulted in comfort being provided, probably in a separate 'Comfort' spoken by the loved one, as in *Fonteinne amoureuse.*[1] A similar story pattern might be predicted for the incomplete 'Squire's Tale'; we are explicitly told that the unfortunate falcon, whose story and complaint are quite reminiscent of *Anelida* and in turn of the French *dits,* will eventually be comforted.

Machaut was Chaucer's most forceful model for inserting lyrics in narrative poems. Aside from the complaints mentioned two of his finest short poems are intercalated in longer works: the roundel in *The Parliament of Fowls* (ll. 680–92), and the balade in the Prologue to *The Legend* (F, 249–69). The structures too of Chaucer's lyrics, both separate and inserted, follow forms fixed by Machaut. Of great importance, in addition, is the inspiration that Machaut's shorter poems provided for Chaucer's narrative verse forms: the rhyme royal stanza has a precedent in the large number of Machaut balades which use the seven-line ababbcc form; and several of Machaut's individual complaints are among the few significant predecessors of Chaucer's decasyllabic couplets.[2]

Machaut's influence is also found in important elements of style beyond the mechanics of versification. The musical quality of the roundel in *The Parliament,* for instance, savours of Machaut's influence. Indeed with many of the passages in Chaucer's poetry where the lyric quality dominates, contemporary French influence is strongly suggested. For example, even if one did not know that Antigone's song in *Troilus* was inspired by a lay of Machaut, he might well intuit the fact. Throughout the song one feels a subordination of sense to melody without concomitant degeneration into nonsense, as in the last stanza:

> *'But I with al myn herte and al my myght,*
> *As I have seyd, wol love unto my laste,*

[1] I develop this point in an essay, '*Anelida and Arcite*: A Narrative of Complaint and Comfort,' *Chaucer Review,* V, 1970, 1–8.

[2] Machaut's lyrics are edited by V. F. Chichmaref, *Guillaume de Machaut: Poesies lyriques,* 2 vol, Paris 1909.

> *My deere herte, and al myn owen knyght,*
> *In which myn herte growen is so faste,*
> *And his in me, that it shal evere laste.*
> *Al dredde I first to love hym to bigynne,*
> *Now woot I wel, ther is no peril inne.'*   (II, 869–75)

With these lines one might contrast the dialectic spirit of the 'Canticus Troili' of Book I, adapted from a sonnet of Petrarch. The first stanza sets the tone:

> *'If no love is, O God, what fele I so?*
> *And if love is, what thing and which is he?*
> *If love be good, from whennes cometh my woo?*
> *If it be wikke, a wonder thynketh me,*
> *When every torment and adversite*
> *That cometh of hym, may to me savory thinke,*
> *For ay thurst I, the more that ich it drynke.'*   (I, 400–6)

The French-inspired lyric element found in *Troilus* is a notable factor in distinguishing the poem from the *Filostrato*.[1]

Other aspects of Chaucer's style—diction, syntax, use of rhyme—also were affected by his French models, more than is commonly thought. D. S. Brewer and others have rightly asserted the importance of the English romance tradition to Chaucer's style. Brewer shows particularly how the first twenty lines of *The Book of the Duchess* are imbued with a native romance character.[2] Passages throughout the poem are susceptible to comparable demonstration ('There was a king / That highte Seys, and had a wyf, / The beste that mighte bere lyf.') It is a paradox that *The Book of the Duchess*, pervasively informed with French antecedents, strongly sounds the English note. Nevertheless, as Joseph Mersand finds, the proportion of Romance words in Chaucer's works increased significantly after *The Book of the Duchess*.[3] We know also that his versification became more regular in line with Continental practice. It thus seems reasonable

[1] I do not mean to imply, of course, that lyricism is absent from Boccaccio's work; Chaucer's lyricism in *Troilus*, nevertheless, is often of a different quality.

[2] 'The Relationship of Chaucer to the English and European Traditions,' in *Chaucer and Chaucerians*, ed D. S. Brewer, Alabama 1966, esp. pp. 1–15.

[3] *Chaucer's Romance Vocabulary*, Brooklyn 1937. Mersand summarizes his conclusions, pp. 137–8.

to hypothesize that his style in general increasingly incorporated Continental influences, that assimilation of diverse stylistic traits, including the French, played a continuing part in his development as an artist. A comparison of the opening of *The House of Fame* with the beginning of one of Machaut's medium-length *dits*, the *Dit de la fleur de lis et de la Marguerite*, helps to substantiate this suggestion.

In all likelihood Machaut wrote *Lis et Marguerite* to promote the marriage of Philippe of Burgundy with Marguerite of Flanders in 1369.[1] Its 415 lines are mostly taken up with the lover-narrator's celebration of his lady's beauty and virtue; he first compares her at some length to the lily, and then similarly demonstrates her likeness to the marguerite. The evidence is not conclusive that Chaucer knew *Lis et Marguerite*, though it seems highly probable. Perhaps the most important of the French Marguerite poems, it provides numerous close analogues to the discussion of the daisy in the Prologue to *The Legend*; most notably it supplies a unique precedent for Alceste's daisy-like costume.[2] The opening of *Lis et Marguerite* also has interesting similarities in substance and syntax to the beginning of the Prologue. More striking correspondence, however, is found with *The House of Fame*.

The House of Fame opens with the exclamation, 'God turne us every drem to goode!' and continues with a loosely-constructed fifty-one line sentence. Machaut's poem similarly begins with a heroic sentence, his being thirty-four lines long. The sentences of both poets treat the possibilities of determining the hidden causes of natural phenomena; whereas Machaut speculates on the nature of flowers, Chaucer deals with dreams. Additionally suggestive of Machaut are the feminine and complex rhymes which run through Chaucer's sentence, twenty of the rhyme words having distinctively French endings: -iouns, -acles, -aunce, -ions, -esse, -ious, -ures.

Similarities in syntax between these sentences provide additional evidence that Chaucer was experimenting with a French manner using a French model. Machaut starts with a ten-line clause in which an infinitive phrase leads to multiple parallel subordinate clauses:

[1] For the occasion of *Lis et Marguerite*, see James I. Wimsatt, *The Marguerite Poetry of Guillaume de Machaut*, Univ. of North Carolina Studies in the Romance Langs. and Lits., No. 87, Chapel Hill 1970, pp. 50–9. Quotations of the poem are from the edition therein, pp. 15–26.

[2] See *The Marguerite Poetry of Machaut*, pp. 30–5.

> *Qui saroit parler proprement*
> *Des couleurs et le jugement*
> *Faire des fleurs et des flourettes,*
> *Pour quoy les unes sont blanchettes,*
> *L'autre est jaune, l'autre est percette,*
> *L'autre ynde, l'autre vermillette,*
> *N'i a celle qui n'ait verdour*
> *En esté et diverse odour,*
> *Ou qui n'ait ou greinne ou semence,*
> *Ce seroit moult belle science. . . .*   (ll. 1–10)

[He who could speak correctly of colours and make judgments about large and small flowers, as to why some are white, another is yellow, another is light blue, another dark blue, another red, nor are there any which lack verdure in summer and different perfumes, or which have neither pollen nor seed, this would be very fine learning. . . .]

To this series of unanswerable speculations we may compare Chaucer's puzzlement over the causes of dreams, which he expresses in a sequence of relative 'whys':

> *And why th'effect folweth of somme,*
> *And of somme hit shal never come;*
> *Why that is an avisioun*
> *And this a revelacioun,*
> *Why this a drem, why that a sweven,*
> *And noght to every man lyche even;*
> *Why this a fantome, why these oracles,*
> *I not. . . .*   (ll. 5–12)

Machaut and Chaucer both follow their questioning with complex adversative clauses expressing scepticism that even the sages could find answers to the problems presented:

> *Mais je ne congnois creature*
> *Qui tant des secrez de nature*
> *Sache, qui me sceust aprendre*
> *Pour quoy c'est ne la cause rendre,*
> *Comment que c'est chose certeinne*
> *Que pluseurs s'en sont mis en peinne*

> *Et fait tout leur pooir sans feindre,*
> *Mais onques ne poient ateindre*
> *Ad ce que la chose sceue*
> *Fust clerement et congneue. . . .*   (ll. 11–20)

[But I don't know anyone who knows so much of nature's secrets, who could teach me why or explain the cause, although it is certain that many have troubled themselves about it and done all they could without stint, but never could they manage to make the thing clearly known and understood.]

> *. . . but whoso of these miracles*
> *The causes knoweth bet then I,*
> *Devyne he; for I certeinly*
> *Ne kan hem noght, ne never thinke*
> *To besily my wyt to swinke,*
> *To knowe of hir signifiaunce*
> *The gendres, neyther the distaunce*
> *Of tymes of hem, ne the causes,*
> *Or why this more then that cause is. . . .*   (ll. 12–20)

Particularly noticeable throughout these involved sentences is the poets' use of run-on lines.

Toward the end of the sentences both narrators again profess mental inadequacy: Geffrey concludes, 'But why the cause is, noght wot I' (l. 52), while Machaut's narrator states, 'Et comment que moult petit vaille / Tel scens com Nature me baille. . . .' (ll. 24–5) ['And although such sense as Nature grants me is worth very little. . . .']. Subsequently, of course, the poems deal with quite different subject matter, and the styles are appropriately diverse. The similarities found in these passages nevertheless show Chaucer experimenting with a French model in style as well as in substance, and producing what seems to me a successful and characteristic effect. It is not, as in much of *The Book of the Duchess*, a case of adapting French material to a stylistic matrix which is essentially English, but rather of incorporating a style modelled at the most basic levels on the French.

Machaut, poetic descendant of Guillaume de Lorris, thus was directly influential on Chaucer in numerous ways. His *dits* provided the main basis for the stories in *The Book of the Duchess* and *The Legend of Good*

Women and for important aspects of the narratives in works like *Anelida and Arcite*. They supplied a precedent for Chaucer's confinement of personification to the diction while repeatedly using Guillaume de Lorris' love story, and a model for the semi-idealized characters of lovers and ladies in works such as *The Book of the Duchess, The Legend, Troilus* and 'The Knight's Tale'. Again, the separate complaints found in several Chaucer poems are greatly indebted to Machaut, as is the Boethian situation involving complainer and comforter that has pivotal importance in *The Book of the Duchess* and *Troilus*. In a more general way Machaut's lyrics supplied models in form and tone for Chaucer's shorter poems and for lyric passages and versification in his longer works. Even on the most basic levels of style Machaut was a major influence. Finally, perhaps Machaut's most important contribution was in supplying the main precedent for Chaucer's comic narrator, a key figure in establishing the tone of the greater part of his imaginative works who in turn provided a chief model for the individualization of the narrators in *The Canterbury Tales*.

These factors, taken together with those previously discussed in which the direct influence of Guillaume de Lorris is apparent, show the combined effect of Machaut and Guillaume on Chaucer's poetry to be of tremendous significance. If one also counts the contributions of works composed in Machaut's modes by Froissart, Granson, and Deschamps, the total is even more impressive. But it would still not have been possible to see Chaucer as basically a product and a continuator of the French tradition of love poetry, which is the way Deschamps' balade represents him, if it were not for the model of Jean de Meun.

Jean's continuation of the *Roman de la Rose* is over four times as long as Guillaume's part. Though none of Chaucer's translation of Jean's portion seems to have survived, he clearly rendered at least some of it into English: the 'heresy' for which the God of Love arraigns Chaucer in *The Legend of Good Women* originates in Jean's part. Chaucer, moreover, incorporated into his works material drawn directly from all parts of Jean's poem. His borrowings, of which Fansler documents several hundred,[1] are strong testimony to Jean's impressive and unique influence on the English poet.

Jean's continuation is comprised mostly of monologues and dialogues involving the Amant, Reason, Friend, False Seeming, the Duenna, Nature, and Genius. The performances of various of these provide the

[1] See esp. Fansler's table, pp. 262–9.

primary inspiration for some of Chaucer's most important characterizations: Pandarus, who combines the functions and personal traits of Friend and the Duenna, and sometimes poses as Reason; the Wife of Bath, whose character and manner find important precedents in the Duenna and the monologue of Friend; and the Pardoner, a lineal descendant of False Seeming. Chaucer also made significant use of Jean's poem for the Prioress, the Merchant, and the Friar. Jean was influential in manifold other respects. We might cite especially the conversational exchanges between Amant and Reason, and Amant and Friend as providing the best model for dialogues in Chaucer like those between the Dreamer and the Black Knight in *The Book of the Duchess*, and between the eagle and Geffrey in *The House of Fame*. Chaucer also used stories in Jean's work for two of the Monk's tragedies and for 'The Physician's Tale'; and Jean suggested numerous of the short exempla and classical references in the English poet's works. As important as these and other contributions that Jean made are, however, his most significant influence on Chaucer's development probably lies in his immense widening of the range of the love poet.

Guillaume de Lorris' subject is a polite love that appealed to the tastes of a courtly society, quite like the love which troubadours and trouvères had celebrated for generations. It involves the passion of a well-bred young man for a beautiful girl whom a coquettish nature and jealous guardians make virtually inaccessible. When Jean takes over the story, he widens its scope to the point that he could aptly term the work a 'Mirror for Lovers' (l. 10651)—an encyclopaedic treatment of the subject of love.

Reason's discussions with Amant which open Jean's section broaden the concerns of the story to include various kinds of love that contrast with Guillaume's love *par amour*: non-carnal love of woman, Christian love, true friendship, and friendship with Fortune. The next two main speakers, Friend and the old Duenna, deal with the practical aspects of sexual love, dispensing to Amant and Fair Welcome pragmatic advice on how to obtain desired results—how to flatter the gossips, to bribe the lady's attendants, to attract men by acting with refinement, to keep lovers on the string, and so forth. Often drawn from Ovid, theirs is advice appropriate to Ovid's treatises on love. Friend also gives his ideas on marriage, which he notes is often the issue of the love affair even though it entails the lady's abdication of mastery. In the subsequent confession of Nature, the character of the speaker as the creative force informing all matter and the binding force which unites the elements and all creatures makes relevant to the main subject such diverse topics as creation, optics, dreams, alchemy, true nobility, death, and the weather. Finally, Genius in his own peculiar way treats of sin and virtue, Heaven and Hell. In Jean's poem thus virtually the whole of creation is subsumed to the subject of love; he showed Chaucer how a poet could be a writer of great diversity while remaining essentially a love poet.

As early as *The House of Fame* Chaucer found in Jean a model for diversifying his poetry of love. Neither Guillaume de Lorris nor Machaut would have found in Fame appropriate matter for a love *dit*. Nor do Chaucer's chief sources for the poem provide a precedent: Nicole de Margival's *Panthère d'Amours* deals only with subjects appropriate to polite love, and Dante's *Divine Comedy* and Boethius' *Consolation* are not love poems. Only in the light of Jean's work can we understand in what real sense the events and sights of *The House of Fame* provide Geffrey with the tidings of love that the eagle promises. The subject which Chaucer's poem explores, Fame, could likewise have supplied material to several of Jean's speakers—to Reason, to Friend, and particularly to Nature. In Jean de Meun's poem of love, as in no other, Fame could find many relevancies.

With *The Parliament of Fowls*, too, while the figure of Nature is only secondarily derived from the *Roman*, Jean's work surely is Chaucer's primary precedent for including in a love poem the diverse attitudes expressed in the birds' assembly concerning the choice of a mate, and indeed for the multiple and contrasting varieties of love and attitudes toward it which form the substance of the whole work.

The diverse approaches to love found in *Troilus* also seem inspired by Jean as well as by Boccaccio. The pragmatism of Pandarus and the hypocrisy of Diomede, both outside the scope of Guillaume de Lorris, find valid counterparts in the poem of Jean de Meun. And while most of Troilus' sentiments accord beautifully with those of Guillaume's Amant, it is only in the confession of Jean's Nature that one can find a Boethian disquisition on Fate and Free Will subsumed under the subject of love (ll. 17059–17874). Nature's confession also supplies a fine precedent for relating the cosmic concord of planets and elements to the human love which Venus promotes, a connection that is made much of in Book III of

Troilus, most notably in the Invocation and in Troilus' prayer at the end of the book:

> '*Love, that of erthe and se hath governaunce,*
> *Love, that his hestes hath in hevenes hye,*
> *Love, that with an holsom alliaunce*
> *Halt peples joyned, as hym lest hem gye. . . .*' (III, 1744–47)

Human love is presented as simply part of the universal order.

The puzzling epilogue of *Troilus*, in addition, finds a significant parallel in Jean's poem. Just as Troilus from his vantage point in the eighth sphere of Heaven looks down and despises 'this wrecched world' (V, 1817), so Genius near the end of the *Roman* contrasts the unchanging Shepherd's Park with the mutable Garden of Mirth that provides the world of the poem. Both poets thus supply explicit criticism of the aims and ideals of the lovers.

Deschamps wrote the lyric celebrating Chaucer as England's poet of love some time in the 1380s, perhaps after the composition of both *Troilus* and *The Legend*, but no doubt before the plan of *The Canterbury Tales* had been conceived. The scope of the love poet as Deschamps evidently conceived it nevertheless also embraces the heterogeneous content of Chaucer's masterwork. At the centre of the *Tales* is the disparate society of the pilgrimage operating under the benevolent rule of a chosen leader, the Host, who is united even with the least, the Pardoner, by a kiss of peace. Tales of love and marriage dominate the story-telling, and there is much of blood-brotherhood (if mostly bad), and of the holy love of saints and martyrs. Even the materials peripheral to the subject fit nicely under the tent of a love poet with the scope of Jean de Meun: the Monk's recitation of Fortune's victims has counterparts in Reason's preachment about Fortune; Jean's introduction to Nature's monologue is a companion to the Canon Yeoman's discussion of alchemy. At the end of the *Tales* the Parson's sermon, calling all to the celestial pilgrimage, and Chaucer's retraction present further parallels to Genius' exposition of the Shepherd's Park which condemns the activities that take up most of the *Roman de la Rose*. Both the Parson and the retraction censure the 'worldly vanitees' with which much the greater part of the *Tales* is concerned.

This is not to say that *The Canterbury Tales* is a French love poem. It is to say that a fourteenth-century French poet could have seen it as legitimately contained within his tradition, and to assert further that the tradition imparts to the bulk of Chaucer's work, including the *Tales*, an important element of coherence.

Ironically, the work of Deschamps himself, whatever he thought of it, could not be gathered as definitely under the rubric 'Love Poetry'. In his work there is a large body of short love lyrics in the manner of Machaut; and there is the *Miroir de Mariage*, eleven thousand lines of an unfinished allegorical treatise mostly directed against marriage, the whole being an inventive derivative of—among other things—the disquisitions of Jean de Meun's Friend and Reason. Such works fit easily into the tradition. But there is also a mass of historical, topographical, domestic, and otherwise topical pieces, many of which are acute and lively but which have no collective centre. The poet in Deschamps, as Muscatine says, is second to the journalist.[1]

The sum of Chaucer's debt to him is not great. Important, though not essential materials for the Wife of Bath and the Merchant were found in the *Miroir*. The alleged use of the *Lai de Franchise* for the Prologue to *The Legend* is doubtful.[2] Some of Chaucer's later lyrics, the envoys to Scogan and Bukton and *Lak of Stedfastnesse*, strongly suggest Deschamps in their topicality and use of the envoy, but even in these Chaucer keeps to the territory of the love poet; he is in no danger of lapsing into Deschamps' journalism.

The influence of Deschamps' work on Chaucer's poetry, then, like that of the other French poets with whom Chaucer had rather certain personal contact—Froissart and Granson—is not of primary importance. It was the older and more original poetry of Machaut and the authors of the *Roman de la Rose* that made the essential French contribution to his work. The only body of literature of more basic influence on Chaucer than their writings is the corpus of English literary materials, both oral and written, that was an integral part of Chaucer's quotidian experience. This corpus is much less susceptible to definition and classification than the French works that Chaucer used. It includes chivalric romances and other native poetry, to be sure, but also the sententious discourses of professional men, the colourful tales and anecdotes of friends and acquaintances, the sermons and other vernacular presentations of the

[1] Muscatine, p. 101.

[2] See Marian Lossing, 'The Prologue to the *Legend of Good Women* and the *Lai de Franchise*,' *SP*, XXXIX, 1942, 15–35.

clergy, and even ordinary conversations in which Chaucer discerned formal properties and thence derived literary values. These supplied components in Chaucer's work that may most appropriately be ident-ified as 'native', though in many cases they are the same as what is called 'bourgeois' or realistic'.

Muscatine eloquently expounds Chaucer's work as an increasingly successful integration of the courtly and the realistic, opposed elements exemplified respectively by Guillaume de Lorris and Jean de Meun. A modification of this view, however, is implicit in the analysis offered in this essay. Particularly as reflected in Chaucer's work, the poems of Guil-laume and Jean occupy common and contiguous, rather than opposing, areas of the poetic sphere. Numerous 'courtly' passages in Chaucer may be traced to Jean; for instance, in *The Book of the Duchess* Jean inspires the lovely lines about Flora and Zephirus who oversee the countless flowers of the garden (ll. 402–9). Guillaume de Lorris, at the same time, is a model for much 'realistic' irony. Under Guillaume's guidance, the reader observes Amant with an arch smile, while Chaucer similarly inspires an ironic attitude toward such of his lovers as Aurelius and Damian, and Palamon and Arcite. The subject matter and style of the poets of the *Roman*, and likewise of Machaut, overlap; and where they do not overlap they are in large part complementary—all three are con-cerned with the great subject of Amour.

Without denying the demonstrated value of Muscatine's theory, I would propose as potentially more significant an hypothesis that Chaucer's poetry presents from the beginning an interplay between English and Gallic elements, the latter supplemented importantly by the Italian. Such interaction of the native and the Continental is perhaps more apparent in the work of other Middle English poets—in *The Owl and the Nightingale, Pearl,* or *Sir Gawain and the Green Knight*—but I think it is not less effective in Chaucer. Blanche and Criseyde, the Eagle and the Rooster, Alison and the Prioress find origins in both traditions, and the combining of them contributes integrally to the complexity and fascination of these figures and the works in which they participate.

Extensive testing of this hypothesis would serve, I believe, to substan-tiate the fundamental importance that I have attributed to the French poets' contributions to Chaucer's work. It could not, of course, negate the significance of numerous other influences. Chaucer may be de-scribed, in Deschamps' words, as a Socrates, a Seneca, and an Ovid; he may also be thought of as a Dante, a Virgil, and a Boccaccio. Nevertheless, at bottom it is his 'translation' and integration of the French tradition into English literature that merits for him the title of God of Love in Albion.

6: Chaucer and the Latin Classics

BRUCE HARBERT

> There saugh I stonden, out of drede,
> Upon an yren piler strong . . .
> The Tholosan that highte Stace,
> That bar of Thebes up the fame
> Upon his shuldres, and the name
> Also of cruel Achilles.
> And by him stood, withouten les,
> Ful wonder hy on a piler
> Of yren, he, the gret Omer;
> And with him Dares and Tytus
> Before, and eke he Lollius,
> And Guydo eke de Columpnis,
> And Englyssh Gaufride eke, ywis;
> And ech of these, as have I joye,
> Was besy for to bere up Troye.
>
> (*The House of Fame* 1456–72)

CHAUCER'S VISION in the House of Fame shows two ancient poets, Statius and Homer, with a crowd of later writers, all of whom share the task of 'bearing up' the fame of the ancient world. 'Tytus' (Dictys Cretensis) is from the fourth century, Dares from the sixth, 'Englyssh Gaufride' (Geoffrey of Monmouth) from the twelfth, and Guido de Columpnis from the thirteenth. All of them treated the story of Troy in Latin prose. Chaucer believed 'Lollius' also to have been the author of a book about Troy. (The error is due to a misreading of a line of Horace quoted by John of Salisbury.)[1]

---

[1] R. A. Pratt, 'A note on Chaucer's Lollius', *MLN* LXV, 1950, 183–7.

This vision illustrates the fact that Chaucer did not make the sharp distinction between 'classical' and 'medieval' to which we are accustomed. Many medieval writers decried the ancient world for its paganism, and regarded study of it as unbecoming to Christians. Chaucer adopts this stance for a moment at the close of *Troilus and Criseyde*:

> *Lo here, of payens corsed olde rites,*
> *Lo here, what alle hire goddes may availle;*
> *Lo here, thise wrecched worldes appetites;*
> *Lo here, the fyn and guerdoun for travaille*
> *Of Jove, Appollo, of Mars, of swich rascaille!*
>
> (TC, V, 1849–53)

But the prevailing attitude was ambivalent, and in spite of their paganism the classical poets were regarded as supreme in their art,[1] a view of which Chaucer again gives us an example in the *envoi* (itself modelled on Statius) to *Troilus and Criseyde*, a few lines earlier than the passage just quoted:

> *But litel book, no makyng thow n'envie,*
> *But subgit be to alle poesye;*
> *And kis the steppes, where as thow seest pace*
> *Virgile, Ovide, Omer, Lucan and Stace.*
>
> (TC, V, 1789–92)

However, while the ancient authors were accorded priority of respect as poets, as sources of information about the past their authority was only regarded as equal to that of more recent writers. So whereas to us it seems natural that such a book as this should contain one chapter on classical literature and a separate one on medieval Latin, Chaucer himself might have been surprised.

It is important to realize from the beginning that the Latin classics did not come to Chaucer as they come to us. We read them in printed texts based on the comparison of a number of manuscripts, and often furnished with explanatory notes drawing on a strong tradition of accurate scholarship. A medieval reader usually had to rely on a single manuscript, which might be full of corrupt readings and have sections of the text

[1] For the canon of classical authors in the Middle Ages, see E. R. Curtius (tr W. Trask), *European Literature and the Latin Middle Ages*, New York 1953, 247–64 and J. A. W. Bennett, *Chaucer's Book of Fame*, Oxford 1968, 138.

missing. Any explanatory matter that the manuscript contained would be written in the margins or between the lines of the text, and might be sparse or inaccurate. As an example of the way in which the classics were available to fourteenth-century readers, I shall examine a single manuscript from that century. I do not suggest that Chaucer knew this manuscript—there is no evidence whatever to suggest that he did—but I introduce it because it illustrates several of the ways in which medieval copies of the Latin classics differed from modern ones.

MS Auct. F.1.17 in the Bodleian Library at Oxford was written in England in the early fourteenth century. It is a large book, with 305 leaves of parchment measuring roughly 14″ by 11″. It is filled entirely with Latin poetry, written in a regular, formal hand with two columns to the page. There are some coloured titles and initials, but no pictures. The main items that it contains are as follows:

(i) *Liber Parabolarum* by Alan of Lille (12th century), to whom Chaucer refers in *The Parliament of Fowls* l. 316.

(ii) *Tobias* by Matthew of Vendôme (12th century), a versification of the book of Tobit.

(iii) Vergil's *Eclogues* and *Georgics*.

(iv) A miscellaneous collection of poems attributed to Marbod of Rennes (12th century).

(v) A number of poems falsely attributed to Vergil, and some epitaphs on Vergil.

(vi) Vergil's *Aeneid*, each book prefaced by a brief medieval verse summary of its action. The manuscript wrongly attributes these summaries to Ovid.

(vii) *Poetria Nova* by Geoffrey of Vinsauf (13th century): a treatise on rhetoric very widely read in medieval England.

(viii) Ovid's *Heroides*, followed by a medieval verse-epistle purporting to be from Deidamia to Achilles: the manuscript leaves no gap between this and the genuine *Heroides*, and so implies that it, too, is by Ovid.

(ix) Ovid's *Epistulae ex Ponto* (lacking the first sixty verses, for which a space has been left in the manuscript), *Amores, Ars Amatoria, Tristia* (lacking most of the fourth and all of the fifth book), and *Metamorphoses.*

(x) Sedulius' *Carmen Paschale* (5th century), an epic poem on the miracles of the Old and New Testaments.

(xi) Prudentius' *Psychomachia* (4th century), an allegorical poem, highly influential in the Middle Ages, on the conflict of vice and virtue.

    This manuscript illustrates many features of the copies of classical authors that were available to Chaucer and his contemporaries. Firstly, the canon of the classical authors was insecure, as we can see from the misattributions to Vergil in (v) and to Ovid in (vi) and (viii). Secondly, the texts are incomplete, as in (ix), where large parts of Ovid are missing. (The scribe seems to have known that the *Epistulae ex Ponto* were incomplete, since he left space for the missing verses, but he did not find a manuscript from which to copy them.) Thirdly, glosses appear sporadically throughout the manuscript, written between the lines of poetry, designed to help the reader construe the Latin. Some pages are thick with glosses, while others have none at all. Fourthly, the texts of all the poems are scattered with corrupt readings. Fifthly, poems from the first, fourth, fifth, twelfth and thirteenth centuries appear in the same collection.

    Chaucer himself describes a manuscript which, like this one, mixes medieval with classical authors. The Wife of Bath tells us of Jankyn, her fifth husband:

> He hadde a book that gladly, nyght and day,
> For his desport he wolde rede alway;
> He cleped it *Valerie* and *Theofraste*,
> At which book he lough alwey ful faste.
> And eek ther was somtyme a clerk at Rome,
> A cardinal, that highte Seint Jerome,
> That made a book agayn Jovinian;
> In which book eek ther was Tertulan,
> Crisippus, Trotula, and Helowys,
> That was abbesse nat fer fro Parys;
> And eek the Parables of Salomon,
> Ovides Art, and bookes many on,
> And alle thise were bounden in o volume.

> (CT, III, 669–81)

    Here stand together the Bible ('Salomon'), Greek Prose ('Theofraste'—the *De Nuptiis* of Theophrastus (fourth and third centuries B.C.), known to the Middle Ages in Latin translation), classical Latin poetry (Ovid), Church Fathers (Tertullian and Jerome), an eleventh-century medical writer (Trotula), Heloise and Walter Map (author of the *Epistola Valerii*, Jankyn's 'Valerie'), both from the twelfth century, and one name, Crisippus, that cannot be identified.

The fact that so wide a range of authors was available to Chaucer makes it more difficult for us to identify the sources of his knowledge about ancient history and mythology. Details which modern readers most readily associate with a classical author may have come to Chaucer from a medieval source. One example will illustrate this: the story of Ariadne in *The Legend of Good Women*. Here, Chaucer borrows from both of Ovid's treatments of the story, in the *Metamorphoses* and the *Heroides*. But Chaucer's version contains elements that are in neither of these, most of which can be paralleled in the Italian translation of the *Heroides*, which Chaucer is known to have used.[1] Some, however, can be paralleled in two other works which he is known to have read: the *Ovide Moralisé* and Machaut's *Jugement du Roi de Navarre*. Moreover, there are anonymous glosses to Ovid which agree with Chaucer in some of his deviations from the classical source. Clearly, it is impossible to tell his source for every detail in his own version, since so many models were available to him.   *→ influence of Ovid remains clear*

[margin: not CT an but le example]

Only when Chaucer unmistakably translates from a classical poet can we be sure that he had read him. When he writes:

> *O Juvenal, lord! trewe is thy sentence,*
> *That litel wyten folk what is to yerne*
> *That they ne fynde in hire desir offence;*
> *For cloude of errour lat hem nat discerne*
> *What best is,*
>
> (TC, IV, 197–201)

the source is plainly Juvenal *Satire* X, 2–4:

> *pauci dinoscere possunt*
> *uera bona atque illis multum diuersa, remota*
> *erroris nebula,*

but this does not imply that he had read the whole of Juvenal. There were available many collections of excerpts from the classics, called *florilegia*. It may have been in such a book that Chaucer found these lines.

[1] S. B. Meech, 'Chaucer and an Italian translation of the *Heroides*', *PMLA* XLV, 1930, 110–28.

In fourteenth-century England, knowledge of the classics was spread by the teaching and writing of the friars, some of whom used to pepper their theological works with classical allusions.[1] Thus, as Miss Smalley suggests, they educated Chaucer's audience, albeit unsystematically, and they may have educated Chaucer himself by extending his knowledge of the classics. One of these friars, John of Wales, wrote a handbook of moral instruction scattered with classical tags called the *Communiloquium*, which may have been known to Chaucer himself. Although Chaucer often refers to Seneca and shows knowledge of his work, especially in 'The Wife of Bath's Tale', R. A. Pratt has shown[2] that all the passages of Seneca that Chaucer uses were quoted by John of Wales in the *Communiloquium*. Chaucer may have known Seneca only from this source, and not at first hand.

We therefore encounter many problems if we try to make a list of the classical works that Chaucer read. In the past, scholars have been too ready to trace a detail in Chaucer to an ancient source, and the extent of his classical knowledge has, I believe, been overestimated. He must, of course, have read more than the passages he actually translates, for it is improbable that he translated every piece of classical writing that he knew, but we cannot know the extent of this 'unrecorded' reading. With these reservations in mind, let us ask how much classical Latin literature we can be certain that Chaucer read.

Of Cicero, he gives clear evidence only of knowing the *Somnium Scipionis*, which is the end of the *De Re Publica*, and which he read together with the commentary of Macrobius. The story of Scipio's dream is told at the beginning of *The Parliament of Fowls* (31ff.), and material from Macrobius' commentary is used in Pertelote's discussion of dreams in 'The Nun's Priest's Tale' (CT, VII, 2923ff.). The story of the two travellers told by Chauntecleer (CT, VII, 2984ff.) is found in Cicero's *De Divinatione*, but Chaucer may equally well have taken it from a medieval writer such as Holcot or Gerald of Wales, both of whom tell it.

The evidence that Chaucer had read Livy is thin. In *The Legend of Good Women* he attributes the story of Lucrece to *Ovyde and Titus Lyvius* (l.

[1] B. Smalley, *English Friars and Antiquity in the early Fourteenth Century*, Oxford 1960.

[2] R. A. Pratt, 'Chaucer and the hand that fed him', *Speculum* XLI, 1966, 619–42.

1683), but bases his version on Ovid. Only one element in Chaucer's narrative which is found in Livy but not in Ovid—the arguments of Lucrece's friends that she is not to blame for having lost her maidenhood —suggests that he might have used Livy as well. Similarly, the Physician's tale of Virginia, although Chaucer names Livy as an authority, is based on the version in the *Roman de la Rose*. Chaucer agrees with Livy against the *Roman* in saying that Virginia's father was absent when she was brought to trial, but this is not enough to establish conclusively that Chaucer was borrowing from Livy direct.

Chaucer frequently mentions *Catoun*, but he did not know the genuine works of Cato. He is referring to the *Disticha Catonis*, a collection of moral epigrams which was composed in the fourth century A.D., but was believed in the Middle Ages to be by Cato. The *Disticha* were widely used as elementary Latin reading matter, and it is very likely that Chaucer read them at school. He uses ignorance of the *Disticha* as an index of poor education in 'The Miller's Tale', saying of the Carpenter:

> He knew nat Catoun, for his wit was rude.
>
> (CT, I, 3227)

These lines in 'The Man of Law's Tale' seem at first sight to imply that Chaucer knew Lucan:

> Noght trowe I the triumphe of Julius,
> Of which that Lucan maketh swich a boost,
> Was roialler ne moore curius
> Than was th' assemblee of this blisful hoost.
>
> (CT, II, 400–3)

In fact, Lucan, far from describing a triumph of Caesar, says explicitly that he did not have one. A triumph is described, however, in the French version of Lucan by Jehan de Tuim.[1] So there is no evidence that Chaucer knew Lucan directly, but he may have read him in this French translation.

He had certainly read some Statius. *Anelida and Arcite* 22–42 has clear verbal parallels with *Thebaid* XII, 519–35, and the description of the Temple of Mars in 'The Knight's Tale', though chiefly based on Boccaccio's *Teseida*, borrows some touches from Statius' description in *Thebaid* VII, 34–73. The passage on the necklace of Harmonia in *The*

---

[1] See Robinson's note to this passage.

Complaint of Mars 245–62 may be based on *Thebaid* II, 265ff., but there are no close verbal parallels, and it is possible that Chaucer was indebted for his information to an unidentified mythographer. Finally, in *Troilus and Criseyde* V, 1485–1510, Chaucer puts into the mouth of Cassandra a complete summary of the action of the *Thebaid*. This need not mean that he had read the whole work, since, as F. P. Magoun has demonstrated,[1] it could equally well be based on the twelve-line Latin arguments that preface each book in many manuscripts of the *Thebaid*, like the arguments to the *Aeneid* included in the manuscript described above. It is certain, then, that Chaucer knew what Statius' poem contained, and that he had read at least some of it.

Chaucer refers in four places to Claudian, three times to the *De Raptu Proserpinae* and once to the *Laus Serenae*, although there is no evidence to confirm that he had read either of these. He had certainly read the Prologue to the *De Sexto Consolatu Honorii*, from which he translates a few lines in *The Parliament of Fowles*, 99–105. R. A. Pratt has suggested that he may have known his Claudian from the *Liber Catonianus*, an anthology of Latin literature widely used as an elementary reader, which contained all of these works.[2]

He twice made substantial use of Vergil. In *The House of Fame* 143–465 he summarized the whole action of the *Aeneid*, with especial emphasis on the love of Aeneas and Dido. As in the case of the *Thebaid*, Chaucer may have relied on an epitome for his knowledge of some of Vergil's poem, but when telling the story of Dido he shows close knowledge of Books I and IV. He also tells the story of Dido in *The Legend of Good Women*, again relying heavily on Vergil, but at the end he translates eight lines from the Letter of Dido in Ovid's *Heroides*.

It was to Ovid that Chaucer owed most. His major borrowings are these:

House of Fame 1918–85 (The House of Rumour) *Metamorphoses* XII, 39–63
Book of the Duchess 62–220 (Ceyx and Alcyone) *Metamorphoses* XI, 410–728
Legend of Good Women 706–915 (Pyramus and Thisbe) *Metamorphoses* IV, 55–166

[1] F. P. Magoun, 'Chaucer's summary of *Thebaid* II–XII' *Traditio* XI, 1955, 409–20.
[2] R. A. Pratt, 'Chaucer's Claudian', Speculum XXII, 1947, 419–29.

Legend of Good Women 1355–65 (Dido's letter) *Heroides* VII, 1–8
Legend of Good Women 1680–1873 (Lucrece) *Fasti* II, 685–848
✳ *Legend of Good Women* 1894–1921 (Ariadne) *Metamorphoses* VIII, 6–182
Legend of Good Women 2185–2217 (Ariadne) *Heroides* X
✳ *Legend of Good Women* 2244–2382 (Philomela) *Metamorphoses* VI, 424–600
Legend of Good Women 2404–2554 (Phyllis) *Heroides* II
Legend of Good Women 2562–2722 (Hypermnestra) *Heroides* XIV

It is clear that Chaucer knew Ovid best among classical authors. But even in his knowledge of Ovid there are striking gaps. Although he called Ovid *Venus Clerk* (*House of Fame*, 1487), he gives no evidence of knowing the *Amores, Ars Amatoria,* or *Remedia Amoris.*

There is one important feature of medieval classical scholarship that we have not yet considered. There were available in the fourteenth century many commentaries on the classics that interpreted them allegorically. These were often copied in the margins of the texts themselves. For example, anyone who read the *Metamorphoses* in a manuscript containing the allegorizations of John of Garland, which were widely known, would find an ingenious moral interpretation of the myth of Pyramus and Thisbe: the mulberry fruit which is turned from white to black when sprinkled by the blood of the dying Pyramus signifies that the delights of love lead to death. Mr C. A. Robson has shown that Dante was familiar with such commentaries and that they influenced his treatment of Ovidian myth.[1] Although attempts have been made to demonstrate the same for Chaucer, as yet no conclusive evidence has been brought forward. More work needs to be done on this subject, but I doubt whether Chaucer will ever be shown to have been much influenced by the allegorists. He was interested in ancient stories for their own sake. In the case of the one moralization that he did certainly read—the *Ovide Moralisé*—we know that he used the parts of the work that translate direct from Ovid, but no parallels have been discovered between Chaucer and the allegorical sections. He seems to have ignored them.

The amount of classical literature that Chaucer certainly knew is, as we have seen, small. One reason for this may be simply that he did not

[1] C. A. Robson, 'Dante's use in the *Divina Commedia* of the Medieval Allegories on Ovid' in *Centenary Essays on Dante* ed C. G. Hardie, Oxford 1965, 1–38.

read classical Latin fluently. This again is something about which we cannot be sure, but since in the past it has often been assumed that Chaucer was an excellent Latinist, I give here some evidence for the opposite view. Firstly, we know that he often used translations when reading Latin—Jean de Meun's translation of Boethius, the *Ovide Moralisé* for the *Metamorphoses*, and the Italian translation of Filippo for the *Heroides*. Secondly, there are some apparent inaccuracies in his translation from Latin, of which these are two examples:

(a)   Vergil (*Aeneid* IV, 180) says that Fame was endowed with 'swift wings', *pernicibus alis*. Chaucer says of Fame:

> *And on hir fet woxen saugh y*
> *Partriches wynges redely.*   (HF, 1391–2)

Chaucer's manuscript of Vergil must have had *perdicibus*, from *perdix* 'partridge', for *pernicibus* 'swift'. *Perdicibus alis* is impossible Latin, and a good classical latinist would be able to spot the error and substitute the correct reading. It may be that Chaucer saw that his manuscript was wrong, but that his imagination was caught by the reference to partridges, and so he decided to retain it. But it is no less possible that his Latin was simply at fault.

(b)   *this was the firste morwe*
> *Of hire gladnesse, and gynning of hire sorwe.*
>
>   (LGW, 1230–1)

These lines, referring to the day when Aeneas and Dido hunt together, are based on Vergil *Aeneid* IV, 169–70:

> *ille dies primus leti primusque malorum*
> *causa fuit*

'That day was the first cause of death and sufferings'. Chaucer has misread *leti* as the genitive of *letus* 'happy' (usually so spelt in medieval manuscripts: *laetus* in modern printed texts), whereas in fact it is from *letum* 'death'. Again, it is possible that Chaucer altered Vergil deliberately, but it is equally possible that he misunderstood him. It may be, therefore, that while Chaucer's Latin was adequate for the technical language of medieval works on such subjects as astronomy or mythology, whose syntax was simple, he had difficulty with the more complex writing of classical authors.

We know nothing of Chaucer's education, although a plausible suggestion made by Edith Rickert is that he attended St. Paul's School, where he would have had access to the books bequeathed to the school by William de Toleshunt in 1328 and William Ravenstone in 1358, which contained many classical authors.[1] Knowledge of Latin was in the fourteenth century strongest among clerks, where there was a wide range of competence, extending from that of friars like John of Wales who had fluent Latin and a good knowledge of classical authors to that of the country priests who could barely construe their massbooks. That laymen could be good latinists is shown by the case of Gower, who knew Ovid's works well and himself wrote a long Latin poem. But laymen who read classical Latin cannot have been numerous, especially since learning the language was made more difficult by the absence of systematic dictionaries such as we now use.[2] Chaucer's competence in Latin lay, I suspect, in the middle range, below that of Gower.

Another striking feature about the list of Chaucer's classical borrowings is that they mostly occur early in his career, in *The Book of the Duchess* and *The House of Fame*, the stories in *The Legend of Good Women*, (which are generally agreed to have been written before their Prologue), and two stories written early but later incorporated into *The Canterbury Tales*, those of the Physician and the Manciple. None of these is among Chaucer's best work, and in them he often translates laboriously from the Latin. In *The Parliament of Fowles*, which is probably later,[3] and belongs among his great poems, he is more independent of his classical model, and summarizes Cicero rather than translating him. In *Troilus and Criseyde* and 'The Knight's Tale', classical borrowings form a far smaller proportion of the total work, and include little close translation. Chaucer may have progressively lost interest in the classics because he found reading them difficult, and was more absorbed in the French and

[1] Edith Rickert, *Chaucer's World*, 1948, 121–6.

[2] On the question of lay literacy, see M. B. Parkes, 'The Literacy of the Laity' ch. V of *Literature and Western Civilization*, ed D. Daiches and A. K. Thorlby, *II The Medieval World*, 1973.

[3] J. D. North, 'Kalendres Enlumyned ben they' *RES* N.S. XX, 1969, 270–74. North's suggestion (pp. 268–9) that the legend of Hypermnestra may be a late work is less attractive, since it seems improbable that Chaucer intended this work to be associated with a particular day.

Italian writers whom he could read more easily. He may also have found the influence of Ovid and Vergil too overpowering, so that they cramped his own initiative. He may have preferred lesser writers —Boccaccio, Machaut, Deschamps—whose material he could make his own more easily. We know that he had read at least some of the *Divine Comedy* but made little use of it. Later English writers have felt similarly overpowered by Milton.

In making these early translations from the classics Chaucer was serving his apprenticeship, and it is not surprising that we find in them some weak poetry, where he was cramped by the attempt to reconcile English metre with close translation from Latin. Ovid's couplet

> *Cingitur interea Romanis Ardea signis*
> *et patitur longas obsidione moras*
>
> (*Fasti* II, 721–2)

appears in Chaucer as four lines, of which the words in roman type are mere padding:

> *Whan Ardea beseged was aboute*
> *With Romeyns,* that ful sterne were and stoute,
> *Ful longe lay the sege, and lytel wroughten,*
> So that they were half idel, as hem thoughten;
>
> (LGW, 1694–97)

At times, Chaucer seems bored with the whole enterprise:

> *What shulde I more telle hire compleynyng?*
> *It is so long, it were an hevy thyng.*
> *In hire Epistel Naso telleth al.*   (LGW, 2218–20)

However, there are many successful moments in his translation, like the rendering of Ovid's gnomic *audentes forsque deusque iuuat* (*Fasti* II, 782) in terse, colloquial English:

> *Hap helpeth hardy man alday*   (LGW, 1773)

or the description of Venus

> *Goynge in a queynt array,*
> *As she had ben an hunteresse,*
> *With wynd blowynge upon hir tresse;*   (HF, 228–30)

whose last line is both accurate translation and vivid English poetry in its own right.

Success is often achieved by a slight deviation from the source, like the simile that Chaucer invents for the whispering of Pyramus and Thisbe through the wall that separates them,

> *a soun as softe as any shryfte* (LGW, 745)

which has no precedent in Ovid, or the picture of them saying goodnight:

> *The colde wal they wolden kysse of ston* (l. 768)

where Chaucer has achieved a greater tactile force by introducing explicit mention of *colde* and *ston*.

Often, the whole character of an episode is changed, like that of the Cave of Sleep from *Metamorphoses* XI. In Ovid's version, Juno's messenger Iris comes to the god of sleep and addresses him in a hushed, respectful voice:

> *Somne, quies rerum, placidissime, Somne, deorum*
> (*Metamorphoses* XI, 623)

Chaucer changes the messenger into a man, in keeping with medieval custom, and makes the scene boisterous and comic:

> *This messager com fleynge faste*
> *And cried, "O, ho! awake anoon!"*
> *Hit was for noght; ther herde hym non.*
> *"Awake!" quod he, "whoo ys lyth there?"*
> *And blew his horn ryght in here eere,*
> *And cried, "Awaketh!" wonder hye.*
> *This god of slep with hys oon ye*
> *Cast up, axed, "Who clepeth ther?"*
> *"Hyt am I," quod this messager.* (BD, 178–186)

Similarly, in his account of the House of Rumour (*House of Fame* 1918–85), Chaucer has depicted a more lively, earthy place than the House of Fame in Ovid, which was his model.

Let us now turn from these isolated details to study Chaucer's handling of a complete myth. In his treatment of Dido and Aeneas in *The Legend of Good Women*, we see him bringing ancient material up to date, so that it

will appeal to the taste of his own time. He excludes ancient customs that
were alien to the experience of his first readers and replaces them with
medieval ones, thus diminishing any note of strangeness that the exter-
nals of Vergil's narrative might have, which would distract a reader's
attention from the human interest of the legend.

Where Vergil's Dido sends to Aeneas' ships animals for sacrifice
(*munera laetitiamque dii, Aeneid* I, 636), Chaucer removes this pagan notion
by saying the animals are for food (l. 1093), adding a gift of wine. Similarly, Vergil's Aeneas first sees Dido enthroned in a temple dispensing
justice, but Chaucer depicts her as praying. When Aeneas is about to
leave her, Chaucer's Dido *seketh halwes* (l. 1310), that is, she visits shrines,
a common medieval devotional practice. The sinister rites described by
Vergil are omitted.

Much of the supernatural machinery is omitted in Chaucer's version.
He excludes both the debate in heaven between Venus and Juno in
which they agree that Aeneas must be commanded to leave Dido and set
sail for Italy, and the appearance of Mercury to Aeneas bearing this command. In Chaucer, Aeneas' reason for leaving Dido is not the will of the
gods, but simply that he has grown tired of her:

> *This Eneas, that hath so depe yswore,*
> *Is wery of his craft withinne a throwe;*
> *The hote ernest is al overblowe.*

> (ll. 1285–87)

He merely pretends to Dido that he has had a vision, as an excuse for
leaving her. Chaucer retains two other divine interventions: Venus' gift
of invisibility to Aeneas when he first sees Dido, and the episode where
Cupid, disguised as Ascanius, Aeneas' son, comes to Dido's court, and
makes her fall in love with Aeneas. Chaucer is sceptical about these episodes, and excuses himself for reproducing them by saying that he finds
them in his source (ll. 1020–22; 1139–45).

For Vergil, the love of Dido and Aeneas is only one episode in the
greater story of the founding of Rome, of which the gods are the instiga-
tors. By decreasing the role of the gods, Chaucer has transformed this
epic material into romance, where human sentiment is all-important. By
depicting Aeneas as a liar, he increases our sympathy for Dido. In this he
was perhaps influenced by Ovid's *Heroides*, where the story is told from
her point of view, and by the traditional treatment of Dido in medieval

love-poetry as one of the great love-heroines of history. Similarly, in *The Book of the Duchess*, Chaucer focuses attention more on Alcyone than does Ovid.

Chaucer also reshapes the narrative so that it follows medieval conventions of story-telling. When a feast occurred in a story, it was common practice to give an elaborate description of it, as is done, for instance, in *Sir Gawain and the Green Knight*. When an author intended not to describe fully something that was a recognized topic for description, he could nonetheless toy with his audience's expectation that the convention would be observed. This device too was conventional, and Chaucer uses it when speaking of the feast given by Dido for Aeneas:

> *What nedeth yow the feste to descrive?* (l. 1098)

Chaucer gives only a brief description of the feast and the entertainment that followed, as does Vergil, but adds at the end a significant touch of his own:

> *Ful was the feste of deyntees and rychesse,*
> *Of instruments, of song, and of gladnesse,*
> *Of many an amorous lokyng and devys.* (ll. 1100–2)

The last line evokes the courtly atmosphere of the medieval feast with its flirtatious conversation, called by the *Gawain*-poet 'luftalkyng'. Conventional also is a discussion between Dido and Aeneas:

> *For in his bed she lyth a-nyght and syketh;*
> *She axeth hym anon what hym myslyketh.* (ll. 1292–93)

This has no parallel in Vergil, but in medieval narrative the 'bolster conversation' was a common motif.

Medieval audiences also greatly appreciated a description of a hunt, and to appeal to this taste Chaucer has introduced direct speech into the hunting-scene, to evoke its atmosphere more vividly. The language is colloquial and excited:

> *The herde of hertes founden is anon,*
> *With "Hay! go bet! pryke thow! lat gon, lat gon!*
> *Why nyl the leoun comen, or the bere,*
> *That I myghte ones mete hym with this spere?"*
>
> (ll. 1212–15)

The most radical kind of adaptation that Chaucer makes alters the depiction of Aeneas and Dido so that they conform more closely to the standard types of hero and heroine in medieval romance. Dido is idealized:

> *This noble queen, that cleped was Dido,*
> *That whilom was the wif of Sytheo,*
> *That fayrer was than is the bryghte sonne,*
> *This noble toun of Cartage hath bigonne;*
> *In which she regneth in so gret honour,*
> *That she was holden of alle queenes flour,*
> *Of gentillesse, of fredom, of beaute;*
> *That wel was hym that myghte hire ones se;*
> *Of kynges and of lordes so desyred,*
> *That al the world hire beaute hadde yfyred;*
> *She stod so wel in every wightes grace.*
>
> (ll. 1004–14)

This hyperbolical language reminds one of any number of descriptions of romance heroines, like Emely in 'The Knight's Tale' (CT, A, 1033ff.), or, to take a non-Chaucerian example from the fourteenth century, of Queen Heurodis in *Sir Orfeo*:[1]

> *The fairest leuedi, for the nones,*
> *That miht gon on bodi & bones,*
> *Ful of loue & of godenisse;*
> *Ac no man may telle hir fairnise.*
>
> (ll. 53–6)

Similarly, Aeneas is made into an ideal lover in his outward behaviour,

> *That feyneth hym so trewe and obeysynge,*
> *So gentil, and so privy of his doinge,*
> *And can so wel don alle his obeysaunces,*
> *And wayten hire at festes and at daunces,*
> *And whan she goth to temple and hom ageyn,*
> *And fasten til he hath his lady seyn,*
> *And beren in his devyses, for hire sake,*

---

[1] Ed A. J. Bliss, Oxford 2nd ed 1966.

> *Not I not what; and songes wolde he make,*
> *Justen, and don of armes many thynges,*
> *Sende hire lettres, tokens, broches, rynges . . .*

(ll. 1266–75)

We find the type of the ideal lover similarly exemplified by Palamon, by Troilus, and by Dorigen.

Although it is Dido who first falls in love with Aeneas, Chaucer invents a scene where Aeneas pleads with Dido for her love, in keeping with the convention of medieval romance that a lady should hold her lover at a distance and humiliate him before yielding. Whether this was in fact likely in Dido's case, and what psychological processes might underlie such a *volte-face* on her part, are questions that Chaucer ignores. He is simply writing to a recipe:

> *For there hath Eneas ykneled so,*
> *And told hire al his herte and al his wo,*
> *And swore so depe to hire to be trewe,*
> *For wel or wo, and chaunge hire for no newe,*
> *And as a fals lovere so wel can pleyne,*
> *That sely Dido rewede on his peyne.*

(ll. 1232–7)

In handling the legend of Dido, then, Chaucer makes numerous adaptations to suit it to the taste of his own time, but he has not remoulded the story so as to show it in a more revealing light. The translations from the classics in *The Legend of Good Women*, and The Manciple's and Physician's Tales, though they have successful moments, are among Chaucer's weakest narrative poems. When a classical borrowing forms part of a larger work, as in *The Book of the Duchess* or *The House of Fame*, for instance, it gains added meaning from its juxtaposition with other elements. The Manciple's and Physician's Tales, and the Legends of Good Women, though formally part of larger works, are not related to their context in any way that would enrich their significance. It was later in his career, when using Boccaccio, that Chaucer came to construct narratives that contain their own ironies, and are greater than their sources. But it was in making these early translations from the classics that he learnt that skill and independence in handling the work of other authors that was eventually to produce 'The Knight's Tale' and *Troilus and Criseyde*.

7: Chaucer and the Medieval Latin Poets

Part A: PETER DRONKE

WHILE CHAUCER'S READING of the Roman poets has been studied in some detail,[1] his reading of medieval Latin poetry has never been systematically investigated.[2] And yet Chaucer's knowledge and understanding of this poetry, as of Italian poetry, was quite exceptional for a vernacular poet of his time. In this essay there can be no question of a comprehensive study, nor of conjectures to reconstruct the full range of the medieval Latin poetry Chaucer may have read. Rather, the approach will be a qualitative one: to consider certain important authors, works and genres with which Chaucer was acquainted, and to indicate something of what he saw in them and how they helped to fructify his art.

I. Cosmological Poetry

There is evidence that Chaucer had read the three most outstanding Latin epics of the twelfth century: the *Cosmographia* of Bernard Silvestris (also known as *De Mundi Universitate*); the *De Planctu Naturae* and *Anticlaudianus* of Alan of Lille.[3] These three are cosmic epics; their setting is

[1] Cf. especially E. F. Shannon, *Chaucer and the Roman Poets*, Cambridge, Mass. 1929.

[2] Particular influences and debts have been noted in the major editions, and discussed in certain detailed studies, such as those of J. A. W. Bennett, *The Parlement of Foules*, Oxford 1957; id., *Chaucer's 'Book of Fame'*, Oxford, 1968); A. C. Friend, 'Chaucer's Version of the Aeneid', *Speculum* XXVIII, 1953, 317–23; D. Bethurum Loomis, 'Saturn in Chaucer's "Knight's Tale"', *Chaucer und seine Zeit: Symposion für Walter F. Schirmer*, ed A. Esch, Tübingen, 1968, pp. 149–61; R. K. Root, 'Chaucer's Dares', *Modern Philology* XV, 1917–18, 1–22; C. Wood, *Chaucer and the Country of the Stars*, Princeton 1970.

[3] *Cosmographia*: the edition of C. S. Barach and J. Wrobel, *De Mundi Uni-*

heaven as well as earth; they describe journeys from earth into the higher spheres and firmament, and thence back to the sublunary world; they are filled with celestial beings, goddesses and genii. They were poetry of a kind not previously attempted. There had been many narratives of otherworld visions and otherworld journeys in early medieval tradition, including a number in poetic form.[1] But in these there was scarcely cosmology, scarcely a sense of the workings of the universe or an attempt to convey those workings through a fabled account. Bernard's and Alan's transformation of poetic otherworld vision into cosmological epic was stimulated by other kinds of writing. Macrobius had shown them how a journey into the beyond, containing a moral and political message, could be extended into discussion of the nature and influence of the firmament, stars and planetary spheres. Boethius' *Consolation of Philosophy* had inspired not only the 'mixed' form, alternating prose and verse, of Bernard's *Cosmography* and Alan's *Complaint*: Boethius had shown how in fictional guise a serious insight was possible into the relations between the changeless world and the transient one, and shown how the fictive heroine, Philosophia, could be a protagonist who partakes in both these worlds, and at the same time the poet's instructress in metaphysics, vexed or affectionate, and an aspect of his own process of understanding.[2] Martianus Capella's *Marriage of Mercury and Philology* had also contributed to the enjoyment of the mixed form, to the peopling of the heavenly regions with exotically described mythical beings, and to the incorporation of didactic matter in a story set in the skies. But the profoundest influence on Bernard and Alan was Plato's *Timaeus*: there they could find an unsurpassed attempt to give an account of the cosmos and its creation in mythopoeic terms.

---

versitate, Innsbruck 1876, is often defective; in citations I correct where necessary from the early and excellent MS Bodley Laud Misc. 515; *De Planctu Naturae*: both the edition in Migne, P.L. 210, 431–82, and that of T. Wright, *The Anglo-Latin Satirical Poets*, Rolls Series 1872, II, 429–522, need to be consulted; the text often remains problematic. The *Anticlaudianus* exists in a critical edition, by R. Bossuat, Paris 1955.

[1] Cf. especially C. Fritzsche, 'Die lateinischen Visionen des Mittelalters bis zur Mitte des 12. Jahrhunderts', *Romanische Forschungen* II, 1886, 247–79; III, 1887, 337–69; A. Rüegg, *Die Jenseitsvorstellungen vor Dante*, 2 vol, Einsiedeln 1945.

[2] This psychological interpretation of Boethius' Philosophia is suggested by

The three epics (Bernard writing in the 1140s, and Alan, imitating and in a sense continuing Bernard's work, in the following decades)[1] are often thought of as stemming from the school of Chartres. This is true in the sense that Bernard, teaching in Tours, shared the metaphysical interests of Thierry of Chartres, to whom he dedicated his chief work, and that Alan was a 'Porretan', a disciple, that is, of Gilbert of Poitiers, who like Thierry had been head of the school of Chartres. The two poets share the passion of the Chartres philosophers for *integumenta* (literally 'coverings'): fables that mean more than themselves, fables through which ethical and cosmological insights can be conveyed. Their three poems form as it were a triptych, offering *integumenta* of the creation[2] (*Cosmographia*), degeneration (*De Planctu*), and renewal of the cosmos (*Anticlaudianus*). The underlying parallels with the Christian scheme —creation, fall, redemption—never become explicit: here the Christian account is neither affirmed nor excluded; specifically Christian allusions are present, but never central to the action. Bernard and Alan sought an 'objective correlative' of a different kind from the accepted Christian one—one that would be self-sufficient, at least as *integumentum*. As metaphysical constructs, their epics have a strange duality: on the one hand creation, degeneration and renewal are seen in terms of a vast web of celestial influences, on the other they are seen naturalistically. The two perspectives co-exist: they are made complementary and so, in effect, relativized. At work in the cosmic events is a series of celestial beings—or are they metaphors for natural forces? The central figure among these beings, in all three poems, is Natura, and she remains deliberately ambiguous. Like Boethius' Philosophia, she belongs in part to a divine world, in part to a mutable, and in part to the poet's consciousness, penetrating both.

Abelard, P. L. 178, 760 c, and stated more fully by Jean de Meun in the Preface to his translation of Boethius, *Mediæval Studies* XIV, 1952, 171.

[1] I accept the datings proposed by Marie-Thérèse d'Alverny, *Alain de Lille: Textes inédits*, Paris 1965, p. 34: *c.* 1160–70 for the *De Planctu*, 1182–3 for the *Anticlaudianus*.

[2] Strictly speaking, the re-creation: lines such as 'Rursus et ecce cupit res antiquissima nasci / Ortu Silva novo' (I, 1. 35–36) would seem to imply a cyclic conception of the cosmos, its disintegration followed, at the end of an aeon, by the possibility of renewal.

The three poems were widely diffused in the thirteenth and fourteenth centuries, they were glossed and commented like classical texts, adapted, and even—in the case of the *Anticlaudianus*—dramatized. What did they mean to Chaucer? They showed Chaucer how a meaning beyond fable —a philosophical meaning—could be embodied in fabled matter without explicit reference to a Christian frame. This was something that had not quite its equivalent in Jean de Meun (however much he borrowed from Bernard and Alan), or Boccaccio, or even Dante. In detail, Bernard and Alan share some of Chaucer's preoccupations and intellectual problems.

Like Bernard, Chaucer returns again and again to the question of how human affairs are controlled and conditioned, and how this control and conditioning leave room for freedom of will. This concern that the two poets share is reflected in the passage where Chaucer explicitly adapts some lines of Bernard:

> *Heaven writes with stars and figures everything*
> *that can proceed from the law of fate.*
> *It signals in what manner and what tenor*
> *the stellar motion may impel all ages.*
> *In the stars pre-exists an order that a longer*
> *age may unfold in intervals of time:*
> *the sceptre of Phoroneus, the strife of the Theban brothers,*
> *the flames of Phaethon, Deucalion's flood . . .*
> *In the stars lies Priam's majesty, Turnus' daring,*
> *Ulysses' cunning, and the strength of Hercules . . .*
> *There Greece pursues its learning, Rome its wars.*
> *There Plato seeks first causes, there Achilles fights,*
> *the generous hand of Titus scatters wealth;*
> *the maiden brings forth Christ, God's image and exemplar,*
> *giving the ages a true deity;*
> *a lavish God provides the world Pope Eugene,*
> *and in that gift alone gives everything.*[1]

---

[1] *Cosmographia* I, 3, 33ff. (Barach-Wrobel p. 16; Laud Misc. 515, fol. 188r −v). The first lines cited should read:

> *Scribit enim celum stellis, totumque figurat*
> *Quod de fatali lege venire potest.*

In 'The Man of Law's Tale', the Sultan of Syria falls heatedly in love with the Christian princess Constance, without having seen her, because merchants have told him of her beauty and perfection. The narrator comments (190–203):

> *Paraventure in thilke large book*
> *Which that men clepe the hevene ywriten was*
> *With sterres, whan that he his birthe took,*
> *That he for love sholde han his deeth, allas!*
> *For in the sterres, clerer than is glas,*
> *Is writen, God woot, whoso koude it rede,*
> *The deeth of every man, withouten drede.*
>
> *In sterres, many a wynter therbiforn,*
> *Was writen the deeth of Ector, Achilles,*
> *Of Pompei, Julius, er they were born;*
> *The strif of Thebes; and of Ercules,*
> *Of Sampson, Turnus, and of Socrates*
> *The deeth; but mennes wittes ben so dulle*
> *That no wight kan wel rede it atte fulle.*

As in the Sultan's privy council in the tale (211), 'Diverse men diverse thynges seyden', both of Bernard's outlook and of Chaucer's. At the one extreme, Dorothy Bethurum Loomis claims that 'What Chaucer and Bernardus Sylvestris have in common is the complete determinism that both 'The Knight's Tale' and *De Universitate* exhibit', and speaks of 'Bernard's enthusiasm for a completely controlled universe'.[1] At the other extreme Chauncey Wood reduces Bernard's preoccupation with the problems of determinism to a Boethian view of providence, and claims that the passage of Bernard just cited 'is nothing more or less than an account of world history up to the time of the Incarnation that emphasizes the apparent vagaries of this world in order to show the ultimate propriety of all these events when they are consummated by the birth of Christ'.[2] I have tried to show the complexity of Bernard's

---

(deleting Barach-Wrobel's full stop after *figurat*: the antecedent of *quod* is *totum*).

[1] *Art. cit.* pp. 159, 155.

[2] *Op. cit.* p. 214.

enquiry into determinism, and the critical, questioning aspect of his imagination, in a detailed study elsewhere.[1] Here I can offer only some observations on the two passages cited.

That Bernard is not a complete determinist is clear from many places in the *Cosmographia*—as when the goddess Urania shows her companion Natura 'What in the will may be free and what determined, and what may be of uncertain outcome'[2]—as well as from a careful reading of what is set in the stars. Certain historical events are written there: the reign of Phoroneus and the war of Thebes at the opening of the passage, the birth of Christ near the close (Bernard's playfully overdone compliment to Pope Eugene III, that his papacy was 'predestined', can hardly count as evidence for fatalism); certain physical disasters of fire and flood; the destiny of certain individuals (Plato, or Achilles); certain human qualities (the majesty of Priam, or the daring of Turnus); and certain national characteristics (as of Greece and Rome). That some great historical events and physical cataclysms were fated to happen, that nations and individuals have predictable characteristics which can shape their destinies—this is indeed to concede something to determinism, at least as hypothesis (note the expressions 'can proceed', 'may impel', 'may unfold'—*venire potest, agat, explicet*—at the opening of the passage). But it is very far from 'complete determinism'.

In Chaucer's adaptation the thought becomes more definite and doom-laden: for the Man of Law, what lies in the stars is 'the deeth of every man'. Only 'the strif of Thebes' has the same import as in Bernard; Achilles, Hercules and Turnus are mentioned, but for their deaths, not for their bravery; the other names and deaths do not occur in the Latin, they are Chaucer's additions. The lines suggest that the Man of Law is a gloomy fatalist; yet even here I think Chaucer has a playfully revealing moment as distinctive in its way as Bernard's hyperbole about the fated pope. For the Man of Law's first premise is, as soon emerges, false: the Sultan in the story does not die for love (at least in the usual meaning of this phrase): he is successful in his wooing; he dies because his fanatic

---

[1] *Fabula Veritas: Explorations into the Uses of Myth in Medieval Platonism,* Leiden-Köln, 1974, ch. iv: 'Fables of Destiny').

[2] *Cosmographia* II, iv, 35–36 (Barach-Wrobel p. 40; Laud Misc. 515, fol. 201v):

> *Que sit in arbitrio res libera, quidve necesse,*
> *Quid cadat ambiguis sub casibus.*

mother murders him.

Fatalism there is, but Chaucer means us to see it is exaggerated. Moreover, it is only one perspective on the story told; another, equally exaggerated, is seen in the narrator's histrionic appeals, at many turns in the action, to divine intervention and 'wonderful myracle' ('Who saved Danyel in the horrible cave? . . .'); yet another, in his smirking human view of Constance's virtue, when for a moment he sees her as hedged neither by fate nor miracle:

> *They goon to bedde, as it was skile and right;*
> *For thogh that wyves be ful hooly thynges,*
> *They moste take in pacience at nyght*
> *Swiche manere necessaries as been plesynges*
> *To folk that han ywedded hem with rynges,*
> *And leye a lite hir hoolynesse aside,*
> *As for the tyme,—it may no bet bitide.*   (708–14)

These perspectives—the fatalistic, the pious, and the prurient—are made relative and complementary. In a similar way throughout Bernard's works the perspective of the universe controlled by celestial laws and physical laws, and the perspective in which

> *God made the elements, the fiery stars, in such a way*
> *that man should not be subject even to the stars*[1]

are relative and complementary, and the relation between these perspectives is explored imaginatively. In Chaucer, the complementariness can be perceived not only within a narrative but in the comparison and contrast between narratives: if in 'The Knight's Tale' he presents a lover's fate as manipulated by a malevolent god—and here again, as Professor Bethurum Loomis has suggested, Chaucer may owe his picture of Saturn to Bernard Silvestris[2]—in *Troilus and Criseyde* he shows the decision of a lover to commit himself to love as freely willed:

---

[1] *Mathematicus* 643–4, ed B. Hauréau, Paris 1892, p. 31:
> *Sic elementa Deus, sic ignea sidera fecit,*
> *Ut neque sideribus subditus esset homo.*

Art. cit. p. 157. Nonetheless, Chaucer could also have found Bernard's details in some widely diffused Latin translations of Arabic astrological writings (Abu Ma'shar, Alchabitius, 'Picatrix'); the planetary attributes of Saturn are also outlined in some detail in *Anticlaudianus* IV, 463–83.

> *For with good hope he gan fully assente*
> *Criseyde for to love, and nought repente.*   (I, 391–2)

In yet another poem, *The Complaint of Mars*, Chaucer shows the planets
Mars and Venus themselves not as manipulators but almost as victims of
the celestial laws: their conjunction and separation (as planets and as
lovers) take place in obedience to a higher power in the face of which
they are helpless. They are subject to the same passions as they influence
in the sublunary world. While Chaucer's development of these paradoxes is his own, the sense that the planets are subjects rather than rulers
is apparent in both Bernard's and Alan's cosmology: in Bernard it is the
divine hand (*divina manus*) that allots the planets their courses, their
nature and behaviour (*naturam moresque suos*), and what each may influence in the world; in Alan Natura shows how firmament, stars and planets serve her, and perform their duties in obedience to her command.[1]

Chaucer's debt to Alan's epics becomes explicit in *The House of Fame*
and *The Parliament of Fowls*. In the first, Chaucer, carried into the heavens
by an eagle in his dream, approvingly mentions the *Anticlaudianus*, alongside Martianus Capella, as an accurate celestial guidebook:

> *And than thoughte y on Marcian,*
> *And eke on Anteclaudian,*
> *That sooth was her descripsion*
> *Of alle the hevenes region,*
> *As fer as that y sey the preve;*
> *Therfore y kan hem now beleve.*   (985–90)

In the *Anticlaudianus* Prudentia (also named Fronesis), the embodiment
of human wisdom, makes a journey through the spheres; like Chaucer,
she beholds in 'this eyr . . . many a citezeyn' (*aerios cives*, IV, 274), 'aye-
rissh bestes' (*aerio vestiti corpore*, IV, 282). Understandably, the eagle bids
Chaucer not to be afraid of these: they are not only the *daimones* 'of
which that speketh Daun Plato' but, as Alan explains, the fallen angels,
who are still dangerous to mankind. To reach the ether, Prudentia must
leave below her this region of the *daimones*,

> *passing the space of air where skies, overcast,*
> *weave darkness in their night, where pendant clouds*

[1] *Cosmographia* I, 3, 137ff. (Barach-Wrobel p. 19; Laud Misc. 515, fols.
189v–190r); *De Planctu*, P.L. 210, 448–9; Wright II, 460–1.

> *gather their rains, where showers of hail advance,*
> *where winds contend . . .*   (IV, 332–5)

So, too, for Chaucer:

> *Tho gan y loken under me*
> *And beheld the ayerissh bestes,*
> *Cloudes, mystes, and tempestes,*
> *Snowes, hayles, reynes, wyndes,*
> *And th'engendrynge in hir kyndes . . .*   (964–7)

The 'engendrynge' of the phenomena is revealed to Prudentia gradually, in the course of her ascent.

But why, from among the numerous descriptions of 'the hevenes region' that Chaucer knew, does he single out the *Anticlaudianus* and Martianus Capella as specially—and even, it would seem, unexpectedly—reliable? There is one point on which Alan and Martianus are in accord, which had become a vexed point of controversy in twelfth century cosmography.[1] The ethereal region and the firmament are fiery —was it possible, then, that they should contain anything cold? For Chaucer this was poetically important in that his House of Fame was to be built upon 'congeled matere', 'a roche of yse' (1126, 1130); for the twelfth century cosmographers, the crucial question was whether the Genesis account of God setting 'the firmament in the midst of waters' was physically conceivable, or had to be demythologized. Alan was one of those who believed that in this highest sphere the natural laws of physics were transcended: in a long topical and polemical passage (V, 306–72) he makes Prudentia 'marvel at the waters joined to fire / by undivided ordering of space'. Are they in the form of mist or vapour (as Thierry of Chartres had argued)? Are they a mere illusion (as William of Conches had—Alan believes falsely—claimed)? Prudentia accepts the view of Bernard Silvestris, 'that the heavenly moisture / retains the look of crystal and the form of ice' (*quod celicus humor / Cristalli retinet speciem glaciemque figurat*—*Anticlaudianus* V, 352–3).

In Martianus, the problem is less explicit: it is that Saturn is the coldest of the planets, and yet Saturn's orbit, described as a celestial stream, 'its leaden water on a misty, chilled and sluggish course' (I, 14), is closest to the ethereal fire. By cosmological argument, therefore, Saturn should be

---

[1] See especially E. Jeauneau, 'Note sur l'école de Chartres', *Studi medievali*, 3a serie V 2, 1964, 847ff.

hotter than the rest. Bernard Silvestris, in his commentary on Martianus, resolves the anomaly: Saturn is cold because he is nearest the 'congealed waters' (*aque congelate*) in which God set the firmament.[1] This commentary, which survives in only one, fragmentary copy, is unlikely to have been known to Chaucer; yet from the text alone he would have seen that Martianus, like Alan, thought 'congeled matere' possible even so near the fiery region. Alan makes this thought explicit (IV, 468ff.): in the sphere of Saturn, 'winter burns, summer grows cold, heat freezes'. The context in Martianus may likewise have been suggestive for Chaucer's narrative: while the 'house of fame' itself has its origins in Ovid's *Metamorphoses*, here in Martianus Mercury and Virtue begin their celestial journey, traversing the spheres in search of Apollo, from the Delphic oracle, the 'loquacious caverns' (*loquacia antra*) where 'the fortunes of cities and of nations, of all kings and of every people', are displayed (I, 11).

Another medieval Latin poem also stimulated some of Chaucer's images of celestial ascent: the ninth century Eclogue of 'Theodulus'[2]—a name which may well be a wordplay on the German 'Gottschalk' and so reveal the author as Gottschalk of Orbais († 869), the tragic lyrical poet who was persecuted for his writings on predestination. The Eclogue is a contention between 'falsehood' and 'truth': between the shepherd whom Chaucer names 'of Athenes daun Pseustis' (HF, 1228; *ab Athenis pastor cognomine Pseustis, Ecl.* 4), who sings of pagan myths, and the shepherdess Alithia, who counters each of his strophes with a biblical parallel, and at last wins the 'flyting' by singing of Christ's incarnation, for which Pseustis knows no parallel. The Eclogue became a popular school-text from the eleventh century to the sixteenth[3]—the known manuscripts approach two hundred—so it is not surprising that certain juxtapositions remained in Chaucer's memory:

> *I neyther am Ennok, ne Elye,*
> *Ne Romulus, ne Ganymede,*

[1] This passage is printed by Jeauneau, who discovered the commentary, *art. cit.* pp. 860–1.

[2] Ed J. Osternacher, *Theoduli Eclogam*, Urfahr/Linz 1902.

[3] J. Osternacher, *Neues Archiv* XL, 1916, 331–76, lists 176 extant MSS and mentions further lost MSS and references in medieval library catalogues; moreover, he describes 93 printed editions of the Eclogue that appeared between 1481 and 1544.

> *That was ybore up, as men rede,*
> *To hevene with daun Jupiter,*
> *And mad the goddys botiller.*   (588–92)

In the Eclogue Enoch, 'snatched up from the earth', is mentioned together with Elias, and ten lines later comes Ganymede, 'borne up into heaven' by Jupiter and made 'butler of the gods'.[1] For another ascent, the unhappy one of Daedalus and Icarus, the words of the Eclogue (103):

> *Et cadit in pelagus; gemuit sub pondere fluctus—*

(and he fell into the sea; the wave moaned beneath his weight) are closer to Chaucer (HF, 922–4) than anything in Ovid's account.

These, however, represent only minor, incidental reminiscences from Chaucer's medieval Latin reading. A more profound influence can be perceived in *The Parliament of Fowls*. Here the explicit reference is to Alan's *De Planctu*, as authority for the appearance of 'goddesse Nature':

> *And right as Aleyn, in the Pleynt of Kynde,*
> *Devyseth Nature of aray and face,*
> *In swich aray men myghte hire there fynde.*   (316–18)

But both of Alan's epics have left memorable traces in this, Chaucer's most philosophical poem. The influence lies in thought rather than language: Alan's flamboyantly virtuoso style, with its cascades of wordplay, word-variation and conceit, would seem to have made little impact on Chaucer. It is not only the look of Natura that Chaucer remembers, or her surpassing radiance and beauty: her robe (*peplum*) may well have suggested to him the whole notion of a 'parliament of fowls'. For on that robe, iridescent in its colours, 'was celebrated a council of living creatures' (*animalium celebrabatur concilium*); and while her mantle is covered with fishes and her tunic with images of man and the other land-animals, the *peplum* is entirely a parliament of birds: *Illic aquila . . . Illic accipiter violentia et tyrannide a subditis redditus exposcebat . . .*[2] A detailed comparison of Chaucer's birds and their attributes and behaviour with those described on Natura's *peplum* would exceed the compass of this essay. Rather I would ask, what are the poetic implications of Chaucer's having brought

[1] *Ecl.* 65–68, 77–80.

[2] There was the eagle . . . There the sparrowhawk, with violence and tyranny, demanded tribute from its subjects. *De Planctu*, P.L. 210, 435–6; Wright II, 437–9.

Natura's robe to life?

All that Natura wears, taken together, is an epitome of the cosmos in its fulfilled and perfect state—its 'natural' state. For Alan, far more than for Bernard, Natura is not only one of the forces—divine and at the same time physical—at work in the creation of the cosmos, but subsists within the created cosmos as a mediatrix, who keeps all things in balance and accord and who embodies their moral-natural norm. It is in Alan's *Complaint* that she elaborates in detail the ways in which she is God's vicegerent on earth.[1] Chaucer's lines

> *Nature, the vicaire of the almyghty Lord,*
> *That hot, cold, hevy, lyght, moyst, and dreye*
> *Hath knyt by evene noumbres of acord*   (379–81)

are an epitome of much of Alan's thought; yet it may be significant that Chaucer's expressions here are closer to Boethius' invocation to the God who governs 'this world by perdurable resoun' (*Consolatio* III, m. 9) than to anything in Alan. In Chaucer's translation of Boethius:

> Thow byndest the elementis by nombres proporcionables, that the coolde thinges mowen accorde with the hote thinges, and the drye thinges with the moyste . . .

This solemn, ultimately Boethian, sense of a divine function fulfilled in the cosmos lies behind the comedy of manners revealed in the birds' debate.

It is a debate about love and the right behaviour of lovers. On this, too, Alan's *Complaint* has a special bearing. Alan, more explicitly than Bernard, assigns not only Natura but Venus a role in the cosmic creation: she is Natura's appointed deputy, even as Natura is God's.[2] But this successive delegation and physical realization means that all is more precarious than in the immutable, ideal world situated in the divine mind. Venus grows weary of working only at Natura's behest, and discovers the joys of adulterous and perverted loves.

The role of Venus in relation to Natura is important to Chaucer's poem, though his thoughts are more elusive than Alan's. In the 'nature-opening' of medieval love-songs the convention had been to contrast the love of birds mating in spring, the perfect expression of spontaneous joy, with the complexities and pains of human love: the world of Venus,

[1] P.L. 210, 445–6; Wright II, 455–6.

[2] P.L. 210, 456ff.; Wright II, 475ff.

subtler and more refined, more premeditated and more entangled than
Natura's world, has lost its primitive innocent joy. Chaucer, by a profoundly artistic irony, makes the birds, Natura's birds, exhibit the complications, a wide spectrum of *human* attitudes to love; and paradoxically
Natura's most prized birds are also the most complicated, those for
whom decisions in love are difficult and tortuous; it is the lower ranks of
the birds who are truly 'natural', uninhibited—though these ranks
include idealists too. In Alan's *Complaint* something of this diversity is
conveyed through the figure of Hymenaeus, the god of weddings,
whom already Martianus Capella had celebrated in his opening invocation as a principle of universal concord. In Alan he is Natura's brother,
and shares her 'infinite variety': he is young, mature, and old, mirthful
and serious, great and small of stature, his clothes now poor and now res-
plendent.[1] The imperfect and ambiguous aspects of Alan's Venus are suggested in Chaucer by the juxtapositions among Venus's personified
attendants:

> *I saw Beute withouten any atyr,*
> *And Youthe, ful of game and jolyte;*
> *Foolhardynesse, Flaterye, and Desyr,*
> *Messagerye, and Meede, and other thre . . .*   (225–8)

and by setting the alluring goddess in a sultry temple whose walls are
filled with legends of ill-starred loves.

Alan, in the *Complaint*, does not give Natura a setting of her own: she
floats down into the dreamer's vision 'from the inner palace of the
changeless world'. It is in the *Anticlaudian* that Natura's setting is poetically important, as it was to be in *The Parliament*. For Alan as for
Chaucer, her dwelling is in an earthly paradise, a joyous world of never-
fading flowers and 'blosmy bowes', of ravishing bird-song and gentle
breezes. 'No man may there waxe sek ne old': the garden is, in Chaucer
as in Alan, an embodiment of the goddess's attributes, an embodiment of
her immortal aspect in a perfect mortal form.[2] But Chaucer has a subtle
detail that goes beyond Alan, or indeed deliberately contradicts him:
where in Alan's garden Natura has a house made of gold, silver and
gems, in Chaucer's, 'Of braunches were here halles and here boures'
(304).

[1] P.L. 210, 471–2; Wright II, 502–4.
[2] *Anticlaudianus* I, 55ff.; cf. PF, 183ff.

A deeper, though less palpable, debt to the *Anticlaudianus* becomes apparent in the movement of Chaucer's poem. Chaucer in his dream first makes a celestial journey, an ascent of the spheres, like Scipio in his *Somnium* and Prudentia in Alan's fantasy. And the direct result—the reward —of that ascent for Chaucer is the vision of the garden 'ther as swetnesse everemore inow is', the garden that includes both Venus's temple and Natura's 'hil of floures'. So, too, in the *Anticlaudianus* Prudentia's ascent has as its goal a return to earth, carrying down from heaven the idea of the *novus homo*, and concludes with the recreation of Natura's paradise in the world. For Chaucer as for Alan, the end of the heavenward journey is not contemplation for its own sake, but the return to Natura and 'commune profit', the renewal of the earth. If many details of the *Parliament* were stimulated by the *De Planctu*, the dynamics of the poem reflect a profound reading of the *Anticlaudianus*.

II. *Trojan Poetry and Rhetoric*

Only the briefest glance is possible here at Chaucer's explicit use of other medieval Latin poets. In an important article published two decades ago, A. C. Friend suggested a relation between Chaucer's depiction of the story of Aeneas in the first Book of *The House of Fame* and the Latin *Ilias* of Simon Chèvre d'Or. Simon, who had composed his *Ilias* between 1152 and 1155, revised and enlarged his poem in the following years, when he had become a Victorine in Paris.[1] Like Chaucer, he gives a condensation of the *Aeneid*, beginning in chronological order with the destruction of Troy, a condensation rich in rhetorical 'brevitas-formulae' comparable to those of Chaucer (*shortly of this thyng to pace . . . shortly for to tellen . . . hyt were a long process to telle . . .*). As Friend showed, there are parallels in the way various narrative details from the *Aeneid* are summarized, and both Chaucer and Simon show Dido as filled only with tragic erotic tenderness as she goes to her death. But such an unvergilian, more Ovidian, conception of Dido is not uncommon in the Middle Ages, and the differences of tone and quality between the English and the Latin verses are considerable: Simon's summarizing has a mechanical staccato effect where Chaucer gathers his story-matter into a swift, sweeping

[1] *Art. cit.* (n. 1) p. 317. Simon's revised text was printed by A. Boutemy, *Scriptorium* I, 1946–7, 267–88.

legato. Friend, however, was able to point to one remarkable narrative detail which, it would seem, only Chaucer and Simon share: during the storm at sea, Venus, afraid for her son Aeneas, beseeches Jupiter to save the Trojan fleet, and Jupiter solaces her and relieves her fear. It is not the kind of detail Chaucer tends to invent afresh: did he adopt it from Simon's *Ilias*? The question remains problematic, in that this scene occurs only in Simon's enlarged version of his poem, of which today not more than one (thirteenth-century French) manuscript survives. Until we have a comprehensive picture of the medieval Latin poems on Trojan themes —many of them remain unpublished—we cannot discount the possibility of an indirect, rather than direct, relation between the two works.

With another medieval Latin Trojan poet, however, Chaucer's direct knowledge and debts are certain. As R. K. Root established more than half a century ago, the 'Dares' to whom Chaucer refers in *The Book of the Duchess*, *The House of Fame*, and *Troilus and Criseyde*, is in fact the epic *Frigii Daretis Ylias* of Joseph of Exeter, completed between 1188 and 1190.[1] By meticulous analysis Root showed the passages where Joseph's influence could be discerned. In *The Parliament of Fowls* the trees in the garden of Chaucer's dream are named, and each is swiftly characterized. While there are several catalogues of trees in Roman poetry that Chaucer will have known, as well as one in Boccaccio's *Teseida*, certain phrases—*the hardy asshe, the boxtre pipere, the olyve of pes, the dronke vyne* —can be paralleled only in Joseph's characterization of the trees of Troy (I, 513ff.): *fraxinus audax, cantatrix buxus, oliva concilians, ebria vitis*. Similarly, the portraits of the Trojan heroes and heroines have their own literary tradition, and Chaucer, giving his portraits of Diomede, Criseyde, and Troilus (TC, V, 799–840), assuredly drew on several sources, especially on the *Roman de Troie*. Yet again, as Root showed, certain details—Diomede's stern voice, the comparison of his valour with that of his father Tideus, and especially the enchanting phrase used of Criseyde—

> *And with hire riche beaute evere more*
> *Strof love in hire ay, which of hem was more—*

must have been stimulated by expressions that can be found only in

[1] R. K. Root, *art. cit.* (n. 1); cf. BD, 1070; HF, 1467; TC, V, 1765ff. A critical edition of Joseph's works has recently been published by Ludwig Gompf: *Joseph Iscanus, Werke und Briefe*, Leiden-Köln 1970.

Joseph of Exeter.[1] The importance of Root's demonstration, in my view, lies not so much in the particular links he has shown as in the light that investigation of this kind can throw on Chaucer's craft. Chaucer was a *doctus poeta* of a rare kind: a poet with an inclination towards the methods both of the literary critic and the textual scholar. Collating the variants of narrative detail and of expression in his authors, he establishes his own eclectic text. At the same time, he was not constrained by the scholar's or critic's responsibility towards his originals; thus he was able again and again to turn critical insight into creative discovery, textual comparison into *alchimie du verbe*.

Chaucer's placing of his three portraits is unparalleled in the Trojan tradition; in Root's view, Chaucer introduces them 'somewhat irrelevantly', in Robinson's, they 'interrupt the narrative'.[2] I would suggest that the stanzas serve a poetic, almost a musical, design: static, measured, rhetorically formal, they are a cadenza contrasting with but also bridging two moments of narrative that are different in key: the one where Criseyde's yielding to Diomede is an imminent danger, the other where in effect she has already yielded. Between these moments, the protagonists are made to pass before our eyes and we see Criseyde set between her two lovers: Diomede is dwelt on briefly but very concretely; Criseyde, with tenderness as well as candour: significantly, the loveliest phrase —*that Paradis stood formed in hire yën*—has no parallel in the portrait tradition; Troilus is commended, but in virtually abstract terms and conventional phrases—*hardy as lyoun, trewe as stiel, in no degree secounde in durryng don*—almost as if Chaucer wanted to objectify the way Troilus had ceased to be a living presence in Criseyde's thoughts. For these moments, the rigid manneristic tradition inherited from late antiquity, which Joseph's verse exemplifies, is poetically apt.

One other medieval Latin poet mentioned explicitly by Chaucer is Geoffrey of Vinsauf, an Englishman who composed his 'New Poetics'

---

[1] Diomede: IV, 124–7; Criseyde (Briseis) IV, 156–62; Troilus: IV, 61–64. Joseph's phrase about Criseyde is: *Diviciis forme certant insignia morum*. Root made the ingenious suggestion that the MS Chaucer used will have read, erroneously, *insignia amorum*. According to Gompf's edition (p. 145), however, none of the extant MSS have such a reading. I am more inclined to suspect a piece of creative textual improvement on Chaucer's part.

[2] Root, *art. cit.* p. 6; Robinson (2nd edn, 1957) p. 834.

(*Poetria Nova*) shortly after 1200.[1] More than eighty extant manuscripts
of the work have been noted. Geoffrey included in his verse treatise his
own illustrations of poetic techniques, and it is Geoffrey's heady example
of pathetic invocation, his virtuoso apostrophe to the Friday on which
Richard Coeur-de-Lion was fatally wounded, that Chaucer mis-
chievously misapplies to the situation of Chauntecleer in 'The Nun's
Priest's Tale' (3347ff.). But it is in *Troilus and Criseyde* that he gives Pandarus some lines to speak which are a translation from Geoffrey[2] and
reflect a fundamental premise of his poetic:

> For everi wight that hath an hous to founde
> Ne renneth naught the werk for to bygynne
> With rakel hond, but he wol bide a stounde,
> And sende his hertes line out fro withinne
> Aldirfirst his purpos for to wynne.   (I, 1065–9)

Geoffrey's lines continue:

> the inner man prescribes the design, ordering its unfolding with
> sureness, the hand of the heart forms the whole before the physical
> hand does so. The work exists first as an archetype, then as a physical
> reality. Let poetry see in this image what rule must be given to
> poets.

The lines are an appeal for a functional approach: it is the 'archetype',
the fully organized imaginative conception of the work, in the mind and
heart of the poet, which must order and dictate his modes of expression.
This principle lies behind some of Geoffrey's finest particular insights, as
into the functional, intrinsic quality of 'hidden comparison' (*collatio
occulta*), which should be

> as it were a new, wondrously ingrafted transplantation, where

[1] Ed E. Faral, *Les arts poétiques du XIIe et du XIIIe siècle*, Paris 1924.

[2] This has been challenged by J. J. Murphy, 'A New Look at Chaucer and
the Rhetoricians', *RES*, n.s. XV, 1964, 1–20. But the correspondence with
Geoffrey's Latin (43ff.) is extremely close:

> Si quis habet fundare domum, non currit ad actum
> Impetuosa manus: intrinseca linea cordis
> Praemetitur opus, seriemque sub ordine certo
> Interior praescribit homo . . .

Unless an equally precise equivalent in another work were to come to
light, Chaucer's dependence on the *Poetria* here cannot seriously be doubted.

something assumes its place so surely in the design as if it were born of the theme itself—yet it is taken from elsewhere, though it seems to be from there . . . thus it wavers, within and without, here and there, far and near: it is absent, and present.[1]

On the larger scale, that of theme as against image, Geoffrey shows that the same quality should be striven for when the poet uses a digression (527ff.): it is a matter of departing from the principal theme in such a way that the seemingly far is still near, that the apparently unrelated matter reveals its functional coherence with the rest. Digressions, like hidden comparisons, must be 'compassed by the heart's intrinsic measure'. So, too, poetic language should never be for display: it must serve the meaning and contexture of the poem:

First look at the mind of your word, then at its face—don't trust the face's colour! Unless the inmost colour is at one with the external, meaning there grows base. To paint a word's face is to paint scum, a falsification . . .[2]

Admittedly Geoffrey's *Poetria* also contains much information of a traditional didactic and technical kind, about 'your termes, your colours, and your figures'. Yet the fact that Chaucer chose to adapt from Geoffrey the lines which state his prime principle of functionality suggests that he saw what was truly important in this poetic. This is also borne out by Chaucer's own creative practice. When for example Cassandra tells Troilus the series of Theban sorrows and deaths (TC, V, 1457ff.), it is a digression both 'far and near': while seemingly 'a fewe of olde stories', it gradually reveals itself as a portent for Troilus of frightening cumulative force. When Cassandra has done, the poet passes from the tragedy of Thebes to the imminent one of Troy: Fortune

> *Gan pulle awey the fetheres brighte of Troie*
> *Fro day to day, til they ben bare of joie.* (V, 1546–47)

This is at the same time a 'hidden comparison', concealing and revealing the tragedy of Troilus himself. The echoes from the first moments when love had overwhelmed him—

> *And yet as proud a pekok kan he pulle . . .*
> *For love bigan his fetheres so to lyme . . .* (I, 210, 353)

[1] *Poetria Nova*, 250ff.
[2] *Ibid.* 739ff.

place the 'wondrously ingrafted' psychological meaning here beyond a doubt. It would be far-fetched to claim that Chaucer needed a work like the *Poetria Nova* in order to achieve poetic effects such as these. But if anyone in fourteenth-century England was capable of seeing what was profound in Geoffrey of Vinsauf's poetic, and capable of realizing its finest precepts in his art, it was Geoffrey Chaucer.

Part B: JILL MANN

III. *The Satiric Tradition*

FOR CHAUCER'S KNOWLEDGE of medieval Latin satire there are varying degrees of evidence. He makes direct reference to the *Speculum Stultorum* of Nigel of Longchamps ('Nun's Priest's Tale' 3312–16); he was a contemporary and friend of John Gower and is therefore likely to have read Gower's long Latin poem on the 'estates' of society, the *Vox Clamantis*. His acquaintance with Goliardic satire, on the other hand, has mostly to be inferred from the great popularity and influence of such works as the *Apocalipsis Goliae* or the songs of Walter of Châtillon, and the frequent similarity of subject-matter between his satire and that of the Goliards.[1]

[1] The *Speculum Stultorum* has been edited by J. H. Mozley and R. R. Raymo, Berkeley and Los Angeles 1960, and translated by G. W. Regenos, Austin, Texas 1959, and (in an abridged form) by J. H. Mozley, Oxford 1961. Mozley and Raymo's edition supersedes that by Thomas Wright in Volume I of *The Anglo-Latin Satirical Poets and Epigrammatists of the Twelfth Century*, Rolls series 59, 1872, except for the prose epistle of Nigel, providing a commentary on the poem, which prefaces the work in MS. BM Harleian 2422, and is not printed by Mozley and Raymo. Besides Chaucer's use of Nigel's story of the vengeful cock in 'The Nun's Priest's Tale', Mozley and Raymo draw attention to the similarity between Nigel's description of a 'parliament of birds' (2901–6) and Chaucer's (*Parliament of Fowls*, 311–15).

Walter of Châtillon was an important and influential writer, as his numerous school of imitators indicates (see F. J. E. Raby, *A History of Secular Latin Poetry*, 2nd edition, 2 vol, Oxford 1957, II, pp. 190–204, and K. Strecker, 'Walter von Chatillon und seine Schule', *ZfdA* 64, 1927, 97–125 and 161–89). Walter's works were popular in England, as Strecker's list of surviving MSS makes clear (*Moralisch-satirische Gedichte Walters von Chatil-*

Similarities of subject-matter are not, however, what I am primarily concerned with here;[1] I want to focus instead on the crucial division between Chaucer and the Latin satirists—the difference between their languages. The Latin satirists wrote in the language which was the vehicle for serious culture in the Middle Ages—the language of the Bible, of the liturgy, of the Fathers, of the classical poets and those who strove to imitate them. Latin satire exploited to the full the possibilities of this language, finding its best and most natural expression in parody and burlesque of all kinds.[2] To take a minor example: the *Speculum Stultorum*, like 'The Nun's Priest's Tale', is a beast narrative in a mock-heroic style. But Nigel's burlesque of the 'dies irae' theme, or his parody of the famous Latin hymn by Sedulius beginning 'Cantemus, socii, Domino', are not directly imitable by a vernacular writer.[3] In 'The Nun's Priest's

---

lon, Heidelberg, 1929, pp. v–viii).

For a discussion of the relationship between the works of Chaucer and Gower see John H. Fisher, *John Gower*, 1965, Chapter 5. The *Vox Clamantis* is edited by G. C. Macaulay (John Gower, *Complete Works*, 4 vol, Oxford 1899–1902) and has been translated by E. W. Stockton, *The Major Latin Works of John Gower*, Seattle 1962. For Goliardic satire in general, see the following collections: T. Wright (ed), *The Latin Poems Commonly Attributed to Walter Mapes*, 1841, Camden Society 16; A. Hilka and O. Schumann (eds), *Carmina Burana* (vols 1–2, Heidelberg, 1930–41, vol 3 ed B. Bischoff, Heidelberg 1971); O. Dobiache-Rojdestvensky, *Les Poésies des Goliards*, Paris 1931; K. Langosch, *Hymnen und Vagantenlieder*, Darmstadt 1961; G. F. Whicher, *The Goliard Poets*, New York 1949. The *Apocalipsis Goliae* has been separately edited by K. Strecker, Rome 1928. For a brief discussion and further bibliography, see J. de Ghellinck, *L'Essor de la Littérature Latine au XIIe Siècle*, Brussels 1955, pp. 494ff.

[1] J. A. S. McPeek has pointed out some similarities between Chaucer's works and some Goliardic poems ('Chaucer and the Goliards', *Speculum* 26, 1951, 332–6). Others are to be found in my book on *Chaucer and Medieval Estates Satire*, Cambridge 1973, although I am not there concerned to argue that Chaucer knew any Goliardic poem in particular. Correspondences between the material of the *Vox Clamantis* and Chaucer's *General Prologue* to *The Canterbury Tales* are also noted there.

[2] For a full study of medieval Latin parody, see P. Lehmann, *Die Parodie im Mittelalter mit 24 ausgewählten parodistischen Texten*, 2nd edition, Stuttgart 1963.

[3] *Speculum Stultorum* 405ff. (where the 'day of reckoning' is the first one of

Tale', Chaucer comes very near to reproducing the habitual manner of medieval Latin satire through his elaborate burlesque of poetic rhetoric and philosophical debate. But it is Chaucer's *own* rhetoric and philosophical frame-work which are here made to look comic; he both establishes the tradition and comically demolishes it. The Latin satirists can take religious, philosophical and poetic traditions as 'given' in the language they use.

Chaucer's kinship with the medieval Latin satirists is not therefore a matter of formal correspondences. What has to be examined is the kind of imaginative perception stimulated by the linguistic playfulness of the Latin poets, and the emergence of a similar imaginative quality in Chaucer's writing. In attempting to analyze this, I shall focus comparison on 'The Wife of Bath's Prologue' which has parallels of form and subject-matter in Latin satire, but I shall also indicate how the qualities described extend throughout the *Tales* as a whole.

Gower's *Vox Clamantis* forms an introductory contrast to the spirit of the Goliards. It is also an excellent example of the way in which the use of Latin entails an implicit reference to religious and cultural norms. The poem is presented as a response to the Peasants' Revolt of 1381. Chaos has overwhelmed the garden paradise of England (I, 1–164), and Gower rejects the view that it is due to the blind revolutions of Fortune (II). Instead, he sees the disorder as divine punishment for the vices of English society, and he devotes six lengthy Books to anatomizing these vices in detail. The standards against which he measures contemporary degradation are implicit in his constant appeals to the stories and language of classical literature and of the Bible. Chapters nineteen and twenty of Book VI, which lament the general decay of virtue, are a good example of this. The first expresses moral deterioration through biblical figures (Isaac is supplanted by Ishmael), while the second, following exactly the same pattern, uses the heroes of the classical world (the generous Alexander is succeeded by the greedy Crassus).

Classical literature and the Bible also give authority to the *Vox Clamantis* in a more unusual way. Gower himself claims that he is not responsible for composing the words of the poem, but only for selecting

---

summer, on which cows will feel the need of their tails), and 1075ff. (where Burnellus, triumphing over the murder of his enemy, chants 'Cantemus, socii! festum celebremus, aselli!').

them from other authors and putting them in a connected series—a claim
that is very largely true.[1] He draws mainly on Ovid, Godfrey of Viterbo,
Nigel of Longchamps, and Alexander Neckam ('classical' authors in a
loose sense, but one that would have been acceptable in the medieval
period) while the Bible is represented *via* Peter Riga's versified text,
the *Aurora*. Whatever the original character of the quotations Gower
borrows from these authors, they play the role of 'authorities' in his
work, lending it a dignity and guarantee of age-old truth which free
invention would not have given it. They give sanction to Gower's view
of the world—appropriately so, since this view is static, conservative,
and based on absolute moral certainties. Law and order are not only
principles that Gower admires, but also the governing qualities of his
style. Balance and contrast are its staples; paradox is a sign of anarchy and
unreason.[2] Thus the discussion of faults among prelates in Book III is
structured by contrast—first, between their way of life and that of
Christ, next between the differing treatments accorded by them to rich
and poor.

> *In precio precium nunc est, dat census honores,*
>   *Omneque pauperies subdita crimen habet.*
> *Cum loquitur diues, omnis tunc audiet auris,*
>   *Pauperis ore tamen nulla loquela valet:*
> *Si careat census sensus nichil est sapienti,*
>   *Census in orbe modo sensibus ora premit.*
> *Pauper erit stultus, loquitur licet ore Catonis;*
>   *Diues erit sapiens, nil licet ipse sciat.*   (41–8)

[Nowadays worth is in wealth; a fortune brings honours, while
every vice is attributed to oppressed poverty. When the rich man
speaks, then every ear will listen, while no eloquence is of any use in
the mouth of a poor man. If he lacks money, intelligence does
nothing for the wise man; money nowadays overwhelms speech

---

[1] See II Prol. 75–82.
[2] Thus in the *Vox Clamantis*, the traditional paradoxes on the nature of love
('a sick health, a troubled serenity', etc.) brand it as evil (V, 53ff.); in
Chaucer's *Parliament of Fowls*, on the other hand, they are used to evoke
admiration for the 'wonderful werkynge' of Love (1–7).

with its own brand of wisdom. The poor man will be a fool, though he speaks with Cato's tongue; the rich will be wise, although he knows nothing.]

I have quoted this passage because it has superficial correspondences with Goliardic satire, and shows that Gower was well acquainted with it. The word-play on 'census' and 'sensus', and the kind of perverted logic it implies in those who equate one with the other, the reflections on the power of money, the line borrowed from Ovid which opens the passage and authorizes its subject as belonging to 'serious' poetry—all are familiar Goliard features. But the Goliards differ from Gower in that they take delight in their punning, and in the perverted logic by which they can 'prove', for example, that gluttony ('gula') is an indispensable part of the monastic rule ('regula'). In Gower, word-play is used only to contrast true values with false ones; the heavy repetition emphasises with unalleviated earnestness his conviction that wealth is a poor substitute for wisdom. The Goliards aim to open up our sense of the contrast and tension between spiritual and worldly values, a sense which in the best of their work leads us to an increased awareness of human complexity; Gower aims to eliminate tension, to establish a firm and unambiguous control over his reader's point of view.

This remains true even when Gower allows his sinners a voice; their point of view is given only to be refuted. The use of biblical quotation in the following passage only gives us authority to reject the 'excuse' for the peccadilloes of nuns:

> While they often read the text naïvely, not concerning themselves with the gloss, they think that what is written is permissible for them to perform. Reading of Scripture teaches them to 'Prove everything' [I Thess. 5:21]. Thus because they read it all, they want to try it all. The laws of nature are to increase and multiply, which God in the beginning wrote down from his own mouth [Gen. 1:28]. They want to obey God's Scriptures, and also to fulfil the accustomed laws of nature with a devout spirit.[1]

---

[1]   *Simpliciter textum dum sepe legunt, neque glosam*
          Concernunt, vt agant scripta licere putant:
       Leccio scripture decet illas cuncta probare,
          Sic, quia cuncta legunt, cuncta probare volunt.

Although this passage does in a way make us aware of the mental confusion in which sexual licence and the religious life can exist side by side, it presents the nuns' point of view only in order to criticize that confusion. Their view is severely framed by Gower's own, by his careful choice of vocabulary, and by his modifications:

> Simpliciter *textum dum saepe legunt*, neque glosam
> Concernunt, *vt agant scripta licere* putant.

To any reader of Chaucer, this passage immediately recalls 'The Wife of Bath's Prologue':

> *Men may devyne and glosen, up and doun,*
> *But wel I woot, expres, withoute lye,*
> *God bad us for to wexe and multiplye;*
> *That gentil text kan I wel understonde.*   (26–9)

This is only one of the 'gentil textes' which the Wife manipulates as she wishes, as she puts up an elaborate defence of marriage, and especially of marrying more than once. Both these activities were perfectly respectable in fourteenth-century England, and so the Wife's defence often uses quite respectable arguments. The first part of her Prologue covers much of the material in St Jerome's *Epistle Against Jovinian*, and at times, such as when pointing out that Christ's own celibacy shows that it is permissible to forego the use of one's 'membres of generacion', the Wife makes Jerome's own point. But at other times she makes those of his adversary: she points out that Paul did not command, but only recommended virginity; and asks how virgins are to be born if there is to be no marriage. At such moments, as when she quotes the text bidding her 'increase and multiply', the reader's attitude to her may well take the form that it does towards Gower's nuns—an awareness of another dimension, another point of view from which her selection and manipulation of arguments looks unscrupulous and wilful. But we notice that the reader is not so securely supported in this point of view as he is in Gower; only the Wife's voice is heard, while Chaucer himself is silent. To take only one example of our insecurity: when the Wife claims to approve of the

---

> Crescere nature sunt iura que multiplicare,
> Que deus in primo scripsit ab ore suo;
> Heque dei scripta seruare volunt, quoque iura
> Nature solita reddere mente pia.(IV, 567–72).

biblical injunction to increase and multiply, we *may* recall that Chaucer nowhere mentions that she has had any children, and speculate that her lack of children shows her hypocrisy at this moment. It would be so easy for Chaucer, either here or elsewhere, to give warrant for these speculations by specific reference to her childless state. But in fact he never does so, and the reader is left to wonder.

Unease is increased by the fact that elsewhere in 'The Wife's Prologue' we are not so easily allowed to identify the Wife with the erring Jovinian and ourselves with the superior wisdom of Jerome; for the Wife, as we have seen, takes Jerome's own words out of his mouth. Jerome, for example, deals carefully and seriously with the Apostle's injunction to virginity:

> It is clear why the Apostle said: 'Concerning virgins I have no command of the Lord [1 Cor. 7:25]'—obviously because the Lord had previously said: 'He who is able to receive this, let him receive it [Matt. 19:12]'. The Starter offers the reward, summons to the race, holds in his hand the prize of virginity; he shows a beautifully pure spring, and cries out: 'Who thirsts, let him come and drink [John 7:37]. He who is able to receive this, let him receive it.'[1]

In the mouth of the Wife, Jerome's rhetoric is transformed:

> *Poul dorste nat comanden, atte leeste,*
> *A thyng of which his maister yaf noon heeste.*
> *The dart is set up for virginitee:*
> *Cacche whoso may, who renneth best lat see.*   (73–6)

The drift of what they are saying is differentiated not by a change in content, but by a change in tone. The Wife is perfectly willing to allow the truth of what Jerome says; she simply takes up a different attitude to this truth—that she is quite happy to remain in the rewarding position of second-best. Jerome's argument tries to exclude this attitude *rhetorically* by challenging or alluring us, but it offers no substantial *reason* against its adoption. His argument is thus impotent to refute the Wife here, for she has taken it over.

We can see already that Chaucer has a more flexible attitude to 'authority' than Gower; the Wife of Bath gains our sympathy, even if it is amused sympathy, in her manipulation of texts, and Chaucer, refusing comment in his own person, allows her an autonomy denied to Gower's nuns. Moreover, by taking texts out of context and assigning them to a radically different one, Chaucer transforms their meaning. The 'respect-

[1] *Ep. ad Jov.* I, 12, *Patrologia Latina*, ed Migne, vol 23, col. 228.

able' arguments become suspicious because they are used alongside those of Jovinian, and even more so because they are voiced by a robust widow in red stockings rather than by a sober Church Father conducting an exegetical discussion.[1]

A similar freedom in the face of moral and stylistic rigidity characterizes the *Speculum Stultorum*. Nigel's poem relates the adventures of Burnellus, an Ass who desires to 'improve himself'; he envisages the improvement successively as a longer tail, a university education, or entry into a religious order. The Ass's failure to achieve any of these things is a source of comedy and ridicule. But those who see the poem only as a moral lesson on the folly of Burnellus ignore the fact that a large part of the serious moral and social comment in the poem comes from his mouth; he can analyze the failings of social classes (2559ff.) and of the religious orders (2051ff.), or describe the qualities required by a perfect bishop (1677ff.), with seriousness and competence. Moreover, although it is generally correct to call 'mock-heroic' the style in which Burnellus' adventures are described, there are occasions when the Ass becomes *truly* heroic—as when pity moves him to rescue three thieves condemned to death, and carry them to safety on his back.[2] What we see in Nigel is a sensitivity to the contradictions involved in hard-and-fast categories: wisdom–folly, human–bestial, comic–serious—an awareness that experience shows itself much more complex than such categories allow. Much of his satire is directed against the absoluteness and rigidity of abstract intellectual thought; Burnellus represents the stubbornly intractable 'nature' before which any kind of scholarly 'art' retires defeated.[3] The same defeat of 'art'—ideology, rhetoric, whatever name we choose to give it—is celebrated in 'The Nun's Priest's Tale', and the fact that Chaucer here makes his direct mention of 'Daun Burnel the Asse' is, I think, a sure indication of Nigel's influence on the tale.

[1] Of course Jerome, being human, is not by his circumstances rendered any more immune than the Wife of Bath from the wish to find rational support for his own prejudices; this is one of the ways in which the 'Prologue' encourages us to use the Wife to retort on St Jerome as well as to use Jerome to retort on the Wife. See especially ll. 673–5, and 688–96.

[2] *Speculum Stultorum*, 1805–1912.

[3] See especially Burnellus' career as a university student, *Speculum Stultorum*, 1503–70. For a more detailed presentation of this argument, see my article on 'The *Speculum stultorum* and the *Nun's Priest's Tale*,' *Chaucer Review*, forthcoming.

As a final example of the delight taken by Latin satirists in the fluid use of rhetoric and intellectual argument, of language and of literary texts which seem to claim fixity, I should like to take Walter of Châtillon's poem 'Missus sum in vineam'.[1] It makes an especially interesting comparison with 'The Wife of Bath's Prologue', since it too offers a mock defence—here, of the pursuit of wealth rather than learning. Walter's distinctive contribution to medieval Latin verse-forms was a stanza of three rhythmic lines ending with a hexameter, usually taken from a classical poet. The stanzas in 'Missus sum' end with hexameters from Ovid, Juvenal, Horace, Lucan, Persius, Claudian, or Cato's *Distichs*. For the first nine stanzas, these hexameters seem to fulfil the same sort of function as the borrowings in Gower; they act as 'authorities' in a lively, but conventional, satire on the corrupting effects of money. But the question left dangerously hanging in the fourth stanza—why shouldn't I indulge my bodily demands like everyone else?—is impudently answered in the second half of the poem as Walter announces his intention to renounce scholarship for a life of pleasure. The shift is marked by two stanzas (10–11) whose final lines appear to be Walter's own, rather than borrowings—as if he is rejecting the burden of the past, of centuries of moral earnestness and other-wordliness, in order to assert himself and his own preferences: '*I* prefer fattened meat to wretched beans.' The authorities are then taken up once more, but now they are subjected to his self-assertion. Do you reject wealth, says Walter, because you hope to receive eternal life for it?

> *Heu mentes perdite!   numquid ignoratis*
> *quod semper multum nocuit differre paratis?*

'Lost souls! don't you know that those who are ready can only lose by delay?' The last line is a quotation from Lucan on the advisability, in a military context, of striking while the iron is hot; Walter uses it to 'prove' the folly of deferring gratification. Quotations from Ovid are used to show that lying on a couch with a girl is more fun than study in cold and darkness—'Tutius est iacuisse thoro, tenuisse puellam' (*Heroides* III, 117), or that poverty and love don't go together—'non habet unde suum paupertas pascat amorem' (*Rem. Am.* 749). A quotation from Juvenal on the wealth of Lucan becomes evidence that writers don't have to be poor to be successful (VIII, 79ff.). The abandonment of scholarly

[1] Ed Strecker, *Moralisch–satirische Gedichte*, No. VI.

ambition is justified by a desire to avoid intellectual pride, and a quotation from Claudian shows how pride taints the very virtues which give rise to it ('inquinat egregios adiuncta superbia mores', *Panegyric on the Fourth Consulship of Honorius*, 305). As a climax, the kind of recommendation of cautious moderation dear to classical and medieval authors alike ('inter utrumque tene, medio tutisssimus ibis', Ovid, *Metamorphoses* II, 140 and 137), is transformed by the context into the advice: 'if you can't be rich, at least be comfortably off!'

Only once in this poem does Walter actually *alter* a text in the manner we usually associate with parody. Cato's proverb that life without learning ('sine doctrina') is a shadow of death, becomes a statement on the insubstantial nature of life without riches ('sine divitiis'). This alteration reflects the larger alteration that Walter sees in the accepted beliefs of the society around him, and is one clue to help us see where he stands, and where the reader should stand, in relation to the attitude adopted in the poem.[1] But what concerns us here is not so much Walter's real beliefs on the subject of clerkly poverty (as it is not our concern to determine Chaucer's real beliefs on marriage), but to examine the nature of the comedy in his poem. And this mostly arises from our surprised awareness of the fluidity with which his texts can be moulded to his argument. He does not have to alter their phrasing; like pieces in a mosaic, they simply take on different functions and natures as they are differently arranged —as they are shorn of the context which originally defined their meaning.

Walter does not, I think, necessarily wish the reader to use the original context of his quotations (even if he could always recall it) as a pertinent contrast to their present abuse; this would be to 'fix' the technique in the service of a rigid viewpoint, rather in the way that we have seen Gower use biblical quotations. We cannot simply contrast a correct and an incorrect use of the texts, which we might if they were all used in the same way as the one from Cato's *Distichs*. It is enough for Walter's purpose that the shift to hexameter form proclaims the separateness of his texts, their origin in another literary world, and their borrowed status in this one. The impression given by their use in the mock argument of this poem is of something I can only describe as the promiscuity of reasoning, argument, axiom, quotation, moralizations, and example. Such literary

[1] In fact, in another poem, Walter takes the opposite point of view ('Stulti cum prudentibus', *Moralisch-satirische Gedichte*, No. IV).

and linguistic resources are not tied by some law of nature to the truth, but can serve the cause of 'falsehood' equally well.[1] And if the power of argument is equally good on both sides, how, except by the exercise of personal preference, are we able to *identify* truth and falsehood? The serious world which the Goliards parody assumes the integrity of argument and logic; arguments may be better or worse, but the better the argument, the nearer we shall be to truth and virtue. What the Goliards and Chaucer show us is that a 'good' argument—'good' not just in the sense of 'ingenious', but in the sense that it uses the same materials as the orthodox moralist—may be used to defend a position which is immoral from an orthodox point of view. 'Virtue' is promiscuous in the same way; the desire to avoid the scholar's pride becomes a reason for avoiding his labours, just as humility becomes the Wife's reason for rejecting the chance for the highest way of earthly life. The promiscuity of rhetoric, of logic, moralizing, etymologizing and quoting is a major source of the comic effects in 'The Wife's Prologue', and it is suggestively paralleled by the manipulation of argument and quotation in Goliardic satire, and the kind of freedom in the face of intellectual and moral control which characterizes the *Speculum Stultorum*.

Its importance for Chaucer, however, is inadequately represented by reference to 'The Wife of Bath's Prologue'. Chaucer learned thoroughly the lesson of the determining power of the context, as we can illustrate briefly by setting side by side two passages from *The Canterbury Tales*:

> *A wyf! a, seinte Marie, benedicitee!*
> *How myghte a man han any adversitee*
> *That has a wyf! Certes, I kan nat seye.*
> *The blisse which that is bitwixe hem tweye*
> *Ther may no tonge telle, or herte thynke.*
>
> *Who koude telle, but he had wedded be,*
> *The joye, the ese and the prosperitee*
> *That is bitwixe an housbonde and his wyf?*

It is the force of the context that encourages us not to read the second of these passages (from 'The Franklin's Tale') as sarcastically as the first

---

[1] The use of the quotation from Lucan to justify the demand for present rewards, here made by Walter himself, is in 'Stulti cum prudentibus' attributed to the prelates Walter is satirizing (*Moralisch-satirische Gedichte*, p. 66, v. 14, 4).

(from 'The Merchant's Tale'). And the contrast between them is a measure of the difference between the two worlds that these pilgrims encourage us to inhabit.

An awareness of different interpretations encouraged by different contexts can indeed be said to be the basis on which *The Canterbury Tales* themselves grow—although here we are moving well beyond the techniques, if not beyond the imaginative suggestiveness, of Goliardic satire.[1] Statements or characters or attitudes or values have a correctness within the world of each Tale which is not evident beyond its limits. The courtly lover is taken seriously in the world of 'The Knight's Tale' but becomes a ninny in the world of the Miller. The marital bullying which is amusing in the Wife of Bath becomes disgusting in the husband of 'The Clerk's Tale'. The view that every man should help himself to what is going seems sensible in 'The Reeve's Tale', but mean in the selfless world of the Franklin. And yet the suggestion of 'The Franklin's Tale' that generosity will establish a balanced social harmony is good-humouredly burlesqued in 'The Shipman's Tale', where the same kind of balanced harmony is established by the exercise of selfishness, turn and turn about. The cross-references between the Tales, their shifting focuses on values and differing selections from the rich store of experience, have been described and illuminated by many Chaucer scholars in recent years, and I need not, even if I could, rehearse them here. What I have aimed to do is to point to the awareness that interpretations of the world only make sense in certain contexts, as an essential part of the achievement of medieval Latin satire; to suggest that this went along with an 'opening up' of the sense of different view-points, different orders of experience, and the restricting nature of intellectual and moral classification when confronted with the robust and unclassifiable forms taken by human life; and to indicate that a similar sensitivity to context, in its widest sense, is a fertile principle of *The Canterbury Tales*, at all levels from the single word to the complete Tale. What Latin satire had to offer Chaucer was a contribution to the essential nature of his poetic imagination.

[1] By 'context', I here mean both the literary structure in which a line or passage appears, and also the place of a literary work in a culture as a whole; thus the reactions exploited can range from 'This contradicts a statement on the previous page' to 'Since this tale occurs in the Bible, it must be possible to see a moral meaning behind its apparent immorality'.

8: Transformations: Chaucer's Use of Italian

HOWARD SCHLESS

'INFLUENCE' STUDIES ASSUME a method and approach whose validity must be subjected to constant testing and revaluation. The two traditional procedures, source-hunting and *zeitgeist*, may be used separately or in combination, each procedure ranging from the most direct to the most sophisticated, and with no guarantee whatsoever that, in combination, the degree of sophistication of the one procedure will necessarily evoke an equal sophistication in the other. Such a caveat as this must be made from the start since the major discussions on Chaucer's use of Italian are no exception to the pattern, save perhaps in their concentration on source work.

In general, the one procedure cannot profitably exist without a real awareness of the other: thus, we may find that 'the time-honored sport of source-hunting'[1]—a clean enough chase when one is tracking down a direct borrowing—may, if used excessively or exclusively, rapidly degenerate into an example of the indefatigable in pursuit of the untenable; if, on the other hand, the approach is too generalized, we may be faced with the twin excesses of *zeit* (where the mere fact that two men lived in the same period becomes sufficient warrant for comparison) and *geist* (where the scholar-critic bathes the entire period in the light of his own reflection).

Perhaps not quite so obvious are the dangers involved in a method that, for Chaucerian studies, had its classic expression in that most tempting study, the influence of Dante. This method sought to recreate the thought association, the 'linked atoms,' in the poet's mind at the moment

---

[1] R. L. Hoffman, 'The Influence of the Classics on Chaucer,' *Companion to Chaucer Studies*, ed Beryl Rowland, Oxford 1968, p. 173.

of poetic creation; it is a method whose validity is directly proportional to the scholar's ability to comprehend the vast cultural and social influences at work in an author; it is a method that comes dangerously close to being self-defeating if the scholar assumes or accepts a closed and radically reduced system, one where (for example) only Chaucer and Dante (and, perhaps, a conductive Boccaccio) exist *in vacuo*. We can, I think, see the success and the failure of this method in the work of a single scholar: John Livingstone Lowes. His success can be seen in his later work, that on Coleridge.[1] There, Lowes familiarized himself with all he could find that Coleridge had read or encountered, and he accomplished the astonishing feat of setting forth a universe sufficiently sophisticated that it could be explained by 'linked atoms.' However, ten to twelve years earlier, essentially this same method of association had been applied to Chaucer to give us our major fund of putative ascriptions to Dante; but the very nature of the restricted and *in vacuo* evidence calls into question not only some of these ascriptions but the viability of the 'linked atoms' approach under such limited and limiting conditions.

Since this earlier method of Lowes has had so large an effect, we might pause for a moment to describe it. By this procedure (if I may cite a summary that I have used elsewhere),[2] the lines in a poem that are said to be based on Dante are put forth not on the grounds of direct indebtedness but through the medium of another poem or poems; that is, a clear and acknowledged source (generally Boccaccio, but at times some other spot in the *Divina Commedia*) may contain a word or phrase that is said to remind Chaucer of a more or less similar word or phrase (in Dante), and this is offered as a probable source for some proximate word or phrase in the Chaucerian passage that is under discussion. The assumptions of such a procedure are threefold: first, it must be assumed that Chaucer composed the putatively Dantesque lines from memory (that is, without consulting the text, for this would often demand a more precise parallel than Chaucer gives); secondly, it must be assumed that Chaucer was capable of almost total recall of Dante (though not necessarily of other authors or common knowledge, since these would break the linkage); finally, it must be assumed that on the basis of a limited number of works (usually

[1] J. L. Lowes, *The Road to Xanadu: A Study in the Ways of Imagination*, Boston 1927, etc.

[2] 'Chaucer and Dante,' *Critical Approaches to Medieval Literature*, ed Dorothy Bethurum, New York 1960, pp. 136–7.

Chaucer, Boccaccio, and Dante), treated *in vacuo*, one can reconstruct the creative process of the poet. On the basis of these assumptions, one can then proceed to connect similar words or phrases in Chaucer's known source with others in Dante and thus promulgate the influence of the Italian poet. This is not to say that any ascription based on this kind of *in vacuo* source study is, *ipso facto*, wrong, but, like a successful laboratory experiment that limits itself to only two or three agents, the procedure itself may remain open to question however fortunate one may be in the particular analysis.

More recently, to this *in vacuo* procedure has been added a rather special form of the other approach to 'influence studies,' *zeitgeist*. Here, a line of Chaucer, echoing or perhaps even using a Biblical passage, is compared with the comment of a patristic or exegetical writer explicating that passage. Suggested similarities of understanding are set forth and form the basis for a suggested dependence. As additional confirmation, the Christian spirit of the times and the general desire of medieval man to work out 'the savacioun of my soule' are seen as legitimate grounds for the 'Christianizing' of both the poet and his poetry. The problem here is somewhat more subtle. Patristic studies of Chaucer are certainly not wrong in themselves, but we must constantly remember that they are but one facet of the diamond. What is wrong is to mistake that one facet for the diamond as a whole. We owe a great deal to those who have rediscovered and polished this facet, for a great deal of grinding and buffing has been necessary; but we must be cautious of those who see into the work through that facet only, or who seem finally to be focusing on what the facet reflects. In particular instances, then, highly pertinent readings and relationships have been established by such studies; but to read Chaucer as basically a writer of versified homily, while it may supply a kind of 'high seriousness,' seems to prescribe and prejudge what are acceptable influences and interpretations. One is tempted, on occasion, to reply to such proffered weighty religiousness with the words of Kittredge:

> Great poets, no doubt address themselves to posterity; and posterity is free to interpret them, for its own comfort and inspiration, in any terms it finds useful. But they address themselves, in the first instance, to their immediate contemporaries. . . . What Chaucer meant to his contemporaries is, then, a pertinent question. It stands

at the threshold. If there is an inner shrine, we must enter it through the portal of the obvious.[1]

Kittredge's remark contains both a caution and a directive. Primarily, it warns us against the kind of projective reading that seems to increase with the increasing remoteness of a period and with our consequent lack of detailed information of that time. The critic's search for moral weight and order, as well as the normal desire of any period to see its ideals, problems and principles prefigured in the past, ardently try to fill the real gaps and empty spaces in our knowledge and understanding of that past. Indeed, in the most extreme cases there would seem to be a kind of Gresham's law whereby modern interpretation tends to drive out uncongenial historical facts.

The counterbalance to such projectionism Kittredge rightly sees as based on what is 'the obvious' for contemporaries. But in trying to determine what is obvious, we must first of all recognize that our major source of information is written record which, in the fourteenth century, concentrates on a fairly restricted although very important aspect of the times. Since literacy was principally confined to members of the clergy, it is not surprising that the chief topic and the chief point of view that we have received reflect their interests. Theological discussions, monastic chronicles, church records, these constitute the relatively extensive information that we have on a quite specific part of medieval life and times. Even in record-keeping areas such as law and governmental administration, what has remained is, in a sense, skeletal. Procedure in law or the actual functioning of administration remain, on the whole, just beyond our sight. We know only by hints and indirections what the attitude towards law was during this period, or what were the real tensions and triumphs of an administration developing towards a civil service. How much less do we know, in that age virtually devoid of personal letters and journals or of records of popular or quotidian concerns, about those issues or excitements that were in themselves ephemeral or that failed to achieve a level that contemporaries considered worthy of note. Such things, so vital to our understanding of the times, are lost to us. To say this is not to counsel chaos nor preach despair; it is simply a matter of recognizing the limitations. Without acknowledging our ignorance, without realizing that 'influence studies' are, by the very nature of the

[1] G. L. Kittredge, *Chaucer and his Poetry*, 9th printing, Cambridge, Mass. 1951, p. 80.

evidence available to them, partial, we cannot hope to deal fairly with problems of source or *zeitgeist*. Of these two general categories, the study of sources would seem to be in a far stronger position since it deals mainly with the comparisons within the area of written word and record. But even here, once we move beyond the direct and undoubted borrowing, the source for a particular line may more accurately be found in the largely unrecorded or unregarded world in which the poet daily lived than in some written or literary source.[1] Once we begin to discuss influence in terms of *zeitgeist*, of the spirit of a period, we must be even more cautious, for here we are often unable to observe the culture's complexity in anything like the infinite details and gradations that then existed, and, even more fundamentally, our view is perforce limited to quite specific areas seen under certain quite particular lights.

   This discussion of methodology is, perhaps, 'a long preamble to a tale,' but such is the nature of Chaucer studies that one can not begin to investigate any one area without an almost immediate awareness of the reverberations that are being felt in others such as dating, biography and criticism. With all this in mind, let us turn to what would seem to be a basic historical aspect of the relationship of Chaucer and Italian: the question of when and why Chaucer might have learnt Italian.

                                    II

Hard evidence for the precise dating of Chaucer's poems is slight, although highly probable conjectures have been offered and, on the whole, have been accepted by scholars over the years. It is, to give but two examples, very likely that the *Book of the Duchess* was finished not too long after the death of Blanche of Lancaster, probably about 1369 and certainly not later than 1372; likewise, it is equally probable that an astrological allusion in Book III of *Troilus and Criseyde* indicates that work was in progress in 1385. While these and other conjectures (many of them based on proposed 'occasions' for the individual poems) have been set forth, we must finally admit that our fullest and firmest evidence has led us to deal with the order in which the poetry was written rather

---

[1] See, for example, the ascription of LGW, 1381–83 to Dante (Inf. XIX, 5) and the discussion of outlawry in 'Chaucer and Dante', pp. 141–5.

than with precise dates. Here, a number of the problems of chronology can be resolved by the undoubted evidence coming from Chaucer's own references to previously written poems. But going beyond this often involves the critical evaluations of the individual scholar who feels that poem A is less mature than poem B, or that stylistically Chaucer should move from the restrictions of tetrameter couplets and stanzaic rhyme to the freedom of pentameter couplets.

Influence studies supply yet another means of ordering the poetry. In this case, the more extreme view of Chaucer's development describes a movement from 'the charmed circle of French erotic verse,'[1] through the broadening, humanistic vision of Dante and Italian writers, and ending with the mature realism of English poetry. This 'neat triplicity'[2] (as Kittredge so aptly called it) has been refined by later scholars[3] who have pointed out (for instance) that no account has been taken of Latin works, and that influences do not have clearly defined limits but flow into one another throughout the author's life; nevertheless, the basic paradigm remains, with the French period on one side and the English on the other. The date when Chaucer could have learned Italian is, then, literally central to this problem and to the critical and historical arguments deriving from it.

Indeed, this very centrality should lead us to pose certain questions concerning the assumptions on which the view is founded. Have we, in considering the Italian influence, looked to 'the world of books' at the expense of 'the world of affairs'[4]? What indication do we have (other than our desire for the ought-to-be) that Dante was the first Italian read by Chaucer[5]? or that Chaucer was the first to bring a copy of the *Divina Commedia* into England? or that Chaucer immediately and totally responded to the liberating and humanizing force of Italian poetry[6]?

[1] H. S. Bennett, *Chaucer and the Fifteenth Century*, Oxford 1948, p. 46.

[2] Kittredge, *op. cit.*, p. 26.

[3] A particularly cogent presentation is given by P. V. D. Shelly, *The Living Chaucer*, Philadelphia 1940, pp. 40–1.

[4] The phrases are the titles of Chapters III and II respectively in J. L. Lowes, *Geoffrey Chaucer and the Development of his Genius*, Boston 1934, etc.

[5] The most profitable approach and statement is that given by R. A. Pratt, 'Chaucer and the Visconti Libraries,' *English Literary History* VI, 1939, pp. 191–9.

[6] See, for example, J. S. P. Tatlock, *The Mind and Art of Chaucer*, Syracuse,

What, in fact, is the significance of 1372—the date of Chaucer's earliest undoubted Italian mission and the date most frequently cited as the start of his Italian period?

There is evidence of previous continental journeys in 1366 and 1368, to Spain[1] and perhaps to Italy. If Rickert and Galway are correct about the Italian destination of the latter,[2] the selection of Chaucer for the 1372 mission would have a clearer explanation. As Prof. Lounsbury cogently remarked a century ago:

> [Chaucer] may have become intimately acquainted with the language of that country before he went thither in person. That facilities for studying it, and that from the mouths of native Italians, should not have existed at the splendid court of Edward III, is almost incredible. . . . There is no evidence that ignorance of the language of a people on the part of an envoy accredited to them was looked upon as a qualification for that particular post in the time of Edward III, at least in the case of a person occupying no higher rank in life than did the poet.[3]

But what might those facilities have included, and why should Chaucer have bothered to learn Italian in the first place? If he was still a member of the household of Lionel (Duke of Clarence) around 1366 when negotiations were getting under way with Galeazzo Visconti, lord of Milan

---

1950, p. 10: ' . . . the influence of the three towering Trecentisti [Dante, Petrarch and Boccaccio] who forced him from the ascendancy of fashionable French poetry, promoted the action on him of classical poetry and freed his own literary personality.'

[1] Suzanne Honoré-Duvergé, 'Chaucer en Espagne? (1366),' in *Receiul de Travaux offert à M. Clovis Brunel*, 2 vol, Paris 1955, II, pp. 9–13.

[2] Edith Rickert's interpretation of a 1368 Chancery document granting Chaucer permission to go abroad with the rather large sum of £10 ('Chaucer Abroad in 1368,' *Modern Philology* XXV [1928], pp. 511–12) strongly suggests that Chaucer's trip was to Italy; the suggestion was upheld by Margaret Galway ('Chaucer's Journeys in 1368,' *Times Literary Supplement*, 4 April 1958, p. 183). If this view is correct, Chaucer may well have joined the large and glittering entourage of his former patron, Lionel, Duke of Clarence, whose marriage to Violante Visconti had been celebrated in Milan in the previous month.

[3] *The Parlement of Foules of Geoffrey Chaucer*, ed T. R. Lounsbury, Boston 1877, pp. 6–7.

and Turin,[1] for the marriage of his daughter Violante to Duke Lionel, then acquiring a knowledge of Italian in anticipation of the arrival of the new duchess and her entourage would not have been in the least surprising. And if Chaucer had already entered the King's service—and we know that he had definitely done so by July 1367—what reasons would a member of Edward III's court have for learning the language? The answer, in part, may rest in that side of Chaucer's career concerned with the world of affairs, with the customs and trade that had long been deeply involved with Italians.

For over one hundred years, the English court had been heavily financed by money from Italian banking houses. Records for the reigns of Edward I and Edward II show disbursements of almost £450,000 principally to the Frescobaldi, the Bardi and the Riccardi.[2] While gifts and special trading rights were allowed, these repayments came primarily from the assignment of customs, especially England's chief product, wool.[3] But there can be little doubt that the loans made by these Tuscan merchants (who often acted as royal bankers[4]) were a good deal larger than the disbursements they received, and their companies suffered accordingly. In reviewing these early financial transactions, one is struck by two points: first, the traditional importance of the Italians in the English economy, not only in the court but in the customs and trade as well; secondly, that, in speaking of these men from Florence, Lucca and Pisa, 'it is with the fellow-countrymen and contemporaries of Dante that we are dealing,'[5] men who were at the very heart of the affairs of their city-states, men who might well have known the extremely popular *Divina Commedia*[6] with its incisive political, topical and—for some of them

---

[1] Galeazzo, who lived mainly in Pavia, shared the lordship with his politically more active brother Bernabò. Chaucer visited Milan in 1378 and later wrote of the death of Bernabò in the prison of Galeazzo's son, Gian Galeazzo, in *Monk's Tale*, VII, 2399–2406.

[2] W. E. Rhodes, 'The Italian Bankers in England and their loans to Edward I and Edward II,' *Historical Essays by Members of the Ownes College, Manchester*, ed T. F. Tout and James Tait, 1902, pp. 137–68. See Table Q of loans, pp. 167–8.

[3] *Ibid.*, p. 162.

[4] *Ibid.*, p. 155.

[5] *Ibid.*, p. 138.

[6] The first extant commentary (of Graziolo de' Bambaglioli) appeared

—often personal comments.

The history of the Bardi in Chaucer's own time supports this impression and shows how integral a part of the English court this Italian group had become. From the comparatively complete records available, it would appear that the failure of the Bardi in the 1340's, while not entirely caused by the English crown's debts of almost £94,000,[1] was certainly accelerated by such large unpaid loans. The government, however, did not repudiate these debts. Over the next forty-five years, the Bardi received in direct payments, annuities and loans a total of £62,525[2] and, with certain considerations, the remainder of the debt was settled by Richard II on 24 October 1391 for the sum of 3,000 marks (£2,000).[3]

This is the bare chronology of the affair, but if we look even a little more, we can begin to see just how close to Chaucer's official court life were those Florentines who, like the other alien merchants, 'had varied functions, which were of financial and diplomatic as well as mercantile service to the crown.'[4] Following their failure in 1346, the Bardi

 . . . after ten years of readjustment and diminished activity under

within three years of Dante's death; by 1340, sixteen years later, Jacopo della Lana and Dante's sons, Jacopo and Pietro, had made their explications. '"In the year 1350," sayd Sismondi, "Giovanni Visconti [Violante's uncle] engaged [two theologians, two scientists and two Florentine antiquaries] in the laborious task of explaining and illustrating obscure passages in the *Divina Commedia*."' (cited in J. W. Hales, 'Dante in England', *The Bibliographer*, No. 2, [January, 1882] pp. 37–9.) 'The lectureship on the *Divine Comedy* established in Florence in 1373 lasted for an hundred years' (O. Kuhns, *Dante and the English Poets from Chaucer to Tennyson*, New York 1904, p. 16); others were established in Bologna, Pisa, Piacenza and Venice. Later fourteenth century exegeses include those of Boccaccio, Benevenuto da Imola and Buti (see *La Divina Commedia*, ed C. H. Grandgent, Boston 1933, pp. xl–xli, citing Elizabetta Cavalieri, *la Fortuna di Dante nel Trecento*, 1921). One writer has estimated that there were '115 commentaries in all before 1500' (Arthur Livingston, in *The Divine Comedy*, trnsl. M. B. Anderson, New York 1944, p. v).

[1] Alice Beardwood, *Alien Merchants in England, 1350 to 1377: Their Legal and Economic Position*, Cambridge, Mass. 1931, p. 8.

[2] *Ibid.*

[3] *Ibid.*, p. 9.

[4] *Ibid.*, pp. 3–4.

the king's protection, reorganized their company in 1357. . . . They seem thereafter to have maintained a sure but inconspicuous position as bankers and merchants, first under the leadership of Philip de Bardi, until his death in 1362,[1] and then under that of his son, Walter de Bardi, who was for many years, under both Edward III and Richard II, the king's moneyer.[2]

Walter de Bardi exemplifies the level to which Italians could rise in the English court, with services to the crown in areas in which Chaucer had regular interests. As head of the mint, he was an important official of the crown; but there are other indications of his status at court. Not only did he receive an annuity of £20 from Edward III,[3] but, as well, he 'was sent [in 1367] by the king with Thomas de la Dale of Flanders, to receive from Galeazzo, lord of Milan, the dower of his daughter,' Violante,[4] who was married to Chaucer's first patron, Lionel, Duke of Clarence, in the following year. Or, let us look at an instance two decades later. The 1391 settlement of the court's debt to the Bardi was certainly expedited by Walter's being at once representative of the company and crown official; the company received the 3,000 marks already mentioned, but as well Richard II 'freed Walter de Bardi from certain obligations he had incurred as master of the mint.'[5] For Walter, the ends of court and commerce, of his public and his private self, must have seemed in happiest accord.

The society of the Bardi of Florence was undoubtedly the most important Italian, or indeed foreign, company in England during the fourteenth century.[6] They, above all the bankers of Florence, would have known full well the writings of their compatriot, Dante Allighieri, for (to cite Grandgent):

Critics have hotly debated the question of whether his Beatrice was a real woman. Boccaccio asserts that she was Beatrice Portinari, daughter of Folco Portinari, a wealthy and public-spirited Florentine who died in 1289; before that she was married to a rich banker

[1] A. Sapori, *La Crisi delle Compagnie Mercantili dei Bardi e Peruzzi*, Florence 1926, p. 92, n. 1 [Beardwood's reference].

[2] *Ibid.*, p. 5.

[3] *Ibid.*, p. 6, note.

[4] *Ibid.*, p. 5, n. 6.

[5] *Ibid.*, p. 7.

Ibid., p. 4.

of good family, Simone de Bardi. There is no valid ground for rejecting this statement.[1]

The testimony of Boccaccio and of Dante's son, Pietro, has been almost universally accepted. We must, therefore, recognize that the Bardi family would have had particular reason for knowing the *Divina Commedia* thoroughly; and this circumstance should once more make us treat with great caution the argument that Dante's work was unknown in England before Chaucer's return from his first Italian journey.

The varied activities of the Italian merchants—the Bardi and others—touched most of the areas of the world of affairs in which Chaucer was involved. When, for example, he went off in 1372 to negotiate with the Genoese about the choice of an English port for their commerce, and also perhaps to arrange certain financial dealings for the king,[2] he was accompanied by two Italians, 'Joliamis de Mari, civis Januensis' and 'Jacobi Provan.'[3] The usefulness of the 'civis Januensis' is evident, but what of Provan? Extant records suggest at least a circumstantial answer. Peter and Hugh Provan, merchants from Turin, were among the king's bankers, and Hugh, along with Daniel Provan, were members of the society of the Malbaille in England.[4] It is quite likely that Jacopo belonged to this family engaged in English commerce and court finances, and that he was actively engaged in the royal mission. Certainly he would seem to have been more than a mere guide and translator for the poet since, 'on reaching Genoa, Chaucer was detached from his associates and sent on special business to Florence.'[5]

Negotiating marriage settlements, resolving problems of international

[1] *La Divina Commedia*, ed C. H. Grandgent, rev. edn, Boston 1933, xvii. All references will be to this edition.

[2] A. S. Cook, 'The Last Months of Chaucer's Earliest Patron,' *Transactions of the Connecticut Academy of Arts and Sciences*, XXI, (Dec. 1916), Section 10.

[3] In R. E. G. Kirk's *Summary of the Life Records of Chaucer* (Chaucer Society, Second Series, XXXII, 1900, No. 72) he is referred to as 'Jakes de Ponan, milite.' M⸱nly (*Some New Light on Chaucer*, New York 1926, p. 32) identifies these men as Giovanni [sic] de Mari and Jacopo de Provano of Corignano.

[4] Beardwood, p. 4.

[5] R. K. Root, *The Poetry of Chaucer*, Boston 1927, p. 257. In his edition (xi), Skeat adds Pisa. All three cities were commercial centres; the largest banking houses in Europe at this time were in Genoa and Pisa.

trade, and arranging royal loans through foreign banks were a part of the Italian merchants 'varied functions, which were of financial and diplomatic as well as mercantile service to the crown.'[1] Such court services are in striking parallel to the 'delicate missions at home and abroad'[2] in which esquires of the royal household, such as Chaucer, were regularly employed.

Finally, we must realize that Chaucer, after leaving the king's household, would have continued to encounter the Italian group in his capacity first as Controller of the Customs on Wools, Skins and Hides, and later as Controller of the Petty Custom on wine and other merchandise, for, outside the court, alien merchants (among whom the Italians are outstanding in the fourteenth century) collected the customs in payment of royal debts, or underwrote those English magnates to whom these revenues were unsuccessfully farmed out.[3] As merchants, they were extremely important in the revenue of the English customs, shipping (principally through London, Boston, Southampton and Hull) about one-third of the country's chief export, wool, and bringing in about 20–25 per cent of its chief import, wine. As B. J. Whitwell put it:

> During the whole period [i.e., from the twelfth to the fourteenth centuries], the merchants of Lucca or Florence—better known in formal documents as well as in speech as 'Lombards'—had a great share in the wool trade and derived great wealth from it, much to the indignation of 'true-born Englishmen'—for whom let John Gower speak . . . :
>
> > *L'en porra trop esmerveiller*
> > *En nostre terre a mon avis*
> > *Des Lumbardz, qui sont estranger.*
> > *Q'est-ce q'ils vuillont chalanger*
> > *A demourer en noz paiis*
> > *Tout auci francs, auci cheris,*
> > *Comme s'ils fuissent neez et norriz*
> > *Avesque nous: mais pour guiler*
> > *Moustront semblant com noz amis,*

[1] Beardwood, pp. 3–4.

[2] T. F. Tout, 'Literature and Learning in the English Civil Service in the Fourteenth Century,' *Speculum* IV, 1929, p. 384.

[3] Beardwood, p. 124, n. 1.

> *Et soubz cela lour cuer ont mys*
> *De nost argent et orr piler.*[1]

The foregoing paragraphs are not meant to court chaos by denying any single date but rather to depict, however briefly, the Italian influences in one aspect of Chaucer's non-literary life. From his early days in the households of Lionel and of Edward III, through his years on diplomatic missions and in the customs, Chaucer would have had ample motive and opportunity for learning Italian from 'Lombards' living in England. Nor must one forget, in considering when he might have come upon Trecentisti poetry, the number of English people who travelled to Italy, not just pardoners and wandering friars, but also those who, like the Wife of Bath, journeyed to Rome on pilgrimage, or those who, like the Clerk, had studied at such centres as Bologna 'mater studiorum,' or those who had stayed for years in Italy, like the English mercenaries under Hawkeswood, or those who had been in the entourage of Lionel at the cultivated Visconti court. The fame of the Italian poets read by Chaucer was such that any one of these Englishmen might have been the means by which texts arrived in England—if indeed Italians resident in London and at the court had not already brought in the first renowned flowering of their native vernacular literature.

As with traditional influence studies, the question of when and why Chaucer came to Italian language and literature cannot be restricted, cannot be handled *in vacuo*. But querying methodologies and historical facts, however fundamental, is basically corrective and, in a sense, not immediately concerned with what is our main aim—learning something about Chaucer's poetry, in this case by seeing his response to undoubted Italian sources. Simply to list ascriptions would tell us little; fortunately, such information is available in the notes to standard texts, as well as in special studies recently surveyed by Paul Ruggiers.[2] The present discussion seeks rather to investigate the ways in which Chaucer transformed his sources, reading them with certain poetic predilections and needs that

---

[1] R. J. Whitwell, 'Italian Bankers and the English Crown,' *Transactions* of the Royal Historical Society, New Series, XVII, 1903, pp. 176–7. Whitwell is citing *Mirrour de l'omme*, 25430–40.

[2] Paul G. Ruggiers, 'The Italian Influence on Chaucer,' *Companion to Chaucer Studies*, pp. 139–61. This essential article, with its fine selective bibliography, is by its very nature more presentational than evaluative; it seems, however, to overemphasize Dante.

tell us a great deal about both the poet and his poem. In order to show the range of this response, I have chosen three passages from three different Chaucerian works (*Parlement of Foules, Troilus and Criseyde,* and *The Canterbury Tales*), comparing them with three different Italian works (Boccaccio's *Teseide,* his *Filostrato,* and Dante's *Divina Commedia*) so that we might see what transformation in theme, in characterization, and in tone Chaucer has carried out.

III

When we turn from the question of the Italian influence in Chaucer's 'world of affairs' to the question of Italian influence in Chaucer's 'world of books', past scholarship tells us relatively little of the degree to which Chaucer transformed these borrowings. Yet such transformations not only constitute one of the most important aspects of 'influence' but they also allow us to see Chaucer in the very act of reshaping the poet's design. To use a somewhat inadequate metaphor, Chaucer may take over certain stones or even the general structure of an Italian artist but, although it is first necessary to recognize those stones or that structure, our fuller understanding of the impact of the Italian original is seen when we begin to realize how he sets or shapes those stones or how he adapts the design to his own poetic plan.

Perhaps the most basic transformation is that in which lines are altered and the stanzas are moved around or dropped, producing a quite different meaning and effect. A good example of this is found in the *Parlement of Foules,* that rather astonishing poem that, by the rhetorical device of *divisio,* presents the manifold aspects of *amor.* As will be recalled, the Dreamer in this poem is first carried to the heavens where he is shown the harmony and the 'commune profyt' of universal accord. The major Chaucerian division of 'celestial love or elles love of kynde'[1] is marked by the Dreamer's entrance into the walled garden, with its literally ambivalent gate bearing the promise of the 'blysful place' on the one half and the threat of unfruitful sorrow on the other.

The Dreamer's walk past Cupid's well, past the traditional amatory

[1] *Tr* I, 979. The relationship and importance of this idea has been sensitively investigated by Dorothy Everett, *Essays on Middle English Literature,* ed Patricia Kean, Oxford 1955, esp. pp. 108–10.

personifications, and up to the temple is based, as is the description of the temple itself, on Boccaccio's *Teseida*.[1] In that poem, Palemone's personified prayer travels up to the temple of Venus, there to present its petition. As Robinson and others have noted, lines 183–294 are 'a close imitation of *Tes*[*eida*] vii, st. 51–60, 61–62, 63–66'[2]—but the slight changes and the stanzaic shifting transform the source remarkably. Rather than dealing with the entire passage, we can see what occurs in looking principally at the temple itself. Now, let us remember that Chaucer's audience did not (poor things) have scholarly footnotes to the text; there is little chance that they would have known of Boccaccio, let alone have recognized this description from the *Teseida*. It is necessary to stress this because Chaucer, quite unlike Boccaccio, does not identify the temple as belonging to any particular deity; and that omission, as we shall see, seems quite deliberate.

In the only description of the exterior of the building itself, Chaucer departs from his source in an apparently small but really very significant way:

> *And upon pilers greete of jasper longe*
> *I saw a temple of bras ifounded stronge*   (230–1)

Quite precisely, the temple is not on, though it is within the confines of, the green-walled garden of 'love of kynde'. It is separated from the ground by long, great pillars of jasper. This last point is not in the *Teseida*, which has only

> *E"n mezzo il luogo in su alte colonne*
> *di rame un tempio vide . . .*[3]

[1] While persuasive counterarguments can be made, it seems more likely that Chaucer needed and made use of this separable episode first, and at a later date returned to the *Teseida* for his writing of *The Knight's Tale*.

[2] Robinson continues: 'The Italian passage goes back to the Roman de la Rose; and it is hard to judge whether Chaucer recalled the French poem or only followed it at one remove . . .' (p. 903). Actually, as we shall see, Chaucer does not use stanza 63. All quotations from Chaucer will come from *Works*, ed F. N. Robinson, 2nd edn, Cambridge, Mass. 1957.

[3] *Teseida*, vii, 57, 1–2. Quotations from Boccaccio are from *Tutte le Opere di Giovanni Boccaccio*, a cura di Vittore Branca, Mondadori, 1964. 'In the middle of the place, [Palemone's dream] saw a temple of copper on high columns.' On Boccaccio's use of 'rame,' see *Opere*, ed Salvatore Battaglia,

If we assume that Chaucer made this change intentionally, what then was he attempting? We know that natural objects—plants, stones, gems, and so on—could be understood significantly. Can we say that we have here the first of a number of instances in which Chaucer is transforming his source, that (in other words) jasper has been chosen for the pillars carefully and intentionally? If we turn to the medieval encyclopaedia, in this case to Vincent of Beauvais' *Speculum Naturale*, we find the following explanation of the uses of jasper, based on Arnoldus de Villanova:[1]

> Arnoldus. Iaspis est gemma multorum colorum. sed optimus est viridis et translucens de multis partibus transmittitur. hominem tutum facit . et fantasmata pellit . *luxuriam quoque cohibet . et conceptum prohibet* . est autem virtus eius contra fluxum sanguinis et menstruorm.[2]

What I shall try to indicate in the next few paragraphs is that Chaucer very deliberately transforms the temple of Venus which he found in Boccaccio into a temple of *luxuria* in the *Parlement of Foules*, carefully separating that building from the garden of earthly love by columns of jasper, which 'luxuriam quoque cohibet . et conceptum prohibet.' It is hoped that in so doing we can perhaps begin to understand influence not just as source or simple input, but, as well, as the movements, the artistic consequences that are forthcoming.

The changes continue. Whereas Boccaccio's Venus is representative of 'la vita volottuosa' and is 'quella per la quale ogni lascivia e desiderata,'[3] Chaucer, as we shall see, changes the emphasis just enough so that the

---

Florence 1939, p. 200 n.

Since we lack a translation of the *Teseida*, I shall give my own as 'neutrally' as possible. In the case of the *Filostrato*, I shall use the most easily available translation, that in R. K. Gordon, *The Story of Troilus*, 1934; now in paperback, New York, 1954.

[1] Chaucer certainly knew Vincent (see Pauline Aiken's Yale Ph.D. dissertation, 1934, and the many articles published thereafter) and cites him as an authority (LGW, G307); however, he also knew, or at least knew of, 'Arnold of the Newe-Toun' (CYT 1428).

[2] *Speculum Naturale*, Lib. IX, cap. LXXVII. [My italics.] *Luxuria* has the basic meaning of excess, indulgence, especially with regard to sensual-sexual immoderation.

[3] Cf. *Teseida*, vii, 66, 4–5. The phrases (the voluptuous life, she through whom every lasciviousness is desired) are Battaglia's, *ed cit.*, p. 205 n.

temple in the *Parlement* is consecrated to three deities, Jealousy, Priapus, and Venus, almost equally. The care and plan with which Chaucer remakes each line of Boccaccio[1] is evident as well in the order in which he takes over the stanzas. Chaucer uses, first, stanzas 51–60; then, eliminating 63, follows with 64–66; and finally, he comes back to pick up the examples of lovers given in stanzas 61–62. This rearrangement (along with the changes in the individual lines) almost totally de-emphasizes Venus by making her just one among three gods of this temple of *luxuria*, rather than (as with Boccaccio) the sole goddess to whom the undeified personification 'Gelosia,' the untitled Priapus, the list of unfortunate or unnatural lovers, and the sixty-third stanza, are all subordinated introductions.

Chaucer has the Dreamer wander through the temple, seeing first the altars of 'the bittere *goddesse* Jelosye'[2] then 'The *god* Priapus . . . in a sovereyn place'[3] and then 'in a prive corner . . . Venus.'[4] With obvious intention, Chaucer has the dreamer definitely depart from Venus before he gives a significantly expanded list of lovers. He states

> But thus I let hire [Venus] lye,
> And ferther in the temple I gan espie
>
> That, in dispit of Dyane the chaste,
> Ful many a bowe ibroke heng on the wal . . .   (279–82)

In short, Chaucer has made Venus and (as we shall see) 'la vita volutuosa' but one aspect of the temple of *luxuria*.

But what is Chaucer attempting to delineate by this change from one to three divinities in what I have suggested is a change from a temple of Venus to a temple of excess? He is, of course, carrying out the plan of

---

[1] It should be noted that the reader of *Boccaccio*, having been told from the start that this was the temple of Venus, would connect the subsequent descriptions of dancing youths and maidens, Pazienza, madonna Pace and so on, with the goddess of love; *Chaucer's* readers, not having been given this identification, would have to treat them as more independent images. Chaucer has slightly shifted each of these images, making them almost foreboding, coming closer to suggestive symbol where Boccaccio employs simple allegory.

[2] PF, 252. [My italics.]

[3] PF, 253–4. [My italics.]

[4] PF, 260–1.

divisio, of cataloguing the manifold aspects of *amor*; but beyond that we are being shown the sterility of misguided excess. Here there is no single goal of *natura generans* but a *luxuria* that leads to one of three ungenerative ends. Such excess, if formalistic, ends in Jealousy;[1] if sexual, it ends in lasciviousness; if sensual, it ends in voluptuousness. To maintain these distinctions and to give each aspect of *luxuria* its proper weight is the purpose of the careful rewriting and shifting about of Boccaccio's verses. For this reason, Chaucer's excision of the phrase 'nate di martiri'[2] and the change from 'una donna cruda e ria . . . chiamata Gelosia'[3] to 'the bittere goddesse Jelosye' have quite purposefully divorced this type of fruitless excess from that which is controlled by Venus.

The lasciviousness that results from excessive sexuality is very aptly put under the aegis of Priapus and very carefully distinguished by Chaucer, for Priapus is not evoked in his role as a god of fertility and personification of the fruitfulness of nature. What we are given is an example, an almost comic example, of lasciviousness. Priapus, it will be recalled, 'was represented as a man unusually grotesque, with an enormous and erect sexual organ'.[4] Lemprière adds that

> . . . he received the name of Priapus *propter deformitatem et membri virilis magnitudinem* . . . [At Lampascus, there were] temples erected in his honor. Festivals were also celebrated and the people, naturally idle and indolent, gave themselves up to every lasciviousness and impurity during the celebrations. . . . The Roman revered him more as a god of orchards than licentiousness. A crown painted with different colours was offered to him in the spring, and in summer a garland of ears of corn. An ass was generally sacrificed to him, because that animal, by its braying, awoke the nymph Lotis, to whom Priapus was going to offer violence. . . . He was crowned with the leaves of the vine and sometimes with laurel or rocket. The last of these plants was sacred to him as it is said to raise the passions and excite love.[1]

---

[1] T. A. Kirby, *Chaucer's Troilus: A Study in Courtly Love*, Baton Rouge, Louisiana, *passim*. Thus, at least three of Andreas' *regulae* have this basis: 'II, Qui non zelat, amare non potest. . . . XXI, Ex vera zelotypia affectus semper crescit amandi. . . . XXII, De coamante suspicione percepta zelus et affectus crescit amandi.'

[2] I.e., Love's martyrs. See *Teseida*, vii, 59, 4–5.

[3] *Teseida*, 59, 7–8. A harsh and cruel woman called Jealousy.

[4] *Encyclopaedia Britannica*, Chicago 1950, XVIII, p. 467.

Lamprière notes that he is referred to as *phallus, fascinus, Ithyphallus, ruber* and *rubicundus*, that he was the deity 'who presided over the garden and the parts of generation of the sexes,' and that he is often seen holding a stick, club and scythe. There was scarcely a phallic cult or an example of lasciviousness that did not own the dominance of Priapus. It is the statue of this deity that Chaucer places 'Withinne the temple in a sovereyn place.' The statue itself is described briefly, and with a snicker. Priapus stands

> *In swich aray as whan the asse hym shente*
> *With cri by nighte, and with hys sceptre in honde.*[2]

Having added the rather obvious 'sceptre in hond,' Chaucer proceeds to make two more important changes. Boccaccio, having finished the reference to the attempted seduction, adds the more general fact:

> *. . . e simil per lo tempio grande*
> *di fior diversi assai vide [sc. Palemone's prayer]*
> *ghirlande.*[3]

Chaucer, on the other hand, increases the importance of Priapus' place in the temple by having suppliants in active attendance on him. This is done by transferring Boccaccio's more generalized description of the temple and its flowers directly to Priapus:

> *Ful besyly men gonne assaye and fonde*
> *Upon his hed to settle, of sondry hewe,*
> *Garlondes ful of freshe floures newe.*　　　(257–9)

The offerings recall the multi-coloured crowns, garlands and first fruits that were traditionally offered to Priapus in his role of fertility god of gardens and fields.[4] The second change is a direct result of Chaucer's

[1] *Lamprière's Classical Dictionary*, ed F. A. Wright, New York 1949, pp. 518–19.

[2] PF, 255–6. For the extensive gloss of Boccaccio, see ed Battaglia, p. 201 n.

[3] *Teseida*, vii, 60, 7–8. And likewise, throughout the temple, [Palemone's prayer] saw garlands of quite diverse flowers.

[4] The dual role of Priapus as 'deus hortorum' and 'prudendorum tensio vel passio' is defined in the *Catholicum*, editum a fratre Joanne Januensi, Venetus, 1495, f. 240.

division of *luxuria*, and is seen in lines which Chaucer excises from the
later description of Venus. Boccaccio has

> *e essa [Venus] seco per la man tenea*
> *Lascivia . . .*   (vii, 66, 4–5)

Chaucer, in reducing the longer Italian description of Venus, would
have been careful to dissociate the personified Lascivia from the goddess
since *lascivia*, or excessive sexuality, in Chaucer's temple of *luxuria* is
properly within the realm of Priapus.

In describing Venus, Chaucer not only took out or shifted Boccaccio's
three intervening, introductory stanzas (with the array of lovers), but he
shortened and altered the remaining three as well. The result is (first) that
Venus is relegated to a more equal status with the other god and goddess
of the temple; (second) that Chaucer's concentration of imagery and
excision of references to Lascivia, as well as Venus' beauty and bounte-
ousness, define the sphere which the goddess controls, and (third) that
this sensuality is treated as an empty and meaningless tableau. Both Boccaccio and Chaucer place Venus in a dimly lighted spot, but while the
former makes it the *sanctum sanctorum* of the temple, with its door
guarded by Richezza, for Chaucer it is simply a 'prive corner' in which

> *. . . she lay to reste*
> *Til that the hote sonne gan to weste.*   (265–6)

These Chaucerian lines seem to contrast with the perpetual day of ll.
209–10 ('ne nevere wolde it nyghte, / But ay cler day to any manes
syghte.'). Indeed there is a sense of stasis, of carefully nurtured fragility,
which establishes a direct contrast to the strong and healthy beauty of
Nature that is shortly to be portrayed. But here, Chaucer takes up
Boccaccio's phrase 'avea d'oro crini' and expands it until Venus
becomes an excessively rich, almost lifeless, artifact:

> *And on a bed of gold she lay to reste, . . .*
> *Hyre gilte heres with a golden thred*
> *Ibounden were*   (265, 267–8)

The bed of gold and the golden thread in her 'gilte heres' are Chaucer's
additions. As well, the voluptuousness that both writers are portraying
in the almost nude Venus is undercut only by Chaucer, who brings in
the Dreamer's comically ambiguous 'to my pay,' the localization of l.
272, and the rhetorical shift to understatement in l. 273. The change in

direction can perhaps be more clearly seen if we look at the two passages. Where Boccaccio has

> . . . *e vide lei nuda giacere*
> *sopr'un gran letto assai bello a vedere.*
>
> *Elle avea d'oro i crini e rilegati*
> *intorno al capo sanza treccia alcuna;*
> *il suo viso era tal, che' più lodati*
> *hanno a rispetto bellezza nessuna;*
> *le braccia e 'l petto e' pomi rilevati*
> *si vedean tutti, e l'altra parte d'una*
> *veste tanto sottil si ricopria,*
> *che quasi nulla appena nascondia.*[1]

Chaucer, by a contrast in tone, gives:

> *And on a bed of gold she lay to reste,*
> *Til that the hote sonne gan to weste.*
>
> *Hyre gilte heres with a golden thred*
> *Ibounden were, untressed as she lay,*
> *And naked from the brest unto the hed*
> *Men myghte hire sen; and, sothly for to say,*
> *The remenaunt was wel kevered to my pay,*
> *Ryght with a subtyl coverchef of Valence—*
> *Ther nas no thikkere cloth of no defense.*   (265–73)

Not only has the superb sensuality of Boccaccio's lines been radically
reduced, but the emphasis on 'bellezza' has been removed entirely.
Chaucer's praise is not for this static sensuality but is reserved for Natura,

> . . . *a quene*
> *That, as of lyght the somer sonne shene*
> *Passeth the sterre, right so over mesure*
> *She fayrer was than any creature.*   (299–301)

[1] *Teseida*, vii, 64, 7–8; 65. 'And he saw her lying naked upon a bed, quite
beautiful to see. She had hair of gold, bound round her head without any
plaiting; her face was such that none, with respect to beauty, had greater
praising; her arm, her chest and breasts were seen all strikingly, and the
other part was covered with a very thin cloth so that scarcely anything was
hidden.'

Both poets stress the pandering to the voluptuousness of the senses in this scene; the light must be dim, there must be 'a thousand savours sote,' Bacchus and Ceres must tantalize and support the appetites. Boccaccio, after adding Lascivia and the apple of discord to the tableau, ends with:

> *E tutto ciò veduto, porse il priego,*
> *il qual fu conceduto sanza niego.*[1]

Chaucer simply puts two suppliants on the scene, but he does not say whether the carefully arranged goddess ever breaks the perfect proportion of the tableau to take any notice of them. Nor does the Dreamer particularly care:

> *And, as I seyde, amyddes lay Cypride,*
> *To whom on knees two yonge folk ther cryde*
> *To ben here helpe. But thus I let hire lye,*
> *And ferther in the temple I gan espie . . .* (277–80)

Not till now does Chaucer follow Boccaccio's list of lovers, expanding it from memory or from some as yet unknown list to include heroes of romance as well as other figures from history.[2] The first two, Calyxte and Athalante, having been nymphs of Diana, are pictured on the wall that celebrates those whose bows are 'ibroke'; but they, as well as every other name on Chaucer's list, are examples of those who carried love beyond its natural limits, who were driven to suicide, distraction, incest, treason or death through an excess of love. Not one of these loves was happy; not one of these loves was fruitful; all were either violent or tragic. All end by telling 'in what plyt they dyde' (204), though one can hardly say—with Semiramis, Biblis, Hercules, Scylla, and Candace present—that this is a hagiology of 'Seintes Legende of Cupide' or a presentation of martyred lovers. Chaucer had already put that idea aside when he excised Boccaccio's reference to 'martiri'. Viktor Langhans, though he seems to give undue emphasis to the immorality of those in the paintings in order to strengthen his view of the poem as a *contentio* between moral and immoral love, nonetheless supplies a fine analysis of this particular part of the poem. He points out that those portrayed have broken *Nature*'s code, and he recalls, quite properly, the relationship of

---

[1] *Teseida*, vii, 66, 7–8. And having seen all of this, the prayer presented itself, which was allowed without denial.

[2] 'Chaucer and Dante,' pp. 138–40.

the temple and the glade to the two inscriptions above the gate,[1] though as I have tried to show, the careful re-thinking and re-working of Boccaccio makes virtually every detail of the temple pertinent. Past critics, however, have seen the poem as a contrast (moral and immoral love, courtly and natural love, and so on) and each has been partially right—'partially' in that they have approached the poem as a *contentio* when in point of fact it is a careful analysis (as I have already remarked) of the manifold aspects of *amor*. The poem's topic is explicitly love, and this topic is then divided into its two major units, 'celestial love' and 'love of kynde'. In turn, this last category is then divided into its components: principally, *luxuria* with its three kinds of unfruitful love, and *Natura generans*, with its varieties of progenerative love. All are *within* the area of earthly love, but the pillars of jasper are meant to hold in or contain *luxuria* while at the same time they prevent or check conception and generation. Choosing any two opposing elements of the *divisio* makes it appear that the poem is a simple *contentio*; but such a contrast can be set forth only at the expense of the rest of the poem. Contrast can be properly used if it is recognized that we are only dealing with parts of the whole poem. With this caveat in mind, let us take one final backward look at the *luxuria* passage:

The contrast that Chaucer makes between the fetid air of the temple and the healthy openness of the court of 'this noble goddesse Nature' is immediately evident. The Dreamer leaves the temple and comes into the glade with an obvious sense of relief:

> *Whan I was come ayeyn into the place*
> *That I of spak, that was so sote and grene,*
> *Forth welk I tho myselven to solace.*   (295–7)

Here are no ambiguous divinities nor over-wrought buildings, but an open glade on a hill of flowers where Nature has set her court:

> *Of braunches were here halles and here boures*
> *Iwroughte after here cast and here mesure . . .*   (304–5)

There is no hint of excess here. 'Cast' and 'mesure' are observed by this 'noble empresse, ful of grace';[2] and order and accord are the dominant

[1] Viktor Langhans, *Untersuchungen zu Chaucer*, Halle, 1918, pp. 27–8.

[2] The echoes of the Ave are obvious; it might, however, be recalled that the first inscription over the gate had mentioned that the reward of proper love was arrival at the 'welle of grace,' another common term in Mariolatry.

tones of the remainder of the poem, ending in the poetic harmony of the roundel. Despite all the noise and confusion, every bird had taken

> . . . *his owne place,*
> *As they were woned alwey fro yer to yeere,*
> *Seynt Valentynes day, to stonden theere.*   (320–2)

Each bird has come 'to chese his make'. This is the annual mating, the drive of *natura generans* which itself is in accord with God's edict to prosper and multiply. Nature's divinely approved authority over all living, unperverted things is acknowledged constantly by all who are there assembled. It is stated directly:

> *Nature, the vicaire of the almyghty Lord,*
> *That hot, cold, hevy, lyght, moyst, and dreye*
> *Hath knyt by even noumbres of acord,*

and it is re-stated towards the conclusion:

> *With dredful vois the formel tho answerde,*
> *"My rightful lady, goddesse of Nature!*
> *Soth is that I am evere under youre yerde,*
> *As is everich other creature,*
> *And mot be youres whil my lyf may dure . . .*   (638–42)

As opposed to the threefold 'idolatry' of the temple, there is here but one ruler, God's vicar, who maintains harmony and to whom all creatures willingly subject themselves. This being the realm of Nature and *natura generans*, it soon becomes evident why normal and proper sexual urge has been carefully kept out of the temple of *luxuria*.

Boccaccio's *Teseida*, as I hope has been shown, did not simply supply Chaucer with a prefabricated description of a temple which he then proceeded to translate 'for the nonnes alle'. The passage was meticulously read and thoroughly understood. Whether Chaucer's reading of the passage led him to consider the distinctions and differentiations that he wrote of in the *Parlement*, or whether his general approach to the topic of *amor* suggested that the Italian's view had in some way to be aligned with, or located in, his own schema is a problem that we shall probably never solve. Indeed, the answer to that seems less important than the fact that we have perhaps been able to see this kind of influence in action, to understand a little better influence in the process of transformation.

IV

Chaucer's most extensive debt to any Italian poem is to Boccaccio's *Filostrato*, the primary source for his profound, tender and witty investigation of love's growth in *Troilus and Criseyde*. To read the *Filostrato* is to suspect at once what must have caught Chaucer's imagination: a superbly human story with a polished rhetoric and poetic that could range from the high style of formal invocation to (on at least one occasion) the relaxed style of relatively natural dialogue. But Chaucer's poem is markedly different, and the change involves more than just the narrative; it is above all in the transformation of Boccaccio's characters and in the greater depth that the English poem attains. Here again, what Chaucer used and what he set aside, what he translated and what he transformed, are evidence of influence in the larger sense of that word.

For Chaucer, there are four major characters: Troilus, Criseyde, Pandarus, and the narrator. The narrator is no impersonal voice; on the contrary, he becomes deeply involved in the story, responding, commenting, directing us, the readers, in such a way that we can enter the inner thoughts of the characters and, in turn, respond to the vital emotions of their world. The very presence of this complex narrator —Janus-like in his ability to see into both the world of the reader and the world of the narrative and, in his responses, Trimmer-like in his ability to present the story's characters with sustained creative ambiguity —quite changes the nature of Boccaccio's poem. The *Filostrato* focuses on the three principal characters, the role of the narrator being quite minimized. Long narrative passages exist, of course, but the story is, with rare exception (e.g., iv, 23–25), neutrally presented, even though we come to it by way of Boccaccio's extended prose *proemio* directly addressed to Maria d'Acquino.

Very closely allied to this use of the narrator as medium is a second Chaucerian transformation, one of rhetorical stance—for, where Boccaccio employs almost opposite ends of the rhetorical spectrum—either the direct address of Boccaccio to his *donna* or neutral narration —Chaucer works within the richly ambiguous centre. His created narrator pretends at times to authorial assertion and at times to narrative neutrality, but Chaucer knows that we as readers realize that even though the narrator achieves neither, we remain dependent on his observations. Transforming Boccaccio's juxtaposition of extremes into the more vital complexity of a medial position seems almost a hallmark of Chaucer's use of the *Filostrato* and is to be found in his treatment of both its themes and, as I hope to show, its characters.

Still another fundamental change—and one that may also be allied to the foregoing—concerns the structure of the two poems. Boccaccio, we find, works with four basic units or blocks of rhetoric; roughly in order of length and substance, these are: the speeches and letters of Troilo, the narrative settings, the speeches of Pandaro, and finally those of Cresseida. Boccaccio's characters tend to express themselves in long, almost set pieces of rhetorical elaboration, striking examples of polished amplification which are juxtaposed masterfully in the investigation of a particular situation. As soon as the rhetorical possibilities of one situation are achieved, a unit of narration is used to establish a new setting and circumstance, evoking once more responses of remarkable rhetorical art. Chaucer must have been struck, as almost every reader is, by Boccaccio's skilfulness; but one suspects that there may have been the additional admiration of seeing this skill applied not in Latin prose argument but in poetry in the vulgar tongue concerning the emotional complexities of personal love. Once more, however, Chaucer seems to transform his source, moving from this juxtaposition of units to a more organic structure. Instead of using a series of situations, Chaucer creates a continuously evolving narrative which, by being tied to the over-arching theme of Troy's place in universal history, attains a life and force of its own. This in turn encourages a basic modification of Boccaccio's rhetoric and structure; the expression of the Chaucerian characters, rather than 'merely' responding to a series of critical moments, grows out of constantly more complex and universally more exigent forces.

Not surprisingly, Chaucer's techniques of characterization reflect this pattern of transformation, allowing us to see the direction in which he was moving. To understand this movement and some of its implications more clearly, let us recall the two more or less traditional methods of character presentation: the one is by character revelation, the other by character development. In character revelation—for which, perhaps, the faceted diamond serves as a suitable image—aspects or facets of the character are discovered through a series of situations (instances could be found in many medieval romances, in rogue literature, in early Smollett, for example). Yet though much has been revealed, the character himself is, in effect, the same at the end of the work as at the beginning. Though we have seen the complexity of the diamond by the numerous facets that are placed to reflect various scenes and situations, the diamond itself remains essentially inorganic. In the second method, character development, there is an organic change; that is to say, the character as he enters the work is quite different from the character that comes out of it. Here, the character is affected by the situations, aspects of him naturally develop, that is, out of the nature of him that we have thus far been given, but in such a way that later developments would be absurd before that later moment. (Instances might include such works as *Gawain and the Green Knight, Piers Plowman*, or Fielding novels, to name but a few.) Obviously, such a dichotomy oversimplifies the problem, if only because most works of literature combine characters constructed in varying degrees of, and by, these two techniques; but what I suggest is that Chaucer, in transforming Boccaccio's poem, used this difference of technique to intensify the dynamics of tragedy in his three main characters.

Boccaccio faces his character with a relatively simple tension between the private world of personal (principally sexual) satisfaction and the social world of courtly strictures, propriety and reputation. And, while their full and fascinating responses delineate for us the many shifting stages in between, the characters themselves never basically change under the onslaught of emotions and events. Troilo, for all his passion and his poetry, never really moves from Self to Other. The egocentricity, often the glandular egocentricity, that one might expect at the beginning of the poem continues throughout, both in his soliloquy after hearing of the prisoner exchange ('who now will give comfort to *my* torments . . . to *my* eager longing . . . *I* poor wretch . . . grievous unto *me*') and as well in the last night together ('But meanwhile by whom will *my* sadness be relieved . . . great torment if *I* see thee not').[1] The dominant tone is I-me-mine, not thou-thee-thine; and even when we find a use of we-us-our, the stress seems still to come on the first person singular. Upon this basis of Troilo's personality, Chaucer built an organically developing character,[2] a character who begins as an ardent young

[1] Gordon's translation; my italicization. See *Filostrato*, iv, 36–40, 155.

[2] I am, of course, rejecting the traditional view that sees Troilus as 'the simplest character . . . much the same as in Boccaccio . . . strong and brave,

male struck ('astoned,' 'awhaped') by a beautiful woman across a crowded room, and who ends, disdaining all this world's 'vanitee,' in the eighth sphere of Heaven, the realm of the fixed stars and of that fascinatingly enigmatic group, the virtuous pagans. Chaucer develops Boccaccio's basically bipolar structure into a carefully expanded delineation of the steps, or (to use an even more popular contemporary image) the ladder of Troilus's love.[1] The pattern is quite clear: Troilus develops from the love-struck youth of Book I, through the emotional revolution of Book II, and on to the superb hymn ('O Love, O Charitee') so pointedly and poignantly set at the emotional centre of Book III, then on to the (Boethian) philosophical additions of Book IV, and into the emotional withdrawal and death (even before his bodily death) that forces him from consideration of the individual instance of love to comprehension of the universal idea of Love as 'L' Amor che move il sole e l'altre stelle.[2] This last step, this sudden expansion, is breathtaking; but a moment's reflection shows how the poem's setting has steadily widened from Troilus solitary in his chamber, to the lovers' chamber, to the parliament, to the increasing distance separating Troy from the Greek camp, to Troilus' dissociation from 'real' time and space, and finally to a whole new universal perception that encompasses at once both the Christian and the perfected (albeit pagan) ideal of Love.

This overarching expansion Chaucer did not find carried out in Boccaccio, though he did find in his source a fully achieved expression of the *gradus amoris* pattern which, with significant changes, forms the basis for the love affair itself. Yet even here there is a shift of emphasis that is easily seen: Troilus appears more immature, less accomplished than Troilo; where Troilo's attention is steadily on Cressida the woman, Troilus' is on a Criseyde who becomes for him the way by which love is compre-

---

. . . sentimental . . . the ideal courtly lover.' (Robinson, *ed. cit.*, p. 387.) I prefer to follow Alfred David's "The Hero in *Troilus*," *Speculum* 37, 1962, 566–81.

[1] For a brief account of the *gradus amoris* and the scholarship on the subject, see M. R. Jung, *Etudes Sur le Poème Allegorique en France au Moyen Age*, *Romanica Helvetica* 82, Berne, 1971, pp. 140–6 and notes thereto.

[2] While 'the Love [i.e. God] that moves the sun and the other stars' is Dante's final statement (Par. XXXIII, 145), I do not wish to imply that Chaucer was dependent on the *Divina Commedia* for a view that was so widely held. Quite simply, Dante gives, in this instance as so often, consummate expression to the thought of his time.

hended. The *gradus amoris* of Boccaccio becomes a *scala amoris* for Chaucer, a ladder not unlike that of Plato's Diotima where the individual instance leads upward and outward to a universal abstract. All of Chaucer's changes from Boccaccio's Troilo, all of his additions to the poem, force us to recognize the transformation from a relatively static characterization to the complex growth, the organic development of Troilus.

If the technique of characterization used with Troilus is that of organic development, the technique used with Pandarus is that of character revelation; that is to say, while we have seen his fascinating multiplicity, while we have recognized the range of his responses to situation after situation, still he comes out of the poem as essentially the same person who went in. In technique of characterization, if not in the actual character himself, Chaucer is closer to Boccaccio than he is with any of the other major figures. The difference between Pandarus and Pandaro is of course striking, but it emanates more from two different views of the individual character than from a difference in technique of characterization. For Boccaccio, Pandaro is a youth of high lineage and great courage (ii, 1, 4), Criseida's cousin and therefore of the same generation as the other two. For Chaucer, Pandarus is without age, his position depends principally upon his relationship with a particular group at the Trojan court, and as Criseyde's uncle his obligations shift dramatically from those of Pandaro. This new relationship not only ties him more closely to this marked family, but, with Calchas' flight, he would seem to have the additional responsibilities of *chef de famille*—a family that has already shown a tendency towards inadvertent betrayal. There is an even more fundamental shift that Chaucer makes. Boccaccio's Pandaro is fully developed in his conventional role of the confidant; Chaucer's Pandarus is far more roguish, far more consciously comic, far more the courtier who operates by his wit and verbal skill, the sympathetic *logodaedalus* who seeks the vicarious satisfaction of bringing his niece and the king's son together.

All these, and the many other changes that one could list, are in Pandarus *ab initio*. Throughout the poem, he continues to think at the level of the practical affair, he continues to feel that he should be able to be the master puppeteer, and he is only annihilated by arriving at a situation in which his verbal legerdemain no longer has pertinence (V, 1723–29). His is a world of words and when one moves beyond a realm where words can manoeuvre, he can only disappear, as so many literary rhetors disappear, in silence. Within his own sphere, Pandarus is quite sensitive to subtle implications; he sees, if in a limited way, that Troilus is indeed moving beyond his ken; he is well aware of what natural forces he is setting in motion, of the fact that he is the initiator of a course of action in which Troilus will soon move beyond his control. This is marked by that lovely, indeed tender, scene (III, 250–300, though the first hints are at II, 1646) when Pandarus in effect turns over the governance of Criseyde to Troilus. For all its sympathetic ineptitude, Troilus' control increases in the course of the work, reaching a critical point at the moment of sexual consummation when Pandarus (unlike Pandaro who is not present) retires into the background, settling down with a good book and a sense of accomplishment. Thereafter, Troilus becomes Criseyde's 'walle of stiele,' her protector, but his development continues to grow, even beyond the affair. By the end of the third book, his affair is hymned forth in terms of the Boethian chain of love that holds the universe together (III, 1744–71). In the fourth book, with its large Boethian addition on free will and destiny, we see at once that Pandarus has absolutely no idea of the philosophical distances that Troilus has travelled while off in the temple, moving beyond him so far that the contrast is almost pathetic. Troilus, then, beginning in ignorance, quite below Pandarus in the world of the pragmatic, passes through that sphere in which Pandarus is so superb and supreme, and goes on to realms that Pandarus knows not of. On his own rung of the *scala amoris*, Pandarus is without peer; but that rung is his limit; he is no psychopompos. The way in which Chaucer transformed the individual character of Boccaccio's confidant, as well as the additions that he made (especially those from Boethius) would seem to indicate once more what his plan and understanding of the *Troilus* had become.

And what of the technique of characterization of Criseyde? When we turn to the *Filostrato*, we find Boccaccio again using character revelation. His Criseida is, on the one hand, far more physically and sexually direct; on the other hand, her regard for outward social appearances is more intrusive, and certainly less convincing in the light of the other half of her character. Boccaccio, in fact, stretches out the story by sudden, unreal changes in Criseida from passion to prudery, or vice versa; the former change occurs when social propriety suddenly, or conveniently, comes to her mind; the latter, when Pandaro gives her any excuse, even a simple demand. We seem to be in an either/or world of adolescent responses. The difference in tone can be seen in the meeting that brings the two together for the sexual consummation. In Chaucer, it is the result of the most delicate and intricate manoeuvring by Pandarus and Fate, a manoeuvring that allows Criseyde to maintain a wonderful ambiguity throughout. In Boccaccio, the meeting is arranged and directed by Criseida (iii, 21,1–4; 28; 29,1–2); there is no Pandaro present (24,8), let alone any of the superb lyricism that we find in Chaucer; they embrace in passion (29,8–30,7), and in the shortest possible time, undress and head straight for the bed (31,4).

Boccaccio's Criseida, whether moved by passion or prudery, is more direct. She embodies these two motivations in a quite literal ambivalence; Chaucer on the other hand uses every device at his command (word-play, narrator intrusion, circumlocution, etc.) to avoid defining her motives and to sustain a creative ambiguity that makes her one of the most charmingly enigmatic women in English literature. A great deal of the charm and of the pathos that surrounds her comes from what I have formerly referred to as the dynamic use of different techniques of characterization. Criseyde begins in many ways as the conventional woman, the *donna*, of romance and courtly love poetry. She is the one whose appearance initiates the first sense of love, even in its most elemental form of glandular impact. Under her guidance, at the beginning, Troilus becomes a 'newe man.' But Chaucer does not stop here, or rather he does not allow Troilus to stop here. Troilus' ever-increasing comprehension of love, his idealization of it even at the moment of consummation (in the lyrical 'O Love, O Charitee,' so beautifully prepared for by the invocation and so well advanced by the concluding Boethian 'song' of Book III), and his expansion into the philosophical realms of the fourth book, in point of fact go beyond what Criseyde herself is capable of comprehending. The pity of it all is, of course, that there is a glimmer of hope, the hope that she, Criseyde, can follow Troilus to his universal view as their love (however sweet, however tender) for him becomes Love, the great abstract force which, even in the pre-Christian universe, the virtuous pagan could perceive. The tragedy is, in a sense, that the area of her potential enlargement is too limited; what Troilus is inadvertently demanding of her is more than she has to offer; and in the end she falls back to that stasis of character when, in a kind of reaction of relief, she accepts, in place of the immense responsibility that Troilus had demanded of her, a resignation to the love of the 'sudden Diomede,' one who is close to being Troilus' equal and opposite.

This is not to say that Criseyde is any the less complex than we have read her in the past, any the less a strong and engaging character; if anything, it reinforces these views. In the past, however, we have all too frequently looked only for her simple motivation; we have taken to the phrase 'slidynge of courage' as the very touchstone of her character. And yet, she has her own realm, broader than Pandarus' because she can do more than simply match him in his world of verbal wit and ingenuity. In that world, perhaps, 'slidynge of courage' may supply the reason and the excuse for many of her responses. But beyond this, as we must always remember, she is able to function (for a time at least) within the realm of Troilus as well. And here it would seem that one of the key phrases (if indeed we must live by key phrases) is that 'wommen ben wys in short avysement,' women are 'wise' (however one wishes to translate that) in the short view of things. This, I feel, points up a fundamental aspect of the poem, one that is a logical consequence of the way in which Chaucer read Boccaccio. It is an aspect that we see again and again in Chaucer, as for instance in the *Knight's Tale* when Arcite is willing to settle for the immediate goal while Palamon devotes himself to the long range one: Palamon must suffer what happens between hither and yon, but Arcite, if he attains the hither, never does achieve the yon. This, as we can see, is the problem of *fortune*, *destinee*, and *purveiaunce*, of *hap*, and *cas*, and *aventure*, in Chaucer; a problem that we can only allude to here.

'Wommen ben wys in short avysement'; but the 'long avysement' belongs to Troilus, to that universal view that is dragging him ever forward, and indeed up to the beatitude of the eighth sphere. Within her particular realm, that of 'short avysement,' Criseyde is 'wys.' Nor is this contrast of distance an unusual one, literature is replete with works that stress the truism that in the end women fall in love with the man and then with love, while men are in love with love and then with the woman. In this view, there is the pathos of the human condition, the pity of it all. And Chaucer, I suggest, deepened this pathos, and finally universalized the differences by techniques of characterization that have been discussed here; universalized them, in fact, to the point where we are forced to admit the ultimate presence of a cosmic irony.[1] This is more than the

[1] See the excellent and incisive study by D. C. Meucke, *Irony*, Methuen Critical Idiom Series, 1971.

simple reversal found in the precept that man's wisdom is God's foolish-
ness, and vice versa. Chaucer of course recognizes this, but the question
then is how he attempts to resolve it. The closest he comes to a Dantean
solution, to a view of the divine (or, to use a term more applicable to the
poem, the cosmic) comedy comes with our last view of Troilus:

> *And down from thennes faste he gan avyse*
> *This litel spot of erthe, that with the se*
> *Embraced is, and fully gan despise*
> *This wrecched world, and held al vanite*
> *To respect of the pleyn felicite*
> *That is in hevene above; and at the laste,*
> *Ther he was slayn, his lokyng down he caste.*
>
> *And in hymself he lough right at the wo*
> *Of hem that wepten for his deth so faste;*
> *And dampned al oure werk that foloweth so*
> *The blynde lust, the which that may nat laste,*
> *And sholden al oure herte on heven caste.*   (V, 1814–25)

The *De Contemptu* theme is delicately poised, for it balances between the
body of the work in which we have been so involved and the infinity of
the universe to which we are now exposed. Chaucer had woven the
moral into the whole fabric of the tale, into the plot itself, into the discussions of fortune, and, most essentially, into the differing techniques of
characterization; but until this point, we had been taken only as far as a
virtuous pagan such as Troilus could have gone. Had Chaucer given the
moral explicitly, it would have weakened the dynamic asymmetry of the
techniques of characterization, it would have greatly hindered our
involvement in the story, and it would have destroyed the sudden and astonishing revelation that is made to Troilus (and to us) here at the conclusion. It is this sudden revelation that leads to Troilus' dramatic laugh,
for there is here a hint of divine comedy. But where Dante's comedy
seeks out resolution, harmony and accord, Chaucer's comedy is based
primarily on incongruity. To Troilus, the sudden view of universal truth
makes the worldly falseness and woe ridiculously insignificant. For
Chaucer, cosmic irony is not found only in 'hevene above'; it permeates
and informs every aspect of the world that is his poem. It is (to cite
merely our present case) in the very nature of his transformation of

Boccaccio's characters and his rhetoric, giving us a developing hero who finally goes beyond what even the narrator wishes to have as the poem's end. By going back and comparing Chaucer's source with Chaucer's poem, we can see just how far the Italian influence went. Many years ago, Professor Manly, in a somewhat different context, made an observation that should be kept in mind:

> The great debt of Chaucer to the Italians—and I suspect that his debt to Dante was as great as that to either Petrarch or Boccaccio—was perhaps not so much because they furnished new materials and new models for imitation, as because they stimulated his powers of reflection by forms and ideals of art different from those with which he was familiar.[1]

V

It remains only to discuss, with a certain brevity, the Dantean influence on Chaucer. Such brevity is possible in large part because more scholarly attention has been devoted to this than to any other single 'source'; nor is such attention surprising since there is a natural desire to bring together the age's two greatest poets of the *lingua volgare*, a natural desire that seems to lead all too many Chaucerians to bring in Dante's name in an almost ritualistic fashion. But what is surprising is that careful analysis of the Dantean ascriptions leaves us, in the end, with the sense that Dante's influence is curiously particularized and even, in a way, sparse. Defining this feeling somewhat more closely will help us, perhaps, to see the nature of the influence more clearly. First of all, and most obviously, Chaucer would only rarely have turned to Dante for narrative, for a depiction of the common and less than elevated, or for fictionalized characterization; a poet of narrative, however superb, would not have found that kind of riches, but he would have found superb poetry of the intellect with its sweep of ideas, images, judgements and concepts. To this extent, the nature of the influence is particularized. Secondly, the very scope of Dante's poetry must make us extraordinarily cautious

[1] J. M. Manly, "Chaucer and the Rhetoricians," Warton Lecture on English Poetry XVII, read before the British Academy, 2 June 1926, n. d., p. 5; reprinted in part in *Geoffrey Chaucer*, ed J. A. Burrow, Penguin Critical Anthologies, 1969, pp. 126–30.

when we posit ascriptions. Robinson summarized the problem best in a review, many years ago, of Chiarini's book on the *Hous of Fame* as an imitation of the *Divina Commedia*:

> Dante embodied in his encyclopedic poem nearly all the philosophic doctrine and very much of the current learning of the Middle Ages, and the same ideas were bound to reappear in any poem of the period that dealt, whether seriously or humorously, with philosophic subjects.[1]

Many of the posited ascriptions to Dante, as I have suggested elsewhere,[2] more likely come from common knowledge or a common source.

Granting these preliminary restrictions, what is the nature of Chaucer's dependence on Dante? Speaking in the most general terms, this indebtedness would seem to fall into two major categories: on the one hand, the many shorter images borrowed for their verbal and dramatic force; and, on the other, the few direct adaptations and translations made for purposes of their content.

Chaucer's borrowing of images is widespread but quite specific, and while these eventually come from the whole of the *Divina Commedia*, they are at first drawn chiefly from the opening and closing cantos of Dante's three *cantiche*, with particular emphasis on the opening of the *Inferno*. Such images may vary from the generally recalled scene of the eagle or the gates of the Inferno to the inclusion of a specific phrase such as Dante's 'rider l'oriente'. In almost all cases, however, these images, like the longer adaptations, are assimilated into the general material and shaped to fit Chaucer's poetic intent.

The second category would seem to divide into two groups: the early 'translations' from the *Divina Commedia* which make their appearance in the later poems, and the adaptations (perhaps as much as ten to fifteen years later) from Tractate IV of the *Convivio*. With the possible exception of the Ugolino episode, Chaucer seems to have returned to the material of both these groups for certain specific topics: to the *Paradiso* for the lyric expression of religious adoration, and to Tractate IV for the philosophical discussion of nobility and gentilesse. Obviously, a state-

[1] F. N. Robinson, 'Chaucer and Dante,' *Journal of Comparative Literature* 1, 1903, p. 293.

[2] *Chaucer and Dante: A Revaluation*, unpublished dissertation, Pennsylvania 1956.

ment of so general a nature as this must be hedged about with numerous reservations, not the least of which is that Chaucer regularly turned to other sources as well, combining and moulding the whole to fit the thematic purpose of the individual poem.

Equally, the idea of two major categories can only be entertained if it is fully understood that a number of borrowings have been left out in order to attain a general view of the direction of indebtedness. Granting this, we can perhaps see an early use of short visual images from the *Divina Commedia* which, while it continues throughout Chaucer's writing, is somewhat displaced by his later use of Dante for specific topics. We can, however, be a bit more certain of the relationship as a whole. Chaucer, it would seem, remained always in control of his material. Poetically, he neither attempted to copy the complex structure of Dante's 'four levels of meaning' nor did he attempt, save for a few verses, to write in terza rima or the canzone. To judge from his works, poetry to Chaucer was primarily entertaining, moral, and undoctrinaire; to Dante, however, poetry was a medium for expressing, with even more concentrated power than prose, the fiercely held theological and political doctrines which he had formed into a philosophic whole. It seems fundamentally incorrect to consider that Chaucer, when borrowing an image or even a passage from Dante, of necessity believed the entire doctrine that informed the borrowing. Not only does such a view in many cases seem contrary to the tone of the poem concerned, but it leads to a singleness of interpretation that turns the journey to the Hous of Fame into a spiritual autobiography and makes of Alceste's speech to the god of love a scathing satire that is not borne out by the rest of the *Legend of Good Women*.

Chaucer drew on Dante not heavily but over a long period of time, and, while he was later to employ in part the ideas behind *Convivio IV* and perhaps had early committed to memory the lyricism of St. Bernard's Marian prayer from the close of the *Divina Commedia*, his most extensive indebtedness would seem to lie in his use of the visual and dramatic images that help make Dante's poem the striking literary masterpiece that it is. Below this level of borrowing, one feels that Dante's most profound influence lies in the confirmation of a stylistic technique (inherent in almost all Chaucer's poetry) based upon a primary regard for the actual world of living people, as opposed to the personified abstractions of the closed and conventional world of stylized verse. And yet there is a

manifest difference. Dante depicted the historical personality and made
of him the representative of a particular vice or virtue by placing him in
an allegorical background, while Chaucer sought to create credible,
vital persons of a particular character by placing them in realistic situations that would best delineate them in their entirety. Both men sought
their symbols in the 'world of affairs,' but Chaucer remained a poet primarily interested in people and not doctrines; his is a full view of the life
around him, and if he borrowed from Dante's universal view, he took
that which helped him explain the world of men of which he was so
much a part and of which he, himself, is so much a symbol.

Nowhere is the transformation in tone and purpose better seen than in
Chaucer's version of the Ugolino passage from Inferno XXXIII. This
passage is one of the finest dramatic narratives in the *Divina Commedia*,
'second only to that of Francesca da Rimini in its appeal to popular sympathy,'[1] and similar to the earlier episode in that in both 'we find the
same exclusion of all detail that might blur the one overwhelming
impression to be produced on the reader.'[2] Chaucer's Hugelino passage,
as Professor Spencer has shown,[3] carefully shifts the emphasis away from
the concentrated terror of Dante's description to the sympathetic, one
might almost say sentimental, description of the death of Hugelino's
innocent children. Once their pitiable death has been recounted, the tale
of Hugelino becomes scarcely more than a rapid fulfilment of the
Monk's primary moral, the adversity of Fortune and the downfall of
princes. The direction of the transformation is quite faithful to the general tone of the *Monk's Tale*, for what is stressed throughout the series of
exempla

> . . . is the emotion of pathos. And this is just what we find in
> Chaucer's account of Ugolino.
>
> > *Off the Erl Hugelyn of Pyze the langour*
> > *Ther may no tonge telle for pitee.*
>
> Even if we remember that *langour* had a stronger meaning ('slow
> starvation') to Chaucer than to us, the word *pitee* at once sets the

---

[1] Grandgent, *ed. cit.*, p. 294. To the present writer, the fact that Chaucer
never made use of the Francesca story from *Inferno* V is one of the most
striking problems of the Chaucer-Dante relationship   [2] *Ibid.*

Theodore Spencer, "The Story of Ugolino in Dante and Chaucer," *Speculum* 9, 1934, pp. 295–301.

tone of pathos. And if we think of Dante's *disperato dolor*, we are immediately aware that Chaucer's emphasis will be very different from Dante's.[1]

While Chaucer's principal addition is epitomized by the narrator's interjection:

> *Allas, Fortune! it was greet crueltee*
> *Swiche briddes for to putte in swich a cage!*
>
> (VII, 2413–14)

his principal *change*—and it can hardly be less than intentional, considering that it transforms the very essence of Dante's account—can be seen in Hugelino's tempered grief and Christian submission to the death of his first child:

> *'Allas, Fortune, and weylaway!*
> *Thy false wheel my wo al may I wyte.'*   (VII, 2445–46)

Against this we may set the raw terror that is sustained from the very opening of *Inferno* XXXIII:

> *La bocca sollevo dal fiero pasto*
> *Quel peccator, forbendola a' capelli*
> *Del capo ch" elli avea de retro guasto.*[2]

Tears that are frozen in Dante's Inferno flow copiously for Chaucer's Monk (2430), just as the speechless terror of Dante's 'orribile torre' gives way to the relief of verbalized emotion and the catharsis of the oft-moaned 'allas' and 'weylaway' (2429, 2445). We have moved from the Inferno's closed circle of allegory to the nowhere land of pathos, and from the immediacy of the first person singular to the vicarious exemplum of the third.

Not only is the stark brutality excised for a more Monk-like sense of submission, but the story itself is simplified to the point of melodrama. Hugelino ('the woful fader'), as well as his children, is an innocent victim:

> *Dampned was he to dyen in that prisoun,*

[1] *Ibid.*, p. 296.
[2] *Inf.* XXXIII, 1–3. From the fell repast that sinner raised his mouth, wiping it upon the hair of the head he had laid waste behind. (Carlyle-Wicksteed translation.)

> *For Roger, which that bisshop was of Pize,*
> *Hadde on hym maad a fals suggestioun*   (2415–17)

Fortune is, of course, the real villainess of the piece, and both Bishop
Roger and the people are merely pale agents of her turning wheel.
Nowhere in Chaucer is there the hint of Ugolino's treachery, nowhere is
there the indication that

> . . . horrible as his experience in life has been, we are not for a
> moment to forget that his memory of it is part of his punishment for
> a sin equally horrible, the sin of treachery, and that if we pity him,
> our pity is to be only a passing emotion. . . . The terror, in the Aris-
> totelian sense of the word, which we felt during the recital of his
> narrative, is mingled with the moral terror of Dante, and it is the
> combination of the two that shakes us so profoundly.[1]

For Dante, poetry was a medium for the expression of a unified doctrine,
and Ugolino's guilt in deserting the Ghibelline faction to join the Tuscan
Guelfs against Pisa was as much a part of the purpose of the passage as the
frightful story itself. Probably nowhere in the Chaucer-Dante relationship are the fundamental differences between the two writers so
clearly stressed.

But can we possibly know what begot this transformation from terror
into 'pitee'? A recent, quite brilliant study by Dr. Hope Weissman has
examined Chaucer's 'bad tales' in the light of the enormous stress on the
sentimentality and affective religion found in the painting, art and writing of this period. The melodrama, the almost cloying pathos that threatened to drown all legitimate sentiment in a pool of tears, were dangers
that Chaucer saw and set about to correct by having the burden of excess
evolve from his narrators, in this case the Monk, but elsewhere the
Physician, the Prioress, or the Man of Laws.

> The *Ugolino* [i.e. Chaucer's] is a near perfect expression of late High
> Gothic pathos—Ugolino's "langour" is absolute—but for this very
> reason it is also a profoundly nihilistic tale. Since the Monk's Ugo-
> lino has done nothing, unlike Dante's, he can only suffer; and since
> Ugolino only suffers, unlike Abraham[2] he can do nothing.
> Ugolino's "passion" has no necessary ending, logical or emotional.
> Like *The Monk's Tale* as a whole, it is equally susceptible to infinite

[1] Spencer, *art. cit.*, p. 296.

[2] For the relationship of the Abraham of medieval drama, see Weissman, p.
347 ff.

extension or abrupt curtailment. In the *Ugolino* the Monk himself invokes the second alternative, ostensibly in order to conserve his artistic energies. It is as if Chaucer were making him pun unwittingly on the final moral bankruptcy of his own pathetic tale. To what end does Ugolino suffer? No end whatever.[1]

Whether we accept the whole of this view or not, the important thing is that we attempt to see what lines and colours Chaucer saw when he looked at the picture of Ugolino that Dante had painted, and the poetic consequences of that artistic encounter. For influence is not merely a question of Poet B using Poet A; it is a function of susceptibility, of the individual and his time, of what he can or will see, of what he does and does not use, of assimilation and of stimulation.

[1] Hope Weissman, *Chaucer's Bad Tales: The Aesthetic Forms of Late Medieval Pathos and the Tradition of Sermo Humilis*, unpublished dissertation, New York 1973, pp. 358–9. The importance of pathos and mixed style has been touched on by Charles Muscatine, "*The Canterbury Tales*: Style of the Man and Style of the Work," in *Chaucer and Chaucerians*, ed D. S. Brewer, 1966, esp. pp. 104–13, and in *Poetry and Crisis in the Age of Chaucer*, Notre Dame, Indiana 1972; also by Robert Frank, *Chaucer and the Legend of Good Women*, Cambridge, Mass. 1972, and in his forthcoming study on Chaucerian pathos.

9: Chaucer and Science *

MAHMOUD MANZALAOUI

IT IS NO LONGER NECESSARY to argue, or to demonstrate, the
important role of the science of the Middle Ages in the world-picture
of those times.[1] Nor is it necessary to demonstrate in general terms the
fact that learned and courtly writers possessed imaginations shaped by
the body of their knowledge, including the corpus of the sciences, and
that, furthermore, they made use of these sciences when they came to
shape their own literary productions. Some qualifications must be made,

* The travel, reading, and leisure necessary for the writing of this chapter
were made possible by a summer Research Grant from the Canada Council,
to whom my thanks are gratefully acknowledged. I am also indebted to
Professor W. Meredith Thompson for his reading of the manuscript, and
for a number of judicious suggestions.

[1] Authoritative works on medieval science are: Pierre Duhem, *Le système
du monde*, 10 vol, Paris 1913–59; Lynn Thorndike, *A History of Magic and
Experimental Science*, 8 vol, New York 1923–58; George Sarton, *Introduction
to the History of Science*, 3 vol in 5, Washington 1927–48; L. Massignon and
R. Arnaldez, *La science antique et médiévale*, Paris 1957; A. C. Crombie,
Medieval and Early Modern Science, 2 vol, rev. edn, New York 1959. See also
Francis J. Carmody, *Arabic Astronomical and Astrological Sciences in Latin
Translation: A Critical Bibliography*, Berkeley, California 1956; A. C.
Crombie, *Robert Grosseteste and the Origins of Experimental Science*, Oxford
1953; Aldo Mieli, *La science arabe et son rôle dans l'évolution scientifique mondia-
le*, 2nd edn, Leiden 1966; Mark Aaron Graubard, *Astrology and Alchemy:
two fossil sciences*, New York 1953. In this essay, I have taken it that a reader
who so wishes can acquire a knowledge of the medieval sciences from these
works; I have, in particular, taken for granted the knowledge of astronomy, which can be acquired from works such as Wood's and Curry's: see
p. 228 n. 3 and p. 233 n. 2.

however, to these assertions. For one thing, it must be made clear that the term 'medieval sciences' covers what may be seen as three different types of discipline. First, activities that we still regard as experimentally sound, true in mathematical and quantitative terms, and technologically, or, at least, empirically, useful. Under this head, in their different ways, come observational astronomy, pharmacology, and herbal lore. Only a fraction of medieval science is still accepted as true, so that much more falls under the second head: the pseudo-sciences, a category which includes physiognomy, many aspects of dream lore, lapidary lore, and judicial astrology. All these disciplines entail a detailed study of natural, bodily, or psychological phenomena. For the most part, they involve a closely textured and internally self-consistent logical system based upon a single false axiom; for example, the assumption that a human being has a personality with the traits of any animal with which he shares a physical characteristic; or, that the positions of the planets influence sublunary events; or, that the planets correspond in nature with sublunary entities with which they are consubstantial. The difference between my first and second categories is that beliefs that fall into the second are not substantiated by experimental fact, although the claim is made that it is precisely in the area of verifiable physical data and events that these systems are true. From Hellenistic times to the eighteenth century, the Mediterranean and European worlds appear to have accepted a huge corpus of detailed allegations concerning the physical world, containing a bare minimum of truth (such as the effect of the moon upon ocean-tides) and which was the basis of lucrative and respected professions, such as medicine. In having done so, they were only marginally more silly than our own world: I am thinking of our contemporaries who base their 'demythologized' view so totally on 'scientism' as to take seriously the views of atomic physicists, *qua* atomic physicists, upon sexual ethics; they nevertheless believe equally hazily that there is 'something in' the daily astrological columns of the newspapers (on which no doubt a fair number of glib swindlers live comfortably amongst us), and they also fashionably affect to believe in the characteristics of an 'Age of Aquarius'.

The third category of activities is that in which the theoretical basis is occult, and the teaching deliberately kept esoteric. I suppose that geomancy falls into this group.[1] Though the technique of alchemy involved

[1] For geomantic figures in Chaucer's poetry, see 'The Knight's Tale'. (CT, I, 2043–45). For the beliefs themselves, see Robert Jaulin (with F. Dejean

much of the grim plodding of my second category (as the Canon's
Yeoman tells us), and even a certain measure of my first category—since
it was the alchemists who developed much of the method and the apparatus of empirical science—yet the theoretical basis of this activity is
highly arcane: not only is it non-empirical, but its asseverations are so far
removed from propositional language that we cannot use the word
dogma for them. What could be further from expository clarity, from the
experimental approach and the inductive outlook than the alchemists'
two foundation stones, the Emerald Table, and the description of the
Philosopher's Stone? They run: '. . . Take the stone animal, vegetable,
and mynerall, the which is no stone, neither hath the nature of a stone.
And this stone is like in manner to stones of montaynes, of mynes, and of
plantes [and] animal[s], and it is founde in euery place, in euery tyme, in
euery man, and it is counuertible to all colours, and ther-in ben contened
all elementes, and it is cleped the litell world. And Y wolle name hym by
his propre name, as þe comone peple calleth it, that is to sey, the terme of
an egge, that is to sey, the philosophers egg'; and: '. . . All thynges were
created of o soole substaunce, and of o soole disposicion, the fader
wherof is the sone, and the moone moder, that brought hym forth by
blast or aier in the wombe, the erthe taken fro it, to whom is seid the
increat fader, tresour of myracles, and yever of vertues etc. . . .',[1] I am
well aware that the first of these extracts is said to consist of directions for
the straight-forward chemical process of 'sublimation' and that, in addition, both are assumed to carry a lesson in moral and spiritual purifica-
tion.[2] But this does not make their form and language less obscurantist:

---

and R. Ferry) *La géomancie: Analyse formelle*, Cahiers de l'homme, n.s. IV,
Ecole pratique des hautes études, Sorbonne, Paris 1966.
[1] The 'Philosopher's Stone' and the 'Emerald Table' are part of the pseudo-
Aristotelian *Secretum secretorum*, ed R. Steele, as fascicule V of *Opera hac-
tenus inedita Rogeri Baconi*, Oxford 1920; pp. 113–17. My quotations, with
the modifications indicated in square brackets to bring the English text into
conformity with the more correct reading of the Latin are from the fifteenth-century English version of the *Secretum* in *Bodley MS. Ashmole 396*;
fols. 22v–23. The text is part of a forthcoming edition of the corpus of this
manual.
[2] For Alchemy, see Graubard as on p. 224 n. 1, and J. Ruska, *Tabula Smarag-
dina, Ein Beitrag zur Geschichte der hermetischen Literatur*, Heidelberg 1926;

they do not work by giving readers a literal meaning to which the knowledgeable can further add a symbolic one; they are examples of a prose which is meaningless on the surface because of its planned unintelligibility, but which yields up an arcane meaning to the Adept alone, a deliberate act of logorrhoeic non-communication.

Like all such classifications, my three-fold division of the medieval sciences is a rough and ready one, whose dividing-lines are often straddled by some of the disciplines. As just claimed, alchemy in its different aspects falls into all three. The division of astronomy into observational and judicial was to most medieval scholars apparently a sub-dividing of a subject they regarded as basically one. Medieval dietaries, ostensibly based on the doctrine of humours, contain suggestions which may nutritionally make empirical sense which we can respect—just as Maritain accepts Freudian therapy as valid, while doubting much of Freudian psychoanalytical theory, and emphatically disagreeing with Freud's *Weltanschauung*.[1]

If I start out with this three-fold division, it is for two purposes. The one is to justify this discussion of themes which are sometimes far from 'scientific' by the terminology of an informed modern reader; to show that we are dealing with a culture in which natural philosophy was largely based on inherited authority, in which the cultural outlook yoked together (to echo the title of a book which is our major authority in this

---

Robert Steele and Dorothea Waley Singer, 'The Emerald Table', *Proceedings of the Royal Society of Medicine*, XXI, 1928: reptd. separately, 1928; Paul Kraus, 'Jabir ibn Hayyan', *Memoires de l'Institut d'Egypte*, XLIV–CLV, 1942–43; Sherwood Taylor, *The Alchemists*, New York 1949; E. J. Holmyard, *Alchemy*, Harmondsworth 1957.

For a key to the 'Emerald Table' in the doctrine of solidified *pneuma*, see Sherwood Taylor, pp. 11–16 and 88–90. For alchemical writings as a genre of symbolic *poesis*, see Joseph E. Grennen, 'The Canon's Yeoman and the Cosmic Furnace: Language and Meaning in the Canon's Yeoman's Tale', *Criticism* IV, 1962, pp. 225–40. For the straightforward discursive sense behind alchemical language, see the examples in Bruce A. Rosenberg, 'Swindling Alchemist, Antichrist', *Centennial Review of Arts and Science* IV, 1962; pp. 566–80. There is further material in the works referred to on p. 257 nn. 2 and 3.

[1] Jacques Maritain, 'Freudisme et Psychanalyse', *Quatre essais sur l'esprit dans sa condition charnelle*, Paris 1939.

field)[1] magic and experimental science, so that the Franklin's magician is referred to as a 'philosophre', and it is a witty paradox that the pilgrim Clerk has made no lucrative use of the alchemists' stone although he is a 'philosophre'. The other reason for making this division at the outset is that, blurred though the outlines may be, its distinctions seem to recur in some of Chaucer's own attitudes.

It is true, however, that for the most part, Chaucer does not appear to emphasize the differences in modality of truth in the medieval sciences. To him, this bundle of scientific disciplines and teachings were a portion of that world of practical and intellectual activities of which he was a part, and about which he wrote. As such, he uses it as the raw material of his art. But it would be both an anachronism and a critical misinterpretation to think of him as pure artist, as observer, as *cuor gentil*, and craftsman, with no urgency to shape his experience and knowledge into a pattern of personally apprehended truth. Science, throughout Chaucer's, works seems not only to provide themes of comic or of touching import: it also provides an objective correlative to the inward characteristics of his personages, as, for example, in the physiognomical descriptions of the pilgrims in the *General Prologue*. It is noteworthy that, in comparison with his English contemporaries and immediate predecessors, Chaucer makes a strikingly great use of scientific material. This remains true even if we hold in mind that general survey of the medieval curriculum of learning which constitutes Book VII of Gower's *Confessio Amantis*, and the same poet's dramatic description of Medea's preparation of her witch's brew.[2] Of Chaucer's use of astral influence, Curry writes, 'So far as I know Chaucer is the only medieval writer who motivates narrative action by reference to the stars'.[3] If, in the following century, King James I and Henryson show us the astral gods in their

[1] L. Thorndike, *History of Magic and Experimental Science,* as on p. 224 n. 1.

[2] For Gower's use of the sciences, see George G. Fox, *The Medieval Sciences in the Works of John Gower,* Princeton Studies in English VI, Princeton 1931. I cannot pass by silently the inexcusable fact that it is nowhere made clear in the Haskell House reprint, New York 1966, that this latter is anything other than an original publication.

Walter Clyde Curry, *Chaucer and the Mediaeval Sciences,* enlarged edn New York 1960; p. 193. Curry's work, first published in 1926, remains the basic text for any study of Chaucer's science.

judiciary and intercessory roles, it is because *The Kingis Quair* and *The Testament of Cresseid* are Chaucerian poems. Much is Chaucerian, too, in the manner of such versified scientific manuals as Lydgate's *Secrees of old Philisoffres*.[1] Yet the scientific strand in Chaucer's poetic and narrative art is one of many. It neither predominates in, nor upsets the balance of, the judicious synthesis of medieval attitudes that forms the background to the poems. It has been well-digested by a healthily functioning system —a contrast to the less well-regulated functionings of modern Chaucerian scholars, in which the scientific material is still, alas, churning around in large and conspicuously unassimilated gobbets.

Yet it is not easy to reach a decision on the further questions: to what extent does Chaucer himself accept or reject one or other of the medieval beliefs concerning the physical world? to what extent is his assent, or withholding of it, a firm attitude? how true is it to assert that he sometimes ironically undercuts the medical, astronomical, or magical assumptions upon which his narrative is constructed, as he seems to undercut, or to encourage us to question, courtly and romantic assumptions in similar contexts? One general answer can be made before proceeding further: we shall probably never decisively know, since Chaucer in this matter does not depart from his usual stance, of introducing a questioning even as he asserts an ideal. Only with reserve, and only now and again, does an authorial indication strike one as single-mindedly and openly imperative. The remainder of this essay will attempt to illustrate the variety of uses to which Chaucer put medieval science, and will sometimes offer surmises as to his poetic intentions.

What works of science did Chaucer read? That he read and used the Latin version of Māshā'Allāh's Arabic treatise on the astrolabe is clear; he is also indebted in his own *Treatise on the Astrolabe* to a derivative of John of Sacrobosco's *De Sphaera*. The many physiognomic references, particularly in *The Canterbury Tales*, suggest, as Curry remarks, an acquaintance with the *Secretum secretorum*, of which there are today hundreds of extant manuscripts.[2] But often his learned references are

---

[1] Ed R. Steele, EETS, ES LXVI, 1894. The work is a verse translation of the *Secretum secretorum*; the title is, more accurately, *The Governaunce of Kynges and Prynces.*

Curry (p. 72) is wrong if his slightly uncertain wording is intended to mean that Chaucer had read the physiognomic portions of the *Secretum* in

strings of name-droppings, and his reading of the brief extracts to be found in florilegia can be surmised to have been responsible for his echo of the first aphorism of Hippocrates as the opening words of *The Parliament of Fowls*,[1] and for his use of similar maxims elsewhere. Since we are concerned with the readings of a man who was to make use of scientific lore in imaginative works of his own, as components of quasi-philosophical constructs, we can assume that it is not unlikely that the scientific texts he was most familiar with (perhaps the ones which first fired off his interest in such topics) were those portions of literary works that were concerned with the sciences. There are such passages in works which were crucial in Chaucer's development: the *Roman de la Rose*, Boethius' *Consolatio*, Cicero's *Somnium Scipionis* and, more fully, Macrobius' commentary upon it.

Jean de Meun's Nature, as part of her long confession to Genius, describes the cosmos and its creation by God, the elements, the humours, the influence of the planets upon human character and conduct, dreams, and many other matters (*Roman* ll. 16699–18557, 18867–19024).[2] The scientific lore ranges from a cosmogony to an account of tricks done with mirrors. Like its source, Alanus ab Insulis' *De Planctu Naturae*, the passage contains a reproach to Man for his departure from obedience, and, at its end, it passes up from scientific description to Platonic metaphysics, and thence to Christian theology. It includes a discussion of the ways in which astral preordination can be forestalled by man's freewill and pre-science, and so, following Boethius' arguments (*Consolatio*, Book V) it reconciles science with the Christian faith and with man's power of choice. It thus not only provides a scientific overview, but merges this with the underlying philosophical and spiritual concepts upon which the poem is being constructed: a synthesizing which exactly anticipates the Chaucerian use of science at its most meaningful. In addition, a meteorological passage leads smoothly into a fine dramatic genre-scene, depicting a storm: the merging of scientific data with descriptive poetry and action-

English. Apart from the rehandled version in Book VII of Gower's *Confessio Amantis*, there is no English version of the work earlier than the turn of the fifteenth century; the earliest to contain a physiognomy is *B. M. MS. Sloane 213*, of around 1400.

[1] M. A. Manzalaoui, 'Ars longa, vita brevis', *Essays in Criticism* XII, 1962; pp. 221–24.

[2] I follow Felix Lecoy's edition, 3 vol, Paris 1965–70.

verse is a characteristic of Chaucer, one for which no doubt both he and Jean de Meun were indebted to Boethius. Thus we find in the confession of Nature an anticipation both of the ingredients of Chaucer's science and of the type of poetic and intellectual use which he made of them. When we look at detail we see anticipations of specific motifs which recur in Chaucer: the discussion of trick effects with mirrors and lenses as the true explanation of apparently magical feats (with a reference to the teachings of al-Hasan ibn al-Haytham) is paralleled in 'The Squire's Tale' by the discussion which Cambyuskan's courtiers hold over the gifts which the stranger-knight has brought (CT, V, 225–35). Venus' excuses to Vulcan (*Roman* 18088–100) recall May's pseudo-scientific exonerations of her adultery (CT, IV, 2378–2410). The passage on the repetition of our daytime preoccupations in dreams (*Roman* 18364–94) recalls some of the most effective vignette-poetry in *The Parliament of Fowls* (ll. 99–105); the account of the different causes of dreams (*Roman ll.* 18297–468) and the uncommitted refusal to decide why dreams fall into different classes and are of different levels of seriousness (*Roman* ll. 18469–84) is similarly paralled in *The House of Fame* (ll. 2–56). A fair number of the main ingredients of Chaucer's science are present in seed in the confession of Nature. The most obvious omission is physiognomy, an element made use of elsewhere in the *Roman* (e.g. ll. 1189–96), as there are also passing glances at lapidary knowledge (ll. 1067–80) and arithmetic[1]. But if by physiognomy we mean the detailed, structured, feature-by-feature study which is the characteristic of the pseudo-Aristotelian tradition,[2] and not the freer characterization which appears to derive from folk-tradition,[3] it is noticeable that, as we shall see, there is little of this in Chaucer's earlier work: in his middle work it appears in a sudden, obtrusive manner, while in the later work it is of central signifi-

[1] In *The Book of the Duchess*, the Arabic arithmetician Al-Khwārizmī appears (l. 435) as 'Argus the noble countour'; Chaucer's quasi-mythological figure is thought to derive from the 'mestre Algus' whom the Vielle mentions in the *Roman de la Rose* (l. 13731: and see again l. 16141).

[2] This goes back to the Peripatetic *Physiognomonica* (ed R. Förster in *Scriptores veteres physiognomonici*, 2 vol, Leipzig, 1893; English translation T. Loveday and E. S. Forster, in W. D. Ross, ed, *Works of Aristotle*, 12 vol, Oxford 1908–52; vol. VI, 1913).

[3] Fritz Neubert, 'Die volkstümlichen Anschauungen über Physiognomik in Frankreich bis zum Ausgang des Mittelalters', *Romanische Forschungen* XXIX, 1910–11.

cance. Can we, then, in science as in other matters, consider the influence of the *Roman* to be of significance, and especially so in the earlier works of Chaucer? More to the point, since this is a detail not paralleled in the scientific readings of the encyclopaedic tradition to which De Meun and Chaucer may owe a common debt, is a certain resemblance in the *Roman* to the bantering tone of Book II of *The House of Fame*, which one notes in the piquant and basically ludicrous application, more by the force of sheer garrulity than by any greater relevance, of optical lore to the story of Vulcan's net, in the lecture on distorting mirrors, and in the pompous claim that the lay mind cannot fathom scientific matters (*Roman* 18243–50): in other words, the mumbo-jumbo flavour of the dramatic use of science, occurring in a context where the general concept nevertheless appears to be taken seriously—an ambivalence which is of the very essence of Chaucer's presentation of human preoccupations and attitudes.

If the science of Nature's confessions can speculatively be described as a seed of Chaucer's own achievement in this field, Boethius' *Consolatio* is, on the other hand, a model which Chaucer rarely equals. Boethius' easy and majestic transition from observational detail to poetical description and dramatic involvement in the cosmic or the panoramic picture, is rivalled or surpassed by Dante, but not by the English poet. Chaucer, as we shall see, in his earlier works substitutes a different tonality, or transposes his source-material in some other way. It is not perhaps until Dorigen's diatribe against the apparent disorder in God's creation that we have anything similar in Chaucer: and there, as it should be, it is poetry of the 'third voice', empathetically expressing the mood of an individual character whom the poet has created.

The brief cosmological and oneiretic descriptions in Cicero's *Somnium* form the basis of a vast expansion in Macrobius, whose commentary becomes, from this point of view, a summa, or a small encyclopaedia, of lore concerning not only the cosmos and dreams, but other aspects of science. The scientific detail here, again, may have been as much a source for Chaucer as his reading in more professionally scientific textbooks; here again, it is interesting to compare the dream-lore to the opening of *The House of Fame*. The progression of the expository teachings, elucidating as they do the adventures and vision of Scipio, is anthropocentric, and the relationship to a man's *gnosis* and growth of awareness make the combined Cicero-cum-Macrobius volume a humanistic text, and one with an aesthetic pattern, in a manner which is scarcely true of the textbooks of the medieval scientific curriculum.[1] In the work, science is *utilized*, as it is by Chaucer, and not merely *exposed*: the feel is closer to that of Chaucer than is that of, say, the *Almagest*: a briefer reading of Professor W. H. Stahl's commentated translation of Cicero and Macrobius leaves a student wiser, and closer to Chaucer's imaginative being, than a lengthier reading of the tangle of technicalities in Professor Chauncey Wood's *Chaucer and the Country of the Stars*.[2]

This is not to underrate the importance, in its place, of Chaucer's more technical and more up-to-date scientific knowledge. He is among the few great English poets who have written a scientific treatise; for one work adapted and translated, there must have been many read and assimilated. *The Treatise on the Astrolabe* reveals a fraction of the knowledge and skills that lie behind Chaucer's use of astronomical settings, themes, and character-motivations in his poetry. It is a measure of Chaucer's interest in astronomy that he should have produced a simple exemplar of the scientific treatise, in a language which a young boy could follow. It is nonetheless an unexpected use of his talents. One would have been mildly surprised if Zola had translated a popularization of Darwinian theory, or André Gide had produced a Havelock Ellis manual in simplified French for Algerian boys. If Chaucer is also responsible for *The Equatorie of the Planetis*, a more professional commitment seems implied: but Dr. Derek Price's cogently presented case, in spite of the deeply interesting circumstantial evidence, must at present be termed unproven:[3] Dr. North has demonstrated, indeed, that Chaucer's own narrative uses of astronomy show that he used almanacs, which were popular and

[1] It has recently been pointed out that all the astronomical settings in Chaucer's narrative poetry are placed in the first part of the year, and that this indicates that Chaucer may have relied for them, initially, not upon a technical work, but upon Ovid's *Fasti*, which cover only those months of the year: J. D. North, 'Kalenderes enlumyned ben they: Some Astronomical Themes in Chaucer', *RES*, XX, 1969; pp. 129–54, 257–83, 418–44: the point in question is on p. 438.

[2] Chauncey Wood, *Chaucer and the Country of the Stars: Poetic Uses of Astrological Imagery*, Princeton 1970; reviewed by J. D. North, *RES*, XXII, 1971. Professor Wood's article, 'Chaucer and Astrology,' in Beryl Rowland, ed, *Companion to Chaucer Studies*, Toronto 1968, is a valuable summary with an indispensable bibliography.

[3] *The Equatorie of the Planetis*, ed Derek J. Price, Cambridge 1955.

accessible reference works, and reveal no definite use of equatoria
(North, p. 132).

Much of the detail of the astrological settings and of the character-motivations in the poems, is made clear by a reading of the *Astrolabe*,
especially of such a passage as *A special declaracioun of the ascendent* (II. 4).[1]
Certain details, even cruxes, in the imaginative works, have light
thrown on them by passages in the scientific treatise. The more sensible
of the interpretations of a controversial passage in Troilus' apotheosis is
supported by the use in the *Astrolabe* (I, 17, 39) of the term '8 speer' for
'the first moveable', an interpretation which, in any case, is also supported by the examination of the 'eighte speere' by Aurelius' learned
helper ('Franklin's Tale', *CT*, V, 1280). It is tempting to add to conjectures concerning the position of the planet Venus in *The Parliament of
Fowls* (l. 117)—*northewest* in one manuscript tradition and *north nor west*
in another, though *north north west* is the generally accepted reading—by
noting that for *north-east* and *south-east* the *Astrolabe* (II, 31, 2–3) makes
use of the terms *northe the est* and *south the est*: thus, *north the west* or, by
apocopation, *northewest*, could be a straightforward description of the
most northerly evening position of the planet.

As an exercise in discursive scientific prose, the *Treatise on the Astrolabe*
has already attracted the attention of transformation-generative lin-
guists.[2] Chaucer himself may not be responsible for all the doublets
employed (such as the explanation of *elongation* as *lengthening*: II, 25, 58),
for some of these may be scribal glosses, but he is certainly conscious of

[1] Brief summaries of late medieval astronomical lore are in: the Appendix
to R. T. Davies' edition of the *Prologue to the Canterbury Tales* (1953:
reprinted in J. A. W. Bennett's edition of the *Knight's Tale*, 1954) the
Appendix to Wood's *Country of the Stars* (pp. 298–305), and the works
cited in footnotes in the latter; James Winney's chapter, 'Chaucer's Science', in M. Hussey, A. C. Spearing and J. Winney, *An Introduction to
Chaucer*, Cambridge 1965; and the section on 'The Influence of Chaucer's
Scientific World', in Muriel Bowden, *A Reader's Guide to Geoffrey Chaucer*,
1965. See also Florence M. Grimm, *Astronomical Lore in Chaucer*, Studies in
Language, Literature and Criticism, no. 2, University of Nebraska, Lincoln, 1919: reprinted New York 1970; T. O. Wedel, *The Mediaeval Attitude Toward Astrology, particularly in England*, New Haven 1920, especially
chap. ix. 'Astrology in *Gower and Chaucer*'.

[2] Ruta Nagucka, *The Syntactic component of Chaucer's Astrolabe*, Cracow,
1968.

the need, for clarity's sake, for what he apologetically calls 'superfluite of wordes' (proem, ll. 43–44), an expansiveness which he counters by adopting an otherwise spare phraseology and syntax, fulfilling in fact the claims which the garrulous eagle of *The House of Fame* exaggeratedly makes for his own language (ll. 854–63), where that bird might with more truth have adopted the apology of Jean de Meun's Nature, who admits, after she is many score of lines into her speech, that she is a prolix woman (ll. 17702–08). Nor is Chaucer's prose altogether devoid of the homely vigour which was later to enliven much Elizabethan translation of humanist treatises: 'From this cenyth . . . there comen a maner croked strikes like to the clawes of a loppe [i.e. a spider], or elles like the web of a wommans calle [i.e. hairnet], in kervyng overthwart the almykanteras' (I, 19, 1–5).

Since one's main interest is in Chaucer as artist, the memorable details in his *Treatise on the Astrolabe* are those from which we can try to deduce his attitude towards the truth of a medieval discipline which plays so great a part in his poetry. Here too his ambivalence is in evidence, and should prevent us from holding too incautiously definite an opinion ourselves. If the supplementary propositions, which appear to belong to 1397, are Chaucer's own, then the opening of Section 44 reads as serious exposition of a belief which had already been made less-than-solemn use of in 'The Franklin's Tale': there the process, though it succeeds in altering the face of the Breton Coast, is condemned by the Franklin as 'japes' and 'wrecchednesse' of 'supersticious [i.e. magical, and theologically improper] cursednesse' CT, V, 1271–72): nor are interpretations which attempt to see the Franklin as foolishly naïve in this matter at all convincing. As Wood points out (p. 14), Chaucer, in a passage which is not in Māshā'Allāh (II, 4, 24–56), blames judicial astrologers who weight the evidence to provide the answers their patrons desire. He then roundly condemns judicial astrology with the well-known words 'Natheles these ben observaunces of judicial matere and rytes of payens, in which my spirit hath no feith, ne knowing of her horoscopum' (II, 4, 57–60), terms which, again, remind us of the Franklin's condemnation (V, 1131–34) as worthless ('folye . . . nat worth a flye' . . . 'illusioun') of the very magic which is so important an element in the machinery of his Tale. Wood takes Chaucer to be without doubt a disbeliever in judicial astronomy (p. 17); if this is so, then his scientific adherence is to observational astronomy. Since, as discussed below, he appears to have a more positive anti-

pathy towards alchemy, his intellectual attitude seems to acknowledge
distinctions which correspond to the classification made at the start of
this study. Unfortunately, however clear an intellectual adherence, it
rarely explains the whole stratification of an author's personality as laid
out in his works. Wood himself takes Curry to task for over-simplifying
the matter (p. 3), and in a lengthy discussion (substantially, pp. 3–102) he
indicates ways in which a medieval Catholic writer could remain perfectly orthodox and yet see in planetary influences the psychological
predispositions which a person might or might not discipline with his
free will,[1] and might accept astrology[2] as a measure of metaphorical
truth, or, of course, of raw material for his art. Wood proceeds, in the
accepted Robertsonian manner, to interpret some of Chaucer's uses as
parodical and as morally condemnatory: in the further reaches of these
arguments the present writer certainly cannot go along with him.
North's observations complicate the picture. He reminds us that
Chaucer's astrological settings and motivations are more often than not
added to his sources: the poet deliberately synthesizes inherited narrative
and inherited 'scientific' *Weltanschauung*. In many cases, North's analyses
claim to reveal an astronomical pattern which Chaucer has imposed
upon himself in order to feed and guide his imagination, to illustrate
themes already crystallized in it, and to give cohesion to his narrative (p.
442); yet, as North says, they are at times 'difficult to justify' (p. 131): on

[1] The same 'necessitee condicioneel' is expounded in the *Secretum secretorum*: '. . . How be it that it is necessarye, that some thynges come, never-
theles yf me knewe it ar it come, me myght the lyghtlyer suffre it, or the
prudentlier decline fro it, and so in maner eschewe it and escape it': version
in Bodley MS. Ashmole 396; fols. 13–13v:cf. Steele, p. 61).

[2] I have noticed no teachings which attempt a theological justification of
astrological studies by reference to the Dominical utterance in *Luke 21.
24–25*. There are attempts, however, to link astrology with Scriptural history. Roger Bacon conceives of the Nativity in connection with the conjunction of Jupiter with Saturn; he further discusses the astronomical signs
which accompanied it (*Opus maior*, ed J. H. Bridges; ii.263–64, 267–68). In
the third quarter of the fifteenth century, Regiomontanus made astrological calculations and speculations around the Nativity and the Passion; Pico
della Mirandola upbraids astronomers for applying their lore to Noah's
flood, the Nativity, and the star of Bethlehem. For all this, see Graubard (as
on p. 224 n. 1), pp. 95–96, 143–44, 170. For the Christological application
of physiognomy, see p. 259 n. 1.

one occasion Chaucer produces merely 'a strange piece of whimsy, which he is unlikely to have supposed would even be discovered' (p. 273); on another occasion, there are merely guidelines which the reader would not know of if Chaucer had 'resisted the temptation to leave behind two trifling hints as to his plan' (p. 280). North's detailed study of astrology, overt and arcane, in Chaucer's works, seems to me to vary in degree of persuasiveness: so likewise do his general attitudes. One can agree willingly with his description of the structural role of astrology. It fits in totally with the 'agnostic' view which is Curry's, and offers no difficulties. The use of astronomy to give cohesiveness to Chaucer's poems is illustrated in much of the discussion which is to follow here, even where the instances are primarily adduced in connection with other points. Chaucer in this respect anticipates the modern phenomenon of the artist who makes conventional use of a creed he does not believe in, and does not expect his public to adhere to outside their reading hours: in this, his art would *not* be analogous to Marlowe's utilization of Christianity in *Dr. Faustus*, but, rather, to the exploitation of the Catholic faith, and its ministers and sacraments, by Shakespeare in *Romeo and Juliet*, by Spenser in his *Epithalamium*, and by Hollywood in its films.

The concealed use of astronomy may imply nothing more than an arbitrary scheme similar to the arcane and slightly arch uses made of Homer's *Odyssey* in Joyce's *Ulysses*, and of Euripides' *Ion* in Eliot's *The Confidential Clerk*. But, combined with the 'astronomizing' of borrowed tales and motifs, it suggests a measure of adherence to a tendency to see power—including poetic strength—in an overlying 'country of the stars', similar to the adherence (one would not say 'belief', with the intellectual commitment which that implies) to the numerology which, in the opinion of certain modern scholars, is used somewhat hermetically by Renaissance writers for works which no aesthetically sensitive reader can consciously find enhanced by its architectonic arbitrariness. This is tantamount to saying that although Chaucer does not commit himself to a belief in judicial astrology, he has a hesitant attachment to it and preoccupation with it—perhaps a superstitious regard for it—: North describes Chaucer as being 'at first imbued with a deep sense of the plausibility of astrology' (p. 442) and of thinking much about this. North sees a development in Chaucer's opinions. From one observational example in the *Astrolabe*, he assigns this work to 1393; he finds that Chaucer may in it be 'revealing a growing disillusionment with judicial astronomy'. In the works which Chaucer wrote after 1393–1394, there is no more astrology, North claims (though it would be safer to assert that there is much less of it than before). This is an important specu- lation, for, although Dr. North does not state this, it would see in Chaucer's career a development away from such influences and props after that central point in the chronology of the *Tales* which seems to co- incide with the resolution, in 'The Franklin's Tale', of his preoccupations with the problem of love. If this is so, he shifts away at that point not only from the influences that radiate from the *Roman de la Rose*, and the Middle French dream romances, not only from Macrobius, Boethius and Boccaccio to boot, but also out of an 'astrological' umbra, to a period of considerably more independent vitality, which I take to be represented by 'The Pardoner's Prologue and Tale', 'The Nun's Priest's Tale', and 'The Canon's Yeoman's Prologue and Tale', a period to which I suppose that the 'Retraccioun' also belongs. This raises conceptual and evol- utionary problems which cannot be discussed here. Perhaps it is signifi- cant that the period should not only contain the statement of Christian commitment in the 'Retraccioun', but also the genial satire upon 'scien- tism' in 'The Nun's Priest's Tale', as well as a sustained satire upon alchemists. Alchemy, however, differs from judicial astronomy both in belonging to my third, and not my second, category of medieval sciences, since it is strongly hieratic and vatic in manner, and also in never having been a strong organic element in Chaucer's art.

The most overt statement of a belief in astrological prediction, un- modified by man's will, and only unclear because of the dullness of man's wits, is given by the narrator of 'The Man of Law's Tale' (CT, II, 190–203). The same narrator curses Mars for his cruel hostility to Cus- tance in her first marriage, and blames Luna for the feebleness of her help, together with the heroine's father for not consulting a 'philo- sophre' in 'electing' the time for her voyage (CT, II, 306–315). Curry, in one of his all-too-rare realizations of the predominance of Christian con- cepts in the Middle Ages, is at pains to demonstrate, however, that God's providence is shown in the poem as supreme over astral influence (pp. 190ff.) . It is in Chaucer's interpolations, and not Trivet's original, that the Divine power is emphasized, in an antithetical way which is surely far from being that of a successful 'piece of artistic workmanship' such as Curry considers the tale to be (p. 191). Wood attempts to save the tale from its inconsistencies by arguing that it is a satire upon the Man of

Law's insensitivity, in a close-packed sixty-page demonstration of misdi-
rected learning which is itself an astounding example of insensitivity to
literary tone and likelihood (pp. 192–224). When Chaucer nods, it does
him little service to interpret the movement as a sage wagging of the
beard.

The description of astronomical conditions, at the start of a tale, or
before key moments in its action, was a well-established convention, a
form of rhetorical *amplificatio*, as Wood points out (pp. 78ff).[1] Chaucer's
most striking use of this convention, one in which personality and dramatic context are most vividly portrayed, is in the Prologue to 'The Man
of Law's Tale', where the learned astrological calculations and the observant mother-wit of Harry Bailly both arrive separately at the conclusion
that it is ten o'clock in the morning on 18 April. In fact, the Host's use of
a man's six-foot shadow-length is paralleled in Nicholas of Lynn's prologue to his treatise on the astrolabe, composed in 1386 for Chaucer's
brother-in-law, the Duke of Lancaster;[2] yet the passage is a fine example
of the power of poetry and of psychological delineation combining with
the fascination in scientific method.[3] The most famous of these settings,
however, is the opening to the *General Prologue*, where, as in the calendar
of the *Secretum secretorum*, and in other traditional works, the astronomical details are combined with a vignette of nature.[4] The synthesis
embraces more in Chaucer, since he proceeds to further matters: first he
heightens the tone by the reference to the cult of love, then heightens it
further by the religious associations of the remarks about pilgrimages,
yet he then goes on to undercut the solemnity by the down-to-earth
realism of the descriptions of the inn and of the company in it.

Specific references to the positions of the individual planets either in

[1] In his book, Wood mentions two peripherally relevant works by Rosamund Tuve, but not her *Seasons and Months. Studies in a Tradition of Middle
English Poetry*, Paris 1933.

[2] Cf. North, pp. 130, 425–26.

[3] The pilgrim-narrator himself uses shadow computation in the *Parson's
Prologue* (CT, X, 5–9).

[4] The prose-poems which form the vignettes in the *Secretum* (Steele, 76–80)
derive word for word from a learned source, the Arabic encyclopaedic
Epistles (Rasā'il) of the True Brethren (Ikhwān al-Ṣafā): see a forthcoming
article by the present writer in *Oriens* XXII for 1970 (to be published in
1974).

the signs of the Zodiac or in the computational houses of the heavens,[1] are made at certain high points of action: the Sun is in Taurus when Pandarus visits Criseyde on his first embassy (TC, II, 54ff.); the Moon is in Aries, an unpropitious but dramatically suitable position, when Criseyde makes her promise to return in ten days' time (IV, 1590–96); Venus is in her own house Libra (or, by another interpretation, in the seventh computational house, which is the home of love and marriage) with no planet in bad aspect, when Criseyde first sees Troilus (II, 680ff.). All three passages, and other similar ones, are added by Chaucer as part of his 'medievalizing' of Boccaccio. The summer solstice is at hand when Pluto intervenes to punish May (CT, IV, 2222ff.) in 'The Merchant's Tale', but the winter solstice comes round when Aurelius and the magician set off for Brittany to submerge the rocks (CT, V, 145ff.) in 'The Franklin's Tale' (North, pp. 245–6, 259): no doubt a deliberate contrast in that pair of tales, as Wood (pp. 94f.) notes.

Sometimes a more complex astronomical setting, involving several celestial entities, may be of general impressionistic and symbolic import, rather than having a precise judicial significance. Wood, by implication, seems to support this (p. 90) when he quotes the lines which precede the account of Criseyde's unfaithfulness, with their picture of the sun, the moon, Venus and the Zodiac, with a special reference to one of its signs:

> The brighte Venus folwede and ay taughte
> The wey ther brode Phebus down alighte;
> And Cynthea hire char-hors overraughte
> To whirle out of the Leoun, if she myghte;
> And Signifer his candels sheweth brighte.

(TC, V, 1016–20)

Chaucer's elaborate description of the wiles of Pandarus, in Book III, contains the most outstanding example in Chaucer of the use of judicial astrology by a character to affect the fortunes of the protagonists. When 'upon the chaungynge of the moone . . . the wolken shop hym for to reyne' (III, 515), Pandarus has known this in advance: it is a meteorological prediction reinforced by the knowledge (III, 624ff.) that the Moon, Saturn, and Jupiter are in conjuction in Cancer, the Moon's mansion. In

[1] The great circle of the heavens is divided into twelve stationary houses. The twelve signs of the Zodiac themselves rotate, and thus pass through these stationary houses.

inviting Criseyde, and planning for all that was to follow, Pandarus is surely joining with Fortune as an *executor* of 'wyrdes', so that Chaucer intends irony in his references to the 'goddes wil', the same irony by which Pandarus is allowed to play at being god and Fortune for the hero and heroine in the first three books of the poem, and yet to prove so ineffectual in Books IV and V. Wood's thesis, which undercuts the witty drama of Chaucer's careful construction, by finding the whole matter 'paltry', 'uncataclysmic' and 'unexceptional' (p. 49 and n.) is a Robertsonian misunderstanding of Chaucerian ambivalence.

The astronomical conditions at the nativity of a character are sometimes pointed out by Chaucer, though, as Wood observes (p. 305) (so himself partly undercutting his own elaborate scheme), Chaucer never uses a full horoscope, but only uses references to ascendants, conjunctions, and oppositions. In the very passage which gives the planetary conditions of Criseyde's first sight of Troilus, we are told that Venus was in a propitious position for Troilus when he was born. At Hypermnestra's birth (LGW, 11, 2580), where Ovid's account is innocent of judicial astronomy, the conjunction of Venus and Jupiter give her beauty and gentleness, and suppress the aggressiveness which might otherwise have been endowed by Mars; the position of Saturn in a bad aspect preordains her imprisonment. The astrology is not only related to the 'wirdes' (l. 2580) but is, unusually, combined with an overt, if brief, piece of character-portrayal, and supplies motivation to an inherited tale which had none (Curry, p. 164). The fullest such integrated use of scientific predisposition in a character sketch is in a totally different tone, since it is, of course, in the portrait of the Wife of Bath: born under Taurus, Martian and Venerian, marked on her face and her private parts, and in her character, by the astral conditions of her birth (CT, III, 609–25).[1]

An ancillary contribution of Dr. North's approach to the astrology of Chaucer is its attempt to date the poems through references to significant astral situations. Sometimes the conditions in the poems seem to reflect a real-life occurrence, presumably at or around the moment of composition. North finds datings in eleven different works, all of which he places in the period 1385–94. Some of the datings are distinctly unconvincing:

---

[1] Wood (pp. 172ff.) is helpful, but tails off into an undercutting of his own arguments when he succumbs to his mentor's arguments that the Wife 'is not a character in the modern literary sense at all'.

1391 for the Legend of Hypermnestra, 1395 for *The Parliament*, 1394 for
the opposition of Saturn and Mars mentioned in 'The Man of Law's
Tale'. Others confirm the chronology deduced from evidence elsewhere: correcting some details in Root and Russell's article on the topic,[1]
North fixes Criseyde's supper on the rainy night of the 8th or the 9th of
June 1385, and points out that it is more likely that the downpour was
written about for a poetic delivery at court in advance of the date of the
unusual conjunction. (It would, one supposes, be rather absurd if it had
been publicly recited soon after the night in question, had it in fact
turned out a fine spring night which was still fresh in the memory of the
delighted court.) Thus the question whether the meteorology was
observed or posited becomes relevant to the immediate *aesthetic* effect of
the poem in its original delivery as court entertainment.

The theory of arcane astronomical meanings leads Dr. North to two
allegations of an unexpected nature. He picks on Manly's suggestion[2]
that Elpheta, the name of Cambyuskan's wife in 'The Squire's Tale', is a
form of the Arabic name, al-Fātih, for the star Alpha Coronae Borealis,
and extends this by identifying in star-lists names which correspond with
those of other characters: Algari (Arabic *al-jārī*) for Algarsyf, Calbalacet
(Arabic *Qalb al-asad*, i.e. *Cor Leonis*) for Cambalo, and Cauda Ceti for
Canacee.[3] The rising of the King from table is identified (*sic*) with the
exaltation of Mars on 15 March 1390, for Cambyuskan *is* Mars 'beyond
all resonable doubt' (North, p. 259), the knight who dances with Canacee 'is' Mercury and the princess's damsels 'are' the stars which lie between Cauda Ceti and the ecliptic (North, pp. 260ff.). Whatever private
device may lie at the back of Chaucer's mind, there is scarcely anything
to be said in favour of this as a poetic *interpretation*, for the obvious reason
that no clear-minded reader of 'The Squire's Tale' taken *in toto* is con-

[1] R. K. Root and H. N. Russell, 'A planetary date for Chaucer's Troilus',
PMLA, XXXIX, 1924; pp. 48ff.

[2] North (p. 257 n 1) states that the notion is J. M. Manly, 'Marco Polo and
the Squire's Tale', *PMLA*, XI, 1896; pp. 349ff. In actual fact, there is no
mention of it there: Manly's remark is in his note to *Squire's Tale*, ll.
29–33, in his edition of the *Tales*, New York 1928; p. 598. The name is
found as a star-name in the *Liber astronomicus* ascribed to the early fourteenth-century Richard de Wallingford.

[3] And yet the rising of Canacee from sleep is in fact compared by Chaucer
to the rising of 'the yonge sonne' early in the year (V, 384–86): the lines are
quoted by North, p. 261.

scious that he is reading an account of astronomical events, or of any surrogate for them which he is capable of conceiving or even of adumbrating, while subliminal interpretations are surely out of order in *literary*, as opposed to psychoanalytical and to antiquarian studies.[1] On 'The Nun's Priest's Tale' (which, with its astronomical element, he must presumably—see pp. 237f. above—, want to date earlier than 1393) North has similar things to say (pp. 418ff). The term Gallina, the hen, is used of one of the Pleiades. The seven wives of Chauntecleer are the Pleiades; Chauntecleer is the sun ('He looketh as it were a grym *leoun*': CT, VII, 3179). In Chaucer studies, one man's ingenuity is another man's dottiness: the general lines of this particular interpretation, taken, again only as a private joke of the poet's, might fit in with the generally parodic nature of the tale, and they admittedly add to the self-importance of the cock, the deliberate inversion of the relationship between sublunary and otherworldly, by which all in the farmyard is pride and grandeur, and all in the life of its owner and guardian, the poor widow, is humility and need.

An aspect of Chaucer's astrology which is of particular literary interest is its connection with his use of mythology. There can be no doubt that from the start Chaucer is at home with astrology, both as a science in itself and as a conceptual or an imaginative illustration of (or surrogate for) the order of creation, the providence of God, and the acting-out of His will. In the astronomical order, seven of the classical deities are identified with the planetary powers, but the astronomy transmitted by the Arabs, and its European offshoots, where they are not influenced by literary traditions such as Ovid's, or by philosophical works of the neo-Platonic tradition, give no recognition to 'stellyfyed' mythological heroes, or to the other gods and goddesses such as Juno and Neptune, the principal Olympian absentees. Chaucer's first independent literary use of

[1] I would make two reservations to my assertion: (a) there is a shadowy suggestion of an astronomical identification in the use of the term 'lusty Venus children' for the courtiers (V, 272), and in the information which follows, concerning the planet's position in Pisces; (b) it should be noted, whatever it may be taken to indicate, that there is indeed an insistence on the motifs of astronomical setting and astronomical comparison in the tale: see the lines at the start (V, 47–57: where the astronomy is combined, as in the *General Prologue*, with a spring vignette and a description of the happiness of the birds) and the lines with which the poems breaks off (V, 671–72).

the non-astronomical classical deities is hesitant and almost mocking. Juno's messenger blows his horn noisily into Morpheus' ear, making him open a single eye, with an economy of effort more Disneyesque than Ovidian (*BD*, ll. 182ff.). The narrator, only too worried by his insomnia, is willing to make an offering—albeit 'in . . . game' (l. 238)—to Morpheus or Juno, but the notion of such superhuman powers was, he claims, new to him, and ran counter to his monotheism:

> *For I had never herd spek, or tho,*
> *Of noo goddes that koude make*
> *Men to slepe, ne for to wake;*
> *For I ne knew never god but oon.*
>
> (ll. 234–237)

In the later dream visions and, especially, in the invocations in the proems to the separate books of *Troilus and Criseyde*, the classical deities, particularly the Muses, seem to have become acceptable symbolic and conceptual entities, much as they were to be to the poets of the sixteenth century. In the final line of the three stanzas borrowed from the *Teseida* to describe the apotheosis of Troilus, the imagery of the cosmic heaven of the neo-Platonic writers is seen combined with the notion of Mercury as psychopomp (and, if we are anxious to make a consistent unity of the poem it is difficult not to see all this as a surrogate for entry into the Christian Heaven). However, the younger Chaucer's initial doubt reasserts itself when, twenty-six lines further on in this poem, he refers to Mercury's colleagues in the Pantheon, Jupiter, Apollo and Mars, as 'rascaille'. We are here, of course, outside the narrative, in the second section of envoy, where the narrator's point of view becomes overtly Christian. Chaucer had behind him a not unsimilar attempt at seeing Christian significance beyond the surface-meaning of pagan myths, by his main source-author, Boccaccio himself, in the closing chapters of the *De genealogia deorum*.[1] Nevertheless, the shuffling game with the poet's counters can scarcely fail to surprise us. This is especially so since Chaucer goes so far elsewhere in the process of assimilating the Olympian and the cosmological avatars of the gods to each other, and into the sublunary action of his tales.

Heavy weather has been made of the rhyme royal portion of the *Com-*

[1] Giovanni Boccaccio, *Genealogie deorum gentilium libri*, ed Vincenzo Romano, 2 vol, in continuous pagination, Bari 1951; pp. 797ff.

plaint of Mars.[1] It is a piece of astrological wit-writing. That light *jeux-d'esprit* were written for the late medieval court is clear from some of the other short poems attributed to Chaucer. It is clearer still if we look at some of the occasional verses produced in the next generation by Lydgate. The Ovidian loves of Mars and Venus are superimposed upon the astrological fact of the conjunction of Mars with Venus in her own house, Taurus, such as occurred, for example, in 1385 (North, p. 14): an association which, as in the Wife of Bath's nativity, augurs lustfulness. Further play is produced from the quibbles upon 'chambre' in the two senses of *zodiacal mansion*, and *female genitalia*, from the implied parallel between planetary and sexual *conjunction*, from the approach of Phoebus (standing-in for the non-cosmological Vulcan)[2] to the mansion where the two lovers are. A modicum of *sprezzatura* will save one from burying this aristocratic joke under unnecessary moralistic and academic rubble.

As already mentioned, the intervention of Pluto and Proserpyna in the lives of January and May is preceded by a description of the astronomical setting. The episode itself, however, perhaps shows the classical deities at their most independent, in Chaucer's use, from astronomical beliefs. For this negative reason, it should be noted here. The god and goddess of the underworld are instead assimilated, as Pluto had already been in the romance of *Sir Orfeo*, to the Celtic powers of Annwfn. Close as their intervention is in manner to the Virgilian interventions of deities, and to Renaissance descents of the *deus ex machina*, it is equally close to the interventions of otherworld beings in medieval romance. It is, however, only a repetition in small of the interventions in 'The Knight's Tale', a poem which Chaucer has emphatically 'astrologized' in adapting it from Boccaccio, and is the high point of his literary use of planetary influence.

Into the romance of Palamon, Arcite, and Emelye, the notion intrudes early on (I, 1086: that is, immediately after Palamon sees Emelye, and as part of Arcite's attempt to comfort him in a distress of which Arcite does not yet know the reason) that adversity has been shaped for the two young men by Saturn or by some maleficent celestial configuration ('constellacioun'). Into the action-poetry of the narrative intrudes the largely original Part III, in which the poem alters manner, becoming pic-

[1] Wood, chap. III, pp. 103–60.

[2] Chaucer can hardly have known (Wood, p. 108) the version in Book VIII of the *Odyssey*, where it is Apollo who discovers Mars and Venus *flagrante delicto*.

torial, heraldic, and largely static, and revealing the protagonists, not in horizontal relationship with each other, but in separate vertical relationships with their tutelary spirits. Theseus, in deference to Venus (cf. CT, I, 1814) and to his own more particular deities (cf. CT, I, 1682) builds a temple to each of these three powers, as part of the special lists prepared for the coming knightly battle. In turn, each of the three protagonists comes to the appropriate temple: each at an hour which is governed by the planet in question. The artistic displays in the temples show us that the Venus and Mars to whom, respectively, Palamon and Arcite pray, and (less unquestionably) the Diana to whom Emelye prays, have unpleasant characteristics. More accurately, the astronomical gods are amoral powers; it is their human devotees who can turn these potentials *ad bonum* or *ad malum*. Astrologically, the temples (North, p. 149f.), are the zodiacal houses of the three planetary deities. The three devotional night visits are thus at pseudo-canonical hours, to temples of gods basically planetary, but pictorially celebrated in their fanes by events which are culled partly from classical mythology and history, and which largely show the deities in the exercise of an unappealing power. It is a portrayal for poetic purposes of forms of worship which have never historically existed, but which, conceivably, Chaucer imagines to represent ancient pagan worship. One of its literary functions is to depict the inward reality of the three protagonists where the narrative method of the other parts of the poem left them as flat characters: to reveal the Emelye who is elsewhere a lay figure, and to distinguish two young men who are elsewhere scarcely differentiated. The emblematic treatment of the psychological differences continues when Emetreus and Lygurge arrive to take sides each with one of the two protagonists: they are accoutred in a manner which denotes that they are respectively the followers of Mars and of Saturn. The Saturnine warrior comes to fight on the side of the devotee of Venus. When the scene shifts to heaven, and Venus and Mars contend before Jupiter, Saturn in person sides with Venus. In spite of the sinister nature of his boasts, it seems likely that his intervention is intended as a rectification of the imbalance which, without him, is in Mars' favour.[1] We are told that he

> *Fond in his olde experience an art*
> *That he ful soone hath plesed every part.*

> (CT, I, 2445–45)

[1] For a different interpretation, see Curry, pp. 127–38.

Without doubt, Theseus is the earthly counterpart of Jupiter: it is further to be asked whether Aegeus in his brief but wise intervention (I, 2837–52) is not, in a more shadowy way, a counterpart of Saturn —giving us a pattern of two pentads, an earthly and a divine one, superimposed and reflecting each other. The full realization of wisdom, however, is in the Boethian thoughts of Theseus: the planetary gods, in their nature as cosmic powers, perhaps lack the fullness of personality and of empathy by means of which human beings, in their sublunary natures, reflect the qualities of a God who stands above the planets. The determinism and one-trackedness of the planetary beings preclude their attaining the sense of Providence and of acceptance with which Theseus comes to terms with the cruel facts of existence, from which Chaucer has even excised the final apotheosis of a defeated protagonist, which he had before him in his source, but had already (it seems) chosen to use elsewhere.[1]

If 'The Knight's Tale' is an astronomical poem by virtue of showing human and celestial beings in consubstantial parallelism, *The House of Fame* mingles human and celestial by the more external device of sending its narrator on a skyward journey, thus making him the first human cosmonaut in English literature, ahead of Elizabeth Drury by over two centuries. The cosmology of *The House of Fame* is that of Boethius and Macrobius, and, as in the latter, a close sight of the workings of the macrocosm is regarded here as the same high spiritual reward that it was to be for Troilus. Knowledge is illumination, and the art of poetry is its ancillary: accordingly, Book III is dedicated in vatic terms ('Now entre in my brest anoon!'—ll. 1109) to Apollo as 'God of science and of lyght' (l. 1091). Yet, after the first book, the tonality is whimsical and fantastical: if Book III is not marked by the rich grotesqueries of the middle book, it nevertheless continues to portray the workings of the universe in a surrealist manner in which science and fantasy blend. Even as Boethius'

[1] A documented and much fuller treatment of views which are partly similar to the present ones is in Douglas Brooks and Alastair Fowler, 'The meaning of Chaucer's Knight's Tale', *Medium Aevum*, **XXIX**, 1970; pp. 123–46. The authors attach considerable importance to the doctrine of humours in this poem and see Palamon as morally superior to Arcite: they give to Lygurge and Emetreus a central importance which seems to me out of all proportion to the impact which intrusion of these two characters makes upon the reader.

'wings of philosophy', which transport the initiate into the supernal world, are turned into a large and professorially garrulous bird,[1] the 'tidings' started in the house of Rumour turn into shrill quarrelsome little creatures when they jostle one another as they try to fly out of the windows (ll. 2088ff.—the passage is borrowing from Ovid's *Metamorphoses* XII, 54–5). Mythology and cosmology blend in this fantasy: Phaeton has a driving accident because he is frightened out of his wits when his chariot comes too close to the Scorpion, which we must imagine as a monster-sized arachnid suspended in space (ll. 941ff.). It is perhaps surprising that Chaucer lets pass the chance for further grotesque poetry and does not attempt to describe the 'eyrysshe bestes' (ll. 927–34). Not cosmology alone, but physics, too, is a topic of this poem: the attention to detail makes it comparable to the descriptions of such phenomena as the alternation of night and day, in the 'Life' of St. Michael the Archangel in *The South English Legendary*.[2] The Eagle (ll. 729–852) explains that all these things have a natural locality towards which they gravitate; applying this to sound he explains the nature of sound-waves, and informs his pupil that they move in ever-widening circles towards the skyriding House of Fame. The general resemblance to the speech of Jean de Meun's Nature is clear; there are touches to suggest that the whole matter should not be treated too ponderously ('Take it in ernest or in game', l. 833), and school physics are abandoned for burlesque when the sounds, arrived at Fame's palace, turn into appearances of the people who uttered them (ll. 1076–82).

The entire experience is, of course, in the form of a dream, and, for a successful telling of it, the narrator (ll. 66–80) invokes the help of the god of sleep, this time in less agnostic terms than in the first of the dream-

---

[1] Dr. J. E. Grennen sees the seizing of the narrator by the eagle in medical-poetic terms, as an apoplectic stroke: see his 'Science and Poetry in Chaucer's House of Fame', *Annuale mediaevale*, VIII, 1967; pp. 38–45. This is less persuasive than Dr. Grennen's opinions on alchemy in Chaucer, as expressed in the works listed below in notes 2 and 3 on p. 257.

[2] *The South English Legendary*, ed C. D'Evelyn and A. J. Mill, 3 vol, EETS, CCXXV–VI, CCXLIV, 1956–59; 'St. Michael', ll. 407–412 (p. 415). The science in this section of this thirteenth-century poem consists of cosmology (ll. 391–508), meteorology and physical geography (ll. 50–662); anatomy and the doctrine of humours (ll. 663–728), and psychology, i.e., the doctrine of the three-fold soul of man (ll. 729–96).

visions. But, true to his habitual vacillation, this invocation (ll. 66ff.) is followed by a prayer to the Christian God, including words which are an echo of the *Gloria* (ll. 81f.); while in the Proem (ll. 2–56), there is hesitation over the scientific classification of the different 'ny causes' (to use Dame Prudence's term,—CT, VII, 1395), and the different species, of dreams. Without adhering to any single explanation himself, the narrator reviews different theories: dreams are caused by physical 'complexions', by an imbalance in persons' bodies or their life-styles, by excesses in spiritual disciplines or in the discipline of worldly love: some dreams have a prophetic significance. In connection with dreams, eight terms are used, somewhat imprecisely (ll. 3–12, 40 and 48): *sweven, (a)visioun, revelacioun, drem, fantome, oracle, miracle,* and *figure.* Attempts have been made to relate the terms to those used by Macrobius—five types of *somnium*: *somnium proprium, alienum, commune, publicum* and *generale*; four other classes: *visio, oraculum, insomnium,* and *phantasma (or visum).* Chaucer's own four dream visions seem to come to a man who is preoccupied with a problem, or is reflecting upon something he has read; *The Book of the Duchess* and *The Parliament* seem to reward him with tidings which constitute a half-formulated deepening of an attitude to life; *The House of Fame* grants him, in its way, a vision of the workings of the cosmos; the dream in *The Legend of Good Women* impels the narrator to write the legends. It would be forcing the issue to relate the romantic dream-convention too closely to oneiretic lore, and the fullest treatment of dream-lore elsewhere in Chaucer is, once again, in the region of burlesque.

In 'The Nun's Priest's Tale', the cock and the hen engage in a debate concerning two types of dream interpretation. Chantecleer is a proponent of the premonitory school, as summed up in lines 41ff. of *The House of Fame.* He is convinced that his dream is a warning, and adduces on his side two lengthy exempla and a string of shorter ones. His wife leans towards the medical theories summed up in lines 21ff. of *The House of Fame.* Her husband, in her opinion, is suffering from indigestion; his brain has been affected by the rising of fumes from the stomach; he suffers from an excess of red choler. From diagnosis she proceeds to an equally detailed and learned prescription of treatment demonstrating a knowledge of laxatives and vomitories and of herbal lore, and warning him against pathogenic complications. She is both more scientific, and more up-to-date in the scholastic manner: by contrast, there is little in

her husband's allegations which could not already have been found in
the old-fashioned rhetorical teachings of over two centuries earlier. It so
happens that she is wrong. The predictions in the dream are borne out,
and only Chantecleer's ready wits save him. Not that this must mean that
the Nun's Priest is seriously siding with one against the other, for in this
poem both he and his creator seem to be mocking the regular stock-in-
trade of their professional lives. Heavy weather has again been made of
this tale by Robertsonians who do not see that a serious teacher may
sometimes make fun of his methods, and who find it easier to take this
light-hearted poem as a serious homily on the Primal Lapse. I can only
conclude that the clerics they frequent must be considerably more
solemn-faced than the ones I do. The parodic tone seems obvious: a possible parodic use of astrology has been referred to above; there is parody
of the description of the beauty and manners of the hero and heroine of
romance in lines 2859–75 and 3160–61. Scientific methods—those for
calculating the time—are parodied further when Chantecleer (3187–99)
at 9 a.m. on 3 May, shortcircuits the astronomical indications and knows
by intuition and not by learning, that it is time to crow.[1]

Yet not all of the Princeton solemnity is out of place. In a serious and
straightforward manner, the benefits of spare diet[2] are movingly embodied in the poor widow's way of living, as described at the opening (ll.
2836–46); moderation in food and the acceptance of bare sufficiency are
here shown—before we enter the disorderly microcosm of the poultry
world—as signs of the Beatitudes of poverty and humility.[3]

We may pass at this point to other poetic uses of medicine. There is a
romantic usage of the topic in the statement that in the Garden of Love
there are all health-giving herbs, and there is no human sickness:

There wex ek every holsom spice and gras;

[1] Cf. also ll. 2853–58, with their lighthearted disparagement of the techno-
logical aid provided by clocks, as contrasted with the natural time-keeping
abilities of Chantecleer. See Standish Henning, 'Chaucer and Taurus',
English Language Notes, III, 1965; no. i, pp. 1–4.

[2] One of the most popular sections of the *Secretum secretorum*, much glossed
and scored in the margins of extant manuscript and early printed versions,
and forming the bulk of the partial translation by Johannes Hispaniensis,
produced a century earlier than the full translation, is a prophylactic die-
tary for the healthy (Steele, pp. 64–98).

[3] Cf. p. 243 above.

> *No man may there waxe sek ne old.*
> (*Parliament of Fowls*, ll. 206–7)

A less romantic recurrence of it is the Squire's gauche reference to indigestion, sleepiness and sanguinary excess (CT, V, 337–60). It is to be expected that the Doctor of Physic should be associated with a string of authorities, some Greek and Arabic, others contemporary Englishmen, and that we should be given a sketch of his art, including a good measure of judicial astrology. Concomittantly, we are told of his lack of interest in religious matters, and of his secret agreement with the apothecary—a charge already made against doctors by Matfre Ermengaud in his *Breviari d'Amor* (in a section of the work—ll. 17268–19229—which contains other parallels to the *General Prologue*)[1]: the criticism is one which goes back to the classical comic dramatists. But it is astonishing to find how detailed is Chaucer's description of the course of Arcite's dying sickness (CT, I, 2743–60) until we remember that if health can be the theme of lyric description, so morbid symptoms can be an element in dramatic narrative. In his own person, Chaucer gives us passing references to the doctrine of the humours (e.g. the sanguine complexion of the Franklin, CT, I, 333) and to the brain as a 'tresorye' of imaginings (*House of Fame*, ll. 523–28). The pharmacopoeia is ransacked for narrative elements: a sleep-inducing drug is used by Palamon on his jailor (I, CT, 1470–74) and is given to Hypermnestra by Egistus to use upon Lyno (LGW, 2667–71). Absalom chews cardomom and licorice in order to have a sweet breath (CT, I, 3690). The youngest of the boon companions in 'The Pardoner's Tale' consults an apothecary over rat-poison (CT, VI, 852–67), and Ibn Sina's *Kitab al-Qānūn* is cited (VI, 889–94) for case-histories which might equal in horror the death of the men on whom the poison was actually used. Canacee (V, 470–71, 638–41) makes herbal salves for the falcon's wounds. Of the herbal salve a fine but fruitless metaphorical use is made in the cause of hapless love, in Oenone's letter to Paris:

> *'Phebus, that first fond art of medicyne,'*
> *Quod she, 'and couthe in every wightes care*

---

[1] Matfre Ermengaud, *Breviari d'Amor*, ed G. Azaïs and P. Meyer, 2 vols, Béziers and Paris 1862–81. See the summary of this work by Paul Meyer in the *Histoire littéraire de la France*, XXXII, 16–56. A new edition of the *Breviari* by Dr. Peter Ricketts is expected shortly: I owe the latter piece of information to my colleague, Dr. F. Hamlyn.

> *Remedye and reed, by herbes he knew fyne,*
> *Yet to hymself his konnyng was ful bare;*
> *For love hadde hym so bounden in a snare,*
> *Al for the doghter of the kynge Amete,*
> *That al his craft ne koude his sorwes bete'.*
>
> (TC, I, 659–65)

This is surely that very use of 'termes of phisik'—medical conceits—in a love letter, which Pandarus warns Troilus against using (TC, II, 1036–43).

By contrast with all this, the Host gives us an uninformed layman's view of medicine (CT, VI, 304–17) complete with malapropism and misuse of words.[1] It is clear that medical men and their lore are frequently taken as types of human wisdom, true or assumed. As already seen above, the description of the craft of love with which *The Parliament of Fowls* opens is based on the first of the medical aphorisms attributed to Hippocrates; there are respected 'surgiens' and 'phisiciens' among the wise whom Melibee consults, but, unlike Dame Prudence, they shortsightedly recommend vengeance (*Melibee*, CT, VII, 1004–16); spurious allegations of a pregnant woman's craving and of a treatment of blindness are part of the mendacity of May (IV, 2331–37, 2372–75, 2396–2410). In a non-medical context, the friar of 'The Summoner's Tale' produces the proverbial saw:

> *What nedeth hym that hath a parfit leche*
> *To sechen othere leches in the toun?*
>
> (CT, III, 1956–57)

The process of cure through unpleasant medication—therapy as a 'dark night'—is one of the medical metaphors which Chaucer has inserted at his own initiative into *Troilus*:

> *O, sooth is seyd, that heled for to be*
> *As of a fevre, or other gret siknesse,*
> *Men moste drynke, as men may ofte se,*
> *Ful bittre drynke, and for to han gladnesse,*

---

[1] Cf. the unlettered layman's picture of the dangers of excessive and blasphemously overcurious study, in the words of Nicholas the carpenter (1. 3449–67) with his malapropism 'astromye'.

> *Men drynken ofte peyne and gret distresse;*
> *I mene it here, as for this aventure,*
> *That thorugh a peyne hath founden al his cure.*
>
> (TC, III, 1212–18)

A medical theme of particular interest in medieval romance is 'the loveris maladye/Of Hereos' (CT, I, 1373–74)[1], which figures equally prominently in the medical text-books of the time, Latin and Arabic.[2] Arcite is joined in this sickness by Troilus and Damyan. A description of the effect of sorrow on the body follows after the complaint of the Man in Black (BD, ll. 487–99). Troilus, deepened by his experiences, has no faith in the 'lechecraft' (TC, IV, 436) by which Pandarus suggests he should find himself a new love: this Ovidian remedy (as the Man in Black calls it,—BD l. 568) is no longer to be usefully indicated. While the Man in Black tells us that no physician, 'Noght Ypocras, ne Galyen', can cure him (BD, ll. 571–72), the narrator in the same poem asserts that 'There is phisicien but oon' who may be of avail (BD ll. 39–40)—a line which, *pace* Professors Robertson and Huppé,[3] in this context must surely refer to the narrator's lady-love, even though it is 'Hye God'—equally suitably in that other context—who is 'oure lyves leche' in 'The Summoner's Tale' (CT, III, 1892). Behind the recurrent metaphor of medicine as spiritual or emotional adjustment lies Boethius' use of the same figure: the metaphorical passages in Chaucer's translation (e.g. I prose 2. 1–9; prose 4. 636–39, prose 5, 68–78) have a resonance perhaps not matched by Chaucer when he treats of the same theme in his original poetry.

There is a fine combination of three elements in one stanza of *Troilus and Criseyde*, where medication and magical remedies are mentioned together as two aspects of one lore, and the role of the beloved as leech is archly assumed by Criseyde:

[1] J. L. Lowes, 'The Loveres Maladye of Hereos', *Modern Philology*, XI. 1913–14.

[2] There is, for example, a detailed discussion of the physiological effects of an excess of emotion in a lover, with illustrations from the poets, in the ninth-century Ibn Dawūd al-Isfahānī, *Kitāb al-Zahra*, ed A. R. Nykl, Chicago, 1932: chap. XLII, pp. 299–306.

[3] Bernard F. Huppé and D. W. Robertson, *Fruyt and Chaf: Studies in Chaucer's Allegories*, Princeton 1963; pp. 32–35.

> *Compleyned ek Eleyne of his siknesse*
> *So feythfully, that pite was to here,*
> *And every wight gan waxen for accesse*
> *A leche anon, and seyde, "In this manere*
> *Men curen folk."—"This charme I wol yow leere."*
> *But ther sat oon, al list hire noght to teche,*
> *That thoughte, "Best koud I yet ben his leche".*
>
> (TC, II, 1576–82)

Therapeutic magic, or rather, 'magic naturel' which may either heal or render sick, is also found in the temple of Fame (HF, 1260–80), Classical, Biblical, Arab, and native English in its varieties.

The love-philtre is another element of lore which overlaps the medical-pharmacological and the strictly magical categories. 'Who yaf me drink?', the simple cry of Criseyde when she first sees Troilus, contrasts powerfully with the dithering version of scholastic debate by which she shortly afterwards tries to focus her discursive wits upon the question whether she should return the love of the prince. The brief rhetorical question reverberates with an echo of the legend of Tristan and Isolde. The language of quasi-scientific metaphor is certainly more Criseyde's element than is that of the logicians.

We pass on from this instance to indubitable cases of magic 'proper'. Two tales have magic as a central element, 'The Squire's Tale' and 'The Franklin's Tale'. In the one, as far as we can tell, magic was to be the machinery for depicting marvels and exploits; in the second, we have, on the contrary, one of the most domestic of the tales; yet the magical theme links 'The Franklin's Tale', in a minor aspect, to the unfinished 'Squire's Tale', even as it is linked by its marriage theme, and by certain deliberate contrasts, to 'The Merchant's Tale.'

The only one of the magical gifts which we see put to use in 'The Squire's Tale' is the ring which allows its wearer to understand the language of birds. The sword, the mirror, and the enchanted horse promise more complexity than the story seems able to carry: as they stand, they are the objects of the courtiers' admiring and overassertive speculations. Like Aurelius' brother (and, perhaps, like the Franklin himself), Cambyuskan's courtiers seem unable to distinguish between departures from the uniformity of nature, and sleight of hand. They knowingly explain away the stranger-knight's allegations: possibly, there is in

Chaucer here an element of mockery at those who seize upon science to demystify life: optics, Ibn al-Haytham and Witelo (V, 228–35) can satisfy some, but

> *As soore wondren somme on cause of thonder,*
> *On ebbe, on flood, on gossomer, and on myst,*
> *And alle thyng, til that the cause is wyst.*
> *Thus jangle they, and demen, and devyse . . .*

(V, 258–61)

Yet, conversely, we are made to feel the poetic magic of the chemistry which transforms fern ashes into glass (V, 243–57). Aurelius' ally does not remove the rocks, as Dorigen asks, but, with similar scientific magic, retains the high tide for several weeks. The Franklin himself seems to waver between sleight of hand and thaumaturgy as an explanation.[1] (It might be noted in passing that Shakespeare's Prospero, like Aurelius' clerk, produces a magical entertainment, and that he uses words which echo Chaucer's 'Farewell! al oure revel was ago'; that seventeenth-century magician's method of work depends entirely upon using his allies in the aerial and the spirit worlds.) The breaking of the uniformity of nature through enchantment by Chaucer's 'philosopher' is the logical extension of Dorigen's irrational outburst against the apparent creation of disorder by God in His creating of the black rocks. What seemed to her to be a danger to the security of her married happiness turns out to have been her defences; a fulfilment of her rash wish leaves her exposed to Aurelius: the hocus-pocus of the magician's preparatives are an objective correlative of the illusoriness of her notion of devising an improved order for the world. Conversely, in the moral and social order, the true ethical and emotional orderliness of *gentilesse* spreads outward and downward from the knight Arveragus to the squire Aurelius and thence to the professional magician (V, 1611–12); the psychological 'magic' of *gentilesse* wins the day over the practical magic worked by arcane knowledge and power.

An unclear glimpse is given us into the conditions in which the knowledge of arcane arts circulated. Aurelius' brother recalls that he had caught sight of a work dealing with such matters—apparently, with

[1] For the astrology behind this magical act, see J. S. P. Tatlock, 'Astrology and Magic in Chaucer's *Franklin's Tale*', *Anniversary Papers by Colleagues and Pupils of George Lyman Kittredge*, Boston and London 1913; pp. 339–50.

judicial astronomy in particular—when he was studying at Orleans, where a graduate student who was supposed to be engaged upon 'another craft' left a book upon his desk (V, 113–34). (The book is left 'prively'; does this imply the action was intentional or otherwise?) The picture complements the open, attractively jumbled image of Nicholas's bed-sitter in Oxford, with his musical instrument, his arithmetical paraphernalia, and the astrolabe for the study, one presumes, of observational astronomy.

The poetic exploitation of the theme of magic, even though it involves some criticism of that discipline, contrasts with the wholly satirical treatment of alchemy in 'The Canon's Yeoman's Prologue and Tale'. Again, Chaucer speaks through the persona of his speaker, so that it is difficult to make assertions as to his real opinions. Yet Curry's notion (p. xxiv) that the Yeoman is meant to be laughed at as an ignoramus seems difficult to accept. The false 'common-sense' statements of Harry Bailly and of Chaucer's pilgrim-persona are to be disbelieved where they have against them some clear facts about the personage one or other of them is assessing, and the reader's true vision of the narratives serves to show up the basic naïvety and inadequacy of the views expressed by these two personae.[1] But the Yeoman's vision is not pitted against anything that pulls in a contrary direction. His 'Prologue and Tale' show the folly of devoting time and energy to a search which is, at best, selfishly greedy, and can be a deflection from one's vocation, as it is for the pilgrim canon and for the priest in the Tale, or, worse still, a vehicle for dishonest exploitation of the gullible, as it is for the canon in the Tale. Much else is criticized: the injunction 'Kepeth it secree' (VIII, 1368–78), the misty teachings *ignotum per ignotius* (1447–71); much is made fun of, in a sustained genre-depiction which treats alchemy much as the schoolboys of my generation treated 'stinks'. Chaucer wrote at a time when, as we can judge by the manuscripts produced then, alchemy had become a secular fad that was alarmingly distracting the clergy, as much as the secular fads of today are doing. For anyone conversant with the bizarreries found among the post-Consiliar churchmen and churchwomen of today, no further analogy is necessary. The material was a rich and tempting one

---

[1] This is not to say that the statements of the Host and those of the pilgrim narrator are to be taken throughout in an identical manner. The Host's statements undoubtedly express his *views*. The narrator's *statements* are often almost certainly meant as deliberate sarcasm.

for a fourteenth-century satirist.[1] Just as a contrast between the affective 'magic' of gentilesse and magic in its normal sense, was drawn in the discussion of 'The Franklin's Tale', so a surprising amount of recent criticism has paired off 'The Canon's Yeoman's Tale' with 'The Second Nun's Tale', and seen a contrast between spurious physical alchemy, and the alchemy of personal mortification and *metanoia* in the life of St. Cecilia.[2] Suggestions thus accumulate for seeing Chaucer as a Christian humanist who pits the profundities of human potential against philosophies of life that place the material world too close to the centre of their view of things.[3]

[1] For a different view, see S. Foster Damon, 'Chaucer and Alchemy', *PMLA*, XXXIX, 1924; pp. 782–88.

[2] C. Muscatine, *Chaucer and the French Tradition*, Berkeley, California 1957, pp. 216–17,—see also p. 221; Joseph E. Grennen, 'St. Cecilia's Chemical "Wedding": the Unity of the *Canterbury Tales*: Fragment VII', *JEGP*, LXV, 1966, pp. 466–81: this brings out the use of the term 'wedding' in the alchemists' jargon and their symbolism. See also Bruce A. Rosenberg, 'The Contrary Tales of the Second Nun and the Canon's Yeoman', *Chaucer Review*, II, 1967–68; pp. 278–91.

[3] Recent literature on 'The Canon's Yeoman's Tale' provides one with a spectrum of attitudes and views, ranging from the illuminating to the unacceptable. It is almost a parodic microcosm of Chaucer scholarship at large. The chief contributor in the field is Joseph E. Grennen (see notes 2 above and p. 226 n. 2). His unpublished thesis, 'Jargon Transmuted: Alchemy in Chaucer's *Canon's Yeoman's Tale*' (Fordham University 1960: *Dissertation Abstracts* XXII, 1961; p. 859) is available in Ann Arbor Microfilms 1961. Grennen interprets alchemical allegory as a parallel to the black mass, a mimicking of the Transubstantiation of the Blessed Sacrament. Grennen shows that Chaucer is using the alchemists' jargon to manifest the folly and vice of their practice (a commonsense point that ought to need no stating, but which has been made necessary by the obfuscations of recent critics); it is the alchemists themselves who are undergoing a transmutation of their souls ('Chaucer's Characterization of the Canon and his Yeoman', *Journal of the History of Ideas*, CCV, 1964; pp. 278–884); the first canon is merely a fool, but the second one *is* [sic] the Mercury of the alchemical processes ('The Canon's Yeoman's Alchemical Mass', *Studies in Philology* LXII, 1965; pp. 546–60). For a survey of alchemy as a discipline, see Grennen's 'Chaucer and the Commonplaces of Alchemy', *Classica et Mediaevalia*, XXVI, 1965; pp. 306–33. The early works of Edgar H. Duncan are informative and useful:

No sharper contrast can be found in Chaucer's treatment of the sciences than that between his presentations of alchemy and of physiognomy. The treatment of alchemy is dismissive in tone, and apart from passing references such as in the description of the Clerk of Oxford, it is confined to one section of the *Tales*. The use of physiognomy is confirmative of the characterization as presented by other methods, and, in the later works, is strongly pervasive. Much of the bodily description in the earlier works consists of the cataloguing of beauties in the manner of the popular romances, as parodied later in the description of Sir Thopas. This contrasts with the picking out of salient features which correspond to the Peripatetic teachings on appearance and reality. Even in the early

'Alchemy in the Writing of Chaucer, Jonson and Donne', 1939, is an unpublished Vanderbilt University dissertation; Chaucer's very exact knowledge and wording are stressed in 'The Yeoman's Canon's "Silver Citrinacioun" ', *Modern Philology*, CCCVI, 1940, pp. 241–62; Chaucer's dependence on Arnoldus de Villanova's *De lapide philosophorum*, where the poet himself refers to that author's *Rosarium*, is discussed in 'Chaucer and "Arnold of the Newe Toun" ', *MLN*, LVII, 1942, pp. 31–3. But more recently Duncan has speculated on the possibility that Chaucer's poetry contains a secret message to the Adept: 'The Literature of Alchemy and Chaucer's Canon's Yeoman's Tale: Framework. Theme and Characters', *Speculum*, XLIII, 1968.

Bruce Rosenberg, 'Swindling Alchemist' (as on p. 226 n. 2) sees a true Christian alchemy as an analogue to the Mass, thus making the true alchemist a type of Christ, and a parallel to St. Cecilia (p. 257 n. 2); the second canon is an anti-type of Christ; Rosenberg asserts that Chaucer revered true alchemy and its Great Secret, and criticized only charlatanism. L. M. Olmert ('The Canon's Yeoman's Tale: An interpretation', *Annuale Medievale*, VIII, 1967, pp. 70–94) sees a Satanic nature in the first canon. John Gardner ('*The Canon's Yeoman's Prologue and Tale*: An Interpretation', *Philological Quarterly*, XLVI, 1967) exaggerates the delicacy of the yeoman when he sees a solemn spiritual development in his renunciation of alchemy. My colleague Bruce L. Grenberg ('*The Canon's Yeoman's Tale*: Boethian Wisdom and the Alchemists', *Chaucer Review*, I, 1966) links the theme to one of the major areas of Chaucer's moral and intellectual interests.

See also: Bruce Rosenberg, as on p. 226 n. 2; Pauline Aiken, 'Vincent of Beauvais and Chaucer's Knowledge of Alchemy', *Studies in Philology*, CLI, 1944, pp. 371–89; Judith Scherer Hertz, 'The Canon's Yeoman's Prologue and Tale', *Modern Philology*, LVIII, 1961, pp. 233ff.

works, however, some awareness of the scholastic tradition appears: thus the fair White's face is said to have no '*wikked* sygne' (BD, 1. 917). The physiognomical descriptions of Troilus, Criseyde, and Diomede are, curiously, kept back until the final book (TC, V, 799–840). We know that they are largely borrowed from Joseph of Exeter.[1] From that point on, in Chaucer's work, the use of physiognomy becomes habitual. It is as though with this compact use of an idea mainly inspired from a minor literary source, the full possibility of concentrated character-depiction in this form had been brought home to Chaucer in the later 1380s. Nothing could have better suited the thumb-nail metonymic manner of the *General Prologue*. There we have salient characteristics revealed through build of body, voice, or, more particularly, the features of the head and face, most especially of the eyes. Usually, the characteristics are faults or bad inclinations, as we see in the descriptions of the Monk, the Friar, the Wife of Bath, the Miller, Summoner, and Pardoner. In the case of Madame Eglentyne, the description of beauty and gentle disposition is slyly used for satiric purposes. The physiognomic characteristics of the Franklin are combined with details from the doctrine of humours. In the Tales themselves, there are dramatic and more fluid uses: the physiognomies of Emetrius and Lycurge are, as is to be expected, combined with emblematic features; Alison and Absalom are accorded lively combined descriptions of features, dress, and behaviour; the description of the miller's daughter in 'The Reeve's Tale' is a grotesque use of the tradition.

The last three scientific disciplines here reviewed—magic, alchemy, and physiognomy—belong respectively to the second, the third, and the first of my initial categories. It is helpful to contrast Chaucer's uses of all three of them. In the later works, physiognomy is regularly used as an ancillary to psychological portrayal.[2] Magic is an activity to be somewhat ambivalently digested into narrative art. Alchemy seems to be wholly an object of satire. The impact of science upon the medieval

---

[1] *Troilus and Criseyde*, ed R. K. Root, Princeton 1926, pp. 541–45, and the references cited there; more fully, Root's article, 'Chaucer's Dares', *Modern Philology*, XV, 1917–18, section ii, i.e. pp. 16–18.

[2] A quasi-devotional application of physiognomy is seen in the *Epistula Lentuli*, which gives the physiognomy of Christ: E. Von Dobschütz, 'Christusbilder,' *Texte and Untersuchungen zur Geschichte der altchristlichen Literatur*, Neue Foge III, Leipzig, 1899; p. 319**. The copy of the *Epistula Lentuli* in *Cambridge MS. Dd. 3. 16* follows some abbreviated *Conclusiones* derived from the *Secretum secretorum*.

imagination, however, is most fully seen when the poet has assimilated the various sciences into his referential field, so that they are used easily and naturally in metaphor and general argumentation. Boethius, once again, one surmises, would have been Chaucer's principal teacher in this. As the sun lends light to Venus, so the lady of the *Complaynt d'Amours* (but this is a doubtfully Chaucerian poem) is for the lover the 'Sonne of the sterre bright and clere of hewe'. The teaching of Aristotelian physics, whereby everything has its natural home, makes the narrator say of the formel eagle that 'In hir was everi vertu *at his reste*'. (PF, l. 376). It is suited to the description of Aurelius' love-longing that we should be told of him:

> *His brest was hool, withoute for to sene,*
> *But in his herte ay was the arwe kene.*
> *And wel ye knowe that of a sursanure*
> *In surgerye is perilous the cure,*
> *But men myghte touche the arwe, or come therby.*
>
> (V, 1111–15)

But, to shift to comedy, it is equally apt—if unkind—that before we know of the Canon's alchemical activities, we are told as he canters along to overtake the pilgrims

> *. . . it was joye for to seen hym swete!*
> *His forheed dropped as a stillatorie,*
> *Were ful of plantayne and of paritorie.*
>
> (VIII, 579–81)

It is suitable that the greatest English poet of the fourteenth century should sometimes take a heroic simile from physics, such as the following example from magnetism:

> *Right as, betwixen adamauntes two*
> *Of evene might, a pece of yren set*
> *Ne hath no myght to meve to ne fro—*
> *For what that oon may hale, that other let—*
> *Ferde I, that nyste whether me was bet*
> *To entre or leve . . .*
>
> (PF, ll. 148–53)

Less than Dante, but still very appreciably, Chaucer is a product of the synthesizing and unifying movement which produced, and was itself influenced by, scholastic philosophy and the late-medieval world picture. Hence, his aesthetic practice shows a very detailed intellectual grasp of the science of his day, a discriminating between its different levels of seriousness and usefulness, a personal preoccupation with its relevance to spiritual and humane truths. The artists and intellectuals of our own day are largely in rebellion against the excesses of scientism and technology. The disjunction in our own imaginative picture is not one which would have been readily understood by a writer who was so constantly plotting harmonies and conjunctions.

10: Religion and Philosophy in Chaucer

GEOFFREY SHEPHERD

CHAUCER'S PARDONER KNEW very well what his own audience looked for in religion: they wanted to secure and increase their cattle; to multiply the yield of grain; and to maintain domestic harmony.[1] The religion that the Pardoner had to offer, many people living in England during the fourteenth century—as in all other centuries—were eager enough to accept, even in and on the terms of the offer. People looked for means to ensure prosperity and security in this life; and in the world to come, very similar satisfactions for ever and ever.

The old religion of England had shaped its practices over centuries to accommodate these homely demands. But it could operate at many other levels. Christian thought had penetrated deep and irradiated government, law, education, the structure of society, even trade and war. Religion could be demanding as well as satisfying. It could disturb and soothe consciences that had become dull to private or public duty. It could comfort the dejected and transform sorrow. It could terrify. No doubt for some, it could still proclaim gospel joy. It could suppress, or even sometimes seem to excuse, excesses of pride and cruelty. It had become totally pervasive, emmeshed in complicated and difficult doctrine and incorporated into elaborate and self-sufficient institutions which could provide a respectable living for many sorts of talent. Something like half of Chaucer's Pilgrims in *The Canterbury Tales* have a dependence upon the Church.

Religious observances shaped all sorts of social occasions. The Wife of Bath lived her life in a whirl of religious routine, not only with her own

[1] Prologue to 'The Pardoner's Tale', ll. 352–76.

several husbands at church door, but also with

> *my visitaciouns,*
> *To vigilies and to processiouns,*
> *To prechyng eek and to thise pilgrimages,*
> *To pleyes of myracles and to mariages,*
> *And wered upon my gaye scarlet gytes.*[1]

The tunes of her old dance were set to convenient texts of Scripture and to scraps of monastic morality. And there were of course many more refined pleasures to be had from fourteenth-century religion: from vestments, buildings, paintings, carvings, jewelry, music; in the savoury smells of feasting after fast, in the many sentimentalities of humanized piety.

The word 'religion' still retained a stricter meaning. It could refer to the special way of life of consecrated initiates set apart from the world —to the vocation of monks, friars and nuns. The contrast between religion in this sense and what religion meant and could mean in the life of the nation as a whole was clearly and harshly exposed by Wyclif at the beginning of his *De apostasia* (*c.* 1381). There he distinguished what he considered the essential meaning, as the personal and general following of Christ's law, from the 'private religions' of monks and friars with their sectarian customs and formal observances.[2] Chaucer and Langland and other writers indicate that the discrepancy was commonly apprehended, even if it were defined less specifically. The idea of holiness is not entirely unambiguous in Chaucer. A moral standard of 'verray vertu and clennesse' exacts an obedience no less demanding and praiseworthy than the monastic ideal (LGW, 295–6). There is a certain unreality in associating holiness exclusively with a life in religion (CT, I, 1157). In fact the old assumption of a double standard in moral demands and heavenly expectations, one for clerks, one for laymen, is by the end of the fourteenth century scarcely tenable. The search for perfection and the superior life can now start in the field full of folk. That all Christians in all the estates have a vocation is the theme of Thomas Wimbledon's well-known sermon preached at St Paul's Cross in 1388.

A Wyclifite tract *Octo in quibus seducuntur simplices Christiani* examines

---

[1] 'The Wife of Bath's Prologue', ll. 555–9.
[2] Johannis Wiclif, *Tractatus de apostasia*, ed M. H. Dziewicki, 1889, pp. 2–18.

in some detail the discrepancies between the actual and the ideal and explains how time and institutions have buried the reality of Christ's words under a cake of custom: when Holy Church is spoken of, it is assumed straight-away to refer only to prelates and priests, not to laymen; divine law is taken to mean ecclesiastical ordinances; it is commonly held that in dealing with sin the important thing is to make a formal distinction between venial and mortal sin and then to observe the appointed tariffs of penance. Instead, the tract exhorts simple Christians to see the clear truth of these matters: 'let each man do his business to flee all manner of sin, and have great sorrow and contempt for his sins, and mind on Christ's righteousness and wisdom to know and punish the foulness of sin, and on Christ's passion, death and mercy to forgive sins for true repentance. And let each man put his first trust in Christ's mercy and in his own good life and not in false pardons and vanities.'[1] The material may seem commonplace enough in Christian preaching, but the emphasis belongs to the late fourteenth century and is certainly not peculiar to Lollardy.

The drift marks no simple secularization of religion. Sacerdotalism was still strong and the claims to participate in the process of salvation did not mean that the laity turned away from supernatural values. Rather it implied a further extension of religion into all states of life. Even the last descendants of the barbarians would have claimed that they were all Christians now. What an increasing number of men wanted to discover afresh was the inner reality to which the concepts embodied in the institution of the Church and in Christian practice corresponded. What was the supernaturalism of which the Church spoke but which had been accommodated in familiar external forms? This is the question that bothered Piers when he received the pardon: it is what Will investigated at length in the rest of the poem and what he is still to seek at the end.

Many aspects of fourteenth-century religious life relate to this new enquiry. 'The need for each man to learn some divinity', as Nicholas of Hereford put it, was met by an unprecedented production of religious tracts, confessional and devotional manuals for pious laymen,[2] which from this time forward into the twentieth century was to continue as the

[1] *Select English Works of John Wyclif*, ed T. Arnold, III, Oxford 1871, pp. 447–53.

[2] See W. A. Pantin, *The English Church in the Fourteenth Century*, Cambridge 1955, chap. X & Appendix II.

staple of the booksellers' trade. But the new didacticism affected most writings in the vernacular. The works of the *Gawain*-poet are exemplary: in *Gawain* itself, the old non-monastic ideal of personal worth is restated in contemporary Christian terms; chastity is given a new relevance in *Cleanness*; in *Pearl* the Grace of God transfigures secular courtesy. Such pieces among many illustrate the working out of nominalist morality, where 'to do what is in you' could possess a saving virtue.[1] That such ideals were taken seriously, at least by some, is evident from the careers of the early Lollard knights who in rather extraordinary fashion combined ascetic piety with aggressive professionalism.[2] Chaucer's Knight may be much less of an idealization than he has been made to appear.

The new prospect emphasized contemporary inadequacies. It is this frustration of optimistic expectations that accounts in part for the curiously mixed impression that a study of late fourteenth-century religious life in England produces. It is possible to find it immensely appealing, with a cumulative force that sweeps medieval art and spirituality to the crest of achievement. An English style of architecture and of religious expression come to maturity at this time. In the cause of religion the great town churches were built and decorated. The dedicated workmanship in embroidery, in alabaster, ivory and stone carving, with wood and brass and glass was never surpassed. Many colleges and schools were founded or refounded. In many places, parish life was vigorous. Religious gilds flourished, religious plays grew popular and vernacular preaching acquired a new effectiveness. There was life and energy in the organization of the Church. There were many able and sensible bishops, many clever and productive scholars whose achievements as *calculatores* and as logicians were admired throughout Europe. There were no doubt multitudes of devout Christians of whose names no record remains. Chaucer's description of the Plowman can stand as cenotaph for their number and worth.

Above all, the late fourteenth century is remembered as the time of the English mystics. The work of Richard Rolle lived on after the Black Death especially in the north, and is strongly evident in some of the com-

[1] Heiko A. Oberman, *The Harvest of Medieval Theology: Gabriel Biel and Late Medieval Nominalism*, Cambridge, Mass. 1963, pp. 129–45.

[2] K. B. McFarlane, *Lancastrian Kings and Lollard Knights*, Oxford 1972, pp. 171f, 179f, 186f, 210f.

mentaries of later times. There is a steady stream of writing concerned with the interiorizing of devotion and the cultivation of an affective and intuitive dependency upon God. Walter Hilton in particular, and the author of *The Cloud of Unknowing* display remarkable poise in their re-commendation of the spiritual life and a steady acceptance of English re-ligious traditions. Even when they write for the laity they can take an advanced and knowledgeable piety for granted.

These mystical writings have an importance both in virtue of their own quality and also as an index of the most intense spiritual desires of the time. They were flowers of an ancient strain and grown in secret gar-dens. They spoke of lives that were hid with God. Chaucer seems to know nothing at all about this kind of religion. Nor does Gower or Wyclif. Though there may well have been a heap of hermits in England as Langland suggests, there was no movement comparable with that of the Brethren of the Common Life in the Low Countries. In England *devotio moderna* seems to have been diverted into Bible reading and moral endeavour. Nor was there any saintly mystic like Catherine of Siena, or Bridget of Vadstena or Jean Gerson who in their lifetimes commanded public affairs. The English mystics represent in English life rather a quiet extension into the vernacular of the monastic spirituality of the twelfth century, modified in some detail by movements in the theology of the schools, but in the main, individual, eclectic and unsystematic.

Altogether, prelates and parishioners, craftsmen and mystics, provide evidence enough to write an account of fourteenth-century life which would be that of a golden age of harvest in religion—not an heroic age of saints and martyrs, but a time of fulfilment with some extraordinary achievements. Yet this is not how men wrote about themselves and about religion at the end of the century. If they were not swept with anger over their condition, they were often full of unease. Even the pious were contentious, eager to detect hypocrisy or heresy. There were many of those 'half-humbled, logic-chopping souls' about whom Walter Hilton complained. Already Thomas Bradwardine, who stood in intel-lect above all other Archbishops of Canterbury of the century, had fier-cely and resolutely and perhaps unavailingly opposed the tendencies of his time. The sensible and moral Gower writes sometimes as if in utter despair at the state of the Church within the realm. Wyclif and also his opponents are often bitter and gloomy. 'Pray, pray for England', writes William Flete in 1380 from his exile in Rome. Even Bishop Brinton of

Rochester, an official spokesman of church and state, is anxious and reproachful.

A large sub-literature of complaint survives from the last decades of the century. Often the complaints contradict one another: that the Church is trampled underfoot, or that its ministers are proud and grasping; that the faithful look up and are not fed, or that the friars are always interfering and making matters worse. There was plenty of material for scandal at all levels of religious life. A review of such evidence could readily reveal an age of spiritual corruption, of weak and uncertain faith, of rampant evil—the twilight of Antichrist itself, as Langland and Wyclif and others saw it. The observant Chaucer is tight-lipped. Yet one of his common themes is a moral weariness with his times, and a longing for a lost stability.

> *The world hath mad a permutacioun*
> *Fro right to wrong, fro trouthe to fikelnesse,*
> *That al is lost . . .*
>
> (*Lak of Stedfastnesse*, 19–21)

Once there had been a better age, of faith and honour, peace and harmony. As the war with France dragged on in uneasy truces, there were many attempts to dignify old values with the memories of past achievements. A curious idealism, ill-founded on a sense of ancient pieties and modern despair manifests itself in the negotiations of the Kings of England and France in the last decade of the century[1]—a mood in high policy caught by Philip of Mézières in France, and by Chaucer in the 'Tale of Melibeus'.

The later English Middle Ages fall into two parts about the fourteenth century. The war brought a permanent change in the political temper of the nation. And in religion, the Babylonish Captivity of the Papacy and in particular the Great Schism of 1378, seemed to have bruised the minds of Englishmen irremediably. In earlier times, England had been far enough from Rome and from the local politics of the Papacy to cherish towards the majestic ideal of Rome a certain awe and respect which partly because of Rome's remoteness confirmed Englishmen in their own sense of worthiness and mission. But a century of French Popes at Avignon coincided with a century of Anglo-French wars. Rome lost its sacredness and mystery. The activities of busy officials at the papal courts

---

[1] J. J. N. Palmer, *England, France and Christendom 1377–99*, 1972, pp. 180–91.

became more obvious and were interpreted as an endless interference with English affairs even at the level of parish life, always it seemed to the foreigners' advantage. Operating temporizing and uncertain policies at the level of those with whom it haggled, the papal court could seem a sinister force with agents everywhere. It demonstrated its servility to the politics of solvency when in 1378 the same college of cardinals elected the two rival popes. It became difficult to appeal convincingly to the ancient principles of a divine authority. For forty years practical politics and private interests of all the parties concerned worked through the uncertain pontificates of eight popes towards a business-like compromise. The moral effect of involvement in this process upon thoughtful and pious men in England cannot be measured. Some shock of disillusionment, it can be assumed, reinforced the rising sense of national identity. A new feeling for a stricter, more self-reliant English establishment of religion shows itself in the policies of kings and bishops. With different emphases it is expressed in many writings of the latter end of the century.

The ecclesiastical and political ferment generated an excitement in recognizing the motions of history, in seeking the purpose behind events, and the patterns of the future. The shaking of old stabilities in society and of certainties in belief convinced some men all the more that they were witnesses to the working out of a new temporal order. Events might be bewildering and unpleasant but they were rich in meanings. There were many different ways of looking for them. Some sober clerks studied and commented on Augustine's *City of God* or endeavoured by the light of the authors of antiquity to see the whole destiny of man including the righteous heathen's in universal terms—to acquire the kind of humanist and classical perspective which Chaucer himself seeks.[1] But there was an apocalyptic tinge to many enquiries, and a diffused revival of Joachism with a whole range of millenarian beliefs. Some men convinced themselves that the reign of Antichrist had begun and that the final Doom was imminent. Prophecies and revelations multiply. There is a new concern with ecclesiastical and national myths, with apocryphal history and secret wisdom: with all forms of learning, including astrology and magic, that could claim to interpret the inner history of the times. Chaucer's work gives only momentary reflections from this obs-

[1] See Beryl Smalley, *English Friars and Antiquity in the early Fourteenth Century*, Oxford 1960.

curer world of speculation, but many preachers and political writers as well as the alliterative poets repeatedly display their fascination.[1]

Piers Plowman can indeed be read as a fourteenth-century apocalypse; but Langland seems to attempt to comprehend and embrace all the uncertainties and all the contradictories of the religious life of his time. Primarily no doubt he is concerned with the individual Christian's search for the way in which he can live and think in hope of salvation: in Langland's time it was still difficult to give any acceptable individuation to the ordinary Christian—the *viator* of the theologians—and Langland can only vaguely substantiate the individual purpose as Will. What is important for the present is that Langland is able to record the process of enquiry. The poem discloses the confusion that the poet discovered. The poem is a faithful mirror of the religious life of the time in its fervent and fearful mobility and remains almost as baffling as all the other evidence of contemporary religious experience. A constantly persistent and probing reading and re-reading of *Piers Plowman* affords the best method of understanding this experience; but the poem is almost inexhaustible of meanings and offers us too much for a brief instruction.

It does not account directly for Chaucer's own attitude towards religion nor for the tone of his religious references. Langland is much too reflective and ironic to be counted naïve; yet he is obsessed with his theme. There was no other poem to compose and re-compose but this one, but its unity is demonstrated by his persistence, not by his accomplishment. His own total commitment to his theme excludes an awareness of the kind of detachment and self-limitation that Chaucer's work displays. No doubt at any time an age's obsession will produce in some men an appropriate reaction of reserve or silence. Chaucer, at least in his writing, is such a man. A careful reading of Chaucer suggests that in religion, as in most other fields of human interest, he was quite aware of what was going on, yet he never discloses his commitment in religion and offers few judgements. Some art, like Chaucer's, but unlike Langland's, seems designed to attenuate the prominent issues of contemporary life and thought.

Chaucer's religious writings make a comparatively short list: the *ABC* prayer, according to tradition written for the Duchess Blanche; 'The

---

[1] See Morton W. Bloomfield, *Piers Plowman as a Fourteenth Century Apocalypse*, New Brunswick 1962; Marjorie Reeves, *The Influence of Prophecy in the later Middle Ages: a study in Joachism*, Oxford 1969, pp. 81–8.

Prioress's Tale'; the 'Tale of Melibeus'; 'The Second Nun's Tale'; 'The Parson's Tale'; in an ironic mode, 'The Pardoner's Tale'. There was also we may suppose the lost translation of Pope Innocent's *De contemptu mundi*. All the material he used was old and familiar, guaranteed by its origins. He takes a saint's life and reworks it quite faithfully, adjusting the ingredients to suit contemporary fashions of piety: 'The Second Nun's Tale' of St Cecilia is his one exercise in the favourite literary form of his time; but the virgin martyr here, or the little clergeon of 'The Prioress's Tale', or the other saints aptly invoked throughout Chaucer's *Tales*, all share that quality we give to stained-glass saints: they transmit a diffused light and in their framework contribute to a pretty design.

Chaucer was familiar with the traditional material to be found in the manuals of confession and instruction, but he uses it extensively only in 'The Parson's Tale'. In this composition, and in his incorporations of religious material into other pieces, he shows the same dependence upon existing public formulas in liturgical or devotional use augmented by his own skill in varying the language and increasing illustration. In all his religious writing his inventiveness is manifested chiefly by his ability to present familiar material with a new confidence and an unexpected verbal enrichment.[1] Nor was this achievement small. It was very much admired and imitated by fifteenth-century writers of religious verse.

The success is understandable; but the apparently deliberate and easy acceptance of limits in his religious verse draws attention to the problem with Chaucer. In a society dominated and pervaded by religion, this poet, who above all English poets is often regarded as holding up a steady broad mirror to an age, writes remarkably little that can be recognized as ostensibly religious in material or impulse.

In the past it has been claimed that it is possible to eliminate the problem by assuming that he shared in a jolly medieval Catholicism into which all natural instincts could be healthily christened. Such a claim could only be made now in careless ignorance of the tensions of the time. Alternatively a more fashionable interpretation has been grounded on a modern assumption (which strangely inverts early Renaissance theory) that poetry is an unveiled theology. Accordingly, a millenium of medieval theology has been selectively quarried to frame Chaucer as the representative medieval poet, the summarian of a static civilization. If one

[1] See Patricia M. Kean, *Chaucer and the Making of English Poetry*, II, *The Art of Narrative*, 1972, Chap. 5: 'The Religious Poetry', pp. 186–209.

approach regards Chaucer as the faithful and untroubled son of Holy Church who saw no need to investigate the mysteries of religion, the other turns everything he wrote into parts of a sustained post-Augustinian allegory. From a reader's point of view the second approach is more offensive, for it limits the response necessary for understanding and replaces what Chaucer wrote with a synthetic, unhistorical and preclusive ideology.

Unlike other late medieval writers Chaucer shows a distinct lack of interest in religious allegory. When he uses a story which has a familiar allegorization he will give it a different turn: thus, only briefly, halfway through the 'Tale of Melibeus', he acknowledges the original significance of the ancient allegory of the Figurative Castle of the Soul: ' "Thou has doon synne agayn oure Lord Crist"says Dame Prudence "for certes, the three enemys of mankynde, that is to seyn, the fleesh, the feend, & the world, thou hast suffred hem to entre in-to thyn herte wilfully by the wyndowes of thy body, & hast nat defended thyself suffisantly agayns hire assautes & hire temptaciouns, so that they han wounded thy soule in fyue places; this is to seyn, the deedly synnes that been entred into thyn herte by thy fyve wittes." "[1] But this is not what the Tale is about at all. It is an advocacy of pacificism and toleration, it illustrates prudential action in a world of war and enmity. Chaucer avoids an exemplification of the helpless sinful soul redeemed by the Passion of Christ and produces instead a social and moral lesson: a man can indeed insure his own safety if he behaves with discretion.

Somewhat differently Chaucer turns the old allegory of the wooing of the beggar-maid by the Christ-knight into the story of Griselda. Here the more spiritual aspects of the story in its earlier use emerge so clearly that the reader is embarrassed. The very skill employed to despiritualize the narration produces a chilling effect. This Tale reveals disconcertingly the gap that had opened up by Chaucer's time between the traditional paradigms of holiness and contemporary social morality. Griselda would make an exemplary figure for *anima*, or a saint: Chaucer knows she scarcely makes a wife or mother fit for the late fourteenth-century life. Presumably what Chaucer is interested in presenting is the consequence of choice or compulsion involved in human action, and not in analogical correspondences of meaning.

For Chaucer it would seem that the insistent problems of religion all

[1] 'Tale of Melibeus', ll. 1419–23.

spilled over, in what has later been considered a characteristic English fashion, into morality, into questions of conduct and conscience. He poses the questions but does not answer them. That is why the *Prologue* and the presentation of the Prioress or the Wife of Bath or the Pardoner have proved so engrossing to moralistic critics. Their associations may be religious, but their interest and their interest to Chaucer lies in their morals and manners. A moral indifferentism in principle appears to accompany sympathetic observation and acceptance of the consequences of human action. His stories would have often presented to his audience either a total moral bewilderment (unless he had cultivated detachment), or a cruel amoral determinism (unless he had emphasized compassion). There are still chinks in his narration through which can be glimpsed a black pessimism. The indeterminate values of the surface action facilitate his irony, his volatility and his sophistication. But the charm and gentility of his high clowning cannot conjure away all the incompatibles. The old systems of symbols and analogues which had once been capable of bearing and asserting, solidly and convincingly, the truths of an earlier medieval experience of the moral life, had become unstable and unsatisfying.

Chaucer took at least the business of story-telling seriously. Any man telling a story has to determine most of his material in advance, to preordain its disposition, and to foresee some of the conclusions to which it shall run. The shaping of material and the ordering of incident introduce subordinations and seeming causality into the action narrated. Almost unconsciously, the pattern imposed will be understood by the listener and probably by the composer himself, as actually inhering in the continuum of incidents. The events themselves will appear to control and to produce the characters. In solving technical problems then a story-teller involuntarily conjures up Destiny and Fate and gives them a role in his story.

All well-made stories link arbitrary incidents into a fixed and appropriate order; only in retrospect and perhaps after reflection does the order appear unavoidable and is recognized as predetermined. The recognition should not be too easy. In its telling the story should arouse expectancy, not fulfil precise expectations. It is because a simple recurrent pattern dominates the materials so completely that 'The Monk's Tale' strikes us, as it struck the Host, as monotonously tedious. It is not necessary to insist that 'The Miller's Tale' is theological in intention or construction to realize that the denouement exemplifies how chance in the exposition becomes necessity in the total action.

But there is perhaps some relationship or parallel between Chaucer's achievement as a narrative poet and a theological preoccupation of his time. The shape of most medieval stories is usually illustrated by reference to the Boethian wheel of Fortune. In 'The Monk's Tale' there is a simple series of such stories: in 'The Miller's Tale' several lines of action with this Boethian profile cross each other and finally coincide. But some medieval stories follow instead what has been called an Augustinian pattern where the course of a human action seems to be running towards an extra-human axis.[1] The outcome then is not what happens in a secular ordering of events. It is presented as what God decided shall occur so that some particular in the history of salvation shall be worked out. The Augustinian model assumes a religious interpretation of the flow of events. It assumes a real causality, not simply an arbitrary sequence in time. It is part of Chaucer's achievement in *Troilus and Criseyde* that he combines both models in telling one completely secular story.

As a writer he seems always to have been puzzled by some variation of this question: How does a succession of events make any sense? The issue is implicit in the presentation of the naïve enquirer in *The Book of the Duchess*, as well as in the complaint of the Man in Black. What is the relationship in *The House of Fame* between the fixed, quite arbitrarily fixed, fame and all the living but formless and whirling rumours? In such poems he strains inconsequentiality to the limits. He relies upon the shared experience of dreams, or on some formal parallel, or some contiguity in association to hold the narrative together. In 'The Squire's Tale' which lacks the support that parody gives to 'Sir Thopas', a pure free flow of romance incidents seems to have become eventually unmanageable.

In *Troilus and Criseyde*, he consciously links the writer's problem in authenticating his fiction with the organization of the action of his story. The soliloquy given to Troilus in Book IV, ll. 946–1085 is not a temporary and self-indulgent suspension of narrative progress but an explicit rationalization of the story's shape. What is the meaning of action and what is the purpose of volition within a completely controlled system? It is the humanly unknown God-foreseen future which troubles Troilus. What he fears most is the uncertainty itself. His situation is secular enough, but the argument in the soliloquy is developed within a premiss

[1] See F. P. Pickering, *Literature and Art in the Middle Ages*, 1970, pp. 169–96.

of the possibility of grace and mercy (ll, 949–52, 1079–82) and presented in school terms as the arguments of the great clerks 'That han hir top ful heighe and smothe y-shore' (l. 996). By Chaucer's time in the schools the clerks had indeed played endless subtle variations on these themes. Presumably Chaucer did not follow them closely. Chaucer takes the soliloquy directly from Prose III of Book Five of his own translation of Boethius's *Consolation of Philosophy*, a work which contributed little to the logical and theological discussions in the schools. But it served Chaucer's purpose well. It gives him the central issues which he presents in the form of question, objection and distinction, catching in an awkward vernacular idiom the tone of contemporary scholastic debate.

If God foresees everything, Troilus asks, how can the human will be free to act? But if things can turn out differently from what has been decided, can the divine foreknowledge be other than imprecise and uncertain? Should the problem then be reduced to one of distinguishing cause from effect, of deciding whether things happen because they are foreseen or whether things are foreseen because they are to happen? Yet can this distinction be said to eliminate necessity? And if necessity has to be readmitted how still can the will be free? Troilus is back with the original dilemma. Boethius had given a solution but Chaucer does not allow Troilus in Book IV to adopt it. It may be argued of course that the whole telling of the story eventually achieves a harmony and moves towards a theological solution.

In the schools the clerks probed deeper and wider and more insistently, even though their touch was less healing than Chaucer's. Theological discussion of God's power and man's freewill involved questions of grace, sin and salvation. If salvation depended upon the free gift of God what part did man play in his own salvation? If the will of man is free to choose some good, to what extent can he earn the salvation, or escape the reprobation that is predestined for him? The broad principles of this intricate debate on *meritum de condigno* and *meritum de congruo* are recalled in *Pearl*. A full reward appropriate to the sense of divine justice can be won only in a state of grace comparable with that of the Blessed Virgin, whose sovereignty among the queens of heaven is acknowledged by the Maiden (*Pearl*, ll. 433–56). The partial reward *de congruo* proceeds from God's generosity, not justice, when God accepts human acts as fit ground for His gift of grace: and this is the substance of the eleventh section of *Pearl* (ll. 601–60).

Theology in the fourteenth century could not maintain the nice balance established temporarily by Thomas Aquinas whereby the election of man by God was directly related to His providence which had incorporated man's predestination into God's purpose in ordering creation. In this way Aquinas had been able to present salvation as a rational and intelligible act even if men with their limited capacities would have difficulty in understanding it completely. But the followers of Duns Scotus and William of Ockham could no longer allow themselves the comforts of understanding. The process of salvation could not be scanned by human intelligence. It was inaccessibly remote and therefore morally much more terrifying.

On this account, the problems of freewill, foreknowledge and grace became more insistent in the fourteenth century and appear with endless ramifications. For the Scotists, God's purpose is expressed in terms of will not mind. Will is the means by which sovereignty is manifested. Since God possesses *potentia absoluta*, He elects those He wills to elect absolutely and unconditionally. But because God has also willed for Himself a mode of willing, His *potentia ordinata*, His grace will have already been infused into those He elects. It is His preordaining not His foreknowledge which is absolute. Some free play was allowed to the human will, but its scope was insignificant and irrelevant if set against the operation of God's will.

Ockham made the issue even less tractable intellectually by erasing even more of the familiar categories of early medieval theology. God's powers of foreknowledge and predestination are fused together. What God wills is the truth He is, but what He wills and what He is are equally unknowable. Theology as traditionally conceived becomes impossible. The nature of human reason itself was an indication of the limitations of human enquiry. All that men could know with any degree of certainty was what could be investigated by reason working upon experience. At most reason could talk about God only in terms of probabilities. By the end of the fourteenth century the distrust of reason is well established:

> *And Idel bost is forte blowe*
> *A Mayster of diuinite. . . .*
> *þe more we trace þe Trinite,*
> *þe more we falle in fantasye.*[1]

[1] 'This World fares as a fantasy', *Religious Lyrics of the XIVth Century*, ed Carleton Brown, Oxford 1924, 106, p. 163, ll. 89–90; 95–6.

Faith was set against reason in great variety of inter-relationships, ranging from fideism to a well-developed scepticism. Chaucer, though but a
layman, in his writings probably presents a special but highly characteristic combination. *The House of Fame* in particular produces what must
seem to us an extraordinary blend of realism and empiricism and illuminationism.

Throughout the thirteenth century especially among the great Franciscans there had always been an opposition to the dominant Aristote-
lianism and an attraction towards Augustine's theory of illumination
according to which human knowledge was acquired by a direct irradia-
tion of the mind by the divine light. For Roger Bacon not only moral
and spiritual knowledge but also sense perception was based on this kind
of illumination. In the fourteenth century both theologians like Henry of
Ghent and Archbishop FitzRalph of Armagh, and also scientists working
within the tradition of Grosseteste developed Augustine's theory within
their own special contexts of interest.

Its influence can be felt also in the recrudescence of belief in the reality
and practice of prophecy. If Langland had a theory of poetry he found it
in some form of illuminationism, and so would several other vernacular
writers of the late middle ages. But perhaps the most striking examples of
the catalytic effect of the theory can be seen in some passages of the English mystics. The consequences of nominalist theology were by no means
inimical to mystical endeavour.[1] God is unknown and unknowable. But
when the human will is directed entirely towards God and all its motions
suspended, then from God may come the illumination. 'He may not be
known by reason. He may not be gotten by thought, nor concluded by
understanding; but He may be loved and chosen with the true louely
will of thine heart.'[2]

If the new movements in theology strengthened the need and experience of faith for some gifted men, yet more generally, the *via moderna*
down which Ockham had beckoned also induced various forms of scepticism: clearly a scepticism about the certainty of knowledge and about
human competence—Chaucer expresses doubt on both; in more theological circles, a hesitation about accepting all the comfortingly tra-

[1] See H. A. Oberman, *Harvest*, chap. 10.
[2] *Epistle of Discretion* in Edmund Gardner, *The Cell of Self Knowledge*, 1910,
pp. 107–8.

ditional attributes of God, an almost total confusion about the nature of grace, and a puzzlement about the responsibility of sin and the value of moral endeavour. Startling questions were debated in the schools: Is God the author of sin?; can God command, and then punish for obedience?; can a sinner merit reward?; can God tell a lie?.[1] To such questions, clerks could answer affirmatively. But at the same time they asserted that their answers were worthless, because they were merely solutions to logical exercises about an unknowable God to whom all things were possible. Perhaps common observation should have taught them that exercises train muscles that eventually demand practical work.

Such intellectual permissiveness and voluntaristic morality provoked, naturally enough, some sharp reactions. There were some formal condemnations of Ockhamism, at Avignon in 1326 and in the University of Paris in the 1360s; and in England by the end of the century, through the troubles of King Richard's reign and of the Great Schism, an urge in the dioceses and in the University of Oxford to rediscover and re-establish a theoretical basis for spiritual authority. But the inheritance of the schools was solid and pervasive. The instruments that had led to scepticism were now the instruments that were used to measure authority and to re-assert it. Though the old method of investigation by *questio* almost disappeared and was replaced by more discursive forms of exposition, the syllogism was still regarded as the infallible and universal tool of thought. The Augustinianism of the late fourteenth century is an Augustinianism in the bonds of scholasticism; and the work of the two great protesters against nominalist scepticism and all it stood for emphasize the paradox.

De Causa Dei contra Pelagium by Thomas Bradwardine is a huge, deliberated, vehement book organized to permit the maximum concentration of argument to penetrate the enemy's position most deeply. Although the enemy is identified as the Pelagians all under one banner, Bradwardine takes aim carefully at so inclusive a target that he lists in his first chapter almost all the heresies known to medieval man. But the prime and central heresy is that of those modern Pelagians who, wittingly or unwittingly, by assuming that God is unknowable have in all sorts of ways made man the centre of interest, seen man as source of values and

[1] See K. Michalski, *La philosophie au XIVe siècle*, Minerva Reprint, Frankfurt 1969, pp. 14; 82–98; Gordon Leff, *Bradwardine and the Pelagians: a study of 'De Causa Dei' and its opponents*, Cambridge 1957, pp. 216–27.

capable of managing his own affairs. Few would ever escape so comprehensive and yet particularized an assault as Bradwardine delivered; and certainly not Chaucer in his writings, except on the terms he finally pleads in his 'Retractions' that his 'giltes' should be ascribed 'to the defaut of myn unconning, and nat to my wil'; that his only hope is for 'the grace to bewayle my giltes . . . grace of verray penitence' that can save him through the working grace of Christ.

Bradwardine himself had been brought up, as he confesses, in the modern fashion: 'I rarely heard anything of grace spoken of in the lectures of the philosophers in the schools. . . . Every day I heard them teach that we are masters of our own free acts, and that it stands in our own power to do either good or evil, to be either virtuous or vicious and so on. Towards grace I was still graceless. . . . But afterwards and before I had become a student of theology, the truth before mentioned struck upon me like a beam of grace.'[1]

What Bradwardine is doing in *De Causa Dei* is to re-rationalize the concept of the *potentia absoluta* of God: to deny the contemporary claim that a recognition of *potentia absoluta* makes a systematic theology impossible; to assert instead that a proper understanding of the common principle makes a theology of grace essential. To admit the absolute sovereignty of God is to admit also His absolute grace. The destiny of man whether directed towards salvation or damnation does not come about through human works, but through the gracious will of God. Bradwardine denies all power to natural necessity, to the stars, or to mundane Fate. Yet the will of man is free though completely enveloped. For whereas it is usually assumed that the will of man displays its freedom of choice in dealing with future contingencies and so is in some measure at odds with the predetermined divine order, Bradwardine sees the divine will as operating in eternity and possessing a decisiveness which is totally unaffected by the passage of secular time. The future is as fixed as the past in the divine will. Thus God's will which extends into future contingencies guarantees the contingents with which man's will is involved and guarantees also the freedom of the will in dealing with contingents.

Bradwardine drives a hard clear way as he saw it, avoiding on the one

[1] Thomas Bradwardine, *De Causa Dei contra Pelagium et de virtute causarum ad suos Mertonenses*, ed H. Savile, 1618, I, xxxv, p. 308 C.

hand, the mechanical fatalists who not only argued that everything was determined by an inexorable and impersonal necessity, but also sought to show that by releasing man from any responsible involvement in the divine plan, man could claim a world of his own to manage. In relation to their own circumstances Palamon and Arcite conduct a debate on these lines in 'The Knight's Tale'.[1] On the other hand, Bradwardine seeks also to avoid all those fourteenth-century eclectics, temporizers and compromisers with Pelagianism, the proud logicians who struggled to win a little freewill for man in a world constrained by logical necessity, by manipulating the tenses and moods of human speech.

For Bradwardine the solvent of all paradoxes is grace. The cause of God is maintained above all else by a rigorous demonstration of the working of God's grace into which every detail is locked. God's will enters everywhere. God initiates every act. Grace is the initiative that God holds in all acts of creation, preservation and salvation. His giving of it is entirely gratuitous. It is needed in any human act to make that act good. No act without grace can win grace.[2]

The debt to Augustine is plain, but the book elaborates its themes with all the insistence of scholastic method with tight chains of syllogism and authorities binding up an unbroken progression of proof, so that it reads like a vast geometrical demonstration. We need not assume that Chaucer read or knew much about *De Causa Dei* except to be able to judge fairly enough that the holy doctor had pounded contemporary concern with predestination and grace to the finest theological powder and had reconstituted them in iron and concrete.

But there are passages in *De Causa Dei* where Bradwardine moves beyond the language of the schools and adopts accents that are reminiscent of Augustine as rhetorician, or of Anselm and the spiritual writers of the twelfth century, who could give theology the pulse of devotion. At the end of the long last Chapter 34 of Book Two, he writes:

'What sinner will not trust in thee, O Lord. For I know, Lord, I know, and not without sorrow I confess and recount to thee, that there are yet certain men, namely the proud Pelagians, who prefer to put their trust in men, indeed in themselves. For they say: "If God

[1] 'The Knight's Tale', I. 1080–1333.

[2] See Heiko A. Oberman, *Archbishop Thomas Bradwardine: a fourteenth-century Augustinian: a study of his theology in its historical context*, Utrecht 1957, chaps. VI & VII, pp. 123–85.

with his grace predestines us and our works, and things fall out as He wills, so that we can do nothing without His agency and prevision: and if likewise He can damn us and refuse us good works, or cancel what He allowed us, thrust us on into evil deeds, and bind us when we are cast there: who can then be secure? Who will hope with any sense of confidence, and not rather be in utter despair? But if on the other hand, predestination and reprobation depend upon our own wills, and we alone are the free masters of our own acts without God, then we can be secure; then it will be well with us and we can trust and hope." O vain and deceitful children of men wandering in illusion. Why will you not put your trust in Him who is supremely good, supremely merciful, and full of loving-kindness? &c"[1]

In such a passage the torment of the times becomes apparent. It is not simply the product of perplexity before hard and complicated doctrine, it touches the whole life and experience of men. In the second half of the century, in the years following Bradwardine's death, the moral and spiritual discomfort had if anything increased. The distress and entrapped hopelessness that Chaucer evokes in his fictional woe of Troilus makes the poem a dark and strong, if indirect reflection of the spiritual mood of his time.

In Book IV Troilus had ended his own debate with himself in a renunciation of argument and a cry for mercy to 'almighty Jove in trone' (IV, ll. 1079–82). It was an admission of powerlessness and abjectness which could originate a comfort of sorts. It is an anticipation of Chaucer's conclusion to the whole story, a call for unconditional surrender on the terms laid down by the absolute power. Troilus has the one clear moment of vision when he sees things as they are—an attenuated version of the last hope that Uhtred of Boldon had daringly offered his generation—but of Troilus's ultimate destination we are left in doubt. All the hard cases of this world are left entirely to the mercy and purpose of God.

Many men living and dying at the end of the fourteenth century seem to have found their last consolation in this abject uncertainty. They acknowledged that they were poor caitifs and miserable and uncomprehending sinners. Even the masterful Archbishop Arundel, the hammer of radical philosophy at Oxford, asked in his will to be buried obscurely in the corner of a parish churchyard as a fearful and humble sinner unworthy of funeral honours.[2]

[1] *De Causa Dei*, II, xxxiv, p. 630 A.
[2] K. B. McFarlane, *Lancastrian Kings and Lollard Knights*, pp. 219–20.

Anger moderates the pessimism of the other great protester against nominalist scepticism. John Wyclif is the most important English figure in religion in the late fourteenth century. His proper status in the history of thought is still not established: that he was pronounced heretic after his death gave an exaggerated prominence to some of his policies and has retarded recognition of his more representative qualities. The early reaction against him only succeeded in digging some of his general principles deeper into the soil of English life. Now he deserves, as we have been told, something better than the brown varnish of post-Reformation nonconformist adulation; something more perhaps than the plastic insulation provided by twentieth-century medievalism which often finds him too prickly to handle.

Unlike many teachers in late medieval Oxford, Wyclif was a secular priest. He seems to have been over forty when he became a Doctor of Divinity. His mind and methods were always, like Calvin's, those of a master of grammar and logic rather than those of a traditional theologian. His writings with their strong didactic and polemical vigour suggest that he was much more interested in effective truth than in theological elegance. There was an explosive mixture in his teaching: a programme to which he was grimly committed in all its successive unfoldings; a technique applied at full power without much delicacy in selecting the point of application.

Wyclif's teaching is a culmination of the method developed in the schools, but it came at a time when there was no common body of doctrine left in the schools to teach. He was, and is still, accused of pursuing issues too far; but so did many other contemporary doctors in the schools. What is more disturbing perhaps is that as an academic Wyclif seems to have believed in what he taught. Unlike the 'doctors of signs' whom he scornfully opposed, he regarded academic questions as concerning real issues.

To some of his sophisticated contemporaries he must have seemed rather old-fashioned and simplistic in his approach to theology. But he is the more characteristic of his time in that he must be counted either an eclectic or an original. He followed no school, although he owed much to Bradwardine and to FitzRalph, with both of whom he was ready enough to disagree. In his early days at Oxford he was known as *Joannes Augustini* and that soubriquet indicates a continuing allegiance.

In dealing with the obsession of the century, the question of freewill or

determinism, Wyclif reverts to the old preScotist position and stresses
the divine fore-knowledge as distinct from the fore-ordaining effected
by the divine will. The reversal separates him from the legacy of mod-
ernism discernible even in Bradwardine and instead emphasizes the
Platonism inherent in Augustine. But Wyclif's doctrine on providence is
to be linked in derivation with his other more characteristic doctrines:
his atomism of individual existences, his theory of time, his highly uncertain theology of the eucharist, even his teachings on dominion, the
priesthood, and the worship of images; and above all with his understanding of the nature of Scripture. All rise inexorably from his belief in
real and possible universals.

Wyclif's realism was a doctrine of certitude. His complete and positive
assurance was no doubt part of his fascination during the 1360s for a generation at Oxford bred on scepticism. Wyclif proclaimed afresh much
more briskly and brilliantly than Bradwardine what Ockhamist scepticism had denied 'that the existence of God can be proved by infallible
proof by a pure philosopher',[1] and all that followed from such a position.
For Wyclif unlike Ockham all knowledge, even human knowledge, is
grounded in God's thought. All that God does, creates, wills, purposes, is
also thought by God. His thoughts are the universals or ideas that are
embodied in all that follows from His acts. 'The Idea is an absolutely
necessary truth.'[2] The universals—the Ideas, or Augustine's *eternæ
rationes*—manifest themselves in different forms in a descending order of
reality. Wyclif follows Grosseteste in speaking of them under five modes.
First and supreme, is the Idea itself, the eternal exemplar of reason in God
Himself; second, the universals possessed by the created pure intelli-
gences (of angels) and celestial bodies; third, those universals that inhere
in general forms, and these will correspond with Aristotle's *genera* and
species; the fourth, are those universal substances which may be apprehended in individuals through their accidents; the fifth way of treating
universals would be by regarding accidents as signs; but these would be
no true universals at all, for they lack the reality of being.[3] Thus the

[1] Quoted by J. A. Robson, *Wyclif and the Oxford Schools: the relation of the
'Summa de ente' to the scholastic debates at Oxford in the later fourteenth century*,
Cambridge 1961, p. 142 from S. L. Fortes' notice of Worcester Cathedral
Library MS F. 65, fol. 33r.
[2] Johannis Wyclif, *Trialogus*, ed G. Lechler, Oxford 1869, p. 61.
[3] See S. H. Thomson, 'The philosophical basis of Wyclif's theology', *Jour-*

Ockhamists and all the *secta signorum* are summarily disposed of.

Everything that is or that happens is thought by God, and His thinking is outside time. Since God is omniscient, and His thinking is constrained only by His will, all His thoughts entail reality or the possibility of reality. The real and the possible real will include all which has been, all that is, all which shall be. All these are real to God's mind. In as much as they are thought by God they have an existence and by virtue of the way in which God thinks and is (through His *potentia ordinata*), they cannot be unthought and thus cannot be annihilated. This objection to annihilation is the principle upon which Wyclif's opposition to the current explanation of transubstantiation was based. For since God's knowledge and His act are interdependent, all things are possible; and all things are decreed, and thus exist by necessity.

But although he is predestinarian Wyclif is not a strict determinist. Indeed he always asserted the freedom of man's will. He sought the solution of the dilemma by his treatment of future contingencies. So did they all, Boethius, Troilus; and Bradwardine, FitzRalph and scores of other fourteenth century doctors. Wyclif took particular issue with Fitz-Ralph who had argued, against a rigid predestinarianism, that though the past and the present are governed by the necessity involved in God's foreknowledge, the future is not ruled by necessity and remains uncertain.[1] According to Wyclif, God's knowing includes both certainty and contingency. God wills and thinks contingency. The very futurity which for men identifies contingency exists already in God's thought and will. Thus for Wyclif necessity which must be accounted absolute in one sense is contingent in another. Late medieval logicians it may be observed, were familiar with the notion of a three-valued logic. Wyclif admired many aspects of FitzRalph's thought, but considered FitzRalph had failed despite twenty years' work to solve the problem of contingency 'because he had ignored the ampliation of time.'[2]

---

nal of Religion 11, 1931, 98; J. A. Robson, *Wyclif and the Oxford Schools*, pp. 148–9; cp. Johannis Wyclif, *Tractatus de logica*, ed M. H. Dziewiki, II, 1896, pp. 32–3.

[1] See Gordon Leff, *Richard FitzRalph, commentator of the Sentences*, Manchester 1963, pp. 39–50.

[2] Johannis Wyclif, *De Ente: librorum duorum excerpta*, ed M. H. Dziewicki, 1909, p. 184.

Wyclif's phrase indicates that he counted FitzRalph's failure a failure in logic. 'Ampliation is the taking of a term for one or more things beyond what is actually the case . . .' and according to Albert of Saxony's eighth rule 'all verbs which, although not in the present, have it in their nature to be able to extend to a future, past or possible thing as to a present one, extend the terms to every time, present, past and future.'[1] It is with intellectual instruments of this sort that Wyclif sought to solve existential problems. But it has to be allowed that his ultra-realist metaphysics gave a peculiar force to his confidence in logic. Logic had for Wyclif that glorious power and promise that mathematics had for Newton. It could enable him to think through God's thoughts again.

At Oxford in his early days his confidence was high and infectious. *De Logica*, one of Wyclif's earliest works on a large scale, starts quite simply with a definition of terms, brief accounts of propositions and of arguments, and shows how arguments build up into *scientia*. But then the exposition leaps into advanced logic, the product of centuries of intense and inbred study at medieval universities. Much too much is taken as understood. Established subtleties are submitted afresh to a highly developed but often less than fully explicit technique of analysis.

Although the exposition draws upon all the seven arts, and treats most of the scientific issues of his time, it is plain from the *Proemium* that Wyclif intends to present formal logic as the instrument whereby an understanding of God and of man's dependence upon God can be built up. The revelation of truth by God to man and the method whereby man can most intelligently penetrate this disclosure can be brought together in a close analysis of the words of Scripture. 'I am moved by certain friends of the law of God to compile a tract which shall explain the logic of sacred scripture. For I have noticed that many men who go on to study logic intend in this way to get a better understanding of the commandments of God, yet by reason of the insipid character in the admixture of secular terminology which is used in proving any proposition, they abandon logic on account of its emptiness and uselessness. I intend to whet the minds of the faithful by setting out the methods of proof of propositions which should be drawn from Holy Scripture.' Wyclif goes

---

[1] I. M. Bocheński, *A History of Formal Logic*, trans. Ivo Thomas, Notre Dame 1961, pp. 173–5.

on to summarize the tract in the terms of his profession as a teaching logician:

'And first since the whole variety of method of proof of propositions has its origin in terms, I propose to explain the properties and concepts of the different terms involves; then I shall look at the problem of universals and the predicaments; and then consider the *summulæ*, suppositions, consequences and obligatories; and finally treat the nature of knowledge itself.'[1] All the ingredients of advanced post-Ockhamist logic are here.

Wyclif did not forget his promise in the *Proemium*. He had started with God, come to learn and exult in logic, and thereby had discovered the dominating importance of the Bible. Throughout *De Logica* he is pursuing scriptural truth. Words are the special, supreme commodity—for logic, naturally enough, but also for theology. The concepts that words carried were all real, individually permanent and timeless. So Wyclif is able to turn Ockham upside down. According to Ockham, human knowledge springs from an intuition of an immediate sense perception, from which by a secondary intuition an intellectual understanding is abstracted. With an origin in fallible intuitions, human knowledge is frail, very limited, working at a remove from reality and scarcely able to rise above probabilities. But for Wyclif knowledge proceeds down the ladder of the modes of the universals. Even human knowledge is authenticated by God. The human mind using words replicates in its own fashion God's own process of thought as manifested in the exemplary Idea. Our human difficulties with universals are closely linked with the mysteries of the Trinity. A proper understanding of the individuation and interdependence of the persons of the Trinity would explain also the mode of existence of all created things.

Thus the Son as Logos is the essence of Wyclif's Christology and a key to his theology. According to his realist and intellectualist teaching, Christ has a double aspect. He is the Mediator of a sacred verbalization. The Logos works as the self-consciousness of God, as the divine intellectual reality in which created things are ideally pre-formed. Towards man, Christ is the humanly intelligible verbalization—the Word, the medium and the message. Christ and the Gospel are not to be separated. The whole Scripture authenticated by Christ is the eternal Word in material form; it came down from heaven. The Bible is unassailably true, for it is an actual form of the Logos; and logic is the perfectible instru-

[1] *De logica*, I, 1893, p. 1.

ment of intellectual truth and can be used on Scripture in order to know God.

Many of Wyclif's characteristic phrases have a startling precision once his rigour as an ultra-realist logician is recognized. 'God and his word is all one and they may not be separated.' 'The whole law of Christ is one perfect word proceeding from the mouth of God.' 'Not to know Scripture is not to know Christ, since Christ is the Scripture we ought to know.'[1] For the *doctor evangelicus*, the Bible ensymbolizes and materializes God in Trinity. Through the action of the Holy Ghost its words assail men's consciences directly: 'so faithful people, those meek and humble of heart, of whatever station, cleric or lay, men or women, applying themselves to the logic and eloquence of Scripture, will find there the strength to do well.'[2]

The Bible is to be taken whole, for it is one perfect word. Each part has to be understood as integral. But a discipline is required for understanding. 'The Christian ought to speak according to the authority of the Scripture the words of Scripture according to the form which Scripture itself explains. It follows then that he ought to follow the logic of Scripture, for Scripture thus analysed contains more fundamental, useful, convergent and demonstrable truth than any other science.'[3] Wyclif protests constantly against the improper and unprofitable study of the Bible by the *moderni* who destroy its importance. They read it simply as a collection of easy sayings and ignore its demonstrative rigour. They give it an irrelevant and externalizing gloss which does not weigh the particularity of its actual wording. They assume it is written carelessly without strict regard to case and tense. They do not regard it as an unbroken and complex statement about salvation.[4]

What Wyclif has learned of logic determines what he expects the inerrant Scriptures to offer. The expectations are not narrow. 'Since logic is the medium between grammar and metaphysics, it ought to share in the conditions of both, in the first place by concerning itself with things as the means towards metaphysical understanding, and secondarily by con-

[1] See Paul de Vooght, *Les sources de la doctrine chrétienne d'après les théologiens du XIVᵉ siècle et du début du XVᵉ*, Bruges 1954, chap. VIII, pp. 168–200.

[2] Johannis Wyclif, *De veritate Sacre Scripture*, ed R. Buddenseig, I, 1905, p. 117.

[3] *Ibid.*, pp. 51–2.

[4] J. A. Robson, *Wyclif and the Oxford Schools*, p. 164.

cerning itself with signs as the fulfilment of grammar'.[1] We should say it is as much a comprehensive biblical rhetoric as an extended logic he is after. He does not restrict his desired discipline to formal syllogistics. He acknowledges propositional variety, modal complexity, the whole tissue of hypotheses, subordinations and consequences in utterance. He sought an improved and universal logical instrument to deal with it.

Wyclif does not talk much about poetry. It would be easy to decide that he despised it. But vaguely perhaps, it was perceived both by Wyclif and his opponents that he was making demands upon the analysis of discourse beyond those which traditional scholastic logic could supply. This issue which has never been sufficiently emphasized, emerges in Wyclif's early debates at Oxford with the East Anglian Carmelite Friar John Kenningham. Kenningham's basic charge is that Wyclif is always trying to push interpretation of Scripture beyond what can be fairly proved *de virtute sermonis*, that is, proved by establishing the truth of propositions by the proper use of logical method.

Truth is the conformation of things and signs, Kenningham tritely argues, and quotes a familiar text from Isidore. Poets may indeed confuse and obscure the proper relationship between thing and sign when they attempt to please the ear or wrap the naked truth in difficult figures and so make something else out of it. Thereby they can readily lead their audience into all sorts of error. Kenningham charges Wyclif with repeated recourse to such practices. If Wyclif is not prepared to accept words according to their proper use—*de virtute sermonis*, then he is using them simply *de vi vocis*—in the fashion of a mere grammarian, relying solely on accidence, figure and elocution. Writers of old and poets may be excused sometimes for having used these methods; but the method is dangerous in a search for truth and should not be pushed far.[2]

But Wyclif is not to be impaled on this fork: either syllogistic logic, or school grammar. 'Doctor Kenningham argues that I say that every part of Scripture is true. I grant that; but I differ in my use of terms. He certainly talks *de vi vocis*: but I, in the very language of scripture, say that each part of Scripture is true *de vi sermonis*!—in its whole force of utterance.' The Scripture, Wyclif explains, is not an aggregation of propositions true *de virtute sermonis*, nor a string of Latin constructions

[1] *Ibid.*, p. 149, note 2.

[2] *Fasciculi Zizaniorum Magistri Johannis Wyclif*, ed W. W. Shirley, Rolls Series 1858, pp. 41–2.

effective *de vi vocis*: all the texts of scripture are but part of one whole catholic utterance (*oratio*). It is the truth of the whole utterance that gives truth to the parts.[1] Wyclif reaffirms, in a milieu of high pedantry, Augustine's view of Scripture.

The consequence of Wyclif's teaching, and certainly the most important consequence for literary history, were the translations of the Bible —whatever may have been Wyclif's own part in the work. Once these translations were produced—it is now agreed that they had some currency in the fifteenth century despite prohibition—the content and style of English religious life would be profoundly transformed; and moreover, the imaginable scope of writing in English almost endlessly enlarged. It was a slow business; but perhaps a successful translation of the Bible in a developed culture is always the collaborative work of many generations.

The ecclesiastical debate to which Wyclif contributed powerfully on the fundamental authorization of faith, whether by Scripture or Tradition, had continued throughout the Christian centuries, and had been opened again in the fourteenth, before Wyclif taught at Oxford. His role as an innovator need not be exaggerated: in many aspects of his thought he was a conscious traditionalist. The debate on Scripture was never a simple issue with clearly defined opposing principles. It acquired a peculiar importance in Wyclif's time because of the cultural situation in late fourteenth century England.

In presenting his case for the primacy of Scripture as interpreted by the early Fathers, Wyclif apparently relies upon a pre-condition of sufficient literacy among his contemporaries and upon the general availability of the written text of the Bible. These are rather astonishing assumptions, surely more of a hope than a reality, but Wyclif takes them for granted. He is not satisfied with or diverted by substitutes, by the associative content of religious symbols, with drawings on church walls and picturesque rituals: he deals with the actual words of Scripture. They hold the truth, they operate directly, God is in them. He assumes that they are there for the reading.

The immense response suggests that Wyclif was right. Implicit in his treatment of Scripture is an anticipation, unclear and confused, of the need for a new public and sacred rhetoric, such as the northern Reformers of the sixteenth century established, when Bishop Jewel could

[1] *Ibid.*, pp. 456–7.

claim that Scripture was indeed poetry, a comprehensive and truth-making form of discourse beyond the control of logic.

Chaucer would probably have been surprised at this development. Nevertheless he would have acknowledged that much of his own composition, in theme, presentation, vocabulary and association of meaning was an imitation, even a respectful parody, of religious discourse. It was an aspect of his immense verbal facility and resourcefulness, part of his equipment as a commentator on moral and intellectual events, as a born and highly trained storyteller, not a mythmaker. What Chaucer lacked was the power or opportunity for fundamental invention. If this lack is what Arnold was thinking of when he judged Chaucer deficient of high seriousness, then Arnold was surely right. The lack in Chaucer may also explain the shallowness of the fifteenth-century Chaucerians. The practical political and religious writing in the vernacular during the fifteenth century has much more vigour and variety in conception.

Few poets have disdained the mantle of prophet and legislator so consistently as Chaucer. Few sequestered scholars become so outrageously didactic and polemical as Wyclif in his later years. It is difficult to imagine that these two men, both for a time dependants on John of Gaunt, could ever have had much to say to one another, if they ever met. Yet history draws them together, and in that light they appear as representative of more than themselves, and together curiously complementary.

11: Chaucer and the Visual Arts

V. A. KOLVE

WITHIN ENGLISH MEDIEVAL STUDIES, the sophisticated use of material drawn from the visual arts as evidence admissible in literary analysis dates back only some ten years, to the publication of Professor Robertson's *A Preface to Chaucer*. Important work from several hands has followed, but the inquiry is still young.[1] We are only beginning to understand the issues involved in this double interest in pictures and text, only beginning the hard tasks of scholarship, methodological refinement, and critical response necessary if we would restore what seems once to have been a viable and vital marriage between the two. If the title assigned me here—'Chaucer and the Visual Arts'—points to any relationship more complex than the simultaneous flourishing of several distinct arts within the same historical period, the exact nature of that relationship is yet far from clear. In this essay, I wish to inquire anew into the grounds on which we may justify the use of such evidence, and into the presumptive rules by which we may best proceed in its use.

The road to a truer view of the relationship cannot lie, I think, in a further exploration of inter-art comparisons. As Jean Laude has recently reminded us: 'Absolutely everything distinguishes a literary text from a painting or a drawing: its conception, its method of production, its modes of appreciation, its identity as an object irreducible to any other

---

[1] D. W. Robertson, Jr., *A Preface to Chaucer: Studies in Medieval Perspectives*, Princeton 1963. Charles Muscatine, *Chaucer and the French Tradition*, Berkeley, California 1957, pp. 167–69, had earlier offered some brief generalizations about Gothic form. See also Rosemund Tuve, *Allegorical Imagery: Some Medieval Books and Their Posterity*, Princeton 1966; Robert M. Jordan, *Chaucer and the Shape of Creation*, Cambridge, Mass.: 1967; and Elizabeth Salter, 'Medieval Poetry and the Visual Arts,' *Essays and Studies*, 22, 1969, 16–32.

object, and its autonomous functioning.'[1] That declaration of separatism among the arts could be equally well extended: as with poetry to pictures, so with poetry to sculpture, architecture, music, or any of them to each other. The history of the idea *ut pictura poesis*—'as with painting, so with poetry'—has not been, philosophically speaking, a happy one. Though one art may *aspire* to the condition of another, as practised at certain times and by certain artists, and in the event may even prove to be a source of creative energy and stylistic innovation, nevertheless in the fields of aesthetics and historical criticism, inter-art comparisons have led chiefly to random analogies, dubious generalizations, impressionistic blur. Words are not pigments, extension in time is not the same as extension in space, verbal and visual organization are not interchangeable.[2] The 'sister arts' of poetry and painting—much less architecture or music —are not, and cannot ever be, the same.

This essay is not offered as a further contribution to the history of *ut pictura poesis*, nor does it seek further to dismember that idea into its component confusions and improbabilities. I think we will do better to choose a very different subject: the nature of Chaucer's visual imagination, in so far as that can be deduced from his writings, and the ways in which he manipulates the visual imaginations of his audience in the larger enterprise of his art. The inquiry I propose is into what Chaucer forces his audience 'to see,' in what ways, and to what ends.

Because we can approach such matters only in terms of the visual images Chaucer forces upon *our* minds as we attend to his art, our first

[1] Jean Laude, 'On the Analysis of Poems and Paintings,' *New Literary History*, 3, 1972, 471. This issue, devoted to the relationship between 'Literary and Art History,' contains several essays relevant here, especially those by Svetlana and Paul Alpers, and by Alastair Fowler. The Salter essay mentioned above offers necessary criticism of too easy comparisons, as does a bracing book by F. P. Pickering, *Literature and Art in the Middle Ages*, Coral Gables, Miami 1970. For historical backgrounds, see Rensselaer W. Lee, *Ut Pictura Poesis: The Humanistic Theory of Painting*, repr. New York, 1967, first published in *Art Bulletin*, 22, 1940; and Jean Hagstrum, *The Sister Arts*, Chicago 1958.

[2] I here borrow a phrase from Ralph Cohen, *The Art of Discrimination: Thomson's 'The Seasons' and the Language of Criticism*, Berkeley, California 1964, p. 247. Chapters III and IV of this book offer a close look at the fortunes of *ut pictura poesis* among writers, critics, and painters in the eighteenth century.

(and continuing) task must be to train our eyes on surviving artifacts of a kind familiar to his first audiences. We must move towards some accuracy of medieval imagining—'imaging'—on all levels, even that of incidental, characterizing detail. When Chaucer describes Nicholas's bedroom, we would do well to have some reasonably accurate sense of what a bourgeois house in fourteenth-century Oxford might have looked like, its architecture and furnishings, its style and size. No one in English before him had ever admitted so generously into poetry the sights, sounds, and smells of daily life—the rich variety of its textures and appurtenances—and it is important that we be able to join his first audience in responding to that technical achievement, to that comprehensiveness and sympathy of vision. Many recent picture-books have been helpful in this regard. Joan Evans' *The Flowering of the Middle Ages*, elegantly produced and richly illustrated, may stand as the finest general example, while more specifically, R. S. Loomis' *A Mirror of Chaucer's World*, Maurice Hussey's *Chaucer's World: A Pictorial Companion*, and Ian Serailler's *Chaucer and His World*, have sought to illustrate the persons Chaucer knew, the places he visited, the things he refers to.[1] If we would know the shape of a fourteenth-century dandy's shoe, the look of an astrolabe or tally-stick or pilgrim's badge or medieval walled town, we need look no further.

But more important by far is our need for some reasonable familiarity with the symbolic language current in both the visual arts and the literature of Chaucer's time, for that is made vehicle to meanings deeper than the surface of the story. Like any poet, Chaucer used words to stand for things, but in a fashion characteristically medieval he used some of those things to stand for yet other things—in a language of sign potent to embody within the delightful lies of fiction a vision of truth. Though every art remains itself alone, they often speak about common subjects through a language of things, and iconography is the study of that common tongue. If we would prepare to be fit audience to this central

---

[1] Joan Evans, ed, *The Flowering of the Middle Ages*, New York 1966; Roger Sherman Loomis, *A Mirror of Chaucer's World*, Princeton 1965; Maurice Hussey, *Chaucer's World: A Pictorial Companion*, Cambridge 1967; Ian Seraillier, *Chaucer and His World*, 1967. See also F. E. Halliday, *Chaucer and His World*, 1968; and Brian Spencer, *Chaucer's London* [catalogue of an exhibition at the London Museum, 1972], D. S. Brewer *Chaucer in his Time*, 1964 and 1973.

aspect of Chaucer's art, there is no school but studying the manuscript illuminations, wall paintings, carvings and stained glass of the period, along with the literary texts that shaped (and themselves continued to transmit) those traditions of symbolic meaning. We have more to learn from the visual arts of Chaucer's time than the shape of old St. Paul's window as Chaucer imagines it fashionably cut into the leather of Absolom's shoe.

Both sorts of training are important if, as twentieth-century persons, we would nevertheless seek Chaucer in his own time. We must educate our eyes to the period at large, to the ordinary fourteenth-century world the literature assumes and reflects; and we must learn the symbolic language used in that period, sometimes in a fashion formally explicit, sometimes in a manner covered and complex. Though material for both sorts of training survives in abundance, students of Chaucer labour under one notable disadvantage: no surviving manuscript of his work illustrates the narrative action of any of his poems. Indeed, were it not for a splendid chest front, carved with scenes from 'The Pardoner's Tale' in about the year 1400, and only just recently come to public notice,[1] we should lack any such contemporary 'imagining' at all. I need hardly stress how valuable more evidence of this kind would be, not because any single such image would be definitive in its authority (the mental images formed by readers/auditors agree only in essentials—*a* white crow in *a* gilded cage, not absolutely identical crows in absolutely identical cages) but because such images offer evidence free from anachronism, and because they can tell us, through their choice of subject, what 'places' in a literary text exerted the greatest pressure upon one member of that tale's first audience to imagine, to image, in his mind. Such evidence can tell us what, for one medieval artist at least, constituted the 'governing images' of a given medieval poem.

But 'The Pardoner's Tale' carved in three scenes on that chest front is an exception. We have otherwise only images of pilgrims, responsive to the word-portraits of the *General Prologue* rather than to the tales they tell. Those in the Ellesmere MS are deservedly famous, while the six that survive (from a set once complete) in Cambridge, Univ. Lib. MS G.iv.27, have not been reproduced since their publication by the Chaucer Society in the nineteenth century. That obscurity is unde-

[1] Spencer, *Chaucer's London*, fig. 34 (from a private collection); reproduced in D. S. Brewer *Chaucer*, 3rd (Supplemented) edition, 1973.

served, for although the Ellesmere portraits are skilful, and were made perhaps within a decade of Chaucer's death, these others (from the middle of the fifteenth century) exhibit at least as imaginative a response to Chaucer's text, and have a peculiar energy all their own. The same Cambridge MS contains three pictures of personified Vices and Virtues from 'The Parson's Tale'. (Again, there once were seven, but vandals have cut out the rest.) Several other MSS offer portraits of Chaucer as author; one has a small picture perhaps meant to represent Melibeus; and there is a fine mythographic depiction of Mars, Venus and Jove, in a MS containing the *Complaint of Mars* and *Complaint of Venus*. But the census remains brief, a meagre body of visual material that can be directly connected to our author's works, and none of it, except for the chest front, narrative in its imagining. There might have been more, even of this second kind, had time or despoilers or the fortunes of patrons allowed. The magnificent Corpus MS of the *Troilus*, for example, whose frontispiece shows Chaucer reciting his works to a noble audience in the garden of a palace, has spaces ruled in the text for some ninety narrative images. But they were never made.[1]

This paucity of surviving 'Chaucerian image,' though a cause for regret, is hardly a cause for surprise. The first half of the fourteenth century had seen a great flourishing of English manuscript art, especially in the area of East Anglia.[2] But the second half of the century, during which

[1] For the Ellesmere portraits, see Loomis, *Mirror*, figs. 1, 80–101; he also reproduces the Vices and Virtues pictures from the Cambridge MS., figs. 177–79, and that of Chaucer reciting to the court (from Cambridge, CCC MS. 61), fig. 68. The picture of Mars, Venus and Jove is contained in Oxford, Bodley MS. Fairfax 16. For the Cambridge MS pilgrim portraits see *Autotypes of Chaucer MSS.*, Chaucer Society Facsimiles, 1876. Margaret Rickert's survey of the illuminated Chaucer MSS, published in J. M. Manly and Edith Rickert, *The Text of the Canterbury Tales*, Chicago 1940, I, 561–605, remains indispensable. Brewer, *Chaucer* 1973, reproduces some of the figures from Cambridge University Library Gg.IV.27, and illustrations from a French fifteenth-century MS of the story of Troilus in Boccaccio's *Filostrato*.

[2] See Eric G. Millar, *English Illuminated Manuscripts of the XIVth and XVth Centuries*, Paris and Brussels 1928. Canon F. Harrison, ed, *English Manuscripts of the Fourteenth Century (c. 1250 to 1400)*, 1937, remains a useful introduction; most recently, *Medieval Art in East Anglia 1300–1520*, ed. P. Lasko and N. J. Morgan, Jarroid, Norwich, 1973, (illustrated and annotated exhibition catalogue).

Chaucer wrote his poems, seems to have been unable to sustain that level of production and artistic innovation. Recurring plague (beginning with the Black Death of 1348–1349, and the severe economic depression that followed in its wake), the endless war with France, the political uncertainties of Richard II's reign, the Wycliffite challenge to church authority, all these suggest some causes for the decline. In any case, illuminated books had *always* been very expensive, and thus chiefly commissioned for religious or ceremonial use. So popular a poem as *Piers Plowman* survives today in more than fifty MSS, but only one of these is illustrated, in drawings without artistic pretension of any kind. MSS of Gower's *Confessio Amantis* likewise yield little information concerning what its audiences 'saw' as they listened to its narratives: a standardized confession scene, or the figure seen in King Nebuchadnezzar's dream, normally suffice to decorate even a deluxe MS of the poem. The *Gawain* MS (Cotton Nero A.x.), to whose chance survival we owe our only knowledge of four of the supreme poems of the age, is remarkable in having twelve illustrations, but they are almost childlike in the crudity of their design and colouring, and in several details bear no relation to the texts they accompany.[1] Even those few earlier vernacular poems that had attained, already in the fourteenth century, a kind of 'classic' status and had therefore evolved fairly elaborate programmes of illustrations—most especially the *Divine Comedy*, the *Romance of the Rose*, and Deguilleville's *Pèlerinage de la Vie Humaine*—offer relatively little fresh evidence of how such texts were being read and imagined across the medieval decades: most often, the picture-cycle was simply copied from one manuscript to the next, with only changes in costume, setting, or painting style, to indicate updating. The 'new' response is as likely to be to the picture-cycle itself as to the text it illustrates. The hand of tradition lay heavy upon the productions of the *ateliers*: on almost every artistic level, sometimes including the highest, it was an age of the pattern-book and the copy recopied.

[1] For *Piers*, see Oxford, Bodley MS. Douce 104 (dated 1427); there is also a picture of the dreamer asleep in Oxford, Corpus Christi College MS 201. The illustrations to London, Brit. Mus. MS Cotton Nero A.x. may be seen in facsimile: Sir Israel Gollancz, ed, *Pearl, Cleanness, Patience, and Sir Gawain*, EETS o.s. 162, 1923. Two copies of the *Confessio Amantis* are more generously illustrated than most: Oxford, New College MS 266, and New York, Morgan Library MS M.126. The latter has 70 illustrations to the text which, though late (second half of the fifteenth century) and though undistinguished, are nevertheless interesting in substantive ways.

And so the lack of numerous and well-wrought contemporary 'images' for Chaucer's narratives is by no means anomalous, nor does the lack of such material significantly separate us from his earliest audiences. Few among those who knew how to read would have had access to manuscripts richer than those that have survived, and most of his audience would have had access to no manuscripts at all. Yet these are demonstrably texts that ask their audiences to see, to image, to imagine. The search for a disciplined 'imaging' of Chaucer's narratives, though difficult, is, I think, inescapable.

Our best recourse will be to two special categories of image. We must go to illustrated MSS, where they can be found, to the sources and analogues of his narrative poems, even though these images (by definition) cannot be responsive to those changes in plot, character, or emphasis which we judge to be Chaucer's own. And we must make judicious use of that vast store of conventional imagery, mostly religious, some of it secular, that served to illustrate other ideas current at the time, and known to his first audiences from other texts and other places. How this second sort of image enters his art, how it functions, and what needs it serves—these are the questions that seem to me to hold best promise of illuminating the relationship of literature and the visual arts in the late medieval period, and in the practice of this specific poet. The pictures we shall talk of are to be found 'in the head' rather than on the manuscript page. They are seen with the mind's inner eye—what was called in Latin, the *oculis imaginationis*, or *acies animi*, and in Chaucer's plural, 'thilke eyen of [the] mynde.'[1] *Mental images* formed in response to *verbal stimuli*, they nevertheless draw upon a rich repertory of images which *do* occur in manuscript illuminations and in other media as well, and within contexts often not fictional in kind.

The Middle Ages believed that the memory receives and stores these images just as it does 'real' images known from the visual arts—as being subject to the same kind of memorial simplification and deterioration, and accessible to the same kind of memorial recall. Both can be summoned to mind as mental pictures, without the mediation of words or of material substance; and they can be rapidly sorted, their essential likeness to other images recognized—other crows in other cages, other birds in other cages—without reference to the several distinctive modes of

[1] For provenance of the Latin terms, see Frances A. Yates, *The Art of Memory*, 1966, *passim*; for Chaucer, see *The Man of Law's Tale* [II 552].

experience by which those diverse mental images were acquired. It is by virtue of this transformation alone that we may speak of 'Chaucer's iconography'—his writing by means of conventional pictures. The two kinds of image were understood to share a common mode and ontological status in the memory.

There are, of course, a number of ways in which the memory operates in relation to a literary text. We can all, with varying degrees of skill, retell a story we have read or heard, taking as our goal the recreation of that story in sequence, *as process*. That is an important kind of remembering, and it was particularly valued in an age when social pleasure (as on the Canterbury pilgrimage) often centred upon an amateur telling of tales. But no medieval author of any consequence sought to have his tale remembered in only that way. What we would call the act of critical interpretation—and what then would have been understood as the act of understanding, meditating upon, drawing wisdom from—does not seek a recreation of the original experience in its original form. Rather it attempts to construct a statement radically different in mode, yet as closely as possible equivalent, adequate to make sense of the story in all its detail. For art of the medieval period, this most often implied a movement from the particular to the general, a discovery of the 'fruyt' within the 'chaf,' a pondering of *precisely* what Hecuba is 'to me' or any other man. Any serious medieval artist sought to help his audience discover in his fiction —and hold in their memories—a residue of ideas and feelings more complex than the encapsulated truth of *fabliau* proverb, of Augustinian distinctions concerning cupidity and charity stated at their most general, or even an accurate summary of the action itself.

And it is in this regard that another kind of memory becomes of interest. For if, in respect to a medieval narrative poem, we put to ourselves the question 'What is remembered?', and limit our answer to what comes to mind immediately and intact, requiring no linear reconstruction of the narrative itself, the answer most often concerns something seen with the eye of the mind, something which the narrative caused us to image with particular force as we attended to the verbal process, and which is instantly accessible as image to the memory. Francis Beaumont, in Speght's edition, wrote of Chaucer: 'one gifte hee hath aboue other Authours, and that is, by the excellencie of his descriptions to possesse his Readers with a stronger imagination of seeing that done before their eyes, which they reade, than any other that euer writ in any tongue.' It is a testimony many have echoed, before and since. The author of a courtesy book printed by William Caxton praised Chaucer for that same power: 'His langage was so fayr and pertynente / It semeth vnto mannys heerynge / Not only the worde / but verely the thynge.'[1] *Verba et res*: word *becoming* thing, in an act of visual imagining. There is no temple other than the mind in which the mystery can occur. In the Middle Ages, poetic narrative—which even a printed book, we might note, assumes to be addressed to 'man's hearing'—sought a response from the inner eye: it became at some mysterious juncture in its progress, 'visual.'

It must follow then that some inquiry into medieval conceptions of the imagination—the faculty that can form an 'image' independent of immediate visual stimulus—and into medieval ideas concerning the nature and status of such images, may provide some useful insight into Chaucer's art. My ultimate concern in this essay will be to discuss how such images relate to narrative context in Chaucer's mature practice—I shall attempt to place his particular procedures and preferences within a broad spectrum of medieval possibilities. But first I want to bring together evidence from several very different areas of medieval thought, all of which seems to me to converge upon one central fact: the dignity and importance of the mental image for any discussion of literary effect, and through it, probable artistic intention, in poems of the late medieval period.

We must begin with medieval faculty psychology, for if we would understand how 'the vertu ymaginatif schapith & ymagineth' we must know how that faculty (i.e., power, 'vertu') relates to the other distinctive capacities of man. Boethius' *Consolation of Philosophy* furnished one authoritative answer, the more important to us because Chaucer translated that work into prose, and used its ideas pervasively in his poetic fictions. In Boethius' terms, creatures know a thing, not in *its* own nature, but according to their own distinctive capacity for knowing. If the thing to be known is, for example, another man:

. . . the wit comprehendith withoute-forth the figure of the body of

---

[1] For Beaumont, see Caroline F. E. Spurgeon, *Five Hundred Years of Chaucer Criticism & Allusion, 1357–1900*, Cambridge 1925, I, 146. The second quotation is from Frederick J. Furnivall, ed, *Caxton's Book of Curtesye*, EETS e.s. 3, 1868, 35 (ll. 341–43).

the man that is establisscid in the matere subgett; but the ymaginacioun comprehendith oonly the figure withoute the matere; resoun
surmountith ymaginacioun and comprehendith by an universel
lokynge the comune spece that is in the singuler peces; but the eighe
of the intelligence is heyere, for it surmountith the envyrounynge of
the universite, and loketh over that bi pure subtilte of thought thilke
same symple forme of man that is perdurablely in the devyne
thought . . . the heyeste strengthe to comprehenden thinges enbra-
seth and contienith the lowere strengthe; but the lowere strengthe
ne ariseth nat in no manere to the heyere strengthe.

[V. pr. 4]

A paraphrase may be found useful. At this point in the *Consolation*, Boethius is attempting to explain how man's free will and God's foreknowledge—since either seems to contradict the other—can coexist. The
answer, he tells us, lies in a distinction between ways of knowing. Men
can know by 'wit' (the outer senses), which tell us about phenomena in
their material form—we can see a loaf of bread, touch it, taste it, smell it,
hear it fall to the floor. By virtue of our 'ymaginacioun,' a higher way of
knowing, we can call to mind the image of a loaf of bread we have eaten
in the past, or, by combining diverse such memories, invent an image of
a loaf we have never known—a loaf, let us say, of gold, or a loaf larger
than a castle. This kind of knowing retains the form or figure of a thing,
but divorces it from matter, and in that important sense is a higher faculty than the five 'wits'. It comes nearer to being free of the phenomenal
world. The faculty of 'resoun' is higher still, for it is capable of relating
the image, divorced from matter, to all other associated images, conceiving the universal class of which it is a species. The workings of reason are
ultimately free not only of matter, but of images as well, and its power is
unique to man among earthly creatures. The fourth way of knowing is
possessed only by divine Providence, whose unique faculty—here called
'intelligence'—knows a thing not only as it exists within the world of
matter, and as image, and as universal class but as that thing exists in per-
petuity within the divine thought—the 'symple forme' (close kin to
those of Plato) that exists in advance of, and will endure beyond, the material creation and the categories that man's reason is able to discover
there. In this hierarchy of faculties, each power comprehends all that
which is proper to the power below it, but the lower has no access to the
higher; 'a man is a thing ymaginable and sensible' and 'resonable,' and so

he shares with animals that do not move (like oysters and mussels) a knowledge derived from the senses; with animals capable of movement ('remuable bestis') he shares the power to transform sense experience into mental images, and to remember by their means, for all such creatures, on seeing a thing, are inclined to seek or shun it. But he is separated from these other orders by his rationality: 'resoun is al oonly to the lynage of mankynde, ryght as intelligence is oonly the devyne nature.' [V. pr. 5]

So of these four faculties—*sensus, imaginatio, ratio, intelligentia*—the first three are proper to man's nature—and *memoria* [memory] receives their product in sum. The medieval understanding of that faculty must concern us too, and again some reference to medieval faculty psychology will be helpful. It explained the power to recall in terms of a model of the human brain that varied to some degree across the centuries, and from writer to writer. But even the variant models have a good deal in common, and that described by Bartholomaeus Anglicus, in his great encyclopaedia, *De proprietatibus rerum*, which John Trevisa translated into English near the end of the fourteenth century, is not only important in its own right, but for our purposes sufficiently representative:

> The inner witte [*sensus communis*] is departid a thre by thre regiouns of the brayn, ffor in the brayn beth thre smale celles: the formest hatte ymaginativa, therein thingis that the uttir witte apprehendith withoute beth Iordeyned and Iput togedres withinne . . . the middil chambre hatte logic, therein the vertu estimative is maister; the thridde. . . . is memorativa, the vertu of mynde.[1]

When the inner senses are so described, 'ymaginativa' includes both the power to recall the forms of sense experience as images, separate from their material identities, *and* the power to recombine those forms into forms of things never experienced. In Augustine's famous example, he can picture in his mind Carthage, which he knew, but also, in some approximate way, Alexandria, which he had never seen. This creative

---

[1] The Trevisa translation is at present being edited from MSS for the first time, though it has been available for centuries in the black letter edition of Wynkyn de Worde, published in 1495, STC 1536. I quote from the M.E.D. article on 'imaginatif,' 1(a), pp. 82–3, which prints from London, Brit. Mus. MS Add. 27944. For medieval diagrams of the brain's structure, see Edwin Clarke and Kenneth Dewhurst, *An Illustrated History of Brain Function*, 1972.

aspect of the imagination was called Phantasy by some thinkers, notably Avicenna and Albertus Magnus, and in some models was given a special portion of the brain to itself alone. The second cell of the brain, in the Bartholomaeus version quoted above, houses 'logica,' the Estimative Power, which in other models is sometimes called the Particular Reason, sometimes the Cognitative Power, sometimes Opinion. Its functions variously include *judging* the forms (testing their reliability and correctness as images) and discovering their 'intentions'—a kind of preliminary judgement, experientially conditioned, concerning their tendency to help or harm. This cell presents its findings to the third, 'memorativa,' which stores the images, forms, and intentions, and furnishes them upon demand to the Intellectual Soul—a still higher aspect of man's nature, also understood in terms of a tri-partite model, comprising Reason, Intellect or Understanding, and the Will.[1]

Technical and difficult though even so abbreviated a discussion must be, what matters to our larger investigation is relatively simple: the importance of *mental images* to human understanding, and the importance of memory, which makes them accessible to reason and thence to the will. The persistence of triads must be noted—they honour the Trinity, and constitute the discovery, by medieval man, of the "image" of the Creator in himself. Chaucer's Saint Cecilia, in 'The Second Nun's Tale', offers a variant version, but her shaping purpose is to instruct Tiberius in the mystery of the Trinity, so difficult to comprehend for a mind trained to honour the Roman pantheon. She takes recourse to an example:

> *Right as a man hath sapiences three,*
> *Memorie, engyn, and intellect also,*
> *So in a beynge of divinitee,*
> *Thre persones may ther right wel bee.*
>
> (VII, 338–41)

Memory, imagination, and reason: three faculties of the mind named out of their usual order, but in testimony to their importance, and in assertion of their inseparability. By 'images' most medieval writings on psychology meant what could be recollected of *any* sense experience—our ability to remember sound, smell, touch, as well as sight

---

[1] See Murray Wright Bundy, *The Theory of Imagination in Classical and Mediaeval Thought*, Univ. of Illinois Studies in Lang. and Lit., No. 12, Urbana 1927.

—but the visual seems to have been the most important, the paradigmatic instance that shaped their theories, and which they held foremost in mind. The reasons for this we need also to examine.

These range from the preferences of the classical rhetoricians for metaphors drawn from the sense of sight—it is (says Cicero) the keenest, and such metaphors seem to place before the mind's eye what we hear described—to St. Paul's great cry of faith, 'For now we see through a glass, darkly, but then face to face.'[1] The swiftness of sight, its range and immediacy, all contribute to the value we place upon ordinary vision of ordinary things, but it readily becomes a metaphor for higher kinds of knowing as well. The Christian emphasis on *vision*, though rooted in those moments in Old Testament history in which God shows himself to man, directly or in figure, is heavily influenced as well by Neoplatonic ideas—especially in the conviction that sight is more spiritual than the other senses. St. Thomas Aquinas, for example, praised sight above the rest because it alone neither alters the thing perceived nor is altered by it: its operation is uncompromised by matter.[2] But with respect to the present argument, as to Neoplatonism proper, that fact is merely suggestive of a higher truth, which holds mental images to be superior to immediate visual images, and the constructive power of the imagination to be superior to the reproductive power, in their ability to transcend both sense experience and the images by which it enters the memory. Hugh of St. Victor, in a dialogue on Noah's ark, *De Vanitate Mundi*, has Reason instruct the Soul unequivocally:

> So when you hear yourself invited to 'see,' it is not the sight of this eye [of the flesh] that I would have you think about. You have another eye within, much clearer than that one, an eye that looks at the past, the present, and the future all at once, which sheds the light and keenness of its vision over all things, which penetrates things hidden and searches into complexities, needing no other light by which to see all this, but seeing by the light that it possesses of itself.[3]

[1] Cicero, *De Oratore*, III, 161, cited by E. H. Gombrich in a magisterial essay, '*Icones Symbolicae*,' included in his recent *Symbolic Images: Studies in the Art of the Renaissance*, 1972, p. 167. For St. Paul, see I Cor. 13:12.

[2] See the discussion by Étienne Gilson, *The Christian Philosophy of St. Thomas Aquinas*, trans. L. K. Shook, New York 1956, pp. 203–4.

[3] Hugh of St. Victor, *Selected Spiritual Writings*, trans. by a Religious of C.S.M.V., intro. by Aelred Squire, O.P., 1962, p. 158.

Hugh has in mind, clearly, the image-making and image-remembering faculties as well as the reason working upon the matter they present to it: but the essential material is visual, and he will furnish the reader of his treatises on the ark, a series of complex images to think upon and hold in mind, as preparation for a closer knowing of God. Although the *via negativa* of the mystics necessarily ends by declaring the awesome unlikeness of God to any image we can frame, that stage of the discipline concerns knowledge of the Godhead only. Hugh teaches the earlier stages of the way through meditative image, in common with many others. Witness Walter Hilton, Chaucer's great contemporary, who advises in *The Scale of Perfection*:

'A man schal nought comen to gostli delit *in contemplacion* of [Cristes] godhede but he come *in ymaginacion* bi bitternes and [bi] compassion . . . of His manhede.'[1] [italics mine].

Literary images, being mental images, share some part of this dignity: they reflect a reality not limited to the present and the material; they present the supra-sensual in the form of a figure to be contemplated with the inner eye. As Lady Grace-Dieu says to the pilgrim in *Le Pèlerinage de la Vie Humaine*, at the beginning of a long instruction that will proceed through many such images, 'I must put eyes in your ears.'[2] Indeed, late medieval art sometimes depicts the process of literary composition by showing an author at his desk writing about a subject (often a personified idea) whom he sees standing before him—as apparently real as himself, anything else in the room, or any boy keeping horses in the fields outside. Notable portraits of Guillaume de Machaut and of Boccaccio survive in this kind, the French poet being introduced by the God of Love to his children, *Douce Penser, Plaisance,* and *Esperance,* the Italian poet shown contemplating Lady Fortune (sometimes twelve-handed) who

---

[1] This work too lacks a scholarly modern edition. I cite the *MED* article on 'imaginacioun,' sense 1(d), p. 81, which prints from London, Brit. Mus. MS Harl. 6579.

[2] A poem by Guillaume de Deguilleville, some verses of which were translated by Chaucer. See the translation made by John Lydgate, *The Pilgrimage of the Life of Man*, ed Frederick J. Furnivall, EETS e.s. 77, 83, 1899, 1901, I, 164.

stands before him, or a throng of the historical great who fell from her favour in past time and now press to have their stories told.[1] Such portraits express the conviction that these authors 'invented' by conceiving visually their central subjects; and they testify to the potency of that literary art to make a reader (here an illustrator) see those subjects in turn. We may note a poet himself so construing the process of invention in the *Prison Amoreuse*, where Froissart (whom Chaucer surely knew) expresses his eagerness to communicate in verse to his patron, Wenceslas of Brabant, *'pluiseurs ymaginations'* [several images] he has recently conceived on the subject of love. Chaucer himself wrote a short *debat* between 'Le Pleintif' and 'Fortune' which is called in several of the early MSS *'Balades de Visage sanz Peinture'*—songs that paint portraits without using paints.[2]

But it is Book I of *The House of Fame* that offers the most interesting evidence concerning the way in which the verbal, the visual, and the memorial were linked in Chaucer's mind. More than 330 of its 508 lines are devoted to the story of Vergil's *Aeneid*, described as 'graven' on the walls of Venus' temple—a long section not remarkable for any particular poetic eloquence or power (the *Aeneid* does not readily reduce to 330 lines of verse) but for the ambiguity with which it registers the mode of the experience being described. The beginning is clear enough: the narrator finds the opening lines of the poem engraved upon a tablet of brass ('I wol now singen, yif I kan, / The armes, and also the man . . . ,'). But when the story proper begins, it is narrated in terms of *seeing* rather than reading: 'First sawgh I the destruction / Of Troye, thurgh the Grek Synon,' a change sufficiently disorienting so that when Chaucer returns to the verb 'graven'—'And aftir this was grave, allas!'—one no longer

---

[1] The Machaut portrait from Paris, Bibl. Natl. MS fr. 1584 (ca. 1370), is reproduced in Loomis, *Mirror*, fig. 9. A companion portrait from the same MS, in which Nature presents *Sens*, Music, and Rhetoric to the poet, is reproduced by P. M. Kean, *Chaucer and the Making of English Poetry*, 1972, I, pl. I. New York, Morgan Library MS M. 396, has similar illustrations, from the fifteenth century. For the Boccaccio portrait with Lady Fortune, see Kean, *op. cit.*, II, pl. II; or Pickering, *Literature and Art*, pl. 4a; or Werner Pleister, *Der Münchener Boccaccio* (Munich 1965, p. 106; or see New York, Morgan Library MS M. 343, fol. 35. For Boccaccio with the fallen lords and ladies, consult e.g., Pleister, *Der Münchener Boccaccio*, pp. 72, 144.

[1] Jean Froissart, *Poésies*, ed Aug. Scheler, I, Brussels 1870, p. 323 (l. 3441); see also p. 287. The Chaucer poem is titled 'Fortune' in Robinson's edition.

knows whether we are to understand 'engraved with letters' or 'engraved in pictures' We return to a series of 'I saugh' events, clearly intended to make us 'see' in our turn, and then move out into kinds of experience not accessible to sight alone as he *hears* the sorrow of Creusa's ghost: 'hyt was pitee for to here.' The narrator briefly returns to a 'saugh I,' then to a new medium altogether as he describes a fearful tempest 'peynted on the wal,' and then resumes the 'graven' designation until the point at which he identifies his own poetic act of 'making' with those temple decorations, by use of a verb that belongs to neither poets nor 'gravers' by first right: 'What shulde I speke more queynte, / Or peyne me *my wordes peynte* / To speke of love?' Rhetoric too has its *colours*, and they are used to create another event which, since it cannot be painted, must be understood as either 'heard,' read, or remembered—the long complaint spoken by Dido after she has been betrayed. The verb 'graven' then governs the narration of the story until the very end, when what the narrator has been seeing is defined unequivocally as pictorial rather than verbal in mode:

> *"A, Lord!" thoughte I, "that madest us,*
> *Yet sawgh I never such noblesse*
> *Of ymages, ne such richesse,*
> *As I saugh graven in this chirche;*
> *But not wot I whoo did hem wirche. . . ."*   (470–74)

The *Aeneid* redaction begins with words on brass, and ends with pictures, perhaps on brass, perhaps on glass, perhaps painted on the wall, and between those two points we have at best a shifting sense of what mode of artistic experience is being reported. Reading, seeing, hearing, and remembering, are rendered as interchangeable. This is not, I think, an instance of *ut pictura poesis*, that contest between poetry and painting to imitate the effects most easy and intrinsic to the other. If that were so, it would seek descriptive effects more ambitious (in fact its only major intensity comes in the speeches, 'heard' or read) and it would move far less swiftly through the story. Rather it seems to me to concern a process of imaginative response and intellectual recall—to concern the nature of narrative art in its capacity to preserve within men's memories the famous deeds of the past. In effect, we are shown a poet remembering a poem he has read *as a series of pictures*, by way of creating a new poem that describes those pictures as though they were real. The narrator's experience of the *Aeneid* in Book I of *The House of Fame* offers a medieval paradigm of how narrative poems are made, responded to, and remembered.

We have already examined the close relationship between the imagination and the memory postulated by medieval faculty psychology in its models of the human brain. The work of Francis Yates can point us in a further direction, away from the act of memory *per se* to the formal *arts of memory* complex, virtuoso, and based upon mental images, which the Middle Ages inherited from classical rhetoric, most especially the *Rhetorica ad Herennium*. That treatise was believed to be by Cicero, to be indeed his (lost) 'second rhetoric,' and it contains a treatise on memory entirely at one with his authentic advice elsewhere that orators who wish to train their memories—a faculty essential to effective public speaking—'must select places and form mental images of the things they wish to remember and store those images in the places, so that the order of the places will preserve the order of the things, and the images of the things will denote the things themselves. . . .'[1] Our present interest is probably not usefully directed towards the more extravagant refinements of these systems of *loci* and *imagines*, but rather in the importance for medieval art of the continued currency they gave to certain underlying Aristotelian assumptions: 'the soul never thinks without a mental picture,' for instance, or 'no one could ever learn or understand anything, if he had not the faculty of perception; even when he thinks speculatively, he must have some mental picture with which to think.'[2] If Chaucer had access to the full *Poetria Nova* of Geoffrey de Vinsauf—the matter is under dispute —he found there a substantial section on memory, and advice such as this: 'When I wish to recall things I have seen, or heard, or memorized before, or engaged in before, I ponder thus: I saw, I heard, I considered, I acted in such or such a way, either at that time or in that place: places, times, images, or other similar signposts are for me a sure path which leads me to the things themselves.'[3] Some such generalized understanding of the relation between memory and mental images or visual signs is all that we need postulate for Chaucer, not an interest in the arts of memory *per se*. He would have noticed, for instance, that Boccaccio's

[1] From *De Oratore*, quoted by Yates, *Art of Memory*, p. 2.

[2] From *De Anima*, also quoted by Yates, p. 32.

[3] Geoffrey of Vinsauf, *Poetria Nova*, trans. Margaret F. Nims, Toronto 1967, p. 89.

Teseida, the source of his 'Knight's Tale', devotes the last part of its eleventh book to a 'pictorial' recapitulation of all that has gone before, as prelude to the marriage between Palemone and Emilia which will be celebrated in the final (twelfth) book. Palemone orders a temple to be built on the spot of Arcita's funeral pyre, and wall-paintings within to depict the story of their friendship, imprisonment, love, combat and Arcita's death. Each stage of the story is narrated again in its essentials, but this time as the description of a picture: the images are being *impressed* upon the mind, in more than twenty stanzas of verse. Cato's ancient advice to the orator obtains for the reader/auditor as well: *rem tene, verba sequentur*. Hold fast to the thing [the image of the thing]; the words will follow.[1]

But the formal art of memory acquired a second house, so to speak, in the Middle Ages, reflecting other kinds of importance attributed to the memorial image in that culture. The *ars memoriae* continues to inhabit the handbooks of rhetoric and poetic, but it suddenly makes its appearance as well in treatises on ethics, written for the Christian who would save his soul. Cicero's *De inventione*—his genuine 'first rhetoric'—suggests the four cardinal virtues as subjects especially suitable to the orator, and names *memoria* as one of the three parts of Prudence. The great scholastic treatises that incorporate an art of memory, the *De bono* of Albertus Magnus, and the *Summa Theologica* of St. Thomas Aquinas, follow that lead, but with man's needs as an orator no longer chiefly in mind. They found the rules of the art in the *Ad Herenium*, but transmitted them in the light of the *De inventione*[2]—a learned parallel to the practical needs of a parish culture in which the vast majority of persons were illiterate, but whose religion declared each man's soul to be incomparably valuable, and saw in its eschatology the magnificent exaltation of the humble: the last shall be first, the mighty shall be put down from their seats. Images were made, and defended against the attacks of the iconoclasts across the medieval centuries, as the books of the common people—*libri laicorum*—and they were indispensable in that role, whether the actual medium

[1] For Cato, see a most useful and learned essay by Harry Caplan, 'Memoria: Treasure-House of Eloquence,' in his *Of Eloquence: Studies in Ancient and Mediaeval Rhetoric*, ed Anne King and Helen North (Ithaca, N. Y. 1970, p. 232. For Boccaccio's *Teseida*, see the edition by S. Battaglia, Florence, 1938.

On this change, see Yates, *Art of Memory*, pp. 54–81.

was pigment or glass or wood or spoken word.[1] To paraphrase St. Bonaventura, *images instruct, arouse pious emotions,* and *awaken memories.*[2] The Middle Ages understood the image to be in service to the moral, as well as aesthetic, life of mankind.

Where then shall we locate Chaucer's practice against this range of ideas concerning the image and its function? We must first recognize that there is much in his art that is 'visual,' that invites us to make images in our mind as we read or listen to his narrative. In a fashion consonant with classical rhetorical precept, he seems to have sought imaginative vividness as a special goal: '*ante oculos ponere*,' set it before the eyes.[3] Any description of his aesthetic must include a serious place for this achievement: he did not disdain the surfaces of his fiction, and we should trust no critic who advises us to do so. But among all that material which is vividly seen by Chaucer in the act of invention, and which forces a comparable act of imagining upon his audience, there is a special category of image, far more complex in its effect, which is my real subject here. I mean those images which the auditor/reader recognizes as being 'like'—as being in approximate register with—images known from elsewhere, from other contexts in both literature and the visual arts, *in some of which* their meanings are stipulative and exact, unmediated by the ambiguities of fable. That recognition of likeness, itself pleasurable, invites a further meditation. They are images essential to the action, which through their relationship with other images in other contexts —that is, in their iconographic identity—become central to the action's meaning as well. In *The Canterbury Tales*, there is no writing (except significantly the 'Sir Thopas') which is not organized around one or two of these 'governing' images. It is around them that we find ourselves recre-

[1] Rosemary Woolf, *The English Mystery Plays*, Berkeley, California 1972, pp. 86–101, brings together some documents central to the medieval defence of imagery, and offers a useful further bibliography.

[2] Quoted by Erwin Panofsky, *Early Netherlandish Painting: Its Origins and Character*, Cambridge, Mass. 1953, p. 141. The whole of chapter V ('Reality and Symbol in Early Flemish Painting: "*Spiritualia sub metaphoris corporalium*"') discusses a technique which he calls 'concealed symbolism,' closely related to that I describe in Chaucer's poetry.

[3] See for instance, the *Rhetorica ad Herennium*, ed and trans. Harry Caplan, Loeb Classical Library 403, Cambridge, Mass., 1968, pp. 376, 380, 382, 384, 408.

ating in memory the experience of the fiction, and pondering what it has to tell us about human life.

Limitations on space preclude my offering any adequate example of such an analysis here. Let me name, instead, in summary fashion, some of the images I shall examine in the book these prefatory remarks are drawn from—images which, *in relation to their context*, comprise (to my mind) the essential 'meaning' of a Chaucerian narrative poem. In 'The Knight's Tale', the prison-tower and its adjoining garden; in 'The Reeve's Tale', the runaway horse; in 'The Man of Law's Tale', the rudderless ship and the sea; in 'The Prioress's Tale', the corpse on the dungheap; in 'The Wife of Bath's Tale', the lovely lady and the hag; in 'The Friar's Tale', the carter and his horse; in 'The Summoner's Tale', the fart and the wheel; in 'The Clerk's Tale', the crown and the shift; in 'The Franklin's Tale', the rocks and the garden; and so on.

These are not merely 'decorative' images, nor are they merely metaphors—quick likenesses to be noted and then passed by.[1] Chaucer uses those kinds too, rather sparely, but they are not my subject here. I am pointing rather to scenes that remain in our mind's eye through long actions or descriptions, whose essential function in the story, whether as architecture, or landscape, or costume, or property, or causal event, confers upon them a certain 'covered' quality. They do not call attention to themselves in specifically symbolic ways, but are instead discovered in —uncovered by—the narrative as it moves naturally from its beginning to its end, and the clue to their identity is the way they create a certain residue in the mind. The knowledge necessary to read them in their symbolic dimension is almost never essential to the surface coherence of the story. Chaucer's sense of his audience is not exclusive in that way; it does not address itself to learned and sophisticated men only. But for those with the training and the wit to respond most fully, his later narratives have concealed within them a most powerful intellectual, artistic, and imaginative coherence—deeper than the linear continuities of the plot —to which these images are central. Langland seems to have preferred a very different method, though the memorial use of images is every bit as important to his work: his invention seems to have begun with a number of controlling images—the Field Full of Folk, for example, or the Vision

[1] P. N. Furbank, *Reflections on the Word 'Image'*, 1970, argues convincingly that we should not use the term 'image' for metaphors which do not invite or require visualization.

of Middle Earth, or the Barn of Unity—and a grammatical triad —Dowel, Dobet, Dobest—around which he invents a series of actions capable of exploring the full ambiguity of their potential meaning. Chaucer's own early practice, in the dream-vision poems, bears a certain kinship to this: the narrator is shown images—places, sights, things —that are expressly supra-real, expressly symbolic. But the mature Chaucer of the *Troilus* and *The Canterbury Tales* invented none of his stories, preferring instead to seek within the given fiction those details that could address a generalized truth, and then to work them, through an exercise of rhetorical skill, into commanding images—memorial centres of meaning and meditative suggestion for the entire poem.

But I have touched here upon several matters that must be looked at more closely, if we are properly to assess the consequences of these facts for the historical criticism of Chaucerian narrative. We must talk now about the medieval bases of iconography, and about iconography in relation to literary contexts; and we might well resume with a phrase from St. Thomas Aquinas that concerns a matter already briefly introduced: 'things signified by words have themselves also a signification.' Such meanings, we would say, must be *attributed*: the raw flux of experience, the total multiplicity of phenomena, contain no 'meanings' in advance of the ruminations of the human mind upon them. So we would say now. But the Middle Ages believed otherwise—that meaning was *inherent* in the material creation, because of the Divine Intelligence that created and directs it. Our task is to recover that meaning, to discover that symbolic code. Christ's life and death was, among other things, a 'reading' of the Hebrew Bible, an interpretation of its secret meanings. And all holy writ contained clues to the significance of things. The great encyclopaedias of the thirteenth century represent a scientific tendency that was to grow increasingly important in the later Middle Ages—an interest in more accurate classification, in direct observation, in the literal—yet this older and more conservative inheritance is neither forgotten nor made consciously separate, as though it were knowledge bearing an entirely different relation to reality. Such encyclopaedias incorporated the traditional materials of the bestiaries, lapidaries, and so on, and thus became (among other things) symbolic handbooks to the universe, contributory to a public language of sign that was being fed from other sources as well—a language in which things can function as complex words, in three especial kinds. There is first of all a vocabulary of *attribute*, which allows the ready identification of certain historical or pseudo-historical persons: the crown and the harp that indicates King

David, for example, or St. Catherine with her wheel, or St. Lawrence with the gridiron of his martyrdom. Such objects mean themselves literally, but their significance derives from a history or legend which must be learned. There is also a vocabulary of *symbol*, in which things mean something other than themselves: the Holy Ghost is not a dove, but a dove can stand for the Holy Ghost, in painting or in literature. And finally, there are complex *allegorical figures*, generally abstract ideas expressed in a human form, often accompanied by other conventional symbols: Fortune as a woman blindfolded, beautiful on one side, ugly on the other, turning a wheel in the midst of the sea; or Avarice as an old man wearing torn clothes sitting at a counting table with money.

Any ordinary member of Chaucer's audience would have known a whole language of such signs; they saw them in paintings, carvings and stained glass; they heard them explained *as signs* in sermons, confessional teaching, and didactic literature; they heard them used in covered and ingenious ways just below the surface of narrative and lyric poems not primarily didactic in intent. Only the most ignorant or indolent among them would have failed to be alert to the possibilities of such meaning in Chaucer's art. And indeed, in the earliest of his great poems, *The Book of the Duchess*, Chaucer casts himself as 'obtuse' auditor to just such a narrative, as the man in black tells under the figure of a game of chess, how he lost his wife to death. The image is wholly conventional, and was widely current, but the dreamer persists almost to the end in hearing everything in a literal way. This is not the proper place to investigate Chaucer's reasons for choosing such a strategy in a poem of lament and consolation; for present purposes we may merely declare as certain that the figure of this excessively literal-minded dreamer is not offered as exemplary to Chaucer's own audience. He expected them to understand the icons, the traditional language of symbol through which he sometimes spoke even in his fictional art.

But it is a language that still lacks its equivalent of the multi-volumed *Oxford English Dictionary*, much less the Michigan *Middle English Dictionary* now appearing fascicle by fascicle. Certain ambitious projects concerned with Christian iconography are under way, but the profane iconography of the Middle Ages still awaits systematic attention; and no one to my knowledge has even contemplated a real dictionary of sign in which both categories are intermingled, arranged on no basis more prejudicial than the order of the alphabet.[1] And so one must do what one can, seeking to establish for any image that seems central to the meaning of a poem a comprehensive survey of *all the meanings current* within the relevant period, as an essential step precedent to formal critical analysis. The minimum that we need, and must offer our readers, if they are to be able independently to judge our conclusions, is a horizontal, trans-cultural survey of how and where any such image occurs (if our interest is in Chaucer) in the late-fourteenth and early-fifteenth centuries.

This attention to the full range of contexts in which images were cur-rent is not only necessary, but has a further procedural consequence: it can protect us from a simplistic notion of how imagery functions, and from reductive definitions that summarily divorce images from all that surrounds them. The analogy with verbal language is again to the point: few words are complete sentences in their own right, and even those few —Stop! Help! Alas!—can mean vastly different things according to situation and tone of voice. So too, few visual signs, or their equivalent mental images, are independently precise communications. Not all doves represent the Holy Ghost; some are a sign for the soul; others identify Venus; some signify just themselves, doves and nothing more. It is context that turns a sign into a communication, defining its exact and immediate intent. Signs are otherwise inert, like words listed in a dic-tionary, where *all* possibilities of meaning remain potential. Such lists of words are not the same thing as words in use: in advance of use, no sig-nification (out of the multiple significations potential in almost any word) bears any priority over any other.

And so too with images: they cannot be 'read' except in relation to context. A devotional cross is relatively unambiguous as a sign—it is the central image of Christianity—and yet a crude cross of wood expresses something about Christ's death quite different from the 'meaning' of an elaborately decorated, highly worked cross of gold and jewels. A cross

[1] *The Encyclopaedia of World Art* VII, New York 1963, pp. 770–86, in its ar-ticle on 'Iconography and Iconology,' offers a history of the discipline and a copious bibliography. Beginning students may find particularly helpful the work of such scholars as Émile Mâle, Raymond van Marle, Louis Réau, Adolf Katzenellenbogen, Erwin Panofsky, E. H. Gombrich, Samuel C. Chew, M.D. Anderson, Millard Meiss, Lilian M. C. Randall, Kenneth Varty, and Jurgis Baltrusaitis. R. E. Kaske is presently preparing a volume entitled 'Sources and Methodology for the Interpretation of Medieval Imagery' for the Toronto Medieval Bibliography Series.

above the rood-screen in a great cathedral expresses something different from a cross in a private home, or yet again from a cross by Cimabue now to be viewed only as a part of the fine arts collection of a great museum. A cross without a figure on it, or a cross that displays the regnant Christ of the Romanesque period, a cross displaying the tortured bird-flesh Christ of the Isenheim altarpiece, or the 'black' Christ of the Andes, all mean different things, though in terms of the lexicography of images, they all signify Christ's sacrifice. (And the cross of a modern telephone pole, or two sticks laced together by children in play, must not be confused with them.) Any sign *in use* is inseparable from context: it has a potential for other meanings only in advance of use.

The images of literature—mental images—likewise do not, and cannot, function in lexicographically neutral ways. They are at once delimited *and* increased by the words that create them and surround them. The sound of those words, the level of diction, the harmony of rhyme and metre, the emphasis conferred by accent and rhythm and pause, along with the genre in which the poem is made, and the social milieu in which it is experienced, all of these are part of the sign properly understood. They are intrinsic to the real existence of signs in literature, and cannot be severed from any sign without its falsification, loss of potency, loss of life. Almost all of these factors are within the control of the author, and constitute the complex language through which he speaks. Through them we discover—and, if the art is successful come to share—what and how he feels about what he says. The lexicographical survey, though essential, is only a preparation for the critical act—it is itself based upon a series of such critical acts—in which one must discover which of the possible meanings is most forcibly implied by the total context in which the image occurs, and how that context in turn mediates, complicates, and enriches the simplified lexicographical meaning (the sense *a, b, c,* or *d*) of the image.

And so I would argue that any student concerned with the mental image as a vital link between Chaucer and the visual arts of his time, must take as his subject whole poems, for that is where such images have their only real existence. By way of example, it has recently been demonstrated (correctly) that bagpipes, whose shape is roughly like that of the male genitalia, are part of an iconography of 'the old song'—the carnal life that must be given over before the spiritual life ('Sing ye to the Lord a new song') can begin. But bagpipes are not always and invariably a sign for that idea. The great Apocalypse tapestries at Angers, made in the late fourteenth century, show in their borders the music of the heavenly host—angels playing harps, viols, portative organs, and even bagpipes —and no carnal meaning is there implied. The designer of the tapestry was thinking of them as musical instruments only. We must take care in our lexicography of signs to survey not merely the *full* range of demonstrable symbolic meanings, but also to allow for the *literal* meaning of things, and to respect both the possibility and the dignity of that literal meaning in our critical practice. Context governs.

Though parody flourished in the Middle Ages, with examples ranging from drunkards' masses to scholastic burlesque of erotic love-ideas to satires on the poetry of incompetent minstrels, and clearly was valued for the pleasures of laughter and virtuoso display alone, yet the vast body of artistic narrative produced within those centuries was shaped by the conviction that literature is two-fold in its nature, concerned with both truth and fiction—a duality variously styled in the vernacular as 'fruyt and chaf,' 'doctrine and delit,' 'sentence and solaas.'[1] But the Middle Ages is far from homogeneous as a period; it covers several centuries, which saw enormous changes in man's ability to dominate the physical universe, in his thought about the nature of his existence and the place of art within it. The quest of criticism for the radically singular truth about any single medieval narrative must be attentive to these changes. It must attempt to define, work by work, author by author, period by period, the exact —but multiple, and shifting—relationship between these two quantities, the truth and the lie, the lie that tells truth. This can only be discovered through a close look at actual artistic practice, for the formulas

[1] Robertson, *A Preface to Chaucer*, offers a learned though highly controversial study of this tradition; see also Bernard F. Huppé and D. W. Robertson, Jr, *Fruyt and Chaf*, Princeton 1963. For other views, see Morton W. Bloomfield, 'Symbolism in Medieval Literature,' *MP*, 56, 1958, 73–81; R. E. Kaske, 'Chaucer and Medieval Allegory,' *ELH*, 30, 1963, 175–92; Francis Lee Utley, 'Robertsonianism Redivivus,' *Romance Philology*, 19, 1965, 250–60; Theodore Silverstein, 'Allegory and Literary Form,' and Paul E. Beichner, C.S.C., 'The Allegorical Interpretation of Medieval Literature,' both in *PMLA*, 82, 1967, 28–32, and 33–8; and R. S. Crane, 'On Hypotheses in "Historical Criticism": Apropos of Certain Contemporary Medievalists,' in his *The Idea of the Humanities and Other Essays* Chicago 1967, pp. 236–60.

survive through the whole period largely unchanged, and in their lack of specificity can cover almost any balance struck between the two, almost any relationship established between them. Such formulas, separated from a critical engagement with texts, can tell us next to nothing. They exist to invite that engagement, not to render it unnecessary.

Chaucer's most extensive discussion of that duality is to be found at the end of his tale of Chauntecleer and Pertelotte:

> But ye that holden this tale a folye,
> As of a fox, or of a cok and hen,
> Taketh the moralite, goode men.
> For seint Paul seith that al that writen is,
> To oure doctrine it is ywrite, ywis:
> Taketh the fruyt, and lat the chaf be stille.

(VII, 3438–43)

This brief passage has been taken as a key to Chaucer's aesthetic, but I think carelessly so, without enough attention to what it actually says. However great the medieval 'authority' of that statement—and learned proponents may be adduced in plenty, across the several medieval centuries—those authorities are not speaking here, and certainly not speaking out of their own moments in historical time. We must be alert to the place in which Chaucer introduces these terms, at the end of some 600 lines of his most brilliant and audacious poetry, *all* of it (except for two 'moralities' expressed in the preceeding 7 lines) 'chaf'—a fable in which two chickens and a fox are allowed to speak and behave as though they were human beings, as though they were indeed lovers, villains, and tragic heroes. We must respect as well the clause that introduces the distinction, for what follows is no prescription to the general, but instead (as with many such 'defenses of poetry') an address to those in his audience who may be disposed to think such fictions empty and a waste of time: 'ye that holden this tale a folye.' For *them*—that possible subgroup within any audience—*this* advice. They too have been provided for. But I doubt that he himself read (much less wrote) literature in so exclusive and austere a way, or that he wishes his larger audience to value only those formulaic truths which he does (in the preceding seven lines) deduce: keep your mouth shut; keep your eyes open. The real morality of 'The Nun's Priest's Tale' seems to me *inseparable* from its surfaces, from the letter of its fiction, in which we are made to contemplate our habitual assumptions concerning the grandeur, dignity, and meaningfulness of the human condition in new and ironical lights.[1] It seeks to alter our habitual gestures of self-regard and self-aggrandizement, and in its competence to achieve that effect lies its highest potential for the moral transformation of its audience. The formulaic morals are valid and useful, to be sure, but they do not necessitate 600 lines in which we are made to see ourselves in the guise of chickens behaving as though they were men. You may—Chaucer tells us—throw away all that, if you can find no worth in it. But I think that a witty challenge, not a sober demand. The reference to St. Paul should perhaps bring a smile to our lips—it is outrageously unsuited to the present context—rather than send us scurrying to tomes of the Fathers. No one, I think, has ever argued that Chaucer wrote the Miller's and Reeve's tales *only* in order that we should skip them, though there too he says we may, if we fear we will be offended, 'turne over the leef and chese another tale.' Again he may be seen providing liberty for some, not a moral imperative for all: 'whoso list it nat yheere' will find other tales more to their liking. It is the generosity of a host, not the didacticism of a teacher. Meanwhile, he will get on with his own version of truth, the great 'mateere' of the pilgrimage, to which the Miller and Reeve bring both their persons and their visions of experience—a truth higher than literary decorum, and one which he will not 'falsen' or betray.

For Chaucer thought of himself as a 'makere,' an artisan working in words and rhyme, not a philosopher or preacher. His first professional concern was with the total integrity and finish of the thing made, all of its elements in harmony with each other. A late fourteenth-century miniature from a MS of Nicole Oresme's *Traduction des Ethiques d'Aristote* can illustrate medieval assumptions on this matter: it shows *Art* as a man at his forge and anvil, while *Sapience* is shown as a man at a book contemplating truth, with Christ and the angels visible above.[2] Chaucer wrote in 'The Knight's Tale', in praise of the painting in Diana's temple, 'Wel koude he peynten lifly that it wroghte', and he sought to emulate that art

---

[1] I follow here the lead of E. T. Donaldson in the Commentary appended to his edition of *Chaucer's Poetry: An Anthology for the Modern Reader*, New York 1958, pp. 940–44.

[2] Brussels, Bibl. Royale MS 9505–6, fol. 115 vo (made ca. 1372–74). See also Edgar de Bruyne, *The Esthetics of the Middle Ages*, trans. Eileen B. Hennessy, New York 1969, esp. pp. 131–38.

himself, to 'devise', 'portreye', and 'peynt', in an art that incorporates wisdom, but is not identical with it. When he rejects art (as he does twice, in the 'Melibeus' and 'The Parson's Tale'), he rejects both rhyme and verisimilar fiction, to offer 'doctryne' unambiguous in its means. But elsewhere he did not work, most or even much of the time, within genres that sought Wisdom or Truth as their characteristic end: wisdom, yes, and truth, yes, but of a more tentative and modest kind, not only discovered through, but inevitably qualified by, the letter of fiction. All of his tales are in an important sense Christian—certainly none of them sets up a counter-truth, not even those tales which take place in pagan times. But the degree to which—and way in which—they reflect that highest truth varies: not all of the imaginative worlds he created are Christian 'worlds'. *Troilus and Criseyde*, 'The Knight's Tale', 'The Franklin's Tale', the *fabliaux*, the 'Sir Thopas', invoke different sets of values and obligations than does, say, 'The Second Nun's Tale' of St. Cecilia. Those differences must concern us, or literature itself becomes unnecessary and unprofitable. We need otherwise only read some theory of 'the medieval possible', and waste no time in exposing ourselves to the complexities, ambiguities, and surprises of art.

Our task is not to substitute an explicitly Christian context for the other sorts of context he created, but instead to understand those contexts too as accurately and fully as we can, to ask why a Christian poet might have chosen to create them, and to ask concerning the Christian truths which his fiction introduces—most generally through narrative images iconographic in their import—how they fare within it. I raise this issue here because, in my view, such images constitute the major way in which Chaucer sought to make a fictional construct coterminous with, but not the same as, a literature of wisdom: and the purpose of those images is seldom narrowly didactic. They are used rather to illuminate human experience in all its complexity, sometimes tragic, sometimes comic, sometimes perplexing, sometimes magnificently clear. *The Canterbury Tales* presents no univocal statement, but rather some twenty-three voices, out of a company of nine and twenty, bearing witness to their understanding of life through the fictions they tell. It is held together by the idea of pilgrimage, not by some neat and tidy moral equation. To read the whole of *The Canterbury Tales* in the light of 'The Parson's Tale', as though all the other narratives were merely partial expressions of its truth, intended only to summon its *full* truth to mind, is at once to under-read and over-read the larger work—to render it, against its nature, monotonous in intent and narrow in its sympathies, and to credit it in all its parts with a higher seriousness than it possesses. There can be no question ever about the priority or superior dignity of the Christian truths (or their expression in images) for the culture Chaucer inhabited and served, but he used those images in fictional contexts less in order to reassert that priority (it needed no such defence or assertion) than as part of an assault upon the otherwise inexpressible: that range of experience for which we have no single word, no adequate formula—a view of metaphor that goes back to Cicero—and which the 'mirror of wisdom' on its own cannot adequately reflect. In this undertaking, the fruit and the chaff, the doctrine and the delight, the moral and the matter are inseparable.

And so this essay, though primarily concerned with the symbolic meaning of certain mental images, must conclude with something of a paradox. For I have wished to argue with equal vigour for the primacy of the *letter*, the authority of the whole poem, line by line, in which the fiction and the truth are voiced simultaneously. Our goal as readers must never be to shrink the narrative to an icon, but rather to explore the icon as the vital centre to a work vivid and valuable as a whole. In Chaucer's aesthetic, we may define the 'chaf' as fiction, to be sure, but not as worth-less falsehood, and the 'fruyt' (more conventionally) as generalized truth freed of its fictive particularities. But the second emerges from the first, and most powerfully so through meditation upon the governing images; it does not make of the former something contemptible, to be disposed of or put out of mind, as soon as a paraphrasable moral lesson may be discerned.

A distinguished historian of medieval science, Lynn White, Jr., has written about some changes closely allied to my argument here:

> The later Roman Empire and the early Middle Ages lived not in a world of visible facts but rather in a world of symbols. . . . In such a world there was no thought of hiding behind a clump of reeds actually to observe the habits of a pelican. There would have been no point to it. Once one had grasped the spiritual nature of the pelican, one had lost interest in individual pelicans. The effect upon science of such a view was of course disastrous. . . .
> Then suddenly, toward the middle of the twelfth century, something began to stir in the art of western Europe: a fresh sense of the

immediacies of concrete experience, a new attachment to physical actualities.[1]

He attributes much to the influence of the Franciscans, and describes, as characteristic of the late medieval period, 'an unprecedented yearning for immediate experience of concrete facts'—a matter of the highest consequence for the development of science. Beryl Smalley, too, in her remarkable studies in the history of Biblical exegesis and the activities of English fourteenth-century friars, has documented this developing respect for the literal, the phenomenal, the historical, and has discovered it where perhaps it was least to be expected—in the glosses to sacred texts themselves: 'The words and events of Scripture retain all their symbolic value. But the [thirteenth-century] postillator has diverted his attention. He is treading on earth, with occasional upward glances, instead of floating above it, descending only now and then.'[2] And Morton Bloomfield, more recently, has reminded us in an elegant and eloquent conclusion that the literal sense of fiction alone is *profound*, for it alone contains the possibility of other meanings.[3]

Chaucer's art is responsive to these same new currents of thought and feeling, while remaining conservative in temper as well. Although the surfaces of some of his fictions are as modern as Boccaccio's in the *Decameron*, yet he ultimately never sought so great a freedom from the hierarchies of truth, if Charles Singleton has correctly described Boccaccio's intention in deciding to take his art (the tale-telling and songs) out of the plague-ridden city. Singleton writes: 'The framework of the *Decameron* is the effort to justify and protect a new art, an art which simply in order to be, to exist, required the moment free of all other cares, the willingness to stop *going anywhere* (either toward God or toward philosophical truth).'[4] Chaucer, in his last great work, similarly frees a diverse com-

---

[1] Lynn White, Jr., 'Natural Science and Naturalistic Art in the Middle Ages,' *American Historical Review*, 52, 1947, 424–25.

[2] Beryl Smalley, *The Study of the Bible in the Middle Ages*, 2nd ed Oxford 1952, p. 372. And see her *English Friars and Antiquity in the Early Fourteenth Century* Oxford 1960.

[3] Morton Bloomfield, 'Allegory as Interpretation,' *New Literary History*, 3, 1972, 317.

[4] Charles Singleton, 'On *Meaning* in the *Decameron*,' *Italica*, 21, 1944, 119. Compare Erich Auerbach's essay on Boccaccio, in *Mimesis*, Princeton 1953, chapter 9 ('Frate Alberto').

pany from the exigencies of their real and daily lives. But unlike Boccaccio's elegant young people, virtually indistinguishable from each other and unmarked by the lives they have lived so far, Chaucer's pilgrims bring with them living evidence of who they are and what they have been. He places them on a long road to a cathedral, and creates for them tales which, in terms of the history of style, simultaneously look forward (in the apparent autonomy of their surfaces) and backward (in the symbolic images uncovered by the action, which govern the making and meaning of the tale that embodies them.) Those images allow truth to speak through fable. They join in a more natural and organic way than had ever been true in English literature before, the *visibilia* and the *invisibilia* of the universe, and the human lives lived out within it. If Boccaccio's art in the *Decameron* is the more audacious and new—he lived to repudiate it himself—it is also less rich, less substantial, less resonant in the mind. Chaucer invented, for English literature, a new decorum for the artistic use of symbol, able to incorporate at once both the clarity of Truth and the common light of day.

12: A Reader's Guide to Writings on Chaucer

L. D. BENSON

'TELL CHILD NOT TO BE too learned about Chaucer, for my sake.' So wrote Arthur Hugh Clough in 1853 when he heard that Francis J. Child was planning an edition of Chaucer's works.* Child abandoned the project, but many readers today, confronted by the vast quantity of critical and scholarly work about Chaucer that has accumulated since Child's time, may wish that everyone had been a good deal less learned about the poet, for all our sakes. Whole volumes are necessary only to list the books, monographs, editions, articles, reviews, notes and discussions written in the past century, and new works appear at an increasing rate. A journal, *The Chaucer Review*, is now devoted almost entirely to articles on Chaucer; the annual meeting of the Chaucer Group of the Modern Language Association of America is regularly attended by hundreds of scholars who come to hear papers about Chaucer; and each year *Neuphilologische Mitteilungen* devotes several pages to listing not the works published in the past year but those planned (or threatened) for future years. One can sympathize with G. K. Chesterton's dictum: 'Chaucer was a poet . . . it is possible to know him without knowing anything about him . . . What matters is not books about Chaucer, but Chaucer.'

Yet, that Chaucer does matter so much today is due almost entirely to books about Chaucer, for though it may be possible to know him without knowing anything about him, we can know him only through his works, and without the help of scholarship—linguistic, textual, critical,

---

* Quotations from critics before 1900 are taken from Spurgeon's *Five Hundred Years of Chaucer Criticism and Allusion* (listed in the Bibliography under *Intro.C*). The quotation at the end of this paragraph from G. K. Chesterton is from his *Chaucer* (see Bibliography under *VIII. A.*). The Bibliography contains full descriptions of all works about Chaucer mentioned in the balance of this essay.

and historical—Chaucer would remain, as he was for centuries, accessible only to a few devoted readers. The necessity for scholarly help was recognized almost in Chaucer's own time; his earliest known 'editor,' the copyist Shirley, produced glossed manuscripts of Chaucer's poems early in the fifteenth century. By the first half of the sixteenth century the obvious need for a reliable text led William Thynne to 'search all the libraries in England' for the Chaucerian manuscripts on which Thynne's edition was based. And by the end of the sixteenth century it was clear, as William's son Francis wrote, that Chaucer required editing, 'after the manner of the Italians, who have largely commented Petrarch,' in order that his works 'by much conference and many judgements might at length obtain their true perfection and glory.'

This took longer than Thynne could have imagined, for the early enthusiasm soon waned. Thomas Speght's edition of Chaucer (1598; rev. 1602 repr. 1667) was the last to appear until the eighteenth century, and, as the reader of Caroline Spurgeon's fascinating *Five Hundred Years of Chaucer Criticism and Allusion* soon discovers, Chaucer remained until the later nineteenth century (in the words of an anonymous writer in the year 1819) 'more neglected, less studied, and less known, though none are more talked of' than almost any major English writer. William Wordsworth, who deplored the fact that Chaucer was so 'little known to the world at large,' translated Chaucer in order to make his works more widely available, and his translations (along with those of Leigh Hunt, Elizabeth Barrett Browning, Richard H. Horne, and others) were published in 1841 as *The Works of Geoffrey Chaucer Modernized*. The volume apparently did not have the desired effect, for Walter Pater claimed that in 1864 when he 'chanced upon a rather rare little book called *Chaucer Modernized* . . . Of Chaucer himself and his work he knew very little. "Of course," he added, "I have heard of *The Canterbury Tales*, but I did not know they were considered of sufficient importance to be modernized."'

Pater may have exaggerated somewhat for effect (he reports that his companion, Richard Jackson, found such ignorance natural in a 'Tutor of Oxford') but his story is not incredible. It was only in the middle years of the nineteenth century that a remarkable group of scholars began the serious scholarly study of Chaucer's works that by the end of the century would restore them to a wide reading public and establish Chaucer in the position he holds today—not only one of the best but one of the best known and best loved poets in our language. These scholars mapped out what would be the main concerns in Chaucerian studies for decades to come: in France E. G. Sandras began the systematic study of Chaucer's sources with his *Étude sur Chaucer consideré comme un troubadour* (1859); in America Child published his 'Observations on the Language of Chaucer' (1862), the first extensive study of Chaucer's language; in Germany Bernhard ten Brink's *Chaucer-Studien* (1865) began the serious study of the canon and chronology of Chaucer's works; and in England, where a few years previously N. H. Nicholas had published the first modern biography of Chaucer (that is, one based on a study of the records), F. J. Furnivall founded the Chaucer Society and began the publication of the *Six-Text Edition of the Canterbury Tales* (1867), which laid the foundation for a reliable edition. It was an international effort, nicely symbolized by the fact that Child sent Furnivall the money with which to begin the Chaucer Society, but the centre of activity was Furnivall and his colleagues in England, and the volumes of the Chaucer Society contained most of the important work on Chaucer until the First World War.

I *The Canon*

The first task of Chaucerian scholars was the canon of Chaucer's work. At one time or another over sixty spurious works have been attributed to Chaucer, and early editions contained many 'apocryphal' pieces. 'Of all writers linked with compositions not their own,' wrote F. W. Bonner, 'it is probable that the reputation of Chaucer, as man and author, has been most consistently affected by works falsely attributed to him.' Chaucer's sixteenth and seventeenth-century reputation as a violent anti-Papal satirist was based mainly on his supposed authorship of works such as *The Ploughman's Tale, Jack Upland*, and *The Pilgrim's Tale*. Until well into the nineteenth century, his life was thought to be a romantic affair, including exile in France and an imprisonment for his supposed Wycliffite sympathies, mainly because of deductions made from *The Testament of Love*. And the attitudes of many readers toward Chaucer were shaped by such admired works as *The Flower and the Leaf*, which Dryden translated, *The Cuckoo and the Nightingale*, translated by Wordsworth, and *The Isle of Ladies (Chaucer's Dream)*, which Ruskin so admired he planned to translate it as the finest example of Chaucer's nature poetry. The necessity of sorting the spurious from the genuine had been recognized as early as 1598 by Francis Thynne, and the task was begun by T. Tyrrwhit in the eighteenth century, but the establishment of the canon itself was mainly the work of nineteenth-century scholars, culminating in Skeat's edition and his *The Chaucer Canon* (1900), which removed the non-Chaucerian pieces and established the 'Works of Chaucer' pretty much as we know them today.

This was not entirely a matter of removing the wheat from the tares, for some of the 'Chaucerian Apocrypha' are very fine works indeed, and one unfortunate side effect of this scholarship has been the unjust neglect into which many of these works have now fallen. Derek Pearsall's good edition of *The Flower and the Leaf and The Assembly of Ladies* has brought these poems back to the attention of readers, and there is a recent edition of *The Pilgrim's Tale* by Russell A. Fraser. *The Cuckoo and the Nightingale* (now known better in Wordsworth's translation than in the original) has been edited in a learned journal, but for most readers it and *The Testament of Love* still languish lightly edited and largely unread in the Supplement to Skeat's Chaucer. And those, such as the delightful *Isle of Ladies*, which Skeat did not include, are even less well known today. They deserve better; most of them got into editions of Chaucer because they were thought worthy of that honour, and among them are some of the best late Middle English poems.

Even today the problems of the canon are not completely settled. A number of lyrics still present problems, since for most of them the evidence of authorship is slight and whether or not a poem is genuine depends on the editor's judgement. The triple roundel 'Merciles Beute' (which Bishop Percy first attributed to Chaucer without any external evidence) was accepted as authentic by Skeat but rejected by Aage Brusendorff in his useful *The Chaucer Tradition*. Robinson placed it (along with the 'Proverbs,' which both Skeat and Brusendorff accepted) among the poems of 'doubtful authorship.' E. T. Donaldson prints it as Chaucer's in his edition, noting that it is 'generally accepted' as his, and in one recent paperback edition (*The Laurel Chaucer*, ed Louis O. Coxe) the poem is printed without comment as one of only two representatives of Chaucer's lyric poems.

Brusendorff proposed to add to the canon 'The Balade of a Reeve,' which he printed in diplomatic transcription from the two manuscripts in which it survives (*Chaucer Tradition*, pp. 278–84). The three-stanza poem has a certain charm, but it has found no other supporters. Brusendorff was also convinced that the whole of the English *Romaunt of the Rose* is Chaucer's, its text garbled due to memorial transmission. Skeat had shown that of the three fragments only the first, 'Fragment A,' is probably by Chaucer, and despite Brusendorff and earlier Lounsbury, who argued vigorously against Skeat's position, almost all scholars now agree with Skeat. In his recent parallel-text edition, *The Romaunt of the Rose and Le Roman de la rose* Ronald Sutherland shows that 'A' derives from a French textual tradition different from 'B' and 'C' and thus more firmly than ever places all but fragment 'A' outside the canon.

Given this continual contraction of the canon, one would have thought that the discovery in recent years of the inscription 'Radix Chaucer' in the Peterhouse Manuscript of the *Equatorie of the Planetis* would have caused a great outburst of scholarly activity. The phrase 'Radix Chaucer' may be in the poet's own hand and the work may therefore be a companion piece to the undoubtedly genuine *Treatise of the Astrolabe*. If so, we have an extended piece of Chaucer's prose in a reliable manuscript that could cast important light on his language and prose style. The manuscript is now available in a fine edition by Derek Price, including a study of the language by R. M. Wilson, who demonstrates that the usages are consistent with Chaucer's practices. Herdon's study of diction also supports the attribution, though his argument is weak, and Margaret Schlauch has shown that the style is consistent with the genuine prose works. The evidence clearly indicates Chaucer's authorship, but it is all internal evidence and most scholars still accept the Scotch verdict—not proven—pronounced by Robinson in his second edition. One can only hope that the problem will soon be settled one way or the other.

II   *Texts*

The manuscript variations in Chaucer's works have bedevilled conscientious editors since the time of Caxton, who tells us that his second edition of *The Canterbury Tales* was necessarily based on a different manuscript from the first edition, which he had printed (1478) without

realizing that 'this book was not according in many places unto the book
that Geoffrey Chaucer made.' The Chaucer Society was founded 'to do
honour to Chaucer and to let lovers and students of him see how far the
best unprinted manuscripts of his works differ from the printed texts,'
and Furnivall's *Six-Text Edition of the Canterbury Tales* was the first of
many volumes devoted to this end. With the texts available for study,
the formidable task of classification and collation could begin. The study
of *The Canterbury Tales* culminated in the great eight-volume edition by
J. M. Manly and Edith Rickert, in which all the known manuscripts
were collated, an enormous undertaking for a work surviving in some
ninety often widely divergent manuscripts. Though there are fewer
manuscripts of *Troilus* (nineteen, counting early printed editions), the
problems are almost as formidable, since Chaucer made at least one revision of this work. The studies of R. K. Root (*The Textual Tradition of
Chaucer's Troilus*) led to his edition of the poem, which remains, like
Manly and Rickert's work, an essential tool for the serious student.

   The first major edition to be based on the new manuscript studies was
Walter W. Skeat's monumental Oxford *Chaucer*, whose richly annotated six volumes (plus a supplement containing the apocryphal poems)
remain a most useful aid to the student. F. N. Robinson's one-volume
edition is now the standard text, valuable especially for its extensive bibliographical notes (last brought up to date in the second edition, 1957).
Other editions are now in progress: most notably a Variorum edition
with Paul Ruggiers and Donald C. Baker as general editors. The Variorum—which will take some years to finish—will be of great use. John
H. Fisher is now preparing a new edition of the complete works (including the *Equatorie of the Planetis*). Such new editions will probably differ
significantly from Robinson's text, since ideas about editorial procedures
have greatly changed since the 1930's. Nevertheless, most advanced
students will probably continue to use Robinson's *Chaucer* for some years
to come.

   Until recent years there were relatively few good selections of
Chaucer's poetry for beginning students. A. C. Baugh's *Chaucer's Major
Poetry* and E. T. Donaldson's *Chaucer's Poetry: An Anthology for the
Modern Reader* now handsomely fill this need. Baugh's volume contains
nearly all the verse and is notable especially for its glosses (better than
Robinson's in many cases). Donaldson's edition has a sensibly stan-
dardized text that removes many of the superficial difficulties for begin-

ning readers, and its extensive critical discussions (some hundred pages) are a major contribution to Chaucerian criticism. Robert A. Pratt's *Selections from The Tales of Canterbury and Short Poems*, much more modest in scale, presents an excellent text that incorporates a number of new readings as well as Pratt's generally accepted theory of the order of the tales. Kenneth Kee's even briefer selection is well designed for beginning students, with a full introduction and good explanatory notes.

The Romaunt of the Rose has been re-edited by Sutherland, and Derek Brewer has published a fine edition of *The Parlement of Foulys*, valuable both for its text and its good critical apparatus. None of the other minor works has been re-edited in recent years (apart from those in the selected editions listed above). *Troilus and Criseyde* has been edited for the Everyman's series by John Warrington, and we now have a useful edition of selections by Derek and L. Elisabeth Brewer. Most editorial activity, however, has concentrated on *The Canterbury Tales*, and we now have many good editions designed for beginning students and general readers, the most notable being those by A. C. Cawley, Donald R. Howard (a standardized spelling text with a good introduction), and John Halverson (a very readable edition with helpful notes). The individual tales are now being published in a series edited by Maurice Hussey, A. C. Spearing, and James Winney as 'Selected Tales,' and the volumes that have appeared thus far are very good.

Despite all the editorial attention *The Canterbury Tales* have received, one major problem remains unsolved: the order of the tales. Chaucer obviously intended the tales to be read in some specific order, but even he may not have been sure what it should be, for he never got beyond organizing them into connected 'groups' or 'fragments,' and apparently the scribes of the surviving manuscripts acted as editors, organizing the groups as they chose and thus producing a bewildering variety of orders. Robinson therefore followed the order of the oldest and best manuscript, the Ellesmere, in which 'The Man of Law's Tale' is followed by 'The Wife of Bath's Tale'. The problem is that in many manuscripts (not the Ellesmere) 'The Man of Law's Tale' is followed by an 'Epilogue' that provides an introduction to 'The Shipman's Tale', which, as it stands in the Ellesmere order has no prologue and is far removed from 'The Man of Law's Tale'. The solution proposed by Henry Bradshaw and adopted by Furnivall (hence known as the 'Chaucer Society order') and Skeat was the so-called 'Bradshaw shift' by which 'Group B2' ('The Shipman's

Tale' to 'The Nun's Priest's Tale') is placed between the Man of Law's 'Epilogue' and the Wife of Bath's 'Prologue'. Though the resulting order is supported by no manuscript and was therefore rejected for a number of years, Robert A. Pratt argued persuasively for it (in 'The Order of The Canterbury Tales') and Robinson himself thought it seemed probable that Chaucer was working toward that order (p. viii, 1957 ed.). But only Baugh and Pratt have adopted it in their editions; Donaldson, Howard, and Halverson all retain the Ellesmere order of Robinson's text. Fewer Middle English editors are now 'strict constructionists' dependent upon a 'base text,' and perhaps in the future more editions will adopt the 'Chaucer Society' order; but the question is by no means settled.

Such problems would be easier if it were not for the fact that Chaucer was an unusually careful writer, willing to polish and revise his works over long periods of time. 'The Shipman's Tale', for example, may have been written as early as 1387, but, as Germaine Dempster showed in an important article ('A Period in the Development of the Canterbury Tales Marriage Group and of Blocks B² and C'), Chaucer was still working on the unit to which it belonged as late as 1396. *Troilus* was revised at least once, and the Prologue to *The Legend of Good Women*, written in 1385 or 1386, was fully rewritten almost a decade later (after 1394). All this makes the problem of the chronology of Chaucer's work very difficult indeed (perhaps that is why Tatlock's *The Development and Chronology of Chaucer's Works* remains the standard study, even though many of Tatlock's conclusions are no longer accepted), but it provides proof, rare in Middle English times, that our author was a self-conscious literary artist. Despite the often remarked 'insouciance' (or simple carelessness) of his style, he was willing to labour long to achieve the effects at which he aimed.

III *Language and Versification*

The study of Chaucer's language, which began in a serious way with the work of Child, was vigorously pursued in the late nineteenth century, and most of the major problems were settled by the time of ten Brink's

The Language and Metre of Chaucer. Yet much has been learned since ten Brink's time. Joseph Mersand's *Chaucer's Romance Vocabulary* considers the vocabulary from the standpoint of derivations; Will Héraucourt's *Die Wertwelt Chaucers* considers it from the standpoint of a semantic field and is a model for further studies of this sort. The publication of the *Middle English Dictionary* continues to add to our understanding of the meanings of the words.

Chaucer's syntax and morphology have received a good deal of attention in recent years from students such as Fisiak and Kerkhoff, and it may be that we will some day have a full scale grammar of Chaucer's English. Certainly such a work is needed, though scholars have shied away from that formidable task for many years. There has also been relatively little work on Chaucer's pronunciation (apart from the problem of his final 'e'), though Kökeritz' pamphlet on *Chaucer's Pronunciation* has been a welcome elementary text and the long-playing record has made it possible for students to hear Chaucer read by good scholars. Though advanced students know little more about Chaucer's pronunciation than ten Brink did, beginning students can now learn a good pronunciation more easily than ever.

Likewise, though we have a number of useful reference works (such as Magoun's *Chaucer Gazeteer*) we are still dependent on the old Tatlock and Kennedy *Concordance*, which was based on the now dated Globe edition, and which, like all concordances before the development of computers, offers only sample entries for the most common words (articles, prepositions, and such, which are of great importance to linguistic studies). We do have (in Michio Masui's *The Structure of Chaucer's Rime Words*) good rime indices to *The Canterbury Tales* (based on the Manly-Rickert text) and *Troilus* (based on Root's edition); for the other poems we are still dependent on the indices compiled by Isabel Marshall and Lela Porter for the Chaucer Society.

The most interesting studies of Chaucer's language in recent years are those that approach the language from a stylistic viewpoint, such as Margaret Schlauch's important article on 'Chaucer's Colloquial English: Its Structural Traits.' Dorothy Everett, Ruth Crosby, Paull F. Baum, and others have all made important contributions to our understanding of how Chaucer used his language, which may be more important, after all, than the compilation of concordances and grammars.

Because of the close connection between the problems of Chaucer's language and those of his metre, linguistic studies of his works have almost always had stylistic implications. From the sixteenth to the nineteenth centuries readers of Chaucer could not agree on whether he wrote a regular iambic line but had been betrayed by his scribes or whether, as Thomas Gascoigne explained in 1575, he wrote rhythmical verse ('Being read by one that hath understanding, the longest verse and that which hath most syllables in it will fall to the ear correspondent to that which hath fewest syllables in it ') The studies of Child and tenBrink clarified the use of final 'e' and settled the question (in favour of a regular iambic pattern) until recent years, when James G. Southworth revived the old rhythmic theory and, in an interesting exchange of articles with Donaldson attacked the received doctrine of the final 'e'. Southworth's position has been generally rejected (by scholars like Baum and Mustanoja), but it did demonstrate the necessity for a clearer statement and defence of what we mean when we speak of 'Chaucer's metre.' An attempt at clarification was made by Morris Halle and Samuel J. Keyser from the standpoint of generative grammar, but the generative approach, as usual, naïvely begs the real question, which is not *how* did Chaucer make regular iambic pentameter but *did* he? I. A. Robinson (*Chaucer's Prosody*) has recently argued for a sort of compromise between the rhythmic and iambic positions by arguing for 'balanced pentameter'—a combination of native half-lines with iambic pentameter. But he is not entirely convincing, and we shall doubtless hear more on this subject in the years to come.

The stanzaic patterns of Chaucer's verse have been studied much less frequently than his metre Maynard's 1934 dissertation is the last full study (though Baum considers the subject and there is a fine study by Stanley on the use of the stanza in *Troilus*). Likewise, apart from the important essays by Margaret Schlauch, Chaucer's prose style remains practically untouched. Schlauch has provided useful categories ('plain style' in the *Astrolabe*, 'heightened' in 'The Parson's Tale', 'eloquent' in 'Melibee' and *Boece*) and has argued that Chaucer drew on the rhythmical cadences, the *cursus*, of elegant Latin prose. However, the theory that Old English prose shows the influence of Latin *cursus* has been convincingly refuted by Sherman Kuhn (*Speculum*, XLVII, 188–206), and a re-examination of Chaucer's prose rhythms from Kuhn's linguistic standpoint may now be needed.

IV *Life*

Until the middle of the nineteenth century, when N. H. Nicholas first attempted a biography of Chaucer based mainly on documentary evidence rather than inferences from his works (especially the spurious ones), little was known of Chaucer's life, and legends passed for fact. (The early lives are available in Hammond's *Chaucer: A Bibliographical Manual*.) The systematic search for records of Chaucer's life began in the nineteenth century and yielded the Chaucer Society's *Life Records* (some three hundred documents), was continued in this century by Manly and Rickert, and culminated in 1966 with the publication of the *Chaucer Life Records* by Martin Crow and Clair C. Olson. This volume does not completely replace the old *Life Records*, which contained documents concerning Chaucer's family and will remain useful until Miss Lillian J. Redstone completes her projected edition of records concerning Chaucer's ancestry and family, but it clearly gives us a more detailed record than ever before of Chaucer's life.

Some facts are still unclear. We do not know when Chaucer was born, and opinions range from 1340 to around 1345 (1343 seems most consistent with his testimony in 1386 that he had borne arms for 27 years). Nor do we know what Chaucer was doing from 1360 to 1365, where there is a tantalizing gap in the records. Many scholars believe that Chaucer was a student at the Inns of Court during these years, since though the records have disappeared, there is an early, possibly authentic story that Chaucer, while a student at the Inner Temple, was fined two shillings for beating a Franciscan friar in Fleet Street.

However that may be, we now know what Chaucer was doing in early 1365: he was on a trip to Spain. This came to light in 1955 when Suzanne Honoré-Duvergé discovered that the name 'Chaucer' had been mistranscribed as 'Chaunser' in a document printed in 1890. We are not at all sure what Chaucer was doing in Spain, whether he was fighting with the English forces against Pedro of Castile (as Mlle. Honoré-Duvergé believed), or going on a pilgrimage to the shrine of St James of Compostella (Crow and Olson), or on a diplomatic mission (Thomas J. Garbáty and A. C. Baugh). But what he was doing is less important than the possibility he may have learned something about Spanish literature, especially *El Libro de buen amor*, whose admittedly very general resemblances to *The Canterbury Tales* have intrigued critics since at least the time of George Ticknor (*History of Spanish Literature*, 1849; I, 85–6). Garbáty has noted a possible relation between *Troilus* and the story of Pamphilus and Galatea in *El Libro*, though the relation is indirect, and Chaucerian scholars will doubtless pay more attention to medieval Spanish literature in the years to come.

Although the *Chaucer Life Records* can occasionally provide such hints for literary study, they tell us nothing of Chaucer the poet. Certainly the discovery of the life records and the biography they outlined did affect criticism. The older idea of a 'naïve,' 'childlike' Chaucer could not be squared with the busy civil servant of the documents. 'A *naif* collector of customs,' as Kittredge wrote, 'would be a paradoxical monster.' 'Genial' replaced the nineteenth-century 'sweet' in characterizations of Chaucer, and the poet of simple sincerity became instead the master of irony (which became fashionable about the time that the outlines of Chaucer's life became clear). More important, the documents seemed to reveal not the aristocrat Chaucer was once thought to be but the son of a wine merchant and therefore the social inferior of the audience he addressed. The idea of Chaucer the bourgeois poet with his protective cloak of irony has become almost a cliché of modern criticism. But as Derek Brewer has shown ('Class Distinctions in Chaucer'), fourteenth-century ideas about social strata were much different from ours and the line between landed aristocrats and rich merchants was sometimes difficult to draw (Sylvia Thrupp, *The Merchant Class in Medieval London*). If the documents show us nothing about the poet, they do show us the man moving easily in the court circles to which he belonged.

Nevertheless, for Chaucer's literary biography, for the significant record of the writer and man, we are dependent entirely on his works. Certainly the works can not be used as autobiography (as George Kane has shown). As Kittredge implied in his complaint about those who use the works in this way—'They are determined to take his jesting seriously'—one must not confuse the narrator with the author. Yet it is because of his works that we have some idea of what Chaucer looked like (the portraits in the Ellesmere Manuscript and the Corpus Christi College Manuscript of *Troilus*). Through his works we know something of his friendships, especially with Gower (recently studied by John H.

Fisher in *John Gower: Friend of Chaucer*). And, as Donald Howard has shown, from his works we can learn something of 'Chaucer the Man,' perhaps even of his personality (as Edward Wagenknecht attempts in *Chaucer's Personality*). In addition to the factual summaries of Chaucer's life to be found in most editions, we do have some literary biographies—Marchette Chute's popular *Geoffrey Chaucer of England* and D. S. Brewer's more critical *Chaucer*—and Martin M. Crow is now preparing a full scale biography based on his and the late Clair Olson's work on the *Chaucer Life Records*. Certainly a full literary biography which would add flesh to the Life Records by judicious use of the works is one of our most obvious needs.

V *Learning*

Chaucer's learning—his intellectual and literary interests—must likewise be inferred from his works, for we know nothing of his education (Plimpton's interesting *Chaucer's Education* is necessarily based on informed guess-work) and the only record of his reading is to be found in the traces it left in his poems. Though there have been many scattered articles on Chaucer's intellectual interests (such as R. W. V. Elliott's 'Chaucer's Reading'), there has been no thorough study since Lounsbury's still valuable chapter on 'The Learning of Chaucer.' One of Lounsbury's main tasks was to refute the extravagant claims of Chaucer's early admirers, such as Dryden, who regarded him as 'perfect in all sciences,' and he zestfully proved that Chaucer was often imperfect, much given to inexactitude and misquotation. Certainly from the standpoint of a modern scholar, with his easy access to libraries, dictionaries, and good editions, Chaucer was at best inexact, often preferring a French pony to a Latin or Italian original, even, as R. A. Pratt discovered, possibly leaning on a French version of *Il Filostrato*. Moreover, as Pratt showed in another essay, our ignorance of the manuscript sources Chaucer actually used often leads to misunderstanding, and we either condemn him for errors because he did not have a modern text or praise him for obscure learning when he was actually using some popular *florilegia*.

However, even with low marks because of carelessness and reliance on secondary sources and textbooks, the translator of Boethius, the first philosophical work in Middle English, the author of the *Astrolabe*, the first scientific treatise in English, and the first English admirer of Italian literature was obviously a man of unusually wide intellectual interests, well read in literary works and in 'all this newe science that men lere' (PF, 22).

Furthermore, Chaucer uses his learning in his poetry, not in the older encyclopaedic way of a Jean de Meun or a Gower—a method he comically rejects in *The House of Fame*, where Geoffrey simply refuses to listen to the eagle's lecture on elementary astronomy, 'For I am now to old' (HF, 995). Instead, he makes his intellectual concerns part of the fabric of his verse. His interest in Boethius (last thoroughly studied by B. L. Jefferson in *Chaucer and the Consolation of Philosophy*) leads not only to his translation but to the infusion of Boethian ideas, attitudes, and even whole passages in works such as *Troilus* and 'The Knight's Tale'. Likewise, his ideas about history (studied by Morton W. Bloomfield in 'Chaucer's Sense of History') affect the shape of his works and even the stance of his narrator, as Bloomfield showed in his important article on 'Distance and Predestination in *Troilus and Criseyde*.' And, however one feels about the recent emphasis (perhaps over-emphasis) on Chaucer as a religious poet, there is no doubt that he thoroughly knew the liturgy (Beverly Boyd's *Chaucer and the Liturgy* is a convenient compilation), deeply admired the lives of the saints (see 'Chaucer's Calender of Saints,' by G. H. Gerould), and had a command of religious and theological literature that led not only to 'The Parson's Tale' but to the delightful disputations of the Wife of Bath. The problem of whether Chaucer was, like so many of his friends, sympathetic to Wycliffe's views is still not entirely settled (discussed in R. S. Loomis' 'Was Chaucer a Laodicean?'), but most likely he was a loyal churchman. Attempts to connect him with a tradition of scepticism (Mary E. Thomas, *Chaucer and Medieval Skepticism*) have been unsuccessful, and, as Loomis showed in another essay, there is no basis for the old idea that he was some sort of modern free thinker.

Chaucer's scientific interests also deeply affected his work, and, as W. C. Curry demonstrated in his important *Chaucer and the Medieval Sciences*, medieval theories of medicine and physiognomy sometimes helped shape his descriptions and characterizations. His interest in alchemy produced 'The Canon's Yeoman's Tale' (fully discussed by Edgar H. Duncan) and may have affected 'The Second Nun's Tale' as well (as argued by Joseph E. Grennen). His interest in animal lore, as Beryl Rowland shows, affected many of his poems and his interest in astronomy is apparent throughout his works. The astronomical passages are especially difficult for the modern reader not only because the world view of which it was a part has disappeared (the first chapter of Lowes' *Geoffrey Chaucer and the Development of his Genius* is a great help, as is C. S. Lewis' *The Discarded Image*) but because the astronomical references are unusually detailed and very technical. These have been studied by J. D. North ('Kalendres Enlumined Ben They'), a thorough discussion which should, however, be read in conjunction with H. M. Smyser's fine essay on 'Chaucer's View of Astronomy.' Chauncy Wood's *Chaucer and the Country of the Stars* is an ambitious attempt to show the thematic and metaphoric implications of the astronomical references and contains an especially interesting discussion of *The Complaint of Mars*. Such studies show that though Chaucer may not have been 'perfect in all sciences', he was perfect enough (as John Leyerle has shown) to joke about scientific theories, and some knowledge of medieval science is essential for the full understanding of his work.

VI *Sources*

Chaucer's literary interests have been more fully studied, for an emphasis on sources and analogues characterized much nineteenth and twentieth-century scholarship. Frequently the interest centred on ultimate sources and the histories of the plots, and the Chaucer Society *Originals and Analogues* contains many remote Eastern analogues that reflect this concern. This interest survives in Chaucer studies (as shown by Sigmund Eisner's *A Tale of Wonder: The Sources of the Wife of Bath's Tale*) but most scholars today are more interested in how Chaucer used his immediate sources, the sort of study exemplified in C. S. Lewis' 'What Chaucer Really Did to *Il Filostrato*' and in J. Burke Severs' *The Literary Relations of Chaucer's Clerk's Tale*. Bryan and Dempster's *Sources and Analogues of the Canterbury Tales*, an essential work, is likewise based on this principle, and the texts in this volume are restricted mainly to immediate sources.

Immediate rather than ultimate sources have always concerned students of the minor poems, since, apart from *The Romaunt of the Rose* (printed alongside its French source in Sutherland's edition), the more important minor works are not based on single sources. The chapters by Kittredge and Lowes on *The Book of the Duchess* set forth the sources of that work in some detail, and two impressive volumes by J. A. W. Bennett—*Chaucer's Book of Fame* and *The Parlement of Foules*—provide thorough expositions of the literary background of those works. *The Legend of Good Women* has been studied in a more scattered fashion and has received less attention in recent years, and the chapter in Root's *The Poetry of Chaucer* is still the best comprehensive survey of the poem's sources.

It is unfortunate that the sources of the minor poems have not been gathered in a volume of 'sources and analogues' (Brewer supplies this, on a small scale, for *The Parlement of Foulys* in his edition), for there would be no better introduction to Chaucer's literary milieu. It is unfortunate too that more of Chaucer's analogues have not been translated, since undergraduates with a command of the necessary languages are becoming increasingly rare. There is a good new translation (by Charles Dahlberg) of the *Romaunt de la Rose*. The major analogues of *Troilus*—Boccaccio's *Filostrato* and Benoit's *Roman de Troie*—are translated in R. K. Gordon's *The Story of Troilus*, where they are printed along with Skeat's text of Chaucer's poem. The sources of most of the fabliaux are translated in Benson and Andersson's *The Literary Context of Chaucer's Fabliaux*, and the sources of some of the other tales are translated or summarized in French's *A Chaucer Handbook*. For the most part, however, the study of Chaucer's use of his sources is restricted to scholars, and even they are hampered by the lack of reliable texts, especially since the texts known to Chaucer frequently differ from those available in modern editions. The Chaucer Group of the Modern Language Association of America has long planned to remedy this with the publication of a 'Chaucer Library,' editions of texts based on the manuscript versions known to Chaucer, and this series, under the general editorship of Robert E. Lewis, is now being published by the University of Georgia Press.

In recent years there has been less interest in finding specific sources (most of which are now known) and more attention to how Chaucer used his experience of particular writers and literary traditions. Along with Shannon's *Chaucer and the Roman Poets*, still the most comprehensive study, we now have R. L. Hoffman's *Ovid and the Canterbury Tales*, an attempt to show how Chaucer's reading of Ovid shaped his conception of the *Tales*. In addition to D. S. Fansler's still useful *Chaucer and the Roman de la Rose* and Haldeen Braddy's *Chaucer and the French Poet Graunson*, we now have W. I. Wimsatt's *Chaucer and the French Love Poets*, a careful study of Chaucer's early use of his French reading, and Charles Muscatine's *Chaucer and the French Tradition*, a brilliant demonstration of the critical uses to which the older 'source' and 'influence' studies can be put. One wishes we had a similar book on the Italian tradition; for this we must make do with studies of Chaucer's relation to particular writers, such as Cummings's book on Chaucer's debt to Boccaccio and Schless' more recent study of Chaucer and Dante, or with general surveys, such as Mario Praz' 'Chaucer and the Great Italian Writers of the Trecento.' The best treatments are in studies of particular works, such as the books by Bennett and some parts of Koonce's *Chaucer and the Tradition of Fame*.

Until recently, the English tradition remained largely unexplored territory. That Chaucer had a full command of English colloquial diction was well known (though seldom studied—Schlauch's essay is the only extended treatment), and critics such as Speirs, Muscatine, and, more recently, Ian Robinson in his *Chaucer and the English Tradition*, have noted the artistry of Chaucer's use of common speech. That Chaucer might also have made artistic use of the English literary tradition was seldom considered by earlier critics. That he knew the tradition well is clear not only from 'Sir Thopas' (studied by Laura Hibbard Loomis in her article on that tale in *Sources and Analogues*) but from his occasional use of alliterative lines (noted by Dorothy Everett in 'Chaucer's Good Ear') and of what E. T. Donaldson calls, in the title of his important article, 'The Idiom of Popular Poetry in The Miller's Tale.' The most promising approach to the study of this tradition is Brewer's 'The Relation of Chaucer to the English and European Traditions,' in which a comparison of the opening lines of *The Book of the Duchess* both to its French source and to contemporary English romances shows how much Chaucer owes to the formulas and diction of the English tradition.

VII   *Fourteenth Century Life and Culture*

Finally, scholars have laboured for years to provide a sense of Chaucer's relation to the life and general culture of fourteenth-century England, so that we can understand (to borrow the title of Brewer's useful guide) *Chaucer in His Time*. Early works, such as Coulton's still useful *Chaucer and His England*, have been richly supplemented by more recent works, such as Edith Rickert's valuable collection of contemporary materials (*Chaucer's World*), the much briefer collection in Helaine Newstead's *Chaucer's Contemporaries*, and D. W. Robertson's fine study of *Chaucer's London*. The work of scholars such as J. M. Manly did not, as they had hoped, uncover convincing real-life models for each of the Canterbury pilgrims, but it did bring to the text a wealth of illuminating information from contemporary life. Muriel Bowden's *A Commentary on the General Prologue*, which summarizes much of this material (along with much else) makes fascinating and rewarding reading.

Today—perhaps because of modern printing techniques—scholars have emphasized especially the importance of medieval art to our understanding of Chaucer's time, with a consequent broadening of perspective and the attempt—reflected in the titles—to comprehend the world in which he lived. Rickert's *Chaucer's World* (which contains many plates) was followed by Loomis's *A Mirror of Chaucer's World* (the best of this genre), Hussey's *Chaucer's World*, Serailler's *Chaucer and His World*, Halliday's *Chaucer and His World*, and there is even an Italian *Chaucer e il suo mondo* (by Aurelio Zanco; Turin, 1955; it is, however, a work of general criticism).

The new interest in medieval iconography, strengthened by the solid chapter (and excellent illustrations) in D. W. Robertson's *A Preface to Chaucer*, extends beyond the use of the arts for illustration to an attempt to understand the broader aesthetic relations between the art of Chaucer's time and his own poetry. Robert M. Jordan's *Chaucer and the Shape of Creation* considers this problem in his discussion of Chaucer's ideas of aesthetic form in relation to the forms and theory of architecture in the later Middle Ages. The art of music has received somewhat less attention, though the long-playing record has now made even late medieval music widely available. Clair C. Olson's article on 'Chaucer and the Music of the Middle Ages' is the most thorough examination of the subject, though some of the most interesting pages in Preston's *Chaucer* emphasize the importance of musical forms to Chaucer's early verse.

For obvious reasons, most of the documentary and illustrative material is focused upon *The Canterbury Tales*. In the case of *Troilus*, past scholars found the most important background material in the doctrine of 'courtly love.' W. G. Dodd's *Courtly Love in Chaucer and Gower* defined the concept as it was first used in Chaucerian criticism and helped place the *De Arte honesti amandi* by Andreas Capellanus on countless students' reading lists (usually in J. J. Parry's translation), but it was C. S. Lewis' treatment of the subject in his deservedly famous *Allegory of Love* that convinced most students and critics that love in Chaucer is characterized in an almost programmatic way by 'Humility, Courtesy, Adultery, and the Religion of Love.' Now we are witnessing a powerful reaction against this idea. E. T. Donaldson and D. W. Robertson, who seldom agree on interpretative matters, both flatly reject the received doctrine, Donaldson in an essay called 'The Myth of Courtly Love' and Robertson in an even more explicitly titled essay, 'The Concept of Courtly Love as an Impediment to the Understanding of Medieval Texts.' Robertson's work was part of a symposium on Courtly Love held at the State University of New York at Binghamton, at which one of the participants, the historian John F. Benton (whose article on 'The Court of Champagne as a Literary Center' destroyed many previously unquestioned assumptions about the historical relations of Andreas and Marie) concluded his survey of the historical evidence: 'As currently employed, "courtly love" has no useful meaning, and it is not worth saving by redefinition. I would therefore like to propose that "courtly love" be banned from all future conferences.' Some of us might prefer to ban all future conferences, but that will not happen, and one suspects that somehow 'courtly love' will remain a concern of Chaucerians, perhaps even more in the future than in the past as we attempt, if not to redefine it, at least to find some suitable substitute. As Lowes showed long ago, 'The Loveres Maladye of Heroides' actually did exist, though it has now gone the way of the vapours, and the symbolic gestures and traditional attitudes of Chaucer's lovers are, as Steadman demonstrates, part of a convention of literary conduct—of rhetoric if not of life—that must be understood. That Chaucer's ideas of literary conduct were more complex than Dodd or even Lewis might have granted is now clear (from the studies of Bennett, Howard, and others), but our understanding of what they were is still incomplete.

VIII   *Interpretative Criticism*

This effort to consider Chaucer in the cultural context of his own time
has become one of the dominant emphases in interpretative criticism
since the Second World War. The interpretation of Chaucer is a field
too vast for any but the most general survey. A detailed account of critical opinion on even one of the Canterbury pilgrims (of the sort Florence
Ridley supplied for the Prioress) would take more pages than this whole
chapter. I can therefore attempt only a general survey of the more
important trends in Chaucer criticism—a procedure I realize is both
unfairly selective and bound to distort, for the best critics are eclectic in
method and do not fit easily into schools or trends. Even the chronological approach I shall use is misleading, for the best critics are still read with
profit and delight (as the many reprints show) long after younger critics
with other approaches have come to dominate, so far as new publication
is concerned. The reader will therefore easily recognize the crude over-
simplification in this scheme: Criticism of Chaucer began in this century
('appreciation' rather than 'criticism' characterized earlier work), and
was dominated by American scholars such as Kittredge, Lowes, and
Root until the late thirties or early forties. Then, beginning mainly in
England, came the 'New Critical' phase and at the same time, in both
England and Germany, appeared a new sort of historical study. We
now seem to have passed fully into this 'New Historical' period, dominated by what Helaine Newstead calls 'the two R's of modern criticism,
Rhetoric and Religion.'

It may seem paradoxical to label contemporary criticism 'New Historical,' for we live in a time that seems increasingly determined to
ignore history, and literary history—the study of sources, influences,
and biographical problems—has always been a major concern of Chaucerian scholars. But those earlier historical critics managed to keep their
historical studies and their critical judgements neatly compartment-
alized. As we have noted, in the late nineteenth and early twentieth
centuries the 'simple,' 'naïve' Chaucer was replaced by Chaucer the
genial master of realism. The fashion was to divide his literary biography
into the early French period, in which he imitated French love poetry,

the middle Italian period, in which the example of Italian renaissance literature liberated him from French allegorizing ('A time of originality,' Kittredge wrote), and the culminating English period, in which he freed himself from bookish conventions and 'His genius turned to English life and English character' (Kittredge, p. 27). The early works could be studied from the standpoint of literary history, but that was of little use to the study of the later works, which concerned 'life' directly. 'There is even a sort of paradox in it,' Chesterton mused, 'that in his vigorous youth, he was formal; in his comparatively crippled and limited old age he was free. . . . We see him gradually breaking those flowery chains of his youth and then living to sow such wonderful wild oats in his old age' (p. 114).

Paradoxical as it may have seemed, the scheme was powerfully attractive to teachers in the newly formed English departments of the time. It was as if Chaucer himself epitomized the whole course of English literature from medieval conventionalism to renaissance originality to modern realism. And, as persuasively argued by Kittredge in *Chaucer and His Poetry* (still one of the few indispensible books of criticism), Chaucer's poetic career was crowned with the two major genres of later English literature, *Troilus*, 'an elaborate psychological novel,' and the drama of *The Canterbury Tales*, 'a human comedy, in which the pilgrims are the *dramatis personae*.'

Whatever the validity of these assumptions, they produced, and still produce, first-rate criticism. The works of scholars such as Kittredge, as Burrow notes, mark the beginning of 'academic' criticism, as distinguished from the work of nineteenth-century scholars, many of whom (like Furnivall) had no regular university appointments. But it was also a 'public' sort of criticism, and some of the most famous critical books of the time—Kittredge's *Chaucer and His Poetry*, Manly's *New Light on Chaucer*, Lowes' *Geoffrey Chaucer and the Development of His Poetry*—were originally series of public lectures, often given in a university setting but intended for audiences more general than a classroom affords and based on the assumption that Chaucer is a poet accessible to any lover of poetry. Contemporary criticism, even the most 'literary' sort, is far more often narrowly technical and academic. The type of criticism that scholars like Kittredge employed—an emphasis on Chaucer's realism, on his dramatic form of expression, on his geniality and common sense—is the sort that lends itself to public delivery, to broad generalization rather

than close analysis (which these scholars reserved for their articles), and
the virtues of this type of criticism—clarity, urbanity, tact—are those of
a good public lecture. We are fortunate this was the case; Chaucer's
popularity is due in large measure to this sort of criticism, and many of
the best critics of Chaucer have continued this 'public' tradition. B. H.
Bronson's *In Search of Chaucer* and Charles Muscatine's recent *Poetry and
Crisis in The Age of Chaucer* were also series of public lectures, and E. T.
Donaldson entitled his collection of essays (many of which were first
delivered as lectures) *Speaking of Chaucer*.

Kittredge and his contemporaries regarded Chaucer himself as a
'public' poet, speaking clearly and directly to all his audiences, those of
the present century as well as the fourteenth. This idea, with its
corollary, that interpretation of Chaucer depends mainly on an informed, sympathetic reading of the text itself, powerfully affected criticism in the decades that followed. So did many other positions of these
critics, who defined the problems and suggested the solutions for a whole
generation. Kittredge stressed Chaucer's artistry, his mastery of literary
form ('We are dealing with a poet who had been through the schools')
and the fact that '*Chaucer always knew what he was about*' and therefore
every detail, rightly considered, will 'fall into decorous subordination
to his main design.' This has sometimes been challenged (notably by
Paull F. Baum), but it is the basis of countless essays on the 'unity' of the
various works, and it had the effect of focusing critical disputes upon the
texts themselves.

Kittredge's appreciation of Chaucer's irony foreshadowed much of
the more recent discussions of this subject (which began with Germaine
Dempster's *Dramatic Irony in Chaucer*), and his discussion of the narrator
in *The Book of the Duchess*, his warning against the 'confusion between
the artist and the man,' contained the suggestion that has been developed
in more recent studies of Chaucer's narrative stance. His emphasis on
Chaucer's realism is now somewhat out of favour (temporarily, I suspect), but his psychological approach to *Troilus* still dominates criticism,
and his idea of Troilus as novel is still with us (as in Spearing's essay on
'Chaucer as Novelist'). Finally, his theory of the dramatic character of
The Canterbury Tales is still powerful. R. S. Lumiansky's *Of Sondry Folk* is
a demonstration that the theory is viable even in today's critical climate,
and few contemporary critics, however they might differ with earlier
scholars on other matters, would completely reject it.

From our vantage point, there are obvious flaws in the critical position represented by Kittredge, Root, and others of their generation. The emphasis on the 'realism' and 'originality' of Chaucer's mature poetry sometimes led to a tendency to undervalue the conventional and traditional elements in his work and to a determination to praise (and to discover) whatever seemed innovative. Most of the lyrics received relatively little attention (and are still too much ignored, as Edmund Reiss showed in his article 'Dusting Off the Cobwebs: A Look at Chaucer's Lyrics'), and even works such as *The House of Fame* and *The Parliament of Fowls* were sometimes treated with more condescension than admiration, either as early experiments redeemed with occasional bits of the humour and realism that characterize the mature works or as *romans à clef* and thus redeemed by 'realism,' even if at second remove. The assumption that these works are primarily imitative did allow critics to study them from the standpoint of sources and influences. Lowes, in *Geoffrey Chaucer and the Development of His Genius* discusses the early works with great verve, combining his zest for source studies with his sound critical judgement—a method he largely abandons in his discussion of *Troilus* and *The Canterbury Tales*, where he follows the fashion of stressing 'life' rather than books.

The 'New Critics' of Chaucer—the generation that reached maturity in the thirties and forties (and made its influence felt most strongly in the fifties)—simply continued the work of Kittredge and his contemporaries, for, like Kittredge, they focused firmly upon the text and assumed that Chaucer shared their own literary values. They differed from their predecessors mainly in having a new set of values. A generation that admired Joyce's fiction, Yeats' poetry, and the critical doctrines in I. A. Richards' *Practical Criticism* and T. S. Eliot's *Tradition and the Individual Poetic Talent* could not regard 'realism' as the highest literary value, was inclined to respect rather than scorn 'tradition,' and found the touchstone of poetic merit in 'complexity.' The 'complexity' that was most admired was 'poetic,' a matter of diction and metaphoric structure, rather than 'narrative,' plot and characterization, and even when these critics carried on lines of interpretation that had been suggested by their predecessors, they notably shifted the focus. Germaine Dempster had followed Kittredge in stressing the 'dramatic' irony of the tales; critics such as A. W. Hoffman and Earle Birney emphasize diction, allusion, and metaphoric structure. Kittredge had stressed the distinction between narrator and author, but now the New Critical Approach to poems as autonomous art objects, distinct from their makers, allowed for a new systematic interpretation of Chaucer's narrative stance from the standpoint of a Swiftian *persona*, the 'Chaucer the Pilgrim' of Donaldson's famous essay. Kittredge's theory that every detail will 'fall into decorous subordination to his main design' was applied not just to plot and character but to the symbolic structure of the tales (as in John Speirs' discussion of 'The Nun's Priest's Tale' in *Chaucer the Maker*), and the expected unity was found more often in theme than in action, as in Ralph Baldwin's widely influential *The Unity of The Canterbury Tales*.

The New Criticism began in England, mainly with Speirs, and has remained strong there, shaping to some degree the works of critics such as A. C. Spearing and John Lawlor and recently producing a number of almost pure *explications de textes*, such as Trevor Whitock's abstemiously ahistorical *A Reading of The Canterbury Tales*, Hoy and Stevens' *Chaucer's Major Tales*, and Ian Robinson's somewhat more historical *Chaucer and the English Tradition*. Usually, however, the techniques of practical criticism are combined with some sort of historical scholarship, either directly, as when Sanford Meech used close analysis along with a careful source study in *Design in Chaucer's Troilus*, or (more often) indirectly, as in the works of critics such as E. T. Donaldson, A. C. Spearing, or Donald Howard, who bring to their analyses an impressive command of literary-historical materials. Raymond Preston's *Chaucer*, one of the first and best of the New Critical books, was New Critical in its techniques of analysis and in the criteria by which the poetry was judged, but it was also a widely learned demonstration of the relevance of the cultural and literary context to our understanding of the works. The success of this work and others that used the tools of New Criticism, such as Muscatine's *Chaucer and the French Tradition*, was a convincing demonstration to those for whom 'complexity' is the prime poetic virtue that a combination of historical scholarship with a sophisticated method of textual analysis yields a richer and more complex reading than does analysis alone.

Moreover, and in this the new generation of critics most significantly differed from their predecessors, the abandonment of 'realism' and 'originality' as tests of literary merit allowed them to appreciate the medieval elements in Chaucer's work. *Troilus*, as Karl Young showed, is more medieval romance than modern novel, and C. S. Lewis's influential *The*

Allegory of Love placed Chaucer's poems in a context of psychological and amatory verse extending back to classical antiquity, with an emphasis on Chaucer's development within the tradition rather than any attempt to break away from it. Critics of Chaucer, taught much about medieval conventions by works such as Curtius' *European Literature and the Latin Middle Ages*, were now not only willing to admire convention but to seek it out in that former temple of realism, 'The General Prologue', which J. V. Cunningham demonstrated ('The Literary Form of the Prologue to the Canterbury Tales') opens with a passage based on the form of the Dream Vision, a genre that earlier scholars thought Chaucer had left behind in his youth.

The new tolerance of medieval forms led to a new appreciation of the fabliaux. Curiously, Chaucer's most realistic works were seldom discussed by those critics who most prized his realism. Certainly they appreciated Chaucer's humour, but even as late as H. R. Patch's *On Rereading Chaucer* (1939) one could write a whole book on Chaucer's humour with only the barest mentions of the fabliaux. They are comic and diverting but not, so it was believed, the stuff of literature. Root thought it unfortunate that Chaucer included the '"cherles tales," which no sophistry can elevate into true art' (p. 176). W. W. Lawrence's *Chaucer and The Canterbury Tales* (1950) was the first extended discussion of the artistry of the fabliaux, which Lawrence regarded as Chaucer's favourite and most successful form. Muscatine's demonstration that the realistic style of the fabliaux is itself a literary convention allowed critics to recognize a further dimension in these tales, and Per Nykrog's proof (in *Les Fabliaux*) that the fabliaux were courtly in origin and audience showed that these tales deserved a more respectful scrutiny. They are now receiving their due. T. W. Craik's *The Comic Tales of Chaucer* and Janette Richardson's *Blameth Not Me* provide instructive analyses, and interpretations of the whole *Canterbury Tales*, such as Helen Corsa's *Chaucer: Poet of Mirth and Morality* and Paul Ruggier's fine book *The Artistry of The Canterbury Tales*, now take full account of the interplay of the fabliaux with the tales of 'sentence' and 'moralitee.'

The new sympathy for medieval literary forms was accompanied by a new sympathy for medieval ideas. The modern study of the history of ideas, beginning in the late thirties and early forties with works such as A. O. Lovejoy's *The Great Chain of Being* (Cambridge, 1936), fostered a respectful relativism toward the ideas of past times, and works such as

Morton Bloomfield's *The Seven Deadly Sins* showed not only that medieval ideas had histories but that an understanding of that history can often illuminate a text (as Bloomfield demonstrated in his essay on *Troilus*). Critics began to interpret Chaucer's poems from specifically medieval standpoints (as in A. L. Kellogg's 'An Augustinian Interpretation of Chaucer's Pardoner' and R. S. Lumiansky's 'Chaucer's Philosophical Knight,' a Boethian interpretation of 'The Knight's Tale') and to stress, as does D. W. Robertson (to whom we must return) the importance of medieval religious thought. In the case of *The House of Fame* and *The Parliament of Fowls* interpretations from the standpoint of medieval thought are now dominant, whether in the exegetical style of Robertson and Huppé (*Fruyt and Chaf*) or Koonce (*Chaucer and the Tradition of Fame*) or the more literary and less dogmatic method of Brewer (in the introduction to his edition of *The Parliament*) or Bennett, who concludes his discussion of Love in *The Parliament* with the assertion—which almost all critics would now accept, however they might interpret it—'The doctrines can be separated from the poetry no more easily than the bouquet from the wine' (p. 186).

Finally, during the thirties critics began the sympathetic examination of Chaucer's rhetoric, which has become so important today. The older view, as expressed in Manly's famous lecture 'Chaucer and the Rhetoricians,' regarded Chaucer's stylistic development as 'a process of gradual release from the astonishingly artificial and sophisticated art with which he began and the gradual replacement of formal rhetorical devices by methods of composition based upon close observation of life and the exercise of the creative imagination' (p. 271). Closer examination showed that this was not true. Traugott Naunin (who shared Manly's distaste for rhetorical devices) demonstrated that the later works had as many rhetorical adornments as the earlier. This (and other studies, such as Marie P. Hamilton's suggestive article) raised the question of whether the earlier works had only the 'thin prettiness' of which Manly complained and whether the later might owe some of the stylistic strength Manly admired to the devices of rhetoric. Wolfgang Clemen, in his fine *Chaucer's Early Poetry*, showed that Chaucer's adaptation of 'the French mode of composition' with its heavy rhetorical flavour created not a thin prettiness but solid poetic structures. Dorothy Everett in 'Some Reflections on Chaucer's "Art Poetical"' showed that in the later poems Chaucer became not less rhetorical but more skilful; he learned to use the rhetorical devices not as appended ornamentation but as part of the fabric of his verse. The new attitude was clear in the prominent position rhetoric received even in introductory books, such as Neville Coghill's pamphlet, *Geoffrey Chaucer*, and its value was shown by the use that more recent critics have made of Chaucer's rhetorical devices.

In these later studies there is little interest in the old business of counting and classifying figures and tropes, which had seemed so important to Manly and Naunin. The difficulty with the quantitative approach is that rhetoric is a descriptive system; one can use it, like M. Jourdain's prose, without knowing it. Moreover, J. J. Murphy has shown that we know very little about Chaucer's rhetorical training, and we assume too easily that he knew exactly those texts printed by ·Faral in Faral's *Les Arts poétiques du xiie et du xiiie siècle* (Paris, 1923) and summarized by Atkins in his *English Literary Criticism: The Medieval Phase* (Cambridge, 1963). Critics of today tend to use rhetoric rather as a means of defining a mode of composition, as does Geoffrey Shepherd in his fine study of *Troilus*; in Payne's important book *The Key of Remembrance*, rhetorical doctrines are used as a means of defining Chaucer's basic ideas of poetry and aesthetics.

Such attempts to define Chaucer's poetics from the standpoint of his own time, now the dominant concern in criticism, mark the end of both the old and New Criticisms. The old 'realistic' assumptions had an obvious basis in fact: Chaucer's representational style does have a marvelously realistic effect that helps build the richly dramatic texture of his mature works. The validity of these assumptions was not disproven when critics like Malone demonstrated the artificiality of the pilgrims but when Muscatine, in *Chaucer and the French Tradition*, showed the inadequacy of the idea that realism was an end in itself for Chaucer. The style of 'bourgeois realism,' Muscatine demonstrated, has an artistic function that we miss if we concentrate solely on the 'realism' and ignore its interplay with the non-representational 'courtly' style that Chaucer also commands. Likewise, the New Critical analysis of complexities, ambiguities, and tensions still produces good criticism (such as Gordon's study of ambiguity in *Troilus*), for Chaucer is a complex, often ironic and ambivalent writer, and we must all be, to some extent, New Critics. But, as Muscatine also showed, these too are part of a more general characteristic of Chaucer's work, the aesthetic expression of his relation to 'the international, Gothic tradition' that underlies the 'typically medieval

dialectic that finds its last great synthesis in Chaucer's capacious poetry'
(p. 10).

Muscatine's emphasis on style, on clusters of related effects and
devices, showed a way to use close critical analysis in Chaucerian narrative; New Criticism had been developed mainly for the analysis of lyric
verse and could never quite be reconciled with Chaucer's orally delivered narrative and its consequently loose verbal style. Muscatine's
emphasis on the effect produced by the Gothic juxtaposition of courtly
and realistic elements also provided a means of understanding Chaucer's
poetic structures, which do not fit easily with modern, New (and old)
Critical ideas about organic unity. Certainly Muscatine found contemporary value in Chaucer's work (it has these or we would not so gladly
read it) but the main thrust of his argument was toward understanding its
stylistic and poetic qualities in the context of its own time.

Muscatine had concentrated almost solely on the French tradition (his
essay on '*The Canterbury Tales*: The Style of the Man and the Style of the
Work' expands the scope) and his focus is almost purely literary. The
consideration of Chaucer within the context of medieval literature continues to be a main preoccupation of critics such as Robert Payne, whose
Key of Remembrance, as we have noted, provides an approach to Chaucer
from the standpoint of medieval rhetorical and literary theory. Other
critics, such as Jordan (*Chaucer and the Shape of Creation*) have attempted
to expand the perspective and to deal with Chaucer in the context of a
more general medieval aesthetic. Jordan's demonstration that Chaucer
knew and to some extent practised a theory of 'inorganic structure' is an
important contribution to the continuing effort to consider Chaucer's
works from the standpoint of medieval rather than modern ideas about
art. The next step—already taken by Muscatine in his most recent book
—is to broaden the perspective even further and to consider Chaucer not
as a fourteenth-century writer but as a writer in the fourteenth century,
reacting to the life of his time as well as its literature and art.

The most thorough attempt to place Chaucer firmly within a medieval frame of reference is D. W. Robertson's *A Preface to Chaucer*, the most
controversial and one of the most important books on Chaucer in the
post-war period. Robertson, basing his argument on theological and
exegetical writings and on the evidence of medieval iconography,
argues for a radical difference between fourteenth- and twentieth-century aesthetics, a difference not in degree but in kind. All serious

medieval literature, he claims, is didactic rather than mimetic, static, and serenely free of tensions and ambiguities, for all medieval literature is, like the Bible, designed to promote Charity (*caritas*) and condemn Cupidity (*cupiditas*). If a work does not obviously serve this end, it is an 'allegory,' with a 'kernel' of truth concealed beneath a 'husk' that must be stripped away with the tools of biblical exegesis. Robertson presents his case with great learning, surveying biblical exegesis from Augustine's *De Doctrina Christiana* (the basic text) through the *Glossa Ordinaria* and beyond and showing the use of these techniques in the interpretation of secular (specifically classical) literature from Fulgentius to Boccaccio's *De Geneologia Deorum Gentilium*. His most impressive body of evidence is drawn from his survey of medieval iconography and his demonstration of the frequent relevance of iconographical conventions to literary texts.

The *furore* raised by Robertson's arguments has yet to subside. It began in scattered articles (such as Morton Bloomfield's 'Symbolism in Medieval Literature'), was developed at length by E. T. Donaldson (who attacked) and R. E. Kaske (who defended a moderate exegetical position) at the English Institute in New York in 1958, and has continued since in reviews and articles (notably by F. L. Utley and A. Leigh DeNeef).

The *furore* might have been less—and the impact of Robertson's ideas more immediate—if he had claimed less for his method. That much medieval literature draws on allegorical conventions is doubtless true, and Robertson's works, along with Rosamund Tuve's impressive *Allegorical Imagery*, show that this fact cannot be ignored. Likewise, most medieval literature (like that of other times) praises virtue and condemns vice. Some medieval works—*El Libro de buen amor*, for example —even promote *caritas* in an explicitly exegetical manner. But it does not follow that all medieval poetry is written in this way. The application of the allegorical method is a discipline of faith rather than criticism; as Boccaccio advised, 'You must persevere . . . If one way does not lead to the desired meaning, take another' (Robertson, 33; similar advice is quoted in Judson Allen, *The Friar as Literary Critic*). Given the indices of the *Patrologia Latina*, the convenient exegetical principle that anything can mean its opposite ('in bono' or 'in malo'), and the ease with which any two sufficiently generalized polarities can be found in any narrative (order and disorder, appearance and reality, yin and yang), not all that much perseverance is needed. All reductionist criticism 'works,' and *Tom Sawyer* (as John Halverson showed) yields the desired meaning as easily as Genesis.

The validity of such an interpretation—and in this case the claim that it is the only valid interpretation—must therefore rest on historical proof drawn from the context in which the work was written. We know that in Chaucer's time not all works were scriptural allegories; some (usually the best) were 'endytinges of worldly vanitees,' and we have Chaucer's own testimony (in his 'Retraccioun') that almost all his major works were of this class. Chaucer knew as well as St Paul and Robertson that all should be written for 'oure doctine,' and he bitterly repented that works like *Troilus* and *The Canterbury Tales*, 'thilke that sounen into synne,' were not. Ordinarily a poet is not the best judge of his own works, but Robertson's theory assumes such a high degree of rationality and conscious design that we must accept the poet's own word and recognize that theology and literature were not the same even in the fourteenth century. But, as Robertson has taught us, we must not make the old error of assuming that literature is a completely autonomous activity, separate from religion and the other forces in the culture that helps produce it.

This, the emphasis on the importance of Chaucer's general cultural situation, is Robertson's main contribution to Chaucer studies, and I suspect that as his method is modified in practice (Huppé's *A Reading of the Canterbury Tales* is considerably less dogmatic than his and Robertson's earlier *Fruyt and Chaf*) his general influence will increase. Few responsible critics today would ignore the religious dimension of Chaucer's thought, even though, like Donald Howard in *The Three Temptations*, they may approach it from a 'non-Robertsonian' position. Likewise, future attempts to define Chaucer's aesthetic assumptions must (as Jordan did) take full account of, and learn from, Robertson's work. As Chaucer criticism moves even further into its new historical phase, the early chapters of *A Preface to Chaucer* (theory and background rather than application) may receive even more frequent and respectful attention.

I expect that criticism of Chaucer will become more historically oriented in the next few years. Certainly the close analysis of Chaucer's verse remains a major preoccupation among younger British critics, and Robertson's method of exegetical analysis is widely popular among younger Americans, in forms ever more Alexandrian in complexity; there will doubtless be more of both forms of criticism in the future. Yet,

Charles Muscatine's recent *Poetry and Crisis in the Age of Chaucer*, which may be as important in the next few years as *Chaucer and the French Tradition* has been in the past, seems more authentically of our own time than the closely analytical studies of both the exegetical and New Critical schools.

Muscatine starts from the proposition that 'The age of literary analysis—the New Criticism—seems to have reached a dead end.' This rings true not because the analytical techniques of the New Criticism are no longer useful (as Muscatine emphasizes, they remain essential for critics of whatever persuasion) but because the poetic values that they served—the ambiguities and tensions that were often taken as the goal of analysis—no longer seem to us the only values, just as the writers the New Critics admired, Joyce and Eliot, are no longer our contemporaries. The writers our time favours (and even the art forms—witness the cinema) are less private and 'literary' and more clearly public and 'social' in their response to the world around them. The great popularity in the West of contemporary Russian writers like Alexander Solshenitsyn, realistic in method and social in theme, seems indicative of the new mood, and in the next few years the critical climate, which seems always to reflect contemporary literary taste, will probably reflect this new mood. The new historical criticism that Muscatine advocates is stylistics, of the sort practised by Auerbach, with style studied not as Chaucer's solution to given literary problems (the main concern of the new historical critics thus far) but as a response to the world in which he lived. There has been a recent growth of interest in Chaucer as a poet responding to his own time, as in John Burrow's *Ricardian Poetry*. It seems very likely that we will see more such works in the future.

This can only be a guess. The criticism of Chaucer is, as I admitted at the beginning of this section, too large and lively a field to categorize, much less to predict. The only certainty is that criticism will continue as part of our necessary dialogue with the past and that, however it continues, no one critic or school of criticism will ever completely comprehend Chaucer. After all—but only after all the qualification of these many pages—Chesterton was right: 'Chaucer was a poet, and what matters is not books about Chaucer, but Chaucer.'

Chaucer: A Select Bibliography

L. D. BENSON

Note

Place of publication is London unless otherwise stated. The following abbreviations have been used.

ELH *English Literary History*
JEGP *Journal of English and Germanic Philology*
PMLA *Publications of the Modern Language Association of America*
RES *Review of English Studies*

THIS BIBLIOGRAPHY LISTS critical and scholarly works on Chaucer in roughly the order in which they are mentioned in the 'Reader's Guide.' A few additional works are listed, but the bibliography is selective. It lists only the more important of the older works, emphasizes books rather than articles in the listing of more recent work, and lists only a sampling of the numerous handbooks, elementary texts, and collections of criticism published in the past few years. Works that are especially suitable for beginning readers are marked with an asterisk.

Intro.A BIBLIOGRAPHY

Albert C. Baugh, *Chaucer*, Goldentree Bibliographies, New York 1968.
  Selected but full and useful.

Eleanor P. Hammond, *Chaucer: A Bibliographical Manual*, 1908. Rpt. 1933.
  Complete to 1908 (must be supplemented by Spurgeon for allusions and early discussions); most useful for full descriptions of early editions and reprints of early lives.

Dudley D. Griffith, *Bibliography of Chaucer: 1908–1953*. Seattle, Washington 1955.
  Continues Hammond; essential for the researcher.

William R. Crawford, *Bibliography of Chaucer: 1954–1963*. Seattle, Washington 1967.
  Continuation of Griffith; notable for good introductory essay on trends in criticism.

*David M. Zesmer, *Guide to English Literature: From Beowulf through Chaucer and Medieval Drama*, With Bibliographies by Stanley Greenfield. 'College Outline' series. New York 1961.
Greenfield's brief, well-annotated bibliography of Chaucer is the best introductory guide.
Rowland's *Companion to Chaucer Studies* (see p. 354, *Intro.E*) contains good bibliographies on selected subjects, and the full notes in Robinson's edition (*II.B*) contain excellent bibliographies to 1957.

Current bibliographies are published in the *PMLA Annual Bibliography*, the MHRA *Annual Bibliography of English Language and Literature*, and the English Association's *Year's Work in English Studies* (the most useful, since items are summarized and criticized). *Neuphilologische Mitteilungen* annually publishes a list of 'Works in Progress.'

Intro.B REVIEWS OF SCHOLARSHIP AND CRITICISM
*Albert C. Baugh, 'Fifty Years of Chaucer Scholarship,' *Speculum*, XXVI, 1951, 659–72.
Excellent survey of scholarship; little concern with interpretative criticism.
*Derek S. Brewer, 'The Criticism of Chaucer in the Twentieth Century,' in *Chaucer's Mind and Art (Intro.D)*.
Good supplement to Baugh, since criticism is the main concern.
Helaine Newstead, 'Chaucer's *Canterbury Tales*,' in J. Burke Severs, *Recent Middle English Scholarship and Criticism: Survey and Desiderata*. Pittsburgh, Pennsylvania 1971.
Brief survey of tendencies.
R. R. Purdy, 'Chaucer Scholarship in England and America: A Review of Recent Trends,' *Anglia*, LXX, 1952–381.
Florence Ridley, *The Prioress and Her Critics*. Berkeley 1965.
Good survey of criticism.
G. G. Sedgewick, 'The Progress of Chaucer's Pardoner, 1880–1940,' *MLQ*, I, 1940; rpt. in Schoeck and Taylor (*Intro.D*).
Still useful survey of critical ideas.
See also the introductory essay in Crawford's *Bibliography* (*Intro.A*); Most of the essays in Rowland's *Companion* (*Intro.E*) are excellent surveys of scholarship and critical opinion on particular subjects; Burrow's *Chaucer* (*Intro.C*) contains a stimulating introductory survey.

Intro.C REPUTATION

William L. Alderson and Arnold C. Henderson, *Chaucer and Augustan Scholarship*, Berkeley, 1970.

Chaucerian scholarship in the eighteenth century.

Earle Birney, 'Is Chaucer's Irony a Modern Discovery?' *JEGP*, XLI, 1942, 305–19.

Derek S. Brewer, 'Images of Chaucer,' in *Chaucer and Chaucerians* (*Intro.D*).

John A. Burrow, ed, *Geoffrey Chaucer: A Critical Anthology*. Harmondsworth 1969.

Contains generous and interesting collection of early opinion.

Caroline F. E. Spurgeon, *Five Hundred Years of Chaucer Criticism and Allusion: 1357–1900*, Cambridge 1925. 3 vol.

The basic work; a fascinating collection.

Intro.D COLLECTIONS OF CRITICISM

Derek S. Brewer, ed, *Chaucer and Chaucerians: Critical Studies in Middle English Literature*, London 1968.

Important collection of original articles.

A. C. Cawley, ed, *Chaucer's Mind and Art*, Edinburgh 1969.

Good collection of both original and reprinted essays.

Arno Esch, ed, *Chaucer und Seine Zeit*, Tübingen 1968.

Original essays.

*Richard J. Schoeck and Jerome Taylor, eds, *Chaucer Criticism*, I: *The Canterbury Tales*, Notre Dame, Indiana 1960. II: *Troilus and Criseyde and the Minor Poems*, 1961.

Excellent collection of reprints of standard articles.

See also Burrow (above) for a good collection of critical opinion in recent as well as early times.

Intro.E HANDBOOKS

*Robert D. French, *A Chaucer Handbook*, 2nd edn. New York 1947.

Though its bibliographies are now dated, this contains much useful information on dating, canon, and sources (many of which are translated or summarized).

*Beryl Rowland, ed, *Companion to Chaucer Studies*. Toronto 1968.

Excellent essays by various hands, with good bibliographies, on a variety of topics.

Maurice Hussey, A. C. Spearing, James Winney, *An Introduction to Chaucer*, Cambridge 1965.
Good introductory essays, though more elementary than either of the above.

I   *The Canon*

I.A   GENERAL STUDIES

Francis W. Bonner, 'The Genesis of the Chaucer Apocrypha,' *Studies in Philology*, XLVIII, 1951, 461–81.
Aage Brusendorff, *The Chaucer Tradition*, Oxford 1925. rpt. 1967.
Technical and intended for advanced students. Treats other matters as well.
Ethel Seaton, *Sir Richard Roos, c. 1410–1482: A Lancastrian Poet*, 1961.
Unconvincing attempt to credit Roos with a number of Chaucerian lyrics.
Walter W. Skeat, *The Chaucer Canon, With a Discussion of the Works Associated with the Name of Geoffrey Chaucer*, Oxford 1900.
Hammond (*Intro.A*) has good bibliographical accounts of the apocryphal pieces.

I.B   EDITIONS OF APOCRYPHAL WORKS

Russell A. Fraser, *The Court of Venus*, Durham, North Carolina 1955.
Contains a diplomatic edition of 'The Pilgrim's Tale.'
*Derek Pearsall, *The Flower and the Leaf and The Assembly of Ladies*, Nelson's 'Medieval and Renaissance' Library. 1962.
Walter W. Skeat, *Chaucerian and Other Pieces*, Oxford, 1897.
A supplementary (seventh) volume to his Oxford Chaucer (*II.B*); contains most of the Apocrypha.

I.C   DOUBTFUL WORKS

Ronald A. Sutherland, ed, *The Romaunt of the Rose and Le Roman de la Rose: A Parallel-Text Edition*, Oxford 1967.
Derek J. Price, ed, *The Equatorie of the Planetis*. With a Linguistic Analysis by R. M. Wilson, Cambridge 1955.
The review by Roland M. Smith (*JEGP*, LVII, 533–37) is a good discussion of the problems of attribution.

G. Herdon, 'Chaucer's Authorship of *The Equatorie of the Planetis*: The Use of Romance Vocabulary as Evidence,' *Language*, XXXII, 1956, 254–59.

Unconvincing (see Joyce Bazire in *Year's Work*, XXXVII, 100–1).

Margaret Schlauch, 'The Art of Chaucer's Prose' in *Chaucer and Chaucerians* (*Intro. D*).

Contains a note on the style of *The Equatorie*.

II *The Text*

II.A TEXTUAL STUDY

F. J. Furnivall *et al.*, eds, *The Six-Text Canterbury Tales*, Chaucer Society, 1868–1877. 8 parts. Rpt. 1967.

Transcriptions of the important manuscripts; for prints of other manuscripts see the full listing of the Chaucer Society publications in Hammond (*Intro. A*).

John M. Manly and Edith Rickert, eds, *The Text of the Canterbury Tales*, Chicago, 1940. 8 vol.

The basic work for serious textual analysis.

J. Mann, *Chaucer and Medieval Estates Satire*. Cambridge, 1973.

Charles A. Owen, Jr., 'The Design of *The Canterbury Tales*,' in *Companion to Chaucer Studies* (*Intro.E*).

Discussion and bibliography of controversy over ordering of the Tales, with his own proposal, differing from both Chaucer Society and Ellesmere orders.

Robert A. Pratt, 'The Order of the Canterbury Tales,' *PMLA*, XLVI, 1951, 1141–67.

Robert K. Root, *The Textual Tradition of Chaucer's Troilus*, Chaucer Society, 1916. Rpt. 1967.

II.B COMPLETE EDITIONS

Walter W. Skeat, ed, *The Complete Works of Geoffrey Chaucer*, Oxford, 1894. 6 vol.

The text of the Oxford Chaucer has been superseded, but the notes and discussions are still of great value.

*F. N. Robinson, ed, *The Works of Geoffrey Chaucer*, 2nd edn. Boston and London, 1957.

The standard text.

II.C SELECTED EDITIONS

*Albert C. Baugh, ed, *Chaucer's Major Poetry*, New York 1963.
   Contains almost all the verse, omitting only *Anelide and Arcite*, all but
   Prologue and Cleopatra of *Legend of Good Women*, a few lyrics, and
   Romaunt of the Rose. Excellent glosses.
*E. Talbot Donaldson, ed, *Chaucer's Poetry: An Anthology for the Modern
   Reader*, New York 1958.
   Less full than Baugh; regularized text. Extended discussions of the
   poems are outstanding.
Robert A. Pratt, ed, *Selections from the Tales of Canterbury and Short Poems*,
   Boston 1966.
   Most of the *Canterbury Tales* and a half dozen lyrics. Interesting for its
   text of the *Tales*.
Kenneth O. Kee, ed, *Geoffrey Chaucer: A Selection of His Works*, New
   York 1966.
   A good elementary text, though brief (six lyrics, seven selections from
   the *Tales*).

II.D INDIVIDUAL WORKS

*Derek S. Brewer, ed, *The Parlement of Foulys*, Nelson's 'Medieval and
   Renaissance' Library. 1960; 2nd edn. Manchester, 1972.
*Robert K. Root, ed, *The Book of Troilus and Criseyde*, Princeton 1926.
   The standard text of *Troilus*.
Robert K. Gordon, ed and tr, *The Story of Troilus*, (*VI.B*). Valuable·for
   the translations of the analogues. The text of *Troilus* is a poorly glossed
   reprint of Skeat's edition.
John Warrington, ed, *Troilus and Criseyde*, 'Everyman's Library'. 1953.
   Modernized spellings; marginal glosses and notes.
Derek S. and L. Elisabeth Brewer, eds, *Troilus and Criseyde, (Abridged)*,
   1969.
   Slightly less than half the text with summaries of omitted passages.
A. C. Cawley, ed, *The Canterbury Tales*, 'Everyman's Library,' 1958.
   Complete text (Robinson's) with marginal glosses and notes.
John H. Halverson, ed, *The Canterbury Tales*, Indianapolis, Indiana 1971.
   Notably readable edition of selections with summaries of omitted
   materials.
Donald R. Howard, ed, *The Canterbury Tales*, Signet paperback, New
   York 1969.

Selections in regularized spelling; good introduction.

Maurice Hussey, A. C. Spearing, James Winney, eds, *Selected Tales from Chaucer*, Cambridge. In progress.

A series of editions of individual tales. Thus far have appeared the 'General Prologue', 'Knight's Tale', 'Miller's Tale', 'Wife of Bath's Prologue' and 'Tale', 'Nun's Priest's Tale', 'Franklin's Tale', each with introduction and explanatory notes.

II.E CHRONOLOGY

Germaine Dempster, 'A Period in the Development of the Canterbury Tales Marriage Group and of Blocks B² and C,' *PMLA*, LXVIII, 1953, 1142–59.

Charles A. Owen, Jr., 'The Development of the *Canterbury Tales*,' *JEGP*, LVII, 1958, 449–76.

J. S. P. Tatlock, *The Development and Chronology of Chaucer's Works*, Chaucer Society, 1907. Rpt. 1967.

III *Language, Style, and Versification*

III.A REFERENCE

Sherman M. Kuhn and John Reidy, eds, *Middle English Dictionary*, Ann Arbor, Michigan 1956 – in progress.

Fascicles A to L have been published.

Francis P. Magoun, Jr., *A Chaucer Gazeteer*, Chicago 1961.

Isabel Marshall and Lela Porter, *A Ryme-Index to Chaucer's Minor Poems*, Chaucer Society, 1887–89. 2 vol.

Masui Michio, *The Structure of Chaucer's Rime Words (III.B)*. Contains indices to the rimes in *Canterbury Tales* and *Troilus*.

Thomas W. Ross, *Chaucer's Bawdy*, New York 1972.

Alphabetically arranged treatments of specific words and topics.

John S. P. Tatlock and Arthur G. Kennedy, *A Concordance to the Complete Works of Geoffrey Chaucer and to The Romaunt of the Rose*, Washington, D.C., 1927. Rpt. 1963.

Bartlett J. Whiting in coll. with Helen W. Whiting, *Proverbs, Sentences, and Proverbial Phrases from English Writings, Mainly before 1500*, Cambridge, Massachusetts 1968.

III.B LINGUISTIC

Gero Brauer, *Studien zum System und Gebrauch der 'Tempora' in der Sprache*

Chaucers und Gowers, Vienna 1970.
Study of use and meaning of tenses.
Bernard ten Brink. *The Language and Meter of Chaucer*, 2nd edn, rev. by
Friederich Kluge; tr. M. Bentinck-Smith. London 1901.
Based on *Chaucers Sprache und Verskunst*, 1881.
Jacek Fisiak, *Morphemic Structure of Chaucer's English*, University of
Alabama 1965.
Technical linguistic study.
Edgar Frey, *Die Verben des Transportsfelds bei Chaucer und König Alfred dem
Grossen*, Zurich 1967.
Technical study of a semantic field.
Will Héraucourt, *Die Wertwelt Chaucers: Die Wertwelt einer Zeitwende*,
Heidelberg 1939.
Interesting study of value system in relation to vocabulary.
Jelle Kerkhoff, *Studies in the Language of Geoffrey Chaucer*, Leiden 1966.
Good for reference on Chaucer's usages.
Kirsti Kivimaa, *The Pleonastic 'That' in Relative and Interrogative Construc-
tion in Chaucer's Verse*. Helsinki 1967.
*Helge Kökeritz, *A Guide to Chaucer's Pronunciation*, Stockholm 1954.
Rpt. 1962.
Excellent elementary guide, mainly for its transcriptions of extensive
passages, which can be used along with Kökeritz' recordings (see
below).
Joseph Mersand, *Chaucer's Romance Vocabulary*, 2nd edn, New York
1939. Rpt. 1968.

III.C RECORDINGS OF CHAUCERIAN ENGLISH
A good recent list of recordings is in the Bibliography to *Chaucer's
Mind and Art* (*Intro.D*). Especially recommended is Kökeritz'
Chaucer Readings (EVA Lexington LE 5505 B). To this list should
be added the recently issued recording of generous selections (2 LP
records) from *Troilus and Criseyde*, read in Middle English by Derek
Brewer, Richard Marquand, Peter Orr, Prunella Scales, and Gary
Watson (Argo Stereo ZPL 1003–4).

III.D STYLISTIC STUDIES
Paull F. Baum, 'Chaucer's Puns,' *PMLA*, LXXI, 1956, 225–46.
Supplemented in *PMLA*, LXXXIII, 167–70.

Ruth Crosby, 'Chaucer and the Custom of Oral Delivery,' *Speculum*,
XIII, 1938, 413–32.
Dorothy Everett, 'Chaucer's Good Ear,' *RES*, XXIII, 1947; rpt. in
Essays on Middle English Literature, ed Patricia Kean, 1955.
Claes Schaar, *Some Types of Narrative in Chaucer's Poetry*, Lund 1954.
Interesting for syntactic analyses of narrative types.
Margaret Schlauch, 'Chaucer's Colloquial English: Its Structural Traits,'
PMLA, LXVII, 1952, 1103–16.
See also the works listed under *VI.D*, 'Literary Traditions,' and *VIII.E*,
'Rhetoric,' since many of them include close analyses of diction and sentence structure.

III.E METRICS
Paull F. Baum, *Chaucer's Verse*, Durham, North Carolina 1961.
E. T. Donaldson, 'Chaucer's Final -e,' *PMLA*, LXIII, 1948, 1101–24.
Attack on Southworth's *PMLA* article (see below); Southworth
replied in *PMLA*, LXIV, 601–9.
Morris Halle and Samuel J. Keyser, 'Chaucer and the Study of Prosody,'
College English, XXVIII, 1966, 187–219.
* Tauno F. Mustanoja, 'Chaucer's Prosody,' in *Companion to Chaucer
Studies* (*Intro.E*).
I. A. Robinson, *Chaucer's Prosody; A Study of the Middle English Verse
Tradition* Cambridge 1971.
James G. Southworth, 'Chaucer's Final e in Rhyme,' *PMLA*, LXII, 1947,
910–35.
See Donaldson above.
——, *Verses of Cadence: An Introduction to the Prosody of Chaucer and His
Followers*, Oxford 1954.
——, *The Prosody of Chaucer and His Followers: Supplementary Chapters to
Verses of Cadence*, Oxford 1962.

III.F STANZAICS
Theodore Maynard, *The Connection Between the Ballade, Chaucer's Modification of It, Rime Royal, and the Spenserian Stanza*, Washington, D.C.
1934.
Eric G. Stanley, 'Stanza and Ictus in *Troilus and Criseyde*,' in *Chaucer und
seine Zeit* (*Intro.D*).

IV *Life*

IV.A LIFE RECORDS

W. D. Selby, F. J. Furnivall *et al.*, *Life Records of Chaucer*, Chaucer Society, 1875–1900. 4 vol. Rpt. 1967.

Martin Crow and Clair C. Olson, *Chaucer Life Records*, Oxford 1966.

IV.B CHAUCER IN SPAIN

Albert C. Baugh, 'Chaucer in Spain,' in *Chaucer und seine Zeit* (*Intro.D*).

Thomas J. Garbáty, 'Chaucer in Spain, 1366: Soldier of Fortune or Agent of the Crown?' *English Language Notes*, V, 1967, 81–7.

——, 'The *Pamphilus* Tradition in Ruiz and Chaucer,' *Philological Quarterly*, XLVI, 1967, 457–70.

Suzanne Honoré-Duvergé, 'Chaucer en Espagne? (1366),' *Recueil de Travaux offert à M. Clovis Brunel*, Paris 1955, II, 9–13.

IV.C GENERAL

*Derek S. Brewer, *Chaucer*, 1953. 3rd (Supplemented) edn, 1973.
   Brief survey of life and works. See also *Chaucer in His Time* (*VII.A*).

——, 'Class Distinctions in Chaucer,' *Speculum*, XLIII, 1968, 290–305.

Marchette Chute, *Geoffrey Chaucer of England*, Rev. ed, 1962.

John H. Fisher, *John Gower: Friend of Chaucer*.
   The general influence of Gower on Chaucer's works.

Donald R. Howard, 'Chaucer the Man,' *PMLA*, LXXX, 1965, 337–43.
   See also 'Chaucer the Pilgrim' in Donaldson, *Speaking of Chaucer* (*VIII.A*) and B. H. Bronson's remarks in *In Search of Chaucer* (*VIII.A*).

George Kane, *The Autobiographical Fallacy in Chaucer and Langland Studies*, 1965.

Jerome Mitchell, *Thomas Hoccleve: A Study in Early Fifteenth-Century English Poetic*, Urbana, Illinois 1968.
   Disproves Chaucer's supposed personal friendship with Hoccleve.

Edward Wagenknecht, *The Personality of Chaucer*, Norman, Oklahoma 1968.

George Williams, *A New View of Chaucer*, Durham, North Carolina 1965.
   Unconvincing attempt to prove the pervasive importance in Chaucer's works of his relation to John of Gaunt.

Surveys of Chaucer's life are also included in most editions (e.g., Robinson's *II.B*) and in many general studies, such as Coghill's *The Poet Chaucer* (*VIII.A*).

V *Learning*

V.A GENERAL

R. W. V. Elliott, 'Chaucer's Reading,' in *Chaucer's Mind and Art* (*Intro.D*).

Thomas R. Lounsbury, *Studies in Chaucer*, New York 1892. 3 vol. Rpt. 1962. 'The Learning of Chaucer,' II, ii, is still useful, as are other parts, such as the study of Chaucer's reputation, III, i.

George A. Plimpton, *The Education of Chaucer: Illustrated from the School-Books in Use in His Time*, Oxford 1935.

Good reproductions and discussions of MSS of common schoolbooks.

Robert A. Pratt, 'The Importance of Manuscripts for the Study of Medieval Education as Revealed by the Learning of Chaucer,' *Progress of Medieval and Renaissance Studies*, Bull. 20, 1949, 509–30.

For Chaucer's use of the *Roman de Troyle* see Pratt's article under *VI.C*.

V.B PROVERBIAL AND POPULAR LORE

Beryl Rowland, *Blind Beasts: Chaucer's Animal World*, Kent State University Press 1971.

Popular lore, tradition, and observation in Chaucer's animal imagery.

Robert M. Lumiansky, 'The Function of the Proverbial Monitory Elements in Chaucer's *Troilus and Criseyde*,' *Tulane Studies in English*, II, 1950, 5–48.

Bartlett J. Whiting, *Chaucer's Use of Proverbs*, Cambridge, Massachussetts 1934.

Study of proverbs in their contexts. Valuable appendices list proverbs in Machaut, the French fabliaux, and the works of Gower. See also Whiting (*III.A*).

V.C PHILOSOPHY AND RELIGION

Bernard L. Jefferson, *Chaucer and the Consolation of Philosophy of Boethius*, Princeton 1917. rpt. 1968.

Morton W. Bloomfield, 'Chaucer's Sense of History,' in *Essays and Explorations* (*VIII.A*).

Beverly Boyd, *Chaucer and the Liturgy*, Philadelphia 1967.
  Brief factual survey of Chaucer's use of liturgical elements.
Gordon H. Gerould, 'Chaucer's Calender of Saints,' in *Chaucerian Essays* (*VIII.A*).
Roger S. Loomis, 'Was Chaucer a Laodicean?' in *Essays and Studies in Honor of Carleton Brown*, New York 1940. Rpt. in Schoeck and Taylor (*Intro.D*).
  On Chaucer's religious views, see also Cottle (*VII.A*).
——, 'Was Chaucer a Free Thinker?' in *Studies in Medieval Literature*, ed MacEdward Leach. Philadelphia 1961, pp. 21–44.
Joseph J. Mogan, Jr., *Chaucer and the Theme of Mutability*, The Hague 1968.
D. W. Robertson, *A Preface to Chaucer* (*VIII.A*).
Mary E. Thomas, *Medieval Skepticism and Chaucer*, New York 1950.
W. Meredith Thompson, 'Chaucer's Translation of the Bible' in *English and Medieval Studies Presented to J. R. R. Tolkien*, ed. N. Davis and C. L. Wrenn, 1962, pp. 183–99.

V.D SCIENCE

*Walter C. Curry, *Chaucer and the Medieval Sciences*, Rev. and enlarged edition. New York 1960. Rpt. 1962.
Edgar H. Duncan, 'The Literature of Alchemy and Chaucer's *Canon's Yeoman's Tale*: Framework, Theme, and Characters,' *Speculum*, XLIII, 1968, 633–56.
Joseph E. Grennen, 'Saint Cecelia's "Chemical Wedding": The Unity of the *Canterbury Tales*, Fragment VIII,' *JEGP*, LXV, 1966, 466–81.
John L. Lowes, *Geoffrey Chaucer* (*VIII.A*).
  First chapter contains an excellent introduction to Chaucer's ideas of astronomy.
*C. S. Lewis, *The Discarded Image: An Introduction to Medieval Literature*, Cambridge 1964. Rpt. 1967.
  Introductory discussion of medieval world view.
John Leyerle, 'Chaucer's Windy Eagle,' *UTQ*, XL, 1971, 247–65.
J. D. North, 'Kalenderes Enlumined Ben They,' *RES*, XX, 1969, 129–54, 257–83, 418–44.
  Full examination of astronomical references, but see Smyser below for some corrections.

*H. M. Smyser, 'Chaucer's View of Astronomy,' *Speculum*, XLV, 1970, 359–73.

Chauncy Wood, *Chaucer and the Country of the Stars: Poetic Uses of Astronomical Imagery*, Princeton 1970.

Interesting attempt to interpret the astronomical references.

VI *Sources*

VI.A COLLECTIONS

Edmund Brock, Thor Sundby, F. J. Furnivall, W. A. Clouston, eds, *Originals and Analogues of the Canterbury Tales*, Chaucer Society, 1872–87. 5 parts. Rpt. 1967.

Useful for distant analogues not in Bryan and Dempster.

*W. F. Bryan and Germaine Dempster, eds, *Sources and Analogues of Chaucer's Canterbury Tales*, New York 1941. Rpt. 1958.

VI.B TRANSLATIONS OF SOURCES

Larry D. Benson and Theodore M. Andersson, eds and trs, *The Literary Context of Chaucer's Fabliaux*, Indianapolis, Indiana 1971. Translations and original texts in parallel.

Derek S. Brewer, ed, *The Parlement of Foulys* (*II.D*).

Appendices contain translations of principal sources.

Charles Dahlberg, tr, *The Romance of the Rose*, Princeton 1971.

Well-annotated prose translation.

Robert D. French, *A Chaucer Handbook* (*Intro.E*).

Summaries or translations of many of the sources.

R. K. Gordon, ed and tr, *The Story of Troilus*, 1934. Rpt. 1964.

Translations of Benoit's and Boccaccio's versions along with Chaucer's text and Henryson's *Testament of Criseyde*.

VI.C. STUDIES

J. A. W. Bennett, *The Parlement of Foules* (*VIII.D*).

——, *Chaucer's Book of Fame* (*VIII.D*).

Sigmund Eisner, *A Tale of Wonder: A Source Study of the Wife of Bath's Tale*, Wexford, Ireland 1957.

George L. Kittredge, *Chaucer and His Poetry* (*VIII.A*).

Esp. chapter i, on *Book of the Duchess*.

C. S. Lewis, 'What Chaucer Really Did to *Il Filostrato*,' *Essays and Studies* by *Members of the English Association*, XVII, 1933; rpt. Schoeck and Taylor (*Intro.D*).

J. L. Lowes, *Geoffrey Chaucer* (*VIII.A*).
Esp. chapters on the early poems.

Robert A. Pratt, 'Chaucer and *Le Roman de Troyle et de Criseida*,' *Studies in Philology*, LIII, 1956, 509–39.

Robert K. Root, *The Poetry of Chaucer* (VIII.A).

J. Burke Severs, *The Literary Relationships of Chaucer's Clerkes Tale*. New Haven, Connecticut 1942. Rpt. 1972.

Claes Schaar, *The Golden Mirror; Studies in Chaucer's Descriptive Technique and Its Literary Background*, Lund 1955.
See also Schaar's *Some Types of Narrative* (*III.D*), which compares Chaucer's narrative techniques to his sources.

Bartlett J. Whiting, *Chaucer's Use of Proverbs* (*V.B*).
Use of proverbs in Chaucer's sources.

VI.D LITERARY TRADITIONS
Classical Literature:
Edgar F. Shannon, *Chaucer and the Roman Poets*, Cambridge, Massachusetts 1929. Rpt. 1964.

Richard L. Hoffman, *Ovid and the Canterbury Tales*, Philadelphia 1967.
Argues Ovidian doctrine of 'twin loves' is important in the *Tales*. See also his chapter on 'The Influence of the Classics on Chaucer' in *Companion to Chaucer Studies* (*Intro.E*).

French:
Haldeen Braddy, *Chaucer and the French Poet Graunson*, Baton Rouge, Louisiana 1947. Rpt. 1968.

Dean S. Fansler, *Chaucer and Le Roman de la Rose*, New York 1914.

*Charles S. Muscatine, *Chaucer and the French Tradition* (*VIII.A*).

James Wimsatt, *Chaucer and the French Love Poets: The Literary Background of the Book of the Duchess*, Chapel Hill, North Carolina 1968.

Italian:
Hubertis M. Cummings, *The Indebtedness of Chaucer's Works to the Italian Works of Boccaccio: A Review and Summary*, Cincinnati, Ohio 1916. Rpt. 1967.

Mario Praz, 'Chaucer and the Great Italian Writers of the Trecento,'

The Monthly Criterion, VI, 1927 rpt. in *The Flaming Heart*, New York 1958.

Paul Ruggiers, 'The Italian Influence on Chaucer,' in *Companion to Chaucer Studies* (*Intro.E*).

Howard H. Schless, 'Chaucer and Dante,' in *Critical Approaches to Medieval Literature*, ed Dorothy Bethurum. New York 1960.

English:

*Derek S. Brewer, 'The Relation of Chaucer to the English and European Traditions,' in *Chaucer and Chaucerians* (*Intro.D*).

E. T. Donaldson, 'The Idiom of Popular Poetry in The Miller's Tale,' in *Speaking of Chaucer* (VIII.A).

Dorothy Everett, 'Chaucer's Good Ear' (*III.D*).

Laura Hibbard Loomis, 'Sir Thopas,' in Bryan and Dempster, *Sources and Analogues* (*VI.A*).

Charles M. Muscatine, '*The Canterbury Tales*: The Style of the Man and The Style of the Work,' in *Chaucer and Chaucerians* (*Intro.D*). Comments on use of colloquial and native diction.

Ian Robinson, *Chaucer and the English Tradition* (*VIII.A*).
    Rather impressionistic emphasis on Chaucer's English qualities.

Margaret Schlauch, 'Chaucer's Colloquial English' (*III.D*).

John Speirs, *Chaucer the Maker* (*VIII.A*).
    Occasional and impressionistic (but influential) comments on Chaucer's colloquial diction.

VII   *Fourteenth-Century Life and Culture*

VII.A GENERAL

*Derek S. Brewer, *Chaucer in His Time*, 1963.

Basil Cottle, *The Triumph of English, 1350–1400*, 1969.

G. C. Coulton, *Chaucer and His England*, 1908. Rpt. with a new bibliography by T. W. Craik, 1962.

*Muriel Bowden, *A Commentary on the General Prologue to the Canterbury Tales*, New York 1948.

F. E. Halliday, *Chaucer and His World*.
    Brief account of life and works, richly illustrated.

Maurice Hussey, *Chaucer's World: A Pictorial Companion*, Cambridge 1967.

Discussion, illustrated by plates, of world of the Canterbury pilgrims, designed to accompany the editions by Hussey *et al.* (*I.D*).

*Roger S. Loomis, *A Mirror of Chaucer's World*, Princeton 1965.

Fine reproductions of fourteenth-century art, with scholarly comments.

John M. Manly, *Some New Light on Chaucer*, Chicago 1926. Rpt. 1952.

Gervase Mathew, *The Court of Richard II*, 1968.

Survey of the general culture of Richard's court.

Helaine Newstead, *Chaucer's and His Contemporaries: Essays on Medieval Literature and Thought*. Greenwich, Connecticut 1968.

Documents, essays on cultural and intellectual backgrounds and on contemporary writers.

*Edith Rickert, *Chaucer's World*, ed Clair C. Olson and Martin M. Crow. New York 1948. Rpt. 1962.

D. W. Robertson, Jr., *Chaucer's London*, New York 1968.

Excellent study of London and its people in Chaucer's time.

Ian Serraillier, *Chaucer and His World*, 1967.

Elementary discussion with illustrations.

VII.B ART

Robert M. Jordan, *Chaucer and The Shape of Creation* (*VIII.A*).

Chapter II and III concern medieval aesthetics and Gothic architecture.

D. W. Robertson, Jr., *A Preface to Chaucer* (*VIII.A*).

Chapters I–III concern medieval art and aesthetics; contains over a hundred reproductions of manuscript illuminations and sculpture.

VII.C MUSIC

Clair C. Olson, 'Chaucer and the Music of the Fourteenth Century,' *Speculum*, XVI, 1941, 64–92.

Raymond Preston, *Chaucer* (*VIII.A*).

Chapter I concerns fourteenth-century music in relation to verse.

VII.D COURTLY LOVE

John F. Benton, 'The Court of Champagne as a Literary Center,' *Speculum*, XXXVI, 1961, 555–91.

——, 'Clio and Venus: An Historical View of Medieval Love,' in *The Meaning of Courtly Love*, ed F. X. Newman. Albany New York, 1968.

William G. Dodd, *Courtly Love in Chaucer and Gower*, Boston 1913.

E. Talbot Donaldson, 'The Myth of Courtly Love,' *Ventures: Magazine of the Yale Graduate School*, V, 1965; rpt. in *Speaking of Chaucer* (*VIII.A*).

Donald R. Howard, *The Three Temptations* (*VIII.C*).

C. S. Lewis, *The Allegory of Love*, Oxford 1936. Rpt. 1948.

John L. Lowes, 'The Loveres Maladye of Heroes,' *Modern Philology*, XI, 1914, 491–546.

*John J. Parry, tr, *The Art of Courtly Love of Andreas Capellanus with Introduction, Translation, and Notes*. New York 1941.

D. W. Robertson, Jr., 'Courtly Love as an Impediment to the Understanding of Medieval Texts,' in *The Meaning of Courtly Love* (as under Benton, above).

Eugene E. Slaughter, *Virtue According to Love—in Chaucer*, New York 1957.
   Useful but uncritical catalogue of doctrinal comments and of Chaucer's views.

John M. Steadman, '"Courtly Love" as a Problem of Style,' in *Chaucer und seine Zeit* (*Intro.D*).

VIII   *Interpretative Criticism*

VIII.A   GENERAL

Paull F. Baum, *Chaucer: A Critical Appreciation*, Durham, North Carolina 1958.

H. S. Bennett, *Chaucer and the Fifteenth Century*, Oxford 1947.

Earle Birney, 'The Beginnings of Chaucer's Irony,' *PMLA*, LIV, 1939, 637–55.

Morton W. Bloomfield, *Essays and Explorations: Studies in Ideas, Language, and Literature*, Cambridge, Massachusetts 1970.
   Reprints of his articles on Chaucer.

Muriel Bowden, *A Reader's Guide to Geoffrey Chaucer*, New York 1964.

Bertrand H. Bronson, *In Search of Chaucer*, Toronto 1960.

John A. Burrow, *Ricardian Poetry: Chaucer, Gower, Langland, and the Gawain Poet*, New Haven, Connecticut 1971.

G. K. Chesterton, *Chaucer*, 1932. Rpt. 1959.

Neville Coghill, *The Poet Chaucer*. 1949. 2nd edn 1968.

*——, *Geoffrey Chaucer*, 'Writers and Their Work', 79. 1956.

Germaine Dempster, *Dramatic Irony in Chaucer*, Stanford, California

1932. Rpt. 1969.

*E. Talbot Donaldson, *Speaking of Chaucer*, New York 1970. Reprinted and new essays. See also his edition (*II.C*).

Gordon H. Gerould, *Chaucerian Essays*, Princeton, New Jersey 1952.

Mary E. Giffin, *Studies on Chaucer and His Audience*, Québec 1956.

M. W. Grose, *Chaucer*, 1967.

Edwin J. Howard, *Geoffrey Chaucer*, New York 1964.

S. S. Hussey, *Chaucer: An Introduction*, 1971.

Robert M. Jordan, *Chaucer and The Shape of Creation: The Aesthetic Possibilities of Inorganic Structure*. Cambridge, Massachusetts, 1967.

*George L. Kittredge, *Chaucer and His Poetry*, Cambridge, Massachusetts 1915. 55th Anniversary edn, with an intro. by B. J. Whiting, 1970.

John Lawlor, *Chaucer*, 1968.

C. S. Lewis, *The Allegory of Love* (*VII.D*).

*John L. Lowes, *Geoffrey Chaucer and the Development of His Genius*, Boston 1934 (English edn: *Geoffrey Chaucer*, Oxford 1934). Rpt. as *Geoffrey Chaucer*, 1962.

Sister Mary Madeleva, *A Lost Language and Other Essays on Chaucer*, New York 1951.

Kemp Malone, *Chapters on Chaucer*, Baltimore 1951.

*Charles Muscatine, *Chaucer and the French Tradition: A Study in Style and Meaning*, Berkeley 1957.

*——, *Poetry and Crisis in The Age of Chaucer*, Notre Dame, Indiana 1972.

Howard R. Patch, *On Rereading Chaucer*, Cambridge, Massachusetts 1939.

Raymond Preston, *Chaucer*, 1952. Rpt. 1969.

D. W. Robertson, Jr., *A Preface to Chaucer* (*VIII.F*).

Robert K. Root, *The Poetry of Chaucer: A Guide to Its Study and Appreciation*, Boston 1906. Rev. edn, 1922. Rpt. 1950.

John Speirs, *Chaucer the Maker*, 1951. Rev. edn. 1960. Rpt. 1967.

John S. P. Tatlock, *the Mind and Art of Chaucer*, New York 1950. Rpt. 1966.

VIII.B THE CANTERBURY TALES

* Ralph Baldwin, *The Unity of the Canterbury Tales*, Anglistica, V. Copenhagen 1955. Rpt. in Schoeck and Taylor (*Intro.D*).

Barbara Bartholomew, *Fortuna and Natura: A Reading of Three Chaucer Narratives*, The Hague 1966.

Helen S. Corsa, *Chaucer: Poet of Mirth and Morality*, Notre Dame, Indiana 1964.

T. W. Craik, *The Comic Tales of Chaucer*, 1964.

J. V. Cunningham, 'The Literary Framework of the Prologue to *The Canterbury Tales,'* *Modern Philology*, XLIX, 1952, 172–81.

Arthur W. Hoffman, 'Chaucer's Prologue to Pilgrimage: The Two Voices,' *ELH*, XXI, 1954, 1–16.

Michael Hoy and Michael Stevens, *Chaucer's Major Tales*, 1969.

Bernard F. Huppé, *A Reading of the Canterbury Tales*, New York 1966.

Alfred L. Kellogg, 'An Augustinian Interpretation of Chaucer's Pardoner,' *Speculum*, XXVI, 1951; rpt. in *Chaucer, Langland, Arthur: Essays in Middle English Literature*, New Brunswick, New Jersey, 1972.

William W. Lawrence, *Chaucer and The Canterbury Tales*, New York 1950.

Robert M. Lumiansky, 'Chaucer's Philosophical Knight,' *Tulane Studies in English*, III, 1952, 47–68.

——, *Of Sondry Folk: The Dramatic Principle in The Canterbury Tales*, Austin, Texas 1955.

Janette Richardson, *Blameth Nat Me: A Study of Imagery in Chaucer's Fabliaux*, The Hague 1970.

*Paul Ruggiers, *The Art of The Canterbury Tales*, Madison, Wisconsin 1965.

Paul T. Thurston, *Artistic Ambivalence in Chaucer's Knight's Tale*, Gainesville, Florida 1968.

Trevor Whittock, *A Reading of The Canterbury Tales*, Cambridge 1968.

VIII.C TROILUS AND CRISEYDE

Morton W. Bloomfield, 'Distance and Predestination in *Troilus and Criseyde*,' in *Essays and Explorations (VIII.A)*.

Ida L. Gordon, *The Double Sorrow of Troilus: A Study of Ambiguities in Troilus and Criseyde*, Oxford 1970.

*Donald R. Howard, 'Courtly Love and the Lust of the Flesh: *Troilus and Criseyde*,' in *The Three Temptations: Medieval Man in Search of the World*, Princeton 1966.

Sanford B. Meech, *Design in Chaucer's Troilus*, Syracuse, New York 1959.

Geoffrey T. Shepherd, '*Troilus and Criseyde*,' in *Chaucer and Chaucerians* (*Intro.D*).

A. C. Spearing, 'Chaucer as Novelist,' in *Criticism and Medieval Poetry*, 1964. Rpt. 1972.

Karl Young, 'Chaucer's *Troilus and Criseyde* as Romance,' *PMLA*, LIII, 1938, 38–63.

VIII.D MINOR POEMS

*J. A. W. Bennett, *The Parlement of Foules: An Interpretation*, Oxford 1957.

——, *Chaucer's Book of Fame: An Exposition of The House of Fame*, Oxford 1968.

*Wolfgang Clemen, *Chaucer's Early Poetry*. Tr C.A.M. Sym. 1963 Translated from a revised version of *Der Junge Chaucer*, 1938.

Constance B. Hieatt, *The Realism of Dream Vision: The Poetic Exploitation of the Dream-Experience in Chaucer and His Contemporaries*, The Hague 1967.

B. G. Koonce, *Chaucer and The Tradition of Fame: Symbolism in The House of Fame*, Princeton 1966.

Edmund Reiss, 'Dusting Off the Cobwebs: A Look at Chaucer's Lyrics,' *Chaucer Review*, I, 1966, 55–65.

D. W. Robertson, Jr., and Bernard F. Huppé, *Fruyt and Chaf: Studies in Chaucer's Allegories*, Princeton 1963.

VIII.E RHETORIC

Dorothy Everett, 'Some Reflexions on Chaucer's "Art Poetical," ' *Proceedings of the British Academy*, XXXVI, 1950; rpt. in *Chaucer's Mind and Art* (*Intro. D.*).

Marie P. Hamilton, 'Notes on Chaucer and the Rhetoricians,' *PMLA*, XLVII, 1932, 403–9.

John M. Manly, 'Chaucer and the Rhetoricians,' *Proceedings of the British Academy*, XII, 1926; rpt. Schoeck and Taylor (*Intro.D*).

James J. Murphy, 'A New Look at Chaucer and the Rhetoricians,' *Review of English Studies*, XV, 1964, 1–20.

Traugott Naunin, *Der Einfluss der mittelalterlichen Rhetorik auf Chaucers Dichtung*, Dissertation, Bonn 1930.

*Robert O. Payne, *The Key of Remembrance: A Study of Chaucer's Poetics*, New Haven, Connecticut 1963.

VIII.F EXEGETICAL CRITICISM

Judson Allen, *The Friar as Literary Critic*, Nashville, Tennessee 1971.

Morton W. Bloomfield, 'Symbolism in Medieval Poetry,' *Modern Philology*, LVI, 1958; rpt. in *Essays and Explorations* (*VIII.A*).

A. Leigh DeNeef, 'Robertson and the Critics,' *Chaucer Review*, II, 1968, 205–34.

Contains useful bibliography of Robertson's works.

E. Talbot Donaldson, 'Patristic Exegesis in the Criticism of Medieval Literature: The Opposition,' in Dorothy Bethurum, ed, *Critical Approaches to Medieval Literature: Selected Papers from the English Institute, 1958–59*, New York 1960. Rpt. in *Speaking of Chaucer* (*VIII.A*).

Donald R. Howard, *The Three Temptations* (*VIII.C*).

John Halverson, 'Patristic Exegesis: A Medieval *Tom Sawyer*,' *College English*, XXVII, 1965, 50–5.

Robert E. Kaske, 'Patristic Exegesis in the Criticism of Medieval Literature: The Defense,' in Bethurum, *Critical Approaches* (see under Donaldson above); partially rpt. in Burrow's *Chaucer* (*Intro. C*).

*D. W. Robertson, Jr., *A Preface to Chaucer: Studies in Medieval Perspectives*, Princeton 1963.

See also Robertson and Huppé's *Fruyt and Chaf* (*VIII.D*).

Rosamund Tuve, *Allegorical Imagery: Some Mediaeval Books and Their Posterity*, Princeton 1966.

Francis L. Utley, 'Robertsonianism Redivivus,' *Romance Philology*, XIX, 1965; rpt. as 'Chaucer and Patristic Exegesis,' in *Chaucer's Mind and Art* (*Intro.D*).

Index

Prepared by Mrs Brenda Hall MA

rhyming techniques 63–7, 329

rhythm, metre in 67–71, 98, 99–101

sentence, solaas in 3, 10–11

significance of images in 308–9

sources for 111–12

surviving manuscripts 86n, 93, 94–5, 325–6

vocabulary 71–83

see also individual parts and General Prologue

Capital letters, medieval conventions in use of 86–7

Caplan, H. 307n

Carminew, Ralph 54

Carmody, F.J. 224n

Carshill, Thomas (Cressell) 51–2n

Catherine of Siena 266

Cato, influence of 143, 180, 181, 307 and n

Cavalieri, Elizabetta, commentary on Dante's *Divine Comedy* 191–2n

Cawley, A.C. 327

Caxton, William 58, 71, 73, 95–6 and n, 99–101, 325–6

Cecilia, St, and Chaucer's concept of women 17–18

Celibacy of the clergy 16–17

Characterization

Chaucer's techniques of 258–9

Chaucer's techniques contrasted with Boccaccio's 209–16

Dante's, Chaucer's contrasted 219–23

French inspiration for Chaucer's 130–1

inconsistencies in presentation of 4

scientific background for 334

Chartier, Alain, influence of Machaut on 118

Chartres, school of 156, 162 and n

Chaucer, Elizabeth 47

Chaucer family, migration to London 38

Chaucer, Geoffrey

appearance 332

association with Lollards 45–7, 54–5

attitude to poetic role 5–8

concept of work as reflection of social pressure 11n

concepts of status as poet 5–12, 109–10

depiction of himself 4, 20

employment of scribe 85, 91

extent of education, learning 28, 147, 245n, 333–5

nature of poetic craft 169, 171–2

origins, life, family relationships 12, 35, 43, 46, 47–53, 190, 191 and n, 194–7, 323, 331–3

significance of English links with Italy for 190–6

threatened proscription of works 92n

Chaucer, Lewis 47

Chaucer, Thomas 47, 52, 56

Chaucer Review, The 321

Chaucer Society 96, 105, 323, 326, 331, 335

'Chaucer's Words to Adam' 93

Chesterton, G.K. 321 and n, 341, 351

Chew, S.C. 312n

Cheyne, John 45–7

Child, F.J. 321, 323, 328

Chomsky, N. 31

Christianity

Chaucer's viewpoint on 244, 257 and n, 317–20

nature, extent of. in medieval